P9-BZC-978

HOW DID THEY DIE?

HOW DID THEY DIE?

by Norman & Betty Donaldson

ST. MARTIN'S PRESS
New York

Copyright © 1980 by Norman and Betty Donaldson
All rights reserved. For information, write:
St. Martin's Press, Inc. 175 Fifth Ave., New York, N.Y. 10010
Manufactured in the United States of America

Library of Congress Cataloging in Publication Data

Donaldson, Norman.
  How did they die?

  1. Biography. 2. Death—Causes. I. Donaldson,
Betty, joint author. II. Title.
CT105.D6   920   79-22871
ISBN 0-312-39488-8

Contents

When we drew our facts largely or exclusively from a single full-length biography, the author and date are cited at the end of the article; when no citation is supplied it can be assumed that several sources, often including press reports, were used.

It is a pleasure to express our appreciation to the many authorities, both in the United States and abroad, who have assisted in resolving the various problems raised by our research.

Finally, we must thank Mr. Thomas J. McCormack, president of St. Martin's Press, for his faith in the book from its earliest beginnings, and to his able assistant, Sarah Clayton. Her enthusiastic help in the final stages, especially in tracking down illustrations, was invaluable.

Abelard, Peter *(Pierre Abailard)* (1079–1142).

The French philosopher and theologian was in his forties when he abused his position as tutor to the young Heloise, niece of Canon Fulbert of Notre Dame. After the birth of their son, Abelard belatedly married her, but Fulbert took his revenge by ordering—some say leading—a band of men into the sleeping Abelard's house and slashing off the offending organs with a razor. Ashamed, Abelard retired to a monastery and ordered his reluctant wife to a convent. He died at the priory of St. Marcel, Chalon-sur-Saône, on 21 April 1142. His fatal illness, a combination of fever and a skin disorder, may have been scurvy. The bones of Abelard and Heloise have been moved several times over the years but now lie together beneath a Gothic canopy in the Père-Lachaise Cemetery in Paris.

Adams, John (1735–1826).

The second president of the U.S. (1797–1801), a short, plump man, Adams was physically one of the healthiest of the presidents. He is also the longest-lived of them all, surviving to the age of 90 years, 247 days. Throughout his career he was reputed to have an abnormally violent temper. In his last years his eyesight began to fail and he complained at times of sciatica and rheumatism. But almost until his eightieth year he took long horse rides, and only toward the end, because of a senile palsy, were his letters written by a secretary. In his last year Adams' arteriosclerosis began to burden his heart, and he spent most of his waking hours sitting upright, supported by cushions, in the armchair in the spacious study of his home, Peacefield, next door to his birthplace in Quincy, Mass. In this position, during the fiftieth anniversary of independence to which he had been eagerly looking forward, he gradually lapsed into a coma. He

1

Tomb of John and Abigail Adams at Quincy, Mass.
LIBRARY OF CONGRESS

died peacefully at sunset on that day, 4 July 1826. His last words are reputed to have been of his former opponent for the presidency, with whom he had in later years become reconciled: "Thomas Jefferson still survives," he murmured, unaware that his successor as president had died a few hours earlier in Virginia. Adams was buried at Quincy in the family tomb.

Adams, John Quincy (1767–1848).

The sixth president of the U.S. (1825–1829) enjoyed the same good health as his father, the second president. Childhood injuries led to a weakened right arm and forefinger, which interfered with his writing throughout his life. In November 1846 Adams collapsed from a stroke in a Boston street but was able to resume his seat in the House of Representatives a few months later.

John Quincy Adams, the sixth President, who died in the House of Representatives. From an 1843 daguerrotype.

THE METROPOLITAN MUSEUM OF ART. GIFT OF
I.N. PHELPS STOKES, EDWARD S. HAWES,
ALICE MARY HAWES, MARION AUGUSTA HAWES, 1937

On 21 February 1848 he was writing at his desk in the chamber when the Speaker rose to put a question. Adams rose at the same moment and then fell insensible into the arms of a neighboring member. He was carried to a sofa, which was moved first to the Hall of the Rotunda to give the dying man more air, then to the Speaker's room, where Adams lay semiconscious for two days with his family in attendance. His right side was evidently paralyzed. Cupping, application of mustard plasters and leeching were resorted to without avail.

"This is the last of earth. I am content," he murmured, and soon afterward, at 7:20 P.M. on 23 February 1848, he died quietly. He was buried in the family tomb at Quincy, Mass.

Adler, Alfred (1870–1937).

At the time of his death the Austrian psychoanalyst was giving a series of popular lectures at Aberdeen University in Scotland. On the morning of 28 May 1937 he set off from the Caledonia Hotel for a brisk walk around the downtown streets. "What a vigorous old boy that is," reflected a Scottish girl on her way to work. At that moment, shortly after 9:30 A.M., she saw him stumble in busy Union Street and lie motionless on the sidewalk. A young theological student who had attended Adler's lectures rushed across the street and loosened his collar. As Adler lost consciousness, he murmured "Kurt," the name of his son. An official, passing by in a streetcar, also hurried across, prepared to sign the death certificate on the spot. Wiser heads prevailed; for so eminent a foreigner an autopsy was surely advisable. Death was caused by degeneration of the heart muscle. Adler's body was taken to Edinburgh Crematorium; the ashes were placed in an urn chosen by his daughter, Alexandra, and left in a beautiful loggia above the chapel.

Agrippina the Younger (A.D. 16–59).

Agrippina, the mother of Nero by her first husband, was accused of poisoning her second husband in A.D. 49 and may have dispatched her third husband (her uncle, Claudius I) by the same means in 54. In 59, Nero plotted her murder by drowning. On about 20 March, simulating a reconciliation, he invited her to come from her estate at Antium (Anzio) to Baiae, west of Naples, where he was celebrating Minerva's five-day festival, and where he embraced her warmly as she disembarked. On her departure after nightfall, the roof of the specially appointed vessel, heavily loaded with lead, fell in on a prearranged signal. One of her maidservants was killed; the other was slain by the crew with poles and oars. But Agrippina escaped with only a shoulder wound; in the confusion she was able to swim away and was picked up by a small boat. Nero, in terror that she would revenge herself on him, or else inform the senate and the people of his crimes, immediately sent Anicetus, a freeman, with an armed band to her nearby villa at Bauli. Though taken unawares, she did not lack courage.

"If you have come to see me," she said, "take back word that I have recovered. If you have come to do ill, I believe nothing against my son. He has not ordered his mother's murder." Thereupon, the captain smote her savagely over the head with his club and, as the centurion drew his sword, she exposed herself. "Smite my womb," she said scornfully and so died.

Her body was cremated the same night, apparently on her dining-room couch, which had been carried into the garden of the villa.

Albert I (1875–1934).

The king of the Belgians (from 1909), a tall muscular man, still athletic at the age of fifth-eight, was a popular monarch. On 17 February 1934 he decided on an impulse to spend the afternoon climbing and drove off from his Brussels palace with his valet, Van Dyck, to a famous wall of rock that overhangs the Meuse valley at Marche-les-Dames. He told Van Dyck he would rejoin him at 4:00 or 4:30, but the wintry twilight descended without his reappearance. The valet searched in the dark along the brambly, boulder-strewn path, then called the palace for help. For several hours the king's aides continued the search until, anxious and exhausted, one of them tripped over a taut rope. Still attached to it was Albert's body, which lay fifty yards down the slope from the foot of the cliff.

Two explanations for the accident were proposed: either the king, reaching the top of the climb, had leaned against a boulder which became dislodged, or a pinnacle around which his rope was belayed had broken off, causing him to fall about sixty feet. After eight hours of procession and religious rites in St. Gudule Cathedral, Brussels, the king was laid to rest in the royal crypt at Laeken.

Albert of Saxe-Coburg-Gotha
(1819–1861).

Queen Victoria's consort was badly shaken when he leaped from a runaway coach on a visit to Coburg in 1860 and was seriously ill with "English cholera" two months later. His sleeplessness and exhaustion were aggravated by domestic and international worries. His son Bertie, the future Edward VII, had become involved with a young actress, and war between the U.S. and Britain over the *Trent* incident was a distinct possibility. The original diagnosis of a feverish cold was replaced by one of "low fever," i.e., typhoid, no doubt contracted from the antiquated sanitary system at Windsor Castle. On 14 December 1861, his consciousness began to fade. At 5:00 P.M. the children were brought to the bed, one at a time, to be smiled upon for the last time. The queen wrote in her diary:

> I bent over him and said to him, "Es ist kleines Fräuchen" & he bowed his head; I asked him if he would give me "ein Kuss" & he did so....Two or three long but perfectly gentle breaths were drawn, the hand clasping mine and...*all, all,* was over....I stood up, kissed his dear heavenly forehead & called out in a bitter and agonizing cry, "Oh! my dear Darling!" and then dropped on my knees in a mute, distracted despair, unable to utter a word or shed a tear!

It was 10:50 P.M.; at midnight the great bell of St. Paul's brought the unexpected news to London's citizens.

Victoria never blamed the doctors. Her husband had worked and worried himself to his death—that was her view, and of all his anxieties the greatest was Bertie, Prince of Wales. She never forgave him.

The coffin was placed in a temporary sarcophagus in St. George's Chapel, Windsor. Final interment (in November 1868) awaited the completion of the magnificent mausoleum at nearby Frogmore.

Alcott, Louisa May (1832–1888).

The U.S. novelist and author of *Little Women* (1868) suffered from vertigo and other maladies for many years. About two years before her death she entered a homeopathic nursing home at 10, Dunreath Place, Roxbury, Boston, where sleeplessness and lack of appetite afflicted her. Despite a permanent writer's cramp in her thumb, she was able to complete the final book in the March family saga, *Jo's Boys* (1886), and to write the last book of all, *A Garland for Girls* (1888). She went to see her dying father in Louisburg Square, Boston, on 1 March and caught a chill by leaving hurriedly without her fur wrap when another visitor was announced. A day or so later she was prostrated by a violent headache, and as Dr. Milbrey Green, whose practice was firmly based on herbs, water and common sense debated whether she was suffering from a stroke or meningitis, she sank rapidly and died at 3:30 A.M., 6 March 1888 (the day of her father's funeral). She was buried on Authors' Hill in Sleepy Hollow Cemetery, Concord, Mass., near the graves of Emerson, Thoreau and Hawthorne.

Aleichem, Sholem *(Solomon Rabinowitz)* (1859–1916).

The Russian-born Yiddish writer fled with his family to Copenhagen in 1914 to escape German harassment. In December of that year, the Jewish community in the U.S. brought the diabetic author to New York. When *The New York Times* began publishing his Mottel stories, his immediate financial worries were abated. Though his health steadily worsened, he wrote feverishly to the end. He died of tuberculosis and diabetes early on 13 May 1916 at 968 Kelly Street in the Bronx. His wish that his body be taken to Europe after the war proved impracticable; it lies in a simple grave in Mount Neboh Cemetery, Cypress Hills, Queens, N.Y.

Alekhine, Alexander Alexandrovich (1892–1946).

The Russian chess master was found dead in his hotel room in Estoril, Portugal, on 24 March 1946, slumped over his chessboard. He had been dining alone when he succumbed to what seemed to be a heart attack, but at autopsy a piece of unchewed meat, three inches long, was found blocking his windpipe. Alekhine was without funds; after a three-week delay, while his wife was unsuccessfully sought, he was buried in Lisbon at the expense of the Portuguese Chess Federation.

Alexander I (1777–1825?).

The death of Aleksandr Pavlovich, Czar of all the Russias, is one of history's great riddles. According to the orthodox account, the genial ruler succumbed to "marsh fever" at an unimposing villa in Taganrog, a small port on the Sea of Azov, where he was wintering with the invalid czarina. An autopsy reported that "accumulation of serum in the brain" consequent upon liver disease was the cause of death, which occurred on 20 November 1825. The body did not leave Taganrog until 10 January 1826, and was not interred in St. Petersburg until 15 May. Rumors that this body was a fake and that the czar was still alive began to circulate almost at once. According to one account, Alexander, who was on record as desiring to quit the throne, made his escape on the yacht of the Earl of Cathcart, one-time ambassador at St. Petersburg.

Nearly eleven years later, a tall distinguished horseman, aged about sixty, was sentenced to twenty lashes for vagrancy at Krasnoufimsk in Siberia after refusing to disclose his identity to the police. Adopting the name Fyodor Kuzmich he became a hermit, gaining a reputation for sanctity, deep learning and an intimate knowledge of Alexander I's court. There were reports, too, of noble visitors traveling from the capital to see him. He died on 1 February 1864 and was buried in a monastery at Tomsk.

Most of the evidence is inconclusive or based on hearsay: that Alexander's surviving courtiers, failing to mourn him in 1825, did so in 1864; that Kuzmich made a deathbed confession; and that Kuzmich's body was secretly moved to Alexander's tomb in 1866. There were press reports in 1965 that the Soviet government was being prevailed upon to have both tombs opened, but these have not been followed up, and the Cathcart family refuses to have its papers examined.

Alexander the Great (356–323 B.C.).

By the time of his death, the young man had carried his empire and the Hellenistic world to India's borders and 500 miles up the Nile. In Babylon, near the hanging gardens of Nebuchadnezzar, he was taken ill with a fever on 18 May 323 B.C. after a prolonged banquet. His illness lasted for eleven days. At first he was able to make the daily sacrifice and even play with dice; on the eighth day he was unable to speak and for two days was unconscious. Stories that he was poisoned did not begin to circulate until six

Days of May (323 B.C.)	18	19	20	21	22	23	24	25	26	27	28
Days of sickness	1st	2nd	3rd	4th	5th	6th	7th	8th	9th	10th	11th
Days he got out of bed	x	x	x	x	x	x	x				
Sacrifices made (to the gods)	x	x	x	x	x	x	x				
Baths taken	x	x	x	x							
Gave orders to his officers	x	x	x	x	x		x				
Days he was able to speak	x	x	x	x	x	x	x				
Days he was conscious	x	x	x	x	x	x	x	x			

Alexander the Great's final illness. A clinical chart reconstructed by Dr. F. Destaing in 1970 from ancient biographies of Alexander.

years after his death, the cause of which has been variously assigned.

In a 1970 study, F. Destaing concludes that Alexander died of a fever and nothing else. Among the candidates (pneumonia, typhus, septicemia, typhoid and malaria) the signs point unerringly to primary malaria. His sarcophagus was exhibited in many countries until Ptolemy had a tomb built for the gold coffin in Alexandria's royal cemetery, where Antony and Cleopatra were later buried.

Allende (Gossens), Salvador (1908–1973).

Allende, who became president of Chile in 1970, was the first freely elected Marxist president in the Western Hemisphere. Following increasing unrest, some of it U.S.-inspired, the military demanded that Allende step down and, when they were defied, on 11 September 1973 they mounted bloody attacks on the presidential palace in Santiago and on Allende's private residence. Afterward, newsmen were invited to see his body, which was sprawled on a blood-soaked sofa in the anteroom of the Moneda Palace's second-floor dining hall, the apparent victim of a self-inflicted shot through the mouth. Yet Allende's last published photograph showed him, automatic rifle in hand, surrounded by his armed guard and apparently resolved to resist to the end, as he had promised to do in his final broadcast.

According to R.R. Sandford in his *Murder of Allende* (1976), Capt. Roberto Garrido led a patrol up the main staircase of the besieged palace toward the entrance of the Salon Rojo, then fired a short burst from his FAL machine gun at a band of armed civilian defenders he had spied through the dense smoke and dust. A bullet struck one of the men in the stomach; others also fired at the man who, as he writhed on the floor, was recognized as the president. A few minutes later he was pronounced dead. By order of the new regime the body was dressed in fresh garments to hide the wounds and the suicide staged by setting the body on the red velvet sofa and firing a shot from Allende's weapon upward through the head. The body now rests in a sealed coffin in the family crypt in the Santa Ines cemetery, Viña del Mar, Chile.

Hans Christian Andersen shortly before his death.

Andersen, Hans Christian
(1805–1875).

The Danish dramatist and author of fairy tales was a hypochondriac and high strung man who never married. Nevertheless, his journals reveal him to have been heterosexual, though timid toward women and ashamed of his sexual feelings. His health began to decline in 1874; first he suffered from bronchitis, later from liver cancer. In June 1875 his friends, Moritz and Dorothea Melchior, took him to their home, Rolighed ("Solitude"), outside Copenhagen, where he had a room with a balcony overlooking the Oresund. On 29 July he took to bed permanently. His hostess found him sleeping peacefully around 11:00 A.M., on 4 August 1875, but he died quietly while unattended a few minutes later. At his breast was found a farewell letter, written forty-five years earlier by the only woman he had ever loved. It was destroyed unread. Andersen is buried in Assistens Cemetery in Copenhagen.

André, John (1751–1780).

The British army major who, with Benedict Arnold, plotted the overthrow of West Point, was captured in civilian clothes within sight of the British lines near the Hudson River on 23 September 1780. Because incriminating papers were found on him he was tried and condemned to death for spying. His appeal to General Washington that he be shot, not hanged, remained unanswered, but the commander-in-chief later explained to Congress that the practice and usage of war made him unable to comply: either André was a spy and had to die a spy's death, or else he was a prisoner-of-war and should not be executed at all.

André, a young man of great charm and fortitude, almost broke down when, on 2 October 1780 at Tappan, N.Y., he first saw the gibbet and realized his desire to face a firing squad had been denied. However, he recovered and helped the hangman (a prisoner called Strickland who had blackened his face with grease to avoid recognition) to adjust the rope, and even supplied a handkerchief for binding his hands. "All that I request of you gentlemen," he said to the officers standing nearby,

Major John André. The self-portrait drawn by the British spy on the day of his execution.

LIBRARY OF CONGRESS

"is that you will bear witness to the world that I die like a brave man." The wagon, containing the black coffin on which André stood, was drawn quickly away, and his body allowed to swing for about half an hour. On 10 August 1821 the grave on the banks of the Hudson was opened. Only the bones and a leather cord, which André had used to tie back his hair, remained to be reinterred in Westminster Abbey. A peach tree whose rootlets had penetrated the coffin and entwined the skull was also taken and replanted in England.

Anne (1665–1714).

Queen Anne of Great Britain and Ireland was a dull-witted, obstinate, but kind woman who endured at least seventeen

The execution of the British spy, Major John André, in 1780. From a contemporary woodcut.

LIBRARY OF CONGRESS

pregnancies in twenty-five years of marriage without producing a single child to survive her. W.B. Saxbe in a 1972 study of the queen concludes that she suffered from a long-standing infection by the bacillus *Listeria monocytogenes*, which causes habitual abortion and meningitis in the newborn. Anne, a hearty eater, became so obese in her later years that she required a pulley to raise her from the drawing room to her bedroom. J. Kemble believes she suffered from a pulmonary embolism arising from thrombophlebitis of the thigh. When she died a few minutes after 7:00 A.M., 1 August 1714, it was probably from exhaustion of toxemia, but even a healthy person would have found her final treatment disabling. In a small room in Kensington Palace, surrounded by seven doctors, ladies-in-waiting and clergymen, she endured cupping, bleeding, blistering with hot irons, shaving of the head, and administration of an emetic. Her body lies in St. George's Chapel, Windsor.

Antonius, Marcus (83?–30 B.C.).

Mark Antony, Roman soldier and statesman, had "married" Cleopatra (q.v.) in 37 or 36 B.C. while still legally joined to his fourth wife, Octavia. The pair lived under constant apprehension of an invasion by Octavia's brother, the Emperor Octavian (later Augustus). He defeated their forces at Actium in 31 B.C. and thereafter their mutual devotion was seriously abraded by the emperor's enticements to each to murder the other. Failing to hold the frontier against the invaders, Antony spent his last night in a drunken orgy. Though he offered battle when daylight came, it was too late; his troops deserted him and he withdrew, as he had before, into Alexandria. In despair, he begged his page, Eros, to stab him, some say because he had heard false reports of Cleopatra's death. Instead, Eros thrust the dagger into his own breast. Thus emboldened, Antony ran his sword into his belly and collapsed, but the wound was not immediately fatal. Coming to his senses, he begged his men to finish him off, but they fled in horror.

Cleopatra heard the news in the mausoleum where she had taken refuge and ordered her dying lover to be brought to her. In the heat of the cloudless Egyptian morning of 1 August 30 B.C. he was hoisted to her window, covered with blood and sweat and

Johnny Appleseed's grave outside Fort Wayne, Indiana.
ALLEN COUNTY–FORT WAYNE HISTORICAL SOCIETY

almost demented by pain. He soon died in her arms. In his last words he advised her to make terms with Octavian and to think not of present misery but of their happy times together. He was buried nearby in a tomb which she was soon to share and which is now covered by the modern city of Alexandria.

Appleseed, Johnny (1774–1845).

According to tradition, by 1801, John Chapman had planted a chain of seedling apple nurseries, in advance of the settlers, from the Allegheny River to central Ohio. He then spent about twenty-five years in north-central Ohio where many of the "Johnny Appleseed" legends originate. On 18 March 1845 he died of pneumonia in the cabin of his old friend William Worth of St. Joseph's township, Allen County, Ind. According to Mr. Worth, Johnny had a fever settle on his lungs which baffled the physician's skill, and in a day or two after taking sick he "passed to the spirit land." A plain walnut coffin was made for him and he was buried in David Archer's graveyard two and a half miles north of Fort Wayne.

Archimedes (287?–212 B.C.).

The Greek mathematician and inventor regarded his contraptions, including the screw (which is still used for raising water in modern Egypt), as less important than his mathematical discoveries. Of these he was proudest of his calculation that a sphere has two-thirds the volume of the cylinder which circumscribes it: this dual figure was depicted on his tombstone at his request. He was killed in his mid-seventies during the capture of Syracuse by Marcellus, despite orders that he be spared.

Plutarch—in a single passage—reports varying accounts of Archimedes' death: that he was so intent on working out a problem drawn in the sand that he failed to notice the Roman invasion; he then refused to obey a soldier's order to follow him to Marcellus until he had worked out the solution, whereupon he was run through by the sword. But Plutarch also reports that he was bearing mathematical instruments to Marcellus when a band of soldiers slew him in the belief he was carrying away gold. He was buried near the Agrigentine Gate in Syracuse, Sicily.

Attila (406?–453).

The king of the Huns, whose empire extended over much of central and eastern Europe, was a squat man with a large head, deep-set eyes and flat nose. Following his marriage to yet another wife, a beautiful young girl named Ildico, a feast and drunken revel took place in his camp on the Hungarian plain. Not until far into the night did the king withdraw to the nuptial chamber. When the guests came to their senses the next day it was near midday. Hours later, when their leader had still not reappeared, the coarse jests gave way to alarm. They broke into the chamber, where they found Attila's naked body flat on its back with arms crossed. Blood had flowed from his nose and mouth and lay congealed on the white fur rug that covered the bed. The terrified bride, heavily veiled, cowered in a corner, unable to offer a coherent account of the night's events.

At first murder was suspected, but no wound could be discovered on the body and the physicians ruled out poison. Not for the first time the king's excesses had brought on a massive nosebleed, but this time, such was his state of stupefaction, he was evidently suffocated. The Huns chopped off their hair and slashed their cheeks in ceremonial grief. After the body had been buried, those who laid it to rest were slain to prevent disclosure of the grave site.

Austen, Jane (1775–1817).

The English mistress of the satirical novel abandoned work on *Sanditon* in March 1817 when she came down with a fever, during which her complexion became "black and white and every wrong colour." In May she left her home in Chawton for Winchester, seventeen miles away, in search of better medical advice. In her College Street lodgings she remained cheerful to the end. "I live chiefly on the sofa," she wrote in her final extant letter, "but am allowed to walk from one room to another." With her sister Cassandra at her side, she died peacefully at 4:30 A.M. on 18 July 1817. Her description of her symptoms fits those of Addison's disease, a functional deficiency of the adrenal cortex for which there was then no adequate therapy. (It was not until 1849 that Thomas Addison, father of endocrinology, first described the condition.) She was buried in Winchester Cathedral.

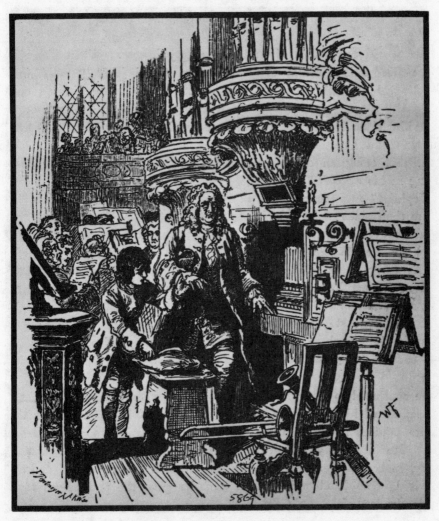

The blind and aged Bach being led to the organ.

NEW YORK PUBLIC LIBRARY

Bach, Johann Sebastian
(1685–1750).

The great German composer and organist, a robust man who
sired seven children by his first wife and thirteen by his second,

This mask of Bach was based on the skull found in St. John's Churchyard, Leipzig.

THE BETTMANN ARCHIVE

lived close to St. Thomas's Church, Leipzig, where he was a cantor for twenty-seven years. In the summer of 1749 his eyes began to fail; the trouble seems to have been glaucoma (excessive pressure within the eye), possibly of the hemorrhagic variety.

During the following winter he submitted to the ministrations of a notorious English quack, "Chevalier" John Taylor (1703–1772), who was then visiting Leipzig. Two operations were performed; both were failures and, to make matters worse, Taylor's subsequent treatment, consisting apparently of repeated incisions, poultices and applications of such irritants as calomel and cantharides, fatally undermined the unfortunate composer's health. Ten days before his death Bach fancied that his sight was temporarily restored. Then he suffered a stroke, followed by a high fever which continued until he died at 8:45 P.M., 28 July 1750. His grave, like his music, fell into oblivion. His widow Anna Magdalena, strangely neglected by her children, went to a pauper's grave ten years later.

When the Johanniskirche in Leipzig was being replaced by a larger church in 1894 it was necessary to disturb the burial ground. By this time, Bach's reputation had been transformed, and a search for his skeleton was made among the 1,400 in the churchyard. An account book disclosure that his coffin was oaken reduced the number of candidates to twelve. One of the skulls strikingly resembled Bach's portrait. The anatomist Wilhelm His directed the sculptor C. Seffner to create a bust of the composer using a plaster cast of this skull as a base. It was satisfactory, whereas a bust of Handel—made in a similar way— failed to fit the cast at all. To clinch the matter, His measured the thickness of flesh at nineteen points on the faces of thirty-seven fresh corpses of both sexes and various ages. Adhering strictly to the median values so obtained, Seffner repeated his likeness of Bach. "This bust," writes K. A. Baer in a 1951 study, "exhibits all the characteristic features known from the portraits and is more lifelike and expressive than any of them."

Bacon, Francis (1561–1626).

During an outing late in March 1616, the English philosopher and man of letters discussed with Dr. Witherborne, a Scottish physician, the possibility of using snow—which was lying thick in the London streets—instead of salt to preserve meat. Alighting from their coach at the foot of Highgate Hill, they purchased a fowl and proceeded to stuff it with snow. Bacon, already cold, became so chilled by the experiment that he took ill and was put to bed at the Earl of Arundel's house at Highgate. Suffering probably from bronchitis and then pneumonia, he steadily declined and died on Easter Sunday, 9 April 1626, in the arms of his oddly named kinsman, Sir Julius Caesar. He is buried near his mother in the little old church of St. Michaels at St. Albans, Hertfordshire.

Balzac, Honoré de (1799–1850).

After years of reluctance, the French writer's mistress, Evelina Hanska, gave in and married him in the Ukraine in March 1850. By then his bronchitis and heart condition were clearly dragging him down. In May they journeyed back to Paris in easy stages. The house in the rue Fortunée had been made ready for them by Balzac's mother, but the sole manservant had gone mad and turned out the maid. They hammered in vain on the door until a locksmith, who had been summoned, forced his way through the crowd and came to their aid. Balzac, almost blind by now, collapsed two days later. Peritonitis and nephritis led finally to gangrene. "Send for Bianchon," he is said to have muttered, in reference to one of his own creations, a physician who appears in *La Comédie Humaine*, his unfinished masterpiece. Victor Hugo came to pay his respects on the evening of 18 August 1850, and late the same night, his body swollen, his face almost black, Balzac died. Evelina had retired; only his mother was with him. Balzac was buried in Père-Lachaise Cemetery on 21 August; Victor Hugo gave the funeral oration.

Bankhead, Tallulah (1903–1968).

The husky-voiced U.S. actress made her last appearances on television talk shows. After a long stay in Maryland at her sister's house, she returned to her New York apartment early in December 1968, her weight down below a hundred pounds. A few days later she was taken, along with her lucky rabbit's foot, to St. Luke's Hospital with Asian flu. She was a difficult patient, screaming at the staff and tearing the intravenous feeding tube from her arm. She died in the intensive-care unit on 12 December and, dressed in her favorite wrapper, was buried beside the lake at her sister's home at Rock Hall, Maryland.

Barnum, Phineas Taylor
(1810–1891).

The U.S. showman rallied after "congestion of the brain" was diagnosed in November 1890, but in April 1891 he realized the end was near. Hearing that he wished to read his own obituary, the New York *Evening Sun* obliged with four columns. The old man, lying in his Bridgeport, Ct., home, greatly relished the account before dying a few days later on 7 April. He was buried beside his wife, Charity, in the beautiful Mountain Grove Cemetery, Bridgeport.

The Barrymores.

The youngest of this eminent U.S. family of actors, **John** (1882–1942), was the first to die. He collapsed in a Los Angeles dressing room on 19 May 1942 while assisting at a rehearsal of Rudy Vallee's radio program. He died ten days later at Hollywood Presbyterian Hospital of a combination of respiratory and kidney ailments. He had been divorced from his fourth wife, Elaine Barry, in 1940 and at the time of his death was plagued by creditors.

Lionel (1878–1954), an artist at heart, broke his hip in 1936 when a heavy metal drawing board collapsed. Thereafter, he achieved success in wheelchair roles, notably in Dr. Kildare movies. On 15 November 1954 he was sitting in the sunshine with his former secretary, Florence Wheeler, on the terrace of her mother's house in the San Fernando Valley near Los Angeles. He was overweight and suffering from congestive heart failure. Suddenly, while reading *Macbeth* aloud to his companion, he suffered a final heart attack and collapsed in her arms. He died at Valley Hospital, Van Nuys, without regaining consciousness.

Ethel (1879–1959) was confined to bed during her last year and a half by arthritis and heart disease. Katharine Hepburn, a regular visitor to Ethel's Los Angeles home, later recalled that she remained beautiful and well-groomed, surrounded by flowers and books in a room kept so cold as to freeze anyone else to death, "but not Ethel." On her last evening she woke from a short nap, grasped her nurse's hand, and asked, "Is everybody happy?

I want everybody to be happy. I know *I'm* happy!" She fell asleep soon afterward and died early on 18 June 1959. All three Barrymores lie in a crypt at Calvary Cemetery, Los Angeles.

Baudelaire, Charles-Pierre (1821–1867).

It was in Paris' Latin Quarter that the French poet—then a young man—contracted the syphilis that killed him twenty-five years later. In his final years his skin was discolored and his joints were affected. The first signs of insanity appeared in 1862. He collapsed in March 1866 while pointing out the rich carvings in a Belgian church to two companions. He returned to Paris in a private railroad car some months later and over the next twelve months suffered a slow death. By early 1867 he scarcely remembered his own name; by April he had lost the will to live; on 31 August he died in his mother's arms. He was buried during a heavy rainstorm in the cemetery at Montmartre.

Beardsley, Aubrey (1872–1898).

The controversial artist of black-and-white illustrations for *The Yellow Book* and Wilde's *Salomé* was too ill to go to church when he was received into the Roman Catholic faith in March 1897. A few days later the thin, tuberculous young man—only twenty-five years old—traveled in stages from Bournemouth, England, to Menton, France, with his mother. His final task, the illustrations for a reissue of *Volpone*, was left unfinished. Toward the end the dying man, propped up in bed, abandoned line-and-wash and resorted to pencil. His reading turned to religious books. His last scrawled letter was to Leonard Smithers, his publisher in London:

Jesus is our Lord & Judge
Dear Friend,
        I implore you to destroy *all* copies of Lysistrata and bad drawings. Show this to Pollitt and conjure him to do same. By all that is holy—*all* obscene drawings.
        Aubrey Beardsley
In my death agony.

He died at the Hôtel Cosmopolitain early on 16 March 1898. His mother wrote: "His marvellous patience and courage…touched all who were near him." After a Solemn Requiem Mass in the cathedral at Menton, his wasted body was carried up a steep hill to a cemetery above the town in sight of the sea. *See* S. Weintraub (1967).

Becket, Thomas à (1118?–1170).

Thomas was an aggressive Archbishop of Canterbury, inimical in his dealings with Henry II. When Thomas condemned and suspended the bishops who had taken part in a ceremony at the king's behest, and elected, moreover, to end his own exile in France, Henry was provoked to an angry outburst which he lived to regret: "Have I no one here who will deliver me from this man?" Four of his knights forthwith set out for Canterbury with murder in their hearts. At the confrontation in Thomas' palace on 29 December 1170, the knights found the archbishop polite but resolute. He was determined by now to become a martyr, and declined to take refuge in the cathedral, whereupon his followers dragged him into the sanctuary there. Nevertheless, he ordered the doors to be reopened so that, when the murderous gang arrived with much clatter of armor, they met no resistance.

"Where is Thomas Becket, traitor to the king and his realm?" they shouted. Undaunted, Thomas descended the steps. "Lo, here I am, no traitor to the king, but a priest."

He refused to remove the excommunication sentences and the suspensions he had imposed on the king's followers but, while indicating his willingness to die, ordered that no one else be hurt. The intruders seized him and attempted to drag him from the church before killing him. Failing in this they brandished their swords, whereupon the martyr inclined his head and lifted his hands in prayer. The first stroke sliced off the crown of his head; even after the second blow Thomas still stood, but a third stroke felled him. "For the name of Jesus and the protection of the Church I am ready to embrace death," he murmured. Another knight, Richard Brito, then smote him with such force that his sword was broken and Thomas's brain exposed. A renegade cleric, Hugh of Horsea, nicknamed "Mauclerk," placed his foot on the martyr's neck and drew out the skull's contents with the point of his sword.

Henry, panic-stricken by what his rash words had led to, fasted and later submitted to scourging. By the end of 1172 he had made his peace with Rome. Thomas was canonized in 1173; in 1220 his remains were moved to a shrine constructed in the chapel at the east end of Canterbury Cathedral immediately behind the high altar.

Beethoven, Ludwig van
(1770–1827).

The cause of the great German composer's deafness, which prevented his playing in public after 1814, was probably otosclerosis—the progressive formation of hard deposits around the tiny stirrup bone of the middle ear. This hinders movement of the tympanic membrane. His final decade began with attacks of bronchitis and rheumatism and thereafter he was seldom

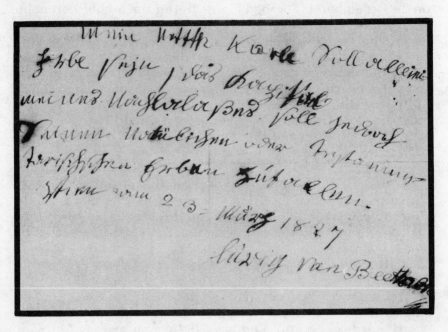

The conclusion of Beethoven's will, which he signed three days before his death.

VIENNA CITY ARCHIVES

Beethoven on his deathbed, from a contemporary sketch.

BRITISH LIBRARY

really well. In July 1826 his nephew Karl tried to kill himself; as soon as the gunshot wound of the head permitted, Beethoven took Karl to his brother Johann's house near Gneixendorf. He made the return journey to Vienna in wintry weather in an open cart. Back in his lodgings in the Schwarzspanierhaus, Beethoven became ill; on 2 December doctors found him with flushed skin, parched lips and unnaturally bright eyes. In the new year he became jaundiced with an enlarged, nodular liver. His abdomen was tapped four times to release accumulated fluid. After receiving the Last Rites on 24 March 1827, he lapsed into a restless stupor, during which he picked aimlessly at the bed covers. At about 6:00 P.M. on the 26th a loud thunderclap roused him for the last time; he sat up and shook his fist at the rattling window, then fell back dead.

At autopsy, Beethoven's limbs were found to be terribly wasted. The liver was shrunken to half its normal size, leathery and greenish-blue, and covered with bean-sized nodules; hence his death was due to liver failure, but the cirrhosis was of neither the alcoholic nor syphilitic type. There was evidence of kidney disease also. S.J. London, in a 1964 study, concluded that the composer had probably suffered from chronic recurrent pancreatitis and an irritable colon associated with irregular drinking bouts. His deeply pock-marked face may have been a symptom not of smallpox but of lupus erythematosus.

Beethoven was buried at Währing on 29 March. In 1863, after the grave had fallen into neglect, his body was exhumed and reburied. In June 1888 the remains of Beethoven and Schubert were removed to the Central Cemetery in Vienna, where they now repose side by side.

Behan, Brendan (1923–1964).

The last years of the Irish rebel, author and monumental tosspot were completely overwhelmed by alcoholism. On Christmas Day 1963 in Dublin he was given Last Rites, but marched out of the hospital to resume his marathon boozing. The following month he was discovered lying in the street with a deep gash in his forehead. By this time he lived in intolerable squalor, seldom even half-sober. In March he collapsed in a tavern and was taken unconscious to Meath Hospital, Dublin, with irreversible liver damage. A misguided friend smuggled a bottle of brandy in to him. A tracheotomy was performed to aid his breathing but he died a few hours later on the evening of 20 March 1964. The death certificate read "fatty degeneration of the liver"; it should have read "suicide." Behan was buried in Glasnevin Cemetery, Dublin.

Belloc, Hilaire (1870–1953).

The French-born writer survived a 1942 stroke and subsequent pneumonia for over a decade. His daughter was preparing Sunday lunch at their home, King's Land, in the village of Shipley, near Horsham, Sussex, on 12 July 1953 when she smelled smoke. Rushing from the kitchen to his study, she found him lying on his back near the fireplace, surrounded by several live coals and his clothes smouldering. He was taken to the

Hilaire Belloc at 83 sitting before the fireplace where his fatal accident occurred.

THE ILLUSTRATED LONDON NEWS

Franciscan-run Mount Alvernia nursing home at Guildford suffering from severe shock and burns of the back. Belloc died on 16 July and was buried at West Grinstead, Sussex.

Benchley, Robert (1889–1945).

The U.S. humorist suffered a series of increasingly severe nose-bleeds before his death of cerebral hemorrhage at Columbia Presbyterian Medical Center, New York, on 21 November 1945. When Benchley's widow and son took his ashes out to Nantucket Island for burial in the spring of 1946, the urn was found to be empty. "My mother was quiet for a while," writes Nathaniel Benchley, "and then slowly she began to smile. 'You know,' she said, 'I can hear him laughing now.'"

Bennett, Arnold (1867-1931).

The English novelist rashly drank water from a carafe while in Paris in January 1931 and suffered a shivering fit on the way back to London. On 3 February he attended a wedding reception and then went to the theater but, "wretchedly ill," he took to his bed that night for the last time. Sir William Willcox diagnosed typhoid fever; gall bladder infection and toxemia followed. For three weeks of his long ordeal Bennett was exhausted by hiccups. Since 1923 he had lived with Dorothy Cheston, the mother of his only child. His estranged wife, Marguerite, who refused him a divorce, journeyed from France, but could get no nearer the deathbed than the foyer of his apartment building, where she spoke to visitors as they came and went. Bennett's brother and sisters were in constant attendance, while the dying man clung to Dorothy's wrist for hours at a time. "Everything has gone wrong, my girl," he whispered. On the main thoroughfare near his flat at 97 Chiltern Court, Clarence Gate, straw had been laid to deaden the noise of steel-rimmed cartwheels. Bennett died at 8:50 P.M., 27 March 1931. His brother Frank took his ashes to Burslem Cemetery, Staffordshire, where they were placed in his mother's grave. It is marked by an unattractive gray granite obelisk on which his death date is shown incorrectly.

Benny, Jack (1894–1974).

The Chicago-born radio and television comedian visited all parts of the U.S. during the summer of 1974. He was already signed up to play the part of an ancient vaudevillian in the movie *The Sunshine Boys*, and the only concern was that he looked too young. Numbness in the hand when he picked up his violin to warm up for a show in Dallas in October caused concern, but a thorough examination back home in Los Angeles failed to find anything wrong. The numbness went away, but stomach pains that had bothered Benny for some time worsened. By early December he was sedated much of the time, but plans for a television special continued as late as the 18th.

Two days later, Mrs. Benny (Mary Livingstone) telephoned Jack's agent Irving Fein with the news that her husband had been found to have cancer of the pancreas and had only about two weeks left. The dying man was not told. Within five days came tidings that Benny was sinking rapidly, and Fein spent a miserable Christmas Day with Benny's lawyer choosing a coffin and sarcophagus for their friend. Benny died at 11:26 on the night of 26 December 1974 at his Holmby Hills estate in Los Angeles.

At the funeral service in Culver City, Bob Hope complained that, for once, Jack Benny's timing was all wrong. "He left us much too soon. He was stingy to the end. He only gave us eighty years, and it wasn't enough." His black-veined marble sarcophagus lies in a mausoleum on a green slope at Hillside Memorial Park, Los Angeles. *See* I.A. Fein (1976).

Bentham, Jeremy (1748–1832).

Only after his memory began to fail in 1831 did the high-spirited English jurist and philosopher lose his boyish enthusiasm. Just before his death on 6 June 1832 at his home—the Hermitage in Queen's Square Place, London—he said to his friend and biographer Sir John Browning, "I now feel I am dying; our care must be to minimize pain...." "After he had ceased to speak," writes Browning, "he smiled and grasped my hand, looked at me affectingly, and closed his eyes." He died with his head resting on his friend's bosom. In his will, Bentham directed that his body be dissected with a view to advancing scientific knowledge and his skeleton used as the foundation of a self-memorial or "auto-icon." Because mummification of the head produced an alteration of facial expression it was replaced by a wax bust; this was set

Jeremy Bentham, whose clothed skeleton is on permanent display at University College, London. The mummified head is kept in the college safe.

UNIVERSITY COLLEGE, LONDON, ENGLAND

atop the padded, articulated skeleton. The lifelike figure, clothed in Bentham's own garments, is on public view in the Cloisters at University College, London. It is seated, wearing a wig and wide-brimmed hat and with the philosopher's favorite cane, "Dapple," across his knees.

Bernadette, Saint (1844–1879).

As a child, Bernadette Soubirous had a series of visions of the Blessed Virgin Mary that led to the foundation of a shrine at Lourdes. From the time she was six years old she had serious difficulty with her breathing; throughout her life her condition was referred to as asthma, but there is no doubt that it was tuberculosis. At sixteen she entered the Hospice of the Sisters of Charity at Lourdes, but her work in the kitchen and infirmary and the constant stream of visitors and sick greatly fatigued her and caused much pain and hemorrhaging of the lungs. "Open my chest and let me breathe," she begged the sisters. In 1866 she entered the Convent of Saint Gildard at Nevers. There she was treated most severely "so as not to encourage her pride" (of which she had none).

In 1873 Mother Adelaide Dons came to Nevers and brightened the last years of Bernadette's life with her kindness. By 15 April 1879 she was only half-conscious with moments of delirium. The following day she could scarcely breathe and was supported upright in a chair with her crucifix bound tightly to her breast. As she died on Easter Day, 16 April 1879, the nuns heard her murmur, "Blessed Mary, Mother of God, pray for me—a poor sinner, a poor sinner...." Bernadette lies in a vault below the tiny chapel of St. Joseph in the convent at Nevers.

Bernhardt, Sarah (1844 or 1845–1923).

In 1886, on her homeward voyage from South Africa, the French actress fell and severely injured her right knee. The ship's doctor recommended that *pointes de feu*—smouldering slivers of burning wood—be applied to the knee. Sarah was prepared to endure the treatment, but the man was so filthy that she hurled a hairbrush at him and drove him from her cabin.

Sarah Bernhardt in the death scene in "La Dame Aux Camellias."
THE BETTMANN ARCHIVE

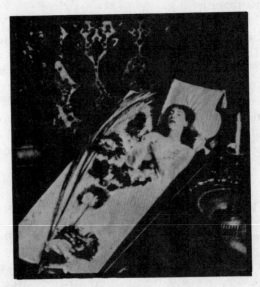

Sarah Bernhardt asleep in her coffin.
THE BETTMANN ARCHIVE

Later this remedy was applied to no avail and over the years the knee caused her great pain, resembling "an animal gnawing my nerves and tendons"; on stage she was frequently obliged to lean on something or someone for support.

In September of 1914 Bernhardt left for Andernos-les-Bains in the Gironde, her leg by this time immobilized in plaster. The next few months should have been tranquil, but her leg was excruciatingly painful and when the cast was removed it was found that gangrene had set in. Amputation was inevitable, but it was difficult to find a surgeon who would operate on a seventy-one-year-old woman with chronic uremia. Finally, Dr. Denucé in nearby Bordeaux amputated the leg on 22 February 1915. Sarah returned to Paris in October 1915 and, despite strong opposition, toured the front lines entertaining the troops. The Boston *Sunday Advertiser* on 18 March 1923 carried the headline BERNHARDT, DYING, ACTS FOR MOVIES. She had taken the part of a clairvoyant in the film *La Voyante*. Too ill to work in the studio, she had the film shot in her Paris home on Boulevard Pereire. On 22 March, emerging from a coma, she announced, "They can now film me in bed." But on the following day it was impossible to continue the production. It was spring in Paris and she asked her son Maurice to cover her with roses, lilacs and Parma violets. A priest administered the Last Rites and, at five past eight on the evening of 25 March 1923, Sarah Bernhardt died. She is buried in Père-Lachaise Cemetery in a plain mausoleum bearing the single name BERNHARDT.

Bierce, Ambrose (1842–1914?).

Richard O'Connor in his 1967 biography of the U.S. writer says, "The greatest fame that Ambrose Bierce achieved was simply vanishing from life, whether deliberately or by mischance." It is possible that Bierce went into Mexico intending to die, for he was seventy-one years old and suffering from asthma. His daughter Helen wrote, "When his hour struck he wanted to go quickly and with none of his friends near to look upon his face afterward."

Late in November 1913 Bierce was granted credentials as an observer with Pancho Villa's rebel army. He arrived at Chihuahua City on 16 December carrying at least $1500 in U.S.

currency. Villa's troops had just occupied the city and the next big fight would be against the federal garrison in Ojinaga. Bierce evidently intended to be there. In a short letter on Christmas Eve he wrote, "Pray for me—real loud." His last letter, dated 26 December, said, "——Expect next day to go to Ojinaga, partly by rail." After that—silence and mystery.

It is probable he did reach Ojinaga, where there was fierce fighting between 1 and 10 January 1914. A photograph of Bierce was shown to one of Villa's officers, who thought he had seen him during the fighting. O'Connor believes it possible that Bierce died in the confusion of battle and was buried in an unmarked desert grave.

Bizet, Georges (1838–1875).

The French composer had long suffered from muscular rheumatism. In May 1875 the pains increased. The abscesses in his throat and mouth from the severe attack of throat angina in 1874 had healed but, complaining of fits of suffocation, he felt that he had to get out of Paris. In Bougival the cool breezy air from the Seine immediately improved his health and spirits. On Sunday 30 May (he had gone swimming the previous day) Bizet suffered an acute rheumatic attack with high fever, extreme pain and almost total immobility of his arms and legs. On Monday night he had an extremely painful heart attack. Dr. Clément Launay applied blisters to the chest. The patient was somewhat better on Wednesday but suffered a final heart attack at about 11:00 P.M.. He died in a coma a few hours later, between midnight and 3:00 A.M. on 3 June. An abscess in Bizet's left ear burst while he was in the coma, leaving traces of blood on his neck. This gave rise to a rumor that he had committed suicide. He was buried on 5 June at the Church of the Trinity in Paris.

Bogart, Humphrey (1899–1957).

The U.S. movie actor owed his lisp to a prisoner he was escorting to detention while in the Navy in 1918. In Boston the handcuffed man smashed him across the face, almost tearing off his upper lip.

For years Bogart had had a dry cough, but by early 1956 his excuse of a "sensitive throat" was no longer convincing. Besides, he was off his food and underweight, and his throat burned when he drank orange juice. After Greer Garson persuaded him to see her doctor, Maynard Brandsma, malignant tissue was detected and an immediate operation was scheduled at Good Samaritan Hospital, Los Angeles. On 1 March in a nine-and-a-half-hour procedure Dr. John Jones removed the diseased portion of the esophagus and repositioned the stomach so that it could be attached to the remaining gullet.

For a time Bogart felt better, but follow-up x-ray therapy nauseated him and he failed to gain weight. Late in November he spent five days in St. John's Hospital, Santa Monica, for what reporters were told was correction of pressure on a nerve caused by scar tissue. Nitrogen mustards were administered in a vain attempt to check the spreading cancer. After that, the actor never left his home at 232 Mapleton Drive, in the Holmby Hills section of Los Angeles.

In her autobiography *By Myself* (1978), Bogart's widow, Betty (Lauren Bacall), has recorded in graphic detail the story of his final weeks. Until the last two days he came downstairs—in a chair wedged inside a dumbwaiter—to join friends and enjoy a martini made with dry sherry. To some of his visitors the sight of "Bogie," reduced almost to skin and bone, was more than they could bear. On Saturday night, 12 January 1957, Katherine Hepburn and Spencer Tracy came, as usual, after everyone else had gone and when Bogart was back upstairs in bed. They stayed with him for forty minutes and later he watched a movie on television. That night he asked Mrs. Bogart to lie beside him. He was terribly restless, his hands continually plucking at his chest. When Brandsma came by early next morning, the dying man told him he never wanted to go through a night like that again.

Bogart's last words to his wife, as he dabbed shakily at his chin with an electric shaver were, "Goodbye Kid. Hurry back." When she returned a few minutes later, after collecting their two children, Stephen and Leslie, from Sunday School, he was in a deep sleep that turned into unconsciousness. At midnight the nurses suggested she rest in the little "nap-room" next to their bedroom. They awoke her at 2:10 A.M., Monday, 14 January 1957, with the news that "Mr. Bogart has just died." In the final minutes his pulse raced and his temperature shot up; he never regained consciousness.

Bogart would have liked his ashes to be cast into the Pacific from his beloved yawl, the *Santana*, but at that date this could not be done legally, and instead his ashes were interred in Forest Lawn Memorial Park, Los Angeles. While the cremation took place miles away, John Huston read the eulogy at a simple service in All Saints Protestant Episcopal Church, Beverly Hills. By his widow's request, the dead man's spirit was symbolized by a model of the *Santana*, which stood in a glass case on the altar rail.

Boleyn, Anne (1507?–1536).

The second wife of Henry VIII and mother of the future Elizabeth I had not been able to present the king with a male heir. Thomas Cromwell, the sovereign's henchman, aware of the king's courtship of Jane Seymour, a lady-in-waiting to Anne, systematically collected, by bribery and threats, the evidence for her destruction. Anne was brought to trial in the King's Hall on 15 May 1536 on charges of adultery with four men, including Smeaton, a court musician; of incest with her brother, Viscount Rocheford; and of plotting the king's death. The four courtiers had been found guilty at an earlier trial; Anne and then Rocheford were condemned to death—the queen by burning or beheading, Rocheford by hanging, drawing (disembowelment while alive) and quartering (dissection).

The king, who undoubtedly believed the atrocious indictments, nevertheless intended to be merciful, and ordered Rocheford (and all the others except Smeaton) to be dispatched by the headsman. For Anne, as befitted her royal station, he sent across the water to Calais for the swordsman there, an expert executioner. Sir William Kingston, Lieutenant of the Tower of London, was unnerved by the queen's gaiety in her last hours. It may, of course, have been no more than hysteria. The moment was delayed from 9:00 A.M. until noon on 19 May 1536, a fact that Anne regretted when she heard of it, "for I thought to be dead, and past my pain." To this, Kingston awkwardly replied, "It should be no pain, it is so subtle." "I heard say," she chattered on merrily, "that the executioner was very good—and I have a little neck." Upon which she laughed shrilly.

Escorted by Kingston, Anne walked down to Tower Green wearing a fur-trimmed gown of gray damask over a crimson petticoat. Her hair was plaited and tucked into a pearl-embroidered netted caul over which she wore a French head-dress. She mounted the steps to the high scaffold with her ladies and addressed the crowd. She would say nothing against her sentence or accuse any man, "But I pray to God to save the King, and send him long to reign over you—for a gentler nor a more merciful prince was there never...." The masked headsman from Calais had already craved her pardon and received his fee. Her headdress and mantle were removed and she was blindfolded. She was led to the block, where she knelt and prayed aloud. The executioner, standing above her, was handed his sword, and with a single, hissing stroke severed her head as a cannon sounded from the battlements. He picked up the head to show that justice had been done, then dropped it into the straw.

Late that afternoon Kingston remembered the body; he had it placed in an old arrow chest and buried beside that of Anne's brother in the chapel of St. Peter-ad-Vincula in the Tower. Some reports have it that friends moved her body secretly to a Norfolk church near her birthplace and buried it beneath an unmarked marble slab. *See* H.W. Chapman (1974).

Boone, Daniel (1734–1820).

When well over eighty years old, the intrepid frontiersman journeyed six hundred desolate miles to spend the winter season trapping in Yellowstone country. The farther slopes of the Rockies intrigued him and he talked of visiting them the following year, but he was beginning to feel intimations of mortality. On one trip with his servant Derry he felt he was going to die and gave instructions as to how and where he should be buried, but after the grave was dug he felt better. Chester Harding, as he was painting the old man's portrait, asked him if he had ever been lost, and received the tart reply, "No, I can't say as ever I was lost, but I was once bewildered for three days." He would sit on the riverbank near his home in St. Charles County, Mo., and watch the brown Missouri roll by, pondering his lack of possessions but aware of the great love of country he had given his children and grandchildren.

A month before his eighty-sixth birthday, Boone was feverish but went to his son Nathan's home nearby as promised. After a

Daniel Boone's grave overlooking Frankfort, Kentucky. Photo by Caufield and Shook.

UNIVERSITY OF LOUISVILLE

generous helping of sweet potatoes he felt sick and retired to the sunny corner room reserved for him in the fine stone house he had helped build. There he died quietly on 26 September 1820. In 1845 Missouri yielded the bones of Daniel Boone and he was interred in Frankfort Cemetery, Kentucky. *See* L. Elliott (1976).

Booth, John Wilkes (1838–1865).

The assassin of Abraham Lincoln (q.v.) was a wild youth, an expert marksman who shot cats and dogs for pleasure. Booth identified himself with the Southern cause after being lionized as an actor in Richmond but, rather than endure possible hardships or bear arms for the Confederacy, he moved north again on the outbreak of the Civil War. In 1864 he plotted with a motley gang to abduct Lincoln, but nothing came of the plan. Booth was consuming astonishing amounts of brandy by this time, and his wild behavior caused at least one official to warn the president against him, but Lincoln took little heed. It was when he called at Ford's Theatre for his mail on the morning of 14 April 1865 that Booth realized the enemy had fallen into his hands. He heard that the White House had reserved a box for the benefit performance that night.

After the assassination, Booth, accompanied by David Herold, lived like a hunted beast for twelve days. Booth's broken leg was set by Dr. Samuel Mudd, who was later imprisoned, and the two fugitives succeeded in crossing from Maryland into Virginia. Very early on 26 April, soldiers surrounded them in Garrett's tobacco barn near Port Royal, Va. Herold surrendered, but Booth refused to come out. The barn was set ablaze and Booth was seen to draw his revolver. A shot was heard and he was dragged out with a bullet wound behind his right ear. He may have been hit by Sgt. Boston Corbett, as that officer claimed, or he possibly shot himself. He was carried to the porch of Garrett's farmhouse, where he died at 3:30 A.M. His last words were, "Tell mother I died for my country. I have done what I thought was for the best." The body was identified by Dr. John F. May of Washington, who had removed a fibroid tumor from Booth's neck the year before and recognized the scar. The damaged vertebra and spinal cord, removed at autopsy, have been preserved.

The body was exhumed from its secret grave under the flagstone floor of an arsenal warehouse, and reburied in the family plot in Greenmount Cemetery, Baltimore, Md., on 26 June 1869.

Boswell, James (1740–1795).

The friend and biographer of Samuel Johnson (q.v.), whose private papers, discovered between 1927 and 1940, reveal him to have been a frank and entertaining diarist, was a good-natured, courteous man of quick perception and remarkable memory. He was also a sot and a roué, an eavesdropper and tattletale lacking in decorum. The dissolute life he began in 1760 with London prostitutes and minor actresses is the material for many a lively page of his *London Journal*, first published in 1950, but his life ended tragically in illness.

W. B. Ober in two medical studies (1969, 1970) records that Boswell contracted no fewer than twelve fresh infections of gonorrhea between the ages of twenty and fifty years. Though he took no precautions against venereal disease, he seems to have avoided syphilis. After his marriage to his cousin Margaret Montgomerie in 1769, he remained faithful to her for almost three years.

She died of tuberculosis in 1789, leaving her husband with five children. On 31 January 1790 he was "sounded; almost fainted"; in other words, repeated inflammation of the urethra had led to a stricture requiring the passage of a metal probe to assist urination. In June of the same year he caught gonorrhea for the last time, but thereafter records no further symptoms.

On 14 April 1795 Boswell was taken ill at London's Literary Club and brought home by coach to No. 122 (now No. 47) Great Portland Street. The early symptoms were chills and fever, violent headache and persistent nausea. Thereafter, until his death five weeks later, Boswell was bedridden. His brother David wrote to William Temple, a friend of James', on 4 May: "I am sorry to say my poor brother is in the most imminent danger; a swelling of the bladder has mortified, but he is yet alive, and God Almighty may restore him to us." On the 8th the dying man scrawled in a barely legible hand the first sentence of a letter to Temple that was completed by dictation to his son: "I would fain write you with my own hand, but realy canot." They were his last written words; the remainder of the message was optimistic, but James Jr. warned Temple in a postscript that his father was "ignorant of the dangerous situation in which he was, and, I am sorry to say, still continues to be."

After a temporary improvement the nausea and vomiting began again and the patient rapidly weakened. On 18 May the younger James wrote to Temple that his father had "expressed a very earnest desire to be lifted out of bed, and Mr. Earle, the surgeon, thought it might be done with safety. But his strength was not equal to it, and he fainted away. Since then he has been in a very bad way indeed, and there are now, I fear, little or no hopes of his recovery." Round his bed as the end approached were his brother David, his elder daughters Veronica (his chief nurse) and Euphemia, and his sons Alexander and James. Boswell died on 19 May 1795; the same day David sent the sad news to Temple:

> I have now the painful task of informing you that my dear brother expired this morning at two o'clock. We have both lost a kind affectionate friend, and I shall never have such another. He has suffered a great deal during his illness, which has lasted five weeks, but not much in his last moments. May God Almighty have mercy upon his soul, and receive him into his heavenly Kingdom.

Ober, evaluating the reported symptoms, suggests the cause of death was "uremia, the result of acute and chronic urinary tract infection, secondary to postgonorrheal urethral stricture." A few days later Boswell was taken on his last, expensive journey (cost: 250 pounds) to the family vault at Auchinleck, near Cumnock, Ayrshire, Scotland.

Brahe, Tycho (1546–1601).

The Danish astronomer died in Prague of an infection caused by a burst bladder. He had neglected to relieve himself before a banquet given on 13 October 1601 by the Baron of Rosenberg, and good manners prevented his leaving the table; he died eleven days later. A fellow student had slashed Brahe's nose in December 1566 during a duel, leaving only the tip intact. Thereafter he wore a prosthesis—a silver-copper shell painted to match his skin. This was missing, probably stolen, when Brahe's body was exhumed in 1901, but a bright green stain caused by copper salts could be seen on the front of the skull. His body lies in the Teyn Church, Prague.

Brahms, Johannes (1833–1897).

The German composer's health began to decline in May 1896. Shocked by the death of his beloved Clara Schumann, he was further upset at missing part of the funeral ceremony in Frankfurt when, on leaving Ischl, he took the wrong train. He caught a chill at the cemetery from which he never really seemed to recover, though it was cancer of the liver that ultimately caused his death. Following a performance of Brahms' Fourth

Johannes Brahms in later life.

Symphony at a Philharmonic concert in Vienna on 7 March 1897, the conductor, Hans Richter, pointed up to the box in which the composer sat hidden by a curtain. As he stood to acknowledge the endless applause and cheers, "a thrill of awe and painful sympathy" ran through the audience as they recognized from his yellow-brown complexion and greatly changed appearance that this was his farewell.

The old bachelor took to his bed on the 25th under the devoted care of his housekeeper, Celestine Truxa, at 4 Carlsgasse, his Vienna lodgings for a quarter century. All day on 2 April he lay unconscious with his face to the wall. Early on the following morning he turned over with a sudden movement, and two great tears rolled down his jaundiced cheeks. When he died, at 9:30 A.M., the burly figure had become a thin old man. He was buried at the Central Cemetery, Vienna, close to Mozart's monument and the tombs of Beethoven and Schubert.

The Brontës.

Sickness and death overshadowed the lives of **Charlotte Brontë** (1816–1855), **Emily Brontë** (1818–1848), and their brother and sisters, who lived in the gloomy parsonage at Haworth on the windswept Yorkshire moors. Their mother Maria died in 1821 when only thirty-eight years old. The two oldest children, Maria and Elizabeth, died less than four years later from tuberculosis aggravated by their privations at the boarding school for the daughters of clergymen depicted in Charlotte's *Jane Eyre* (1847). The only boy, Patrick Branwell Brontë, ruined by alcohol and laudanum, died rather suddenly, apparently of tuberculosis, on 24 September 1848 at the age of thirty-one.

The stoical Emily, author of *Wuthering Heights* (1848), caught a cold at his funeral but refused medical aid. On 18 December 1848, carrying bread and meat in her apron from the kitchen for the two house dogs, she staggered and fell. The following morning, awakened by the dying woman's moans, Charlotte went out onto the frozen moors to search for heather for Emily's pillow, but could find only a sprig. Even on this, her last day, the doomed woman forced herself to dress and sit by the fire. The comb fell from her fingers into the grate as she tried to use it on her long brown hair and she lacked the strength to retrieve it. The grieving Charlotte, forbidden to say a word about Emily's health, was reduced to writing to her friend Ellen Nussey: "Moments so dark as these I have never known. I pray for God's support to us all." Returning from posting the letter down the lane, Charlotte found her sister writhing in pain. She helped her to the black horsehair sofa. "If you will send for a doctor, I will see him now," Emily gasped. By two o'clock the wildest, most passionate of the Brontës was dead at thirty. She was interred in a crypt under the stone floor of Haworth Church.

Gentle **Anne** (1820–1849) readily admitted she was ill and was eager to have the doctor call. Like Emily she was a victim of tuberculosis. Her last wish was to die by the sea. Charlotte and Ellen took her to lodgings at Scarborough with a night's stop at York, where Anne, the most religious of the sisters, viewed the Minster. She was able to ride in a donkey cart on the sands the day after their arrival at Scarborough but the next morning, 27 May 1849, she felt "a change" and was lifted from her chair to a bed. Like Emily, she died at about two in the afternoon, but her passing was in sharp contrast. "She died without severe struggle," wrote Charlotte in a letter, "assured that a better existence lay before her....I let Anne go to God, and felt He had a right to her. I could hardly let Emily go. I wanted to hold her back then, and I want her back now...." Anne lies high on a hill in St. Mary's graveyard, Scarborough.

For five years, Charlotte, a migrainous, high-strung woman, only 4 feet 9 inches tall, lived alone with her father, who kept largely to his own room. With his reluctant consent, she married Arthur Bell Nicholls, his curate, on 29 June 1854; she survived the wedding by only nine months. Charlotte's death is often ascribed to a chill after a walk in the rain in November, but her pregnancy is a much more likely cause. Though the single word "phthisis" appears on her death certificate, there is no evidence she was actively tuberculous. Throughout the first months of 1855 she was utterly overwhelmed by nausea and vomiting and could neither eat nor drink. Waking from a stupor shortly before her death she found her husband kneeling in prayer by her bed. "Oh," she whispered, "I am not going to die, am I? He will not separate us; we have been so happy." Early on Saturday night, 31 March 1855, her breathing stopped, just three weeks before her thirty-ninth birthday.

In a 1972 study Philip Rhodes, a professor of obstetrics and gynecology, has no hesitation in giving the true cause of death as hyperemesis gravidarum—the excessive nausea of pregnancy, which leads to essential salts and water being lost from the body. It is encountered most frequently in neurotic women. The condition was poorly understood in 1855; today its control poses no difficulty. Charlotte lies beside Emily in the crypt of Haworth Church.

Brooke, Rupert (1887–1915).

Although the best known of the handful of English poets who died in World War I, Brooke did not fall in battle. He joined the Royal Naval Volunteer Reserve as a sub-lieutenant on the outbreak of war in August 1914 and, at the time of his death, was serving in the Mediterranean. An attack of dysentery, while he was encamped at Port Said in early April 1915, weakened him considerably. Shortly afterward a swollen lip, probably an in-

Rupert Brooke's grave on the Greek island of Skyros.

fected mosquito bite, developed into a general septicemia. By 22 April Brooke was comatose on board the *Grantully Castle,* a troop transport lying off the Greek island of Skyros, with inflammation of the right side of the face and neck. A smear was examined; the organism responsible was a "*Diplococcus* morphologically resembling a *Pneumococcus.*"

In late afternoon the patient, wrapped in blankets, was hoisted overboard into a picket boat and transferred to a French hospital ship, the *Duguay-Truin,* which lay a mile away in Trebuki Bay. Brooke became the sole patient of the dozen surgeons on board. He was handed over with the exhortation that their charge was a precious one; "he's our best young poet and the apple of Winston's and Sir Ian's eye." Telegrams were sent to those eminent men (Churchill and Hamilton) with the news that Brooke's condition was "very grave" and that his parents should be told. At 9:00 A.M. on 23 April 1915 the French surgeons cauterized the infected area and an attempt was made to establish a focal abscess in the thigh (to draw away the bacteria in the neck, in accordance with the practice of the time).

But at 2:00 P.M., Brooke's temperature had risen to 106 degrees and he evidently could not last long. He died at 4:46 that afternoon in his airy cabin on the sun deck. The certificate reads: *Oedème malin et septicémie foudroyante* (Virulent edema and fulminating septicemia). Sub-Lt. Rupert Brooke, R.N.V.R., was buried that evening in an olive grove on Skyros. He was just one of sixty-six war dead that day; of the five men who made the cairn above his grave, only two survived until the Armistice. *See* C. Hassall (1964).

Browning, Elizabeth Barrett (1806–1861).

Elizabeth Barrett's secret marriage in 1846 to her fellow poet Robert Browning and their subsequent elopement was followed by fifteen happy years, spent mainly in Italy. Her invalidism, which began with an apparent spinal injury at the age of fifteen when she was saddling her pony, was greatly diminished during the first years of her marriage. Later, her predisposition to chest ailments returned, to such an extent she regarded herself as a "drag chain" on the plans of her active husband, six years her junior, and began to dread that his deep love might become eroded. That he remained constant to the end must have greatly heartened her in the final days, and contributed to her marked gaiety as she expired.

Following a stay in Rome, Elizabeth caught a cold, which led to bronchitis and a suspected abscess of the lung. The seriousness of her condition was not evident until the final hours. Robert and a servant woman nursed her in the Brownings' home, the Casa Guidi, in Florence. Early on 29 June 1861, as Robert was feeding Elizabeth consommé from a spoon, he began to wonder whether she recognized him. "Do you know me?" he asked. She kissed him and spoke words of love. He continued to feed her and she put her arms around him, whispering "God bless you" and kissing him repeatedly and vehemently. Robert wrote later: "I said, 'Are you comfortable?' 'Beautiful'...Then she motioned to have her hands sponged—some of the jelly annoying her—this was done and she began to sleep again—the *last*." She died peacefully with a smile on her lips and her head against his shoulder. Her face was "like a girl's" and it was some time before he could believe she was gone.

On 1 July, a crowd of Florentines followed her body to the protestant cemetery, where Walter Savage Landor and Arthur Hugh Clough are also buried. Her tombstone bears the disconcerting inscription: BE NOT AFRAID; IT IS I.

Browning, Robert (1812–1889).

The English poet, a man of sturdy common sense, suffered from recurrent headaches but otherwise, especially in later life, enjoyed excellent health. One afternoon in late November 1889 he caught a cold while walking in foggy weather on the Lido in Venice. Suffering from bronchitis he was put to bed in the Palazzo Rezzonico, the house of his son "Pen." His devoted daughter-in-law Fannie poulticed him regularly until the bronchitis cleared up. But by then Browning's heart was failing. On the afternoon of 12 December a telegram from London announced favorable reviews of his collection *Asolando*. "How gratifying," murmured the poet. Soon thereafter he lost consciousness; that evening, as San Marco's clock struck ten, Browning's massive chest heaved and he died. The Protestant cemetery in Florence had been closed since Elizabeth was laid there; Robert was interred in Westminster Abbey.

Buddha, Gautama (c563–483 B.C.).

Prince Siddhartha, given the title Buddha because he was held to have attained supreme knowledge, left his wife and child at the age of thirty to follow a life of religious contemplation. The prince was taken ill after a rich banquet served to him at Pava by a blacksmith named Cunda. He was overtaken by great pain and weakness, and suffered a "flow of blood," but despite this he made his way to Kusinara in the company of a monk, Anandra. On the outskirts of that village he was forced to rest and begged for water to be brought. A little later, while lying on Anandra's robe beneath a tree, the old man ceased to converse with the villagers who had gathered around, closed his eyes and died quietly.

P.M. Dale believes the most likely cause of the Buddha's death to be a massive hemorrhage. "After the ingestion of a large quantity of irritating food an attack of acute indigestion with violent, painful peristalsis ensued. A sizeable artery, lying in or contiguous to a duodenal ulcer, ruptured and loosed a large quantity of blood into the intestinal tract." The hemorrhage would be slowed when the dying man lay down, but, in the end, "loss of circulating-fluid volume, combined with oxygen deficiency, resulted in the stoppage of cardiac function."

After the Buddha was cremated his ashes were divided, to avoid dispute, into eight equal parts, placed in gold urns and given to the rulers of eight kingdoms.

Burns, Robert (1759–1796).

The Scottish poet is believed to have suffered a severe attack of rheumatic fever around the time his only daughter died in the fall of 1795. In the following June, sleeping badly and suffering from swollen joints, he was sent to what has been described as the meanest, shabbiest little spa in all the world. Brow-Well stood on the Solway Firth ten miles south of Burns' home at Dumfries, near the border with England; it consisted of three cottages and a tank the size of a dining table into which mineral water trickled through an iron pipe. There the poet drank the waters and bathed in the chilly sea. Suffering a recurrence of fever, he hastened home to Dumfries and, too feeble to climb the stairs, was put to bed in the kitchen. His wife Jean Armour was due to give birth to their sixth child at any moment, and Burns wrote his last letter to his father-in-law:

> Do for Heaven's sake, send Mrs. Armour here immediately. My wife is hourly expecting to be put to bed. Good God! What a situation for her to be in, poor girl, without a friend....

Robert Burns died three days later at 5:00 A.M. on 21 July 1796. During his funeral on the 25th his son, Maxwell, was born. In a 1926 study, Sir J. Crichton-Browne declared Burns to have suffered for much of his life from rheumatic endocarditis, an

The mausoleum of Robert Burns in St. Michael's Churchyard,
Dumfries, Scotland.

SCOTTISH TOURIST BOARD

inflammation of the membrane lining the chambers of the heart
and forming the valve leaflets. S. Watson Smith, a distinguished
rheumatism specialist, dismisses alcoholic excess, rheumatic
fever, and venereal disease as possible causes of Burns' death.
According to him, the poet died of subacute infective endocarditis "which has a usual fatal ending in septicemia. In this condition a painful arthritis is not a rare complication." Burns lies in a
mausoleum in St. Michael's Churchyard, Dumfries. *See* R. Scott
Stevenson, *Famous Illnesses in History* (1962).

Burr, Aaron (1756–1836).

The third vice-president of the U.S. had a turbulent life: he lost the presidency by a single vote, killed Alexander Hamilton in a duel, was tried for treason and acquitted on a technicality and, after deportation, wandered penuriously in Europe for four years. On his return he again began practicing law. He recovered quickly from his first stroke in 1830 and at the age of seventy-seven made the headlines when he married a wealthy ex-courtesan, Mrs. Eliza Bowen Jumel, in 1832. He reverted to the habits of his younger years by going through her money at a prodigious rate; after some tremendous quarrels he left her home. A few weeks later he had a second stroke. Eliza brought him home and nursed him to such good effect that he was back to his old ways within a month. Eliza, discovering that he was involved in extramarital affairs, filed for divorce; Burr filed a countersuit. Another stroke paralyzed his left leg and partially paralyzed his left arm.

In the spring of 1836 Burr took up lodgings at Winants Inn in the little village of Port Richmond on Staten Island, N.Y., where he was much spoiled by the other guests, a group of U.S. Navy officers and their wives. A Dutch Reformed minister, the Rev. Dr. P.J. Van Pelt, was friendly and the two men discussed theology by the hour, though Burr resisted Dr. Van Pelt's attempts to convert him. Burr began to fail in the early days of September and on the 13th it was evident to the attending physicians that the end was near. A few minutes after daybreak Dr. Van Pelt, who had been at the dying man's side all night, asked him if he was prepared to accept salvation. Burr, consistent to the last, said with a glint of humor, "On that subject I am coy." A few minutes later he fell asleep and died quietly at 2:00 P.M., 14 September 1836. Two hours before he died the divorce became final. After lying in state in the college chapel he was buried near his parents in the churchyard at Princeton, N.J.

Byron, Lord (*George Gordon Noel Byron*) (1788–1824).

The English poet kept the nature of his deformity a secret during his lifetime. His good looks and athletic prowess were marred by a congenital malformation of the right foot and calf. This he disguised with an inner boot and a padded legging worn under his trousers. From two specimens of these which still survive, Sir Denis Browne in a 1960 medical study concludes that Byron's calf was grotesquely thin, the foot small, narrow and bent slightly inward. These defects, with a probable stiffness and lack of ankle movement, would give him the peculiar sliding gait noted by his friends.

On his way to help the Greeks in their war of independence against the Turks, Byron appears to have had epileptic fits. At Missolonghi, Greece, he suffered a chill from riding in the rain on 9 April 1824; he died at 6:15 A.M. on the 19th, but the postmortem report throws no light on the cause of death. In 1924 Sir Ronald Ross and Dr. G.C. Low independently concluded that Byron succumbed to a virulent form of malaria, and Ross adds that the poet's death was hastened by "remorseless bleeding" and poor medical care. The disease, writes P.M. Dale, was probably picked up the previous autumn at Cephalonia. Byron's body was taken back to England and, refused burial in Westminster Abbey, was interred in the ancestral vault in Hucknall Torkard church, five miles northwest of Nottingham.

When the vault was opened in June 1938, the poet's body was found to be well preserved with the features easily recognizable. Only the arms and lower legs were reduced to a skeleton. One of the observers, A.E. Houldsworth, cited in Countess Longford's 1976 biography of Byron, reported:

> "His sexual organ shewed quite abnormal development. There was a hole in his breast and at the back of his head, where his heart and brains had been removed. These are placed in a large urn near the coffin."

Caesar, Julius (100–44 B.C.).

On 13 September 45 B.C. in his villa at Labicum, the Roman emperor wrote his will, which seems to indicate that however godlike he had become, he sensed his earthly life was drawing to a close. His autocratic rule and tactlessness toward the senators had spawned a conspiracy which was greatly aided when he discharged his Spanish guard in February 44. When the senate met on 15 March, Brutus escorted Caesar to his golden chair-of-state while Trebonius detained Mark Antony to prevent his going to the dictator's aid. The conspirators gathered around Caesar; Cimber yanked his toga from his neck. "This is violence!" cried Caesar. Casca struck with his dagger and missed, but the other conspirators closed in with a hail of dagger thrusts. Cassius stabbed Caesar in the face and Brutus stabbed him in the thigh. When Brutus was about to strike again, Caesar groaned, "You too, my son?" He covered his face with the upper part of his purple toga and unbelted the lower part so that it would cover his legs. Then he fell dead at the base of Pompey's statue.

Caesar had received twenty-three wounds, but a postmortem revealed that only the second—delivered to Caesar's breast by an unknown assassin—was fatal. His body was cremated in front of the Regia at the east end of the Forum.

Camus, Albert (1913–1960).

The French writer and critic won the Nobel prize for literature in 1957 and used the money to buy a picturesque old house in the tiny village of Lourmarin, between Avignon and Aix-en-Provence. He spent November and December 1959 working on his novel *Le Premier Homme*, during which period he exhibited a bizarre black humor, on one occasion having his daughter Catherine climb into a chest to see how one would look in a coffin, and remarking on his preference for burial at Lourmarin rather than for a state funeral.

The publisher Michel Gallimard, with his wife Janine and her daughter Anne, had been staying with Camus, and on 3 January 1960 the Gallimards set off for Paris in their Facel Vega with Camus as their passenger, taking two days for the 470-mile journey. Francine and the children traveled by rail, as Camus had originally intended to do. After a night's stay at Thoissey, near Mâcon, and a lunch stop at Sens, Gallimard drove along the old National Route 5, flat, straight and tree-lined. Discussing insurance, Camus quipped that he would have a hard time buying any, his lungs were so full of holes (since he was 17 he had battled tuberculosis).

Suddenly Janine, sitting in the rear seat with her daughter, felt the car lurch. Police found her half-conscious near the wreck and Anne sixty-five feet away in a field. The car had swerved on the slightly wet surface, smashed into a plane tree and then into a second tree forty feet further on. Camus was thrown against the rear window. He had suffered fractures of the skull and spine and his thorax was crushed. Death must have been instantaneous, but a reporter commented on the look of horror on his face. Michel, bleeding profusely, survived for only six days; Janine and Anne suffered minor injuries. In a suit brought by Camus' heirs Gallimard was found to have been speeding. The road surface was scarred over a distance of 160 feet; debris was scattered over a wide area. The dashboard clock was stopped at 1:54 or 1:55 P.M.

Camus' body was taken for the night to the nearby village of Villeblevin. As is customary when a nonbeliever dies, the Catholic and Protestant church bells remained silent; only the bell in the Lourmarin clock tower tolled. Camus was buried in what had been the Catholic section of the village cemetery. Francine dropped a red rose on the coffin.

The tomb, which bears only the dead man's name and dates, is covered with a profusion of rosemary. *See* H.R. Lottman (1979).

Carnegie, Andrew (1835–1919).

To the Scottish-born giant of American industry the news of the outbreak of World War I was "terrible and shocking." He had worked so hard for peace. Weakened by severe pneumonia, his health rapidly deteriorated, and he longed to return to Skibo, his beloved ancient manorial estate in the northeast corner of Scotland. Because of the war he was never able to make the journey. In the fall of 1916 the Carnegies bought a mansion, Shadowbrook, near Lenox, Mass., and Carnegie's health improved there. In 1919, after the marriage of their daughter, Louisa Carnegie wrote in her diary: "I am left alone with Andrew, so frail and feeble and so very weak." She was grateful that Morrison, Carnegie's devoted valet, had been released from military service and was able to take care of her husband.

On 9 August Carnegie was stricken once again with pneumonia. Both he and Louisa knew that the end was near, but Carnegie was so very tired that he welcomed it. In the early morning hours of 11 August the nurse aroused Louisa and told her she should come to Andrew's bedside. "I was called at 6:00

A.M. and remained with my darling husband, giving him oxygen, until he gradually fell asleep at 7:14," Louisa wrote in her diary, "I am left alone——"

At his own request Carnegie was buried in the Sleepy Hollow Cemetery in North Tarrytown, N.Y. His grave is marked by a Celtic cross cut from stone quarried at Skibo.

Carroll, Lewis (*Charles Lutwidge Dodgson*) (1832–1898).

The English clergyman and mathematician who wrote *Alice in Wonderland* was busy with the second volume of *Symbolic Logic* when he left his rooms at Christ Church College, Oxford, for the last time on 27 December 1897. His customary visit to Guildford to visit his sister at The Chestnuts, Castle Hill, was prolonged by a bad cold. "A feverish cold of the bronchial type," is how he described it on 5 January. But within a week he was upstairs in bed and Dr. Gabb was called in. Carroll had always enjoyed good health, often taking the eighteen-mile walk from Guildford to Hastings even in his last year. But now he could not shake off his cold. His breathing became hard and labored. "Take away the pillows," he said on the 13th. At 2:30 P.M. on 14 January 1898, only a nurse was in the room when his breathing stopped. After the simple funeral at St. Mary's, Guildford, the body of the Rev. C.L. Dodgson was taken on a hand bier up the steep hill to the cemetery. One of the wreaths was from a Mrs. Hargreaves, who signed herself simply—"Alice."

Carson, Kit (1809–1868).

Kit Carson was thrown by his horse over a cliff in October 1867 and had not fully recovered when his wife, Maria, died in April 1868. He took the loss very hard, and on 26 May had a severe heart attack. Two days later, shortly before dawn on the 28th, Brigadier-General Christopher Carson, folk hero and great frontiersman, died peacefully in his own bed at Fort Lyon, Col. He was buried in the cemetery at Fort Lyon, but in 1869 the bodies of Kit and his wife were reinterred in a small burial plot not far from their home in Taos, N.M.

Kit Carson, U.S. frontiersman, in his declining years.
LIBRARY OF CONGRESS

The last home of Kit Carson, from a 1906 photograph.

Caruso, Enrico (1873–1921).

In spite of being very tired and suffering from a heavy cold, the great Italian tenor opened the Metropolitan Opera season on 15 November 1920 as Eléazar in *La Juive*. His increasingly severe chest pains were incorrectly diagnosed by his physician as intercostal neuritis. On 11 December, while singing in *L'Elisir d'Amore* at the Brooklyn Academy of Music, he bled badly from the mouth. His doctor briskly diagnosed "a small burst vein at the tip of the tongue." He appeared in *La Juive* on Christmas Eve at the Metropolitan Opera House, the last time he was ever to sing in public. On Christmas Day 1920 he was in agonizing pain. A physician, Dr. Evan Evans, was found with difficulty. He discovered a condition of acute pleurisy which was developing into bronchial pneumonia. Three days later a gallon of fluid was drawn from the pleural cavity. Caruso began to improve slowly thereafter but early in February 1921 his temperature abruptly rose to 104 degrees. On 12 February he was operated on again.

Deep abscesses, caused by poisonous seepage from the pleura, had to be drained; to facilitate this a four-inch section of rib was cut away.

In May Caruso traveled with his wife, Dorothy, and their baby, Gloria, to Sorrento, Italy, where rest and sunshine worked their miracle. But he allowed the elderly doctor who had attended his mother to probe the old incision with a dirty instrument. His temperature shot up and his doctors insisted a kidney would have to be removed. Because of Caruso's severe pain they decided to leave for Rome. On Sunday 31 July in Naples, where he and his family had stayed overnight, he was in great pain again. His wife begged doctors to probe for an abscess where the old doctor had introduced the dirty instrument, but they refused. He died just before 9:00 A.M. on 2 August 1921 at the Hotel Vesuvio. The cause of death was peritonitis due to the bursting of an abscess at the place Mrs. Caruso had indicated.

The funeral of Caruso, the great tenor, in Naples in 1921. Photo by Radel and Herbert.

LIBRARY OF CONGRESS

Caruso's crystal casket was placed in a chapel in the Del Planto cemetery above Naples. His fellow tenor, Tito Schipa, and other friends arranged for the embalmed body to be dressed in new clothes every year, but in 1927 the widow objected to the long public display of her husband's body. She had a slab of white granite placed over the casket and the mausoleum was locked up.

Casanova, Giovanni Jacopo (1725–1798).

The Italian-born adventurer became librarian to Count Waldstein at Dux in Bohemia in September 1785. Although Casanova was, by then, a quarrelsome and garrulous old man, the count treated him well and paid him handsomely. Nevertheless, Casanova became bored and began to write his memoirs, in which he vividly described his dissolute life. Although he entitled them "The story of my life to the year 1797," the twelve known volumes end with the year 1773. In February 1798 Casanova fell ill. According to John Masters in his 1969 biography, the seventy-three-year-old man, in addition to having had smallpox, pleurisy, pneumonia and probably malaria two or three times, had suffered at least eleven attacks of venereal disease—both gonorrhea and syphilis. These had weakened his genito-urinary tract and the mercury used in the treatment had lowered his resistance. Now, a septic infection, caused by prostatitis, had spread to the kidneys.

After battling the disease alone, Casanova consulted Dr. Hansa, but after one dose of the prescribed medicine, he rejected it as "no good." His friends rallied around and Carlo Angiolini, who had married Casanova's niece, came from Dresden to nurse him. He died on the morning of 4 June 1798; after partaking of the Sacrament he said, "Bear witness that I have lived as a philosopher and die as a Christian." He was buried behind the Saint Barbara Chapel in the little cemetery at Dux. In 1922 a stone bearing his name and the date 1799 was discovered but no trace was found of his remains. A memorial tablet erected recently reads "Jakob Casanova/ Venedig 1725/ Dux 1798.

Casement, Roger (1864–1916).

The Irish patriot, whose execution during World War I made him one of the foremost martyrs of his country's nationalist cause, gained international fame and a knighthood by his exposure of the ruthless white traders in the Congo and Peru.

In 1914 he went to Berlin to get help for the Irish National Volunteers. The Germans sent a shipload of arms for the rebels and Casement traveled back to Ireland on a U-boat in April 1916. The ship with the arms was captured and Casement was arrested at Banna Strand, County Kerry, on 24 April. In June he was tried in London for treason before the Lord Chief Justice, convicted and sentenced to death. His appeal against conviction was dismissed on 18 July. He did not entirely reject the possibility of a last-minute reprieve, but ceased to desire it: "It is better that I die thus on the scaffold." On 3 August 1916 he was hanged at Pentonville Prison, London. His priest, Father Carey, said, "He feared not death; he marched to the scaffold with the dignity of a prince." To Ellis the hangman he appeared to be "the bravest man it fell my unhappy lot to execute."

There has been much controversy over the years as to how much effect diaries reputedly written by Casement had on public opinion. The authenticity of these diaries, which contain detailed descriptions of homosexual practices, has been challenged, but the handwriting does appear to be Casement's.

Despite Irish protests, Casement's body was buried in quicklime within the prison walls, but in February 1965 its exhumation and removal to Ireland were permitted. After a state funeral at which President de Valera gave the oration, Casement was laid to rest on 1 March in Glasnevin Cemetery, Dublin.

Catherine of Aragon (1485–1536).

The first queen consort of Henry VIII (from 1509) gave birth to six children, including two sons; all were stillborn or died in early infancy except for one daughter, born in 1516, who became Mary I. By 1526 Henry wanted to divorce Catherine; Archbishop Thomas Cranmer annulled their marriage on 23 May 1533, four months after Henry had secretly married Anne Boleyn. Catherine, separated from her daughter and her friends, became ill. In 1534 she was removed to damp, cold Kimbolton Castle in Huntingdonshire; there she often lay awake at nights racked with coughing, listening to the howling winds. By the end of 1535 Catherine was very ill, worn out by a feverish restlessness, nausea and sleeplessness. Early on 7 January she woke her maids and asked if it were not near dawn. Alarmed by her manner, they sent for her confessor, who offered to say Mass at once. She insisted on waiting for dawn, at which time she received the Sacrament. At ten she was given extreme unction and prayed for her daughter, the people of England and her husband Henry VIII. At 2:00 P.M. on 7 January 1536 she died.

F. Martì-Ibañez in a 1974 study cites a postmortem finding of a heart "black and hideous" and "a round black thing clinging to the outside." He suggests she suffered a fatal coronary thrombosis, the black excrescence being a subpericardial hematoma. In 1884, when repairs were being made to Peterborough Cathedral, Catherine's body was moved from the lowest step of the high altar to the north choir aisle.

Catherine the Great (1729–1796).

Czarina Catherine II of Russia was a native of Germany. She usurped the throne in 1762, soon after the accession of her dull-witted, almost impotent husband, Peter III. Her children were fathered by a series of a dozen, carefully chosen lovers, and she neither apologized for nor regretted her way of life. She was a courageous woman who, as an example to her subjects, was inoculated with live smallpox virus by the English pioneer Dr. Thomas Dimsdale. In her prime she was a tall, beautiful brunette with blue eyes, but in later years she became very heavy, with grossly swollen legs. She suffered a mild stroke in mid-September 1796.

On 5 November (old style) Catherine was in good spirits when awakened at eight in her St. Petersburg palace. As usual she drank several cups of coffee before retiring to her water closet. When her customary ten minutes' stay had lengthened to nearly an hour, her footman Zotov ventured to peer in. The empress was huddled on the floor, her features suffused with blood, a rattle sounding in her throat. This second stroke proved fatal;

Catherine's pulse began to weaken on the evening of the 6th, and her struggles for breath became more labored. She died at 11:15 P.M. and her embalmed body lay in state until her funeral on 5 December in the Cathedral of Saints Peter and Paul. Catherine's heir, Paul, who had long suspected her of having had a hand in the murder of his putative father thirty-four years earlier, ordered Peter's remains exhumed and the two coffins lay side by side during the Requiem Mass. The tombs are now close together below the cathedral. Catherine's is sealed with a white marble slab bearing a golden cross. *See* V. Cronin (1978).

Cavell, Edith (1865–1915).

The diminutive nurse who became a British heroine was the daughter of an austere country vicar. She helped found a clinic and school for nurses in Brussels in 1907. During the Allied retreat of 1915 she was approached by an underground movement headed by Prince Reginald de Cröy, who asked that she treat and shelter two wounded British soldiers. During the next nine months two hundred soldiers passed through the clinic in their flight to freedom via Holland, all under the noses of the German occupation forces, but at last the secret leaked out. Edith refused to flee; when arrested she disdained to deny the charges, and at the trial of the thirty-five defendants declined to wear her uniform, though it would have doubtlessly helped her.

Five death sentences were pronounced late on the afternoon of 11 October 1915, but three of them were commuted. Edith and an architect, Phillippe Baucq, were selected for immediate execution. The U.S. and Spanish ministers in Belgium argued forcefully with the German military governor, Baron von der Lancken, until well into the night, but to no avail. Edith wrote farewell letters at St. Gilles prison and told her pastor she had welcomed the opportunity for rest and meditation. "I know now that patriotism is not enough; I must have no hatred or bitterness towards anyone." The guards came for her at 6:00 A.M. on 12 October and the secret execution at the Tir National, a rifle range near the city, was hurried through in three minutes. Enlistments in Britain and the U.S. rose spectacularly in the following weeks.

The execution of Edith Cavell by the Germans in 1915, as depicted on this postcard issued in Paris, greatly boosted Allied recruitment.

ROWLAND RYDER

Cavell's body was reinterred in the close of Norwich Cathedral in 1919. To her statue near Trafalgar Square, her final message was added as an afterthought: "Patriotism is not enough."

Charles I (1600–1649).

Charles' marriage to the Catholic Henrietta Maria of France, and his desire to retain ceremony in the Church of England's services, made the English fear their king wished to restore Catholicism. His continual quarrel with Parliament over money for his disastrous foreign wars—he dissolved three Parliaments because they refused to submit to his arbitrary ways—created more ill feeling. In 1642 civil war broke out when Charles attempted to seize five leading members of Parliament. Cromwell led the parliamentary forces (Roundheads) to victory. In 1646 Charles escaped to Scotland but was returned for trial in January 1647. On 20 January 1649 he was brought before a specially constituted high court of justice in Westminster Hall and charged with high treason. On the 27th his execution was ordered as a "tyrant, traitor, murderer and public enemy." After sentence had been passed, he was taken by sedan chair down King Street to the old palace at Whitehall. The guards shouted "Execution! Justice! Execution!" but the crowds watched silently.

Tuesday, 30 January 1649, was a bitterly cold day. Charles put a second shirt over the first so that he might not shiver on the scaffold and be mistaken for a coward. At 10:00 A.M. Colonel Hacker came to tell him it was time to leave, but he had to wait four long hours because the House of Commons had quite forgotten that, the moment Charles I was dead, Charles II would be king. Only after an emergency bill had been rushed through making it illegal to proclaim the fact did the order come for him to mount the black-draped scaffold that had been erected outside the Banqueting House. He tucked his hair under his tall white satin nightcap and asked if the block could not be raised higher so that he might kneel rather than lie. But the block had been set deliberately low to make it easier to kill him if he struggled, and the executioner replied, "It can be no higher, sir." The king placed his neck on the block and asked the executioner to wait until he gave the sign. "Yes, I will, and it please your Majesty." With a final prayer, Charles stretched out his hands; the bright ax fell and his head was severed in a single stroke. A week later he was buried in the Royal Chapel of St. George at Windsor. In 1813 it was discovered that he shared a vault with Henry VIII and Jane Seymour, and that his severed head was still surprisingly well preserved.

Chaucer, Geoffrey (1340?–1400).

At the end of 1399 the author of *The Canterbury Tales* rented a little house in the garden of the Chapel of St. Mary, Westminster. The rent was fifty-three shillings and four pence a year and, with great optimism, he took the little house on a fifty-three-year lease. The optimism was ill-founded as, according to the inscription on his tomb, he died on 25 October 1400, probably of the plague. Though he wrote a retraction of his works on his deathbed, some think that he did so only to please his confessor. He was buried in Westminster Abbey, his tomb becoming the nucleus of the later Poet's Corner.

Chekhov, Anton (1860–1904).

The Russian novelist had long exulted in his bachelor state, though he did have an understanding with Olga Knipper, an actress, who wanted to marry him. He was still undecided when Dr. Shchurovsky told him in May 1901 that his tuberculous condition had deteriorated and that both lungs were now seriously affected. He was advised to take the "koumiss cure" (the drinking of fermented mares' milk) in the Ufa Province of southeastern Russia. To travel on his own would be boring—to marry Olga would be selfish. But Olga was not deterred by the author's poor health prospects and the two were married on 25 May 1901.

By 1904 Chekhov, who had become extremely ill, was confined to his room in their apartment in Moscow. His most recent physician, a German, advised him to travel to Germany for a cure, though he was beyond all help. He left with his wife for the Black Forest spa of Badenweiler, Germany, on 31 May 1904, and though he grumbled about the "stupid" diet of cocoa and porridge he began to feel much better. On 29 June he had a heart attack but seemed to recover after an injection of morphia and gulps of oxygen; the following night he had another attack. He awoke early on 2 July and asked his wife to send for a doctor. At 2:00 A.M. the doctor arrived and administered camphor injections and whiffs of oxygen. He also prescribed a glass of champagne. Chekhov took the champagne, smiled at his wife, remarked that he "hadn't drunk champagne for ages," drained the glass and calmly turned on to his left side. By 3:00 A.M. he was dead. His coffin was delivered to St. Petersburg in a railway wagon labeled FRESH OYSTERS. He was buried in Novodyevichy Cemetery.

Chesterton, Gilbert Keith (1874–1936).

The English writer was an immense man, well over six feet tall and weighing about 300 pounds, with an intellect to match. In the spring of 1936 it had become evident that he was dying. His breathing was labored; he suffered from bronchial catarrh and had sporadic bouts of high temperature. A short trip to Lourdes and Lisieux with his wife Frances and his secretary Dorothy Collins cheered him but did little to improve his health. On 18 March he made his last broadcast, talking about the importance of enjoying life in ordinary times: "Until a man can enjoy himself he will grow more and more tired of enjoying everything else...." By the summer of 1936 Chesterton would drop off to sleep as he worked in his studio at Top Meadow, Beaconsfield, 25 miles west of London, and on waking his thoughts wandered.

On 12 June his wife wrote to Father John O'Connor (the original of Chesterton's fictional detective, Father Brown), "In case you hear the news from elsewhere I write myself to tell you that Gilbert is very seriously ill. The main trouble is heart and kidney and an amount of fluid in the body that sets up a dropsical condition. I have had a specialist to see him, who says that though he is desperately ill, there is a fighting chance. I think possibly he is a little better today. He has had Extreme Unction this morning and received Holy Communion." On 13 June, when Frances came into the room with Dorothy, Chesterton was able to murmur "Hallo, my darling," to the one and "Hallo, my dear" to the other. Then he lapsed into the coma in which he died at 10:15 A.M. on 14 June 1936. After a service at Westminster Cathedral he was buried at Beaconsfield. *See* D. Barker (1973).

Chopin, Frédéric (1810–1849).

The Polish composer's sojourn in Majorca during the winter of 1838–1839 with George Sand was a disaster. The incessant rain, cold weather and poor food caused Chopin's health to grow steadily worse. The community, on discovering that Chopin was consumptive, shunned the pair. As soon as the first fine days arrived and they were able to get away from the island they left for France. In 1839 they settled at Nohant, George Sand's country estate. For seven years they spent the winters in Paris and the summers at Nohant. Chopin's health remained much the same with severe fits of coughing every morning. In 1846 the deep friendship between Madame Sand and Chopin began to disintegrate and by 1847 they separated. Chopin felt that when this long affection and powerful bond had been broken so had his health. He spent 1848 in London and Edinburgh, where he was almost continuously ill. When he returned to Paris in the summer of 1849 the composer Hector Berlioz commented that even the slightest conversation made Chopin alarmingly tired and that he tried in general to make himself understood by signs.

In September 1849 Chopin's friends helped him move to 12 Place Vendôme where he was able to be up and around for part of the first few days, but he was failing rapidly and on 13 October he received the viaticum from the Abbé Alexander Jelowick. His friend (perhaps mistress) Delphine Potocka, on hearing of the gravity of his illness, came from Nice. His sister and her family were with him, and friends and colleagues visited him frequently. His physician, Dr. Jean Cruveilhier, was at his bedside. Chopin was in great pain, gasping and struggling for breath with less and less success. After a long fit of coughing he lay exhausted. The doctor asked him if he suffered; his answer came back faintly, "Plus" ("no more"). A few minutes later, between three and four in the morning of 17 October 1849, he died. He had advanced pulmonary tuberculosis and possibly tuberculous enteritis. Chopin's body was buried in Père-Lachaise Cemetery; his heart, as he had requested, was removed by Cruveilhier and placed in the wall of the Church of the Holy Cross in Warsaw. *See* E.R. Long (1956).

Churchill, Winston (1874–1965).

The prime minister of Great Britain resigned on 5 April 1955. He had survived several strokes, pneumonia, bronchitis and jaundice, and had pulled Britain through the Second World War. But inactivity and boredom dulled his senses and, when he no longer felt needed, age and infirmity took over. In his final ten years he gave up reading; he seldom spoke and when he did it was difficult to understand him. His physician, Lord Moran, describes him entering a room supported by two nurses and helped into a seat: "Very small, almost shrunken, he appeared huddled up in the depths of a big chair. There he sat through the afternoon hours, staring into the fire, giving it a prod with his stick when he felt cold." On his ninetieth birthday, 30 November 1964, hundreds of well-wishers gave him a heartwarming ovation when, clad in a green velvet siren suit, he appeared briefly at a window of his home at 27-28 Hyde Park Gate. But after his birthday he became quiet and withdrawn, unwilling to leave his bed and taking little pleasure in life.

Just after Christmas Churchill caught a slight chill. On 12 January 1965 Moran called in a neurologist, the aptly named Lord Brain, and together they told Lady Churchill that her husband had had a stroke. He developed a bad cough and was put on antibiotics. At first the public was simply informed that Sir Winston was unwell, but on the 15th Lord Moran walked outside to the waiting crowd and read the first bulletin: "After a cold, Sir Winston has developed a circulatory weakness and there has been a cerebral thrombosis." The crowd gasped, "He's had a stroke; old Winnie's had a stroke."

Sir Winston, wearing a green bed jacket and propped up on a dozen pillows, slipped deeper and deeper into unconsciousness. The family was summoned. Roy Howells, the old man's personal attendant, in his book *Churchill's Last Years* (1965) wrote: "It was now the final act. I went into the room where the family was gathered and said, 'I think you had all better come in.' My voice was a little hoarse and I had to repeat myself. They came in one by one to join Lady Churchill and Mrs. Soames [Churchill's daughter Mary], already kneeling on either side of Sir Winston's bed. Slowly the others sank to their knees around the room."

Churchill died a few minutes later, quite peacefully, at 8:00 A.M., 25 January 1965. For three days he lay in state in the Hall of William Rufus, Westminster. On the fourth day he was borne on a gun carriage to St. Paul's. He was buried near his birthplace, Blenheim Palace, in the country churchyard at Bladon, eight miles northwest of Oxford.

Cleopatra (69–30 B.C.).

The most famous queen of Egypt, who was almost entirely Greek by race and culture, captivated in turn Julius Caesar and Marcus Antonius (q.v.) At the time of Antony's death she had taken refuge with her treasure in her almost completed mausoleum not far from her palace in northeast Alexandria. Michael Grant, in his 1972 biography of the queen, casts doubt on the tradition that Egypt's conqueror, Octavian, visited Cleopatra after she had been captured by his agents and brought to the palace. Instead, he sent to her a young emissary, P. Cornelius Dolabella, with the story (probably untrue) that she was to be exhibited in Rome at Octavian's Triumph. The strategem, intended to force her suicide, proved effective.

Cleopatra asked permission to pour a final libation at Antony's tomb. Then, on or about 12 August 30 B.C., she bathed and perfumed herself; dressed in royal robes, she reclined on her golden couch to partake of a final meal. When Octavian soon afterward received her written request to be buried beside her dead husband he knew she was no longer a problem. Guards who hastened to the palace found her lying dead on her couch. One of her ladies, Iras, lay lifeless on the floor; the other, although nearing collapse, was adjusting the diadem on Cleopatra's brow. "Was this well done by your lady?" asked Octavian's emissary in an angry voice. "Exceedingly well," replied the servant, Charmian, "as became a descendant of a long line of kings." She then fell dead.

Plutarch marshals several accounts of her suicide. An asp, hidden in a basket of figs, or concealed in a vase, may have been brought to her. Some say faint puncture marks were found on Cleopatra's arm. No asp was seen, but a possible trail was espied on the seashore nearby. Another theory, which would better account for the death of all three women, was that poison was concealed in a hollow bodkin round which Cleopatra's hair was wound. Octavian believed snake-bite to be the cause of her death and carried into Rome a figure depicting Cleopatra with an asp fastened to her upper arm. Her wish was granted and she was buried beside Antony; Grant believes the graves were located near the mausoleum, which adjoined the temple of Isis in the palace quarter of Alexandria on Cape Cochias.

Cleveland, (Stephen) Grover
(1837–1908).

During Cleveland's second term as U.S. president (1893–1897), the nation faced a severe financial and commercial crisis. For this reason, when Cleveland developed a cancerous growth on the roof of his mouth it was decided to keep the matter secret. Surgery was performed on the corpulent fifty-six-year-old man aboard the private yacht *Oneida* on 1 July 1893 by J.D. Bryant and W.W. Keen. As the boat steamed up the East River, N.Y., with the anesthetized patient propped up in a chair against the mast, a dentist, F. Hasbrouck, extracted the two left upper bicuspids. Then Bryant, working rapidly, removed most of the left upper jaw; this was necessary because of the spread of the disease into the antrum, the cavity below the eye, where a gelatinous mass was discovered.

The president withstood the surgery well and walked unaided from the yacht up to his summer house at Buzzard's Bay, Mass. A second operation, to remove further suspicious tissue, was also carried out aboard the *Oneida*. Curious newsmen were fobbed off with stories of tooth extractions, but after some indiscreet talk on the part of Hasbrouck, the Philadelphia *Press* on 29 August published a remarkably accurate account of the operation. By then, however, Cleveland had been able to address Congress while wearing a rubber prosthesis, which made him look and sound normal, so the story did little harm. It was not until 1917 that Keen published an authoritative report of the operations.

Cleveland's health began to decline in 1907, and he died at his Princeton, N.J., home at 8:40 A.M., 24 June 1908. The certificate listed the cause of death as heart failure complicated by pulmonary thrombosis and edema, but Keen's assistant, Dr. John Erdmann, said Cleveland died of an intestinal obstruction, while yet other sources give the cause as cerebral thrombosis. At any rate, he had no recurrence of the sarcoma. He was buried in the old Princeton Cemetery.

Clift, Montgomery (1920–1966).

The U.S. movie actor was returning from Elizabeth Taylor's home high in Coldwater Canyon, Los Angeles, on 12 May 1956 when his car crashed into a telephone pole. Miss Taylor found him crushed under the steering wheel, his face a bloody pulp. When he began to choke she put her fingers down his throat and brought out two teeth that had lodged there. Clift was taken to Cedars of Lebanon Hospital where he was operated on immediately for face lacerations, a broken nose and a fractured jaw. He had severe cerebral concussion and was put in traction for back injuries.

From then on the actor began to drink heavily. In addition, he had a fourteen-foot medicine cabinet made for his brownstone duplex on East 61st Street in Manhattan to hold the thousands of pills he stocked—some obtained legitimately, some from a drug runner nicknamed "Bird."

Montgomery Clift was bisexual, but in later years his house became a hangout for homosexuals. When Lorenzo James, a black actor, was engaged to take care of Clift in 1963, he ejected the drifters, bought a new lock for the door and attempted to get the house running smoothly.

In 1965 Clift's drinking became heavy again and he was injecting increasingly large amounts of Demerol, which caused him to hallucinate. On 22 July 1966 Monty spent the day alone in his room. At about 1:00 A.M. Lorenzo asked him if he wanted to watch *The Misfits* (in which he had starred with Clark Gable and Marilyn Monroe) on the Late Late Show. "Absolutely not," he shouted. Those were his last words. About 6:00 A.M. on the 23rd Lorenzo tried to awaken him. The bedroom door was locked and he could not break it down: he climbed through the bedroom window by means of a ladder and found Montgomery dead on top of his outsize bed. The New York Medical Examiner's official report stated that Clift was found "lying face up in bed, glasses on, no clothes on. Right arm flexed. Both fists clenched. No evidence of trauma. Rigor present. Underclothes and pants scattered about on floor of bedroom.... No notes, weapons etc."

The body was taken to the city morgue at 520 First Avenue, where an autopsy was performed by Dr. Michael Baden. There was no evidence of foul play or suicide; Clift had died of occlusive coronary artery disease. Dr. Baden added that the dead man had been suffering from a calcium deficiency for four years.

Only 150 people were invited to the private funeral in St. James' Church, Manhattan, though many hundreds waited outside. There were two huge bouquets of white chrysanthemums from Elizabeth Taylor. The actor, a Quaker, was buried in the Friends Cemetery in Prospect Park, Brooklyn; the grave is planted with 200 crocuses and has a simple granite marker. *See* P. Bosworth (1978).

Clive, Robert (1725–1774).

When the East India Company went bankrupt in 1772, the founder of British India returned to England to defend himself in parliament. After an all-night debate it was declared that he "had rendered great and meritorious service to his country." Clive caught a cold in the fall of 1774 while supervising improvements at Oakly, his estate in Shropshire. On 5 November he left for Bath, full of catarrh, but he was too ill even to drink the waters. Two weeks later he was worse, but insisted on going to London. The journey was a nightmare: he was unable to eat or even to swallow. By the time he reached Berkeley Square on 20 November he was suffering acute abdominal spasms. Even larges doses of opium failed to give him much relief. On 22 November about noon, Clive, after taking a purge, was obliged to retire to the water closet. Apparently his pain returned with tremendous violence and in a paroxysm of agony he thrust his penknife into his throat. Clive's family tried to conceal his suicide, and his death remained something of a mystery until recently. He was buried in Moreton Say Church, Salop. *See* M. Bence-Jones (1974).

Coleridge, Samuel Taylor (1772–1834).

The English poet's drug problems seem to have begun when he was eighteen years old. At that time he was given laudanum for the pain of rheumatic fever, with which he was confined to the sick ward of Christ's Hospital, London, for many months. He became addicted to opium, consuming, according to his brother-in-law Robert Southey, as much as two quarts of laudanum a week. His poem "Kubla Khan" was probably written under its influence. In April 1816 James Gillman, a surgeon, was asked to take the poet into his Highgate, London, home to help him overcome his drug problem. Coleridge stayed with the Gillmans until his death eighteen years later. Their tranquil house and garden relaxed him; the doctor's skilled care, which included the small amount of morphine necessary to maintain equilibrium—Coleridge was never able to give the drug up entirely—enabled him to live to the age of sixty-two.

Coleridge's health deteriorated toward the end of his life but his mind remained sharp and clear. He had many visitors, both from Britain and abroad, whom he would receive, immaculately dressed in clerical black, in the parlor set aside for him. During the last few months he was confined to bed. Though often in pain he managed to conceal it. He died at Gillman's home on 25 July 1834. The autopsy showed that the diseased heart nearly filled the left side of the chest and the right side was filled with fluid. A specialist consulted by Molly Lefebure for her 1974 biography of the poet suggests these symptoms might be interpreted as hypertrophy and dilatation of the left heart due to aortic disease or, less likely, high blood pressure. In 1961 Coleridge's remains were moved from Highgate School Chapel cemetery to a vault in St. Michael's Church, Highgate.

Columbus, Christopher
(1451–1506).

The tall, red-headed discoverer of the New World, the greatest navigator of his age, was deeply religious, with a lively sense of curiosity and a love of adventure. But S.E. Morison, a lifelong student of the Genoese admiral, wonders if, in common with many other explorers, he was not motivated by incurable restlessness. What else could have driven him back to the sea when he was nearing the end of his life and plagued by arthritis? Certainly not the gratitude of the Spanish crown.

In 1494, on his second voyage, Columbus became seriously ill. He was taken to the port of Isabela in the Dominican Republic, where he lay feverish, delirious and helpless. It is possible, according to P.M. Dale, that he had typhus. He recovered to find many of his men ill, possibly of syphilis, which was common at that period among the American Indians. On his third voyage he was in great pain with what he described as gout, but was more likely rheumatic fever. On 31 August 1498 he reached Santo Domingo, where he hoped to find peace to recuperate. But there was rebellion on the island which he dealt with forcefully—too forcefully, thought the Spanish envoy when he landed on 23 August 1500 to see bodies swinging from the gallows. He had Columbus manacled and thrown into jail, where his swollen, aching limbs became much worse. After his unsuccessful fourth and final voyage, during which he was marooned in Jamaica for a year, Columbus was reduced to importuning Ferdinand with his claims. Though crippled by arthritis, he followed the court to

The remains of Christopher Columbus lie below the cathedral in Santo Domingo.

LIBRARY OF CONGRESS

Valladolid on a donkey. There, bedridden with grossly swollen limbs and belly, probably suffering from rheumatic heart disease, he made his will on 19 May 1506. The following day he grew suddenly worse. A priest was summoned, a Mass said, and everyone in the little circle of friends and relatives received the last sacraments. The viaticum was administered to the dying admiral and, after the concluding prayer of this last office, Columbus was heard to say: "In manus tuas, Domine, commendo spiritum meum."

The mortal remains of Columbus possess a history of their own; in the words of J.H. Parry, "His bones seem to have traveled about the world almost as much as he did." Columbus was buried in the Church of San Francisco in Valladolid but removed in 1509 by order of his son Diego to a chapel in the monastery of Las Cuevas, Triana. In 1541 the remains of Christopher and Diego were taken, in small lead caskets, to Santo Domingo and interred before the high altar of the cathedral, Christopher on the gospel side. The monument was removed in 1655, when it was feared that the English would capture and sack the city, and it was lost. When Santo Domingo was ceded to the French in 1795 permission was granted to remove the remains to

Havana. A small stone vault was found when the gospel side of the altar was excavated and the remains, assumed to be those of Christopher Columbus, were taken to the cathedral in Havana. When Cuba became independent they were taken to Spain and placed in a modern monument in Seville Cathedral. But in 1877, when the presbytery of the Cathedral of Santo Domingo was enlarged, a small lead casket was discovered with the letters CCA, probably standing for CRISTOBAL COLÓN ALMIRANTE, inscribed on the front and ends.

S.E. Morison in *The European Discovery of America* (1974) writes: "There need be no doubt that the authentic remains of Christopher Columbus are under his monument in the Cathedral of Santo Domingo." Construction was begun in 1948 of a Memorial Lighthouse on a high cliff at the mouth of the Ozama River in the Dominican Republic which will, when completed, be the last resting place of the great admiral.

Conrad, Joseph (1857–1924).

The Polish-born adventurer and author is considered one of the foremost English writers of the sea. He was a delicate child and a high-strung young man who became fatigued easily. In 1890 Conrad was in the Congo where he became severely ill with fever and dysentery. His convalescence was slow and dismal and for the rest of his life his health was to show the permanent effects of the African expedition. On 2 August 1924 Conrad's son Borys brought his wife and newborn son Philip to see him at his eighteenth-century home, Oswalds, at Bishopsbourne in Kent. Conrad was not feeling well and was in bed propped up by many pillows and with the inevitable cigarette smouldering between his fingers. He was calm and relaxed and greeted the young people cheerfully. Borys Conrad in his 1970 biography of his father says that they talked far into the night. "The close and intimate relationship which had always existed between us now seemed closer than before. When I left he took my hand and said: Good night Boy [his name for Borys]—then added, 'You know I am *really* ill this time.'"

Conrad died early on the following morning. Apparently, he had gotten out of bed and was sitting in an armchair when he collapsed. His invalid wife, Jessie, heard him fall and rang her bell, but when his manservant reached the room he was already dead of cardiac failure. He is buried in the Roman Catholic cemetery in Canterbury.

Cook, James (1728–1779).

The priests and chiefs heaved sighs of relief when the English explorer's ships, the *Resolution* and the *Discovery*, sailed from Kealakekua in the Hawaiian Islands; the crew had been very expensive to feed. However, Captain Cook had trouble with his masts and was forced to return to the harbor to make repairs. The Hawaiians were not happy to see the men return; thieving became serious and one night the *Discovery*'s cutter—a large boat—was stolen from her moorings.

Cook, in full uniform and carrying his personal double-barreled shotgun, went ashore accompanied by nine marines to

An artist's impression of the death of Captain Cook in Hawaii.
LIBRARY OF CONGRESS

take King Kalaniopu'u hostage for the return of the boat. The king's favorite wife wailed; two young chiefs pushed him down gently so that he could not walk. Cook urged him on, the chiefs held him back. Then shots were heard further along the beach; an important chief had been killed. The mood of the crowd turned nasty. A warrior rushed up to Cook, menacing him with a dagger. Cook fired small shot at him and the pellets bounced off his tough mat breastplate. The warrior laughed and yelled defiance and the crowd attacked. While Cook faced the blood-hungry natives none would strike him, but as he turned toward the boat a warrior rushed at him from behind, clubbing him violently. As he sank to his knees, half in the water, the warrior stabbed him over and over again. Other natives stabbed him, clubbed him and held him under the water. Only once did he manage to raise his head. It took only seconds, but James Cook, who had circumnavigated the world three times, was dead—at 8:00 A.M. on 14 February 1779. He was buried at sea.

Cooper, Gary (1901–1961).

John Barrymore called him the world's greatest actor; his career spanned thirty-five years during which he made at least ninety-five films. In 1959 he was hospitalized in Hollywood and Boston for abdominal and prostate surgery. He seemed pretty fit by the end of 1960, but in London while filming *The Naked Edge* he complained of feeling cold in his back all the time. He liked *The Naked Edge*—a whodunit—and thought it would be interesting to know how it came out; he was destined never to find out. On his return to Hollywood he maintained a brave front in spite of terrible pain. A cancerous portion of his colon was removed. His face was gaunt and his towering frame became even more angular.

On 27 December Cooper's wife, Veronica (Rocky), was called to the doctor's office, where she learned Gary had an inoperable cancer of the lungs. On 27 February 1961, feeling dreadfully ill, Cooper asked Rocky to tell him what he really had. He didn't bat an eye. In spite of the gravity of his illness, Gary carried out his promise to narrate a television documentary about the West. He was in agony. When he failed to appear at the Academy Awards presentation to receive his special—and third—Oscar, millions knew there was something desperately wrong. Gary was confined to the sunny study in his Holmby Hills house. By the beginning of May he was failing fast but could talk to Rocky and his daughter Maria until the final two days, when he was heavily sedated. At 12:47 P.M., 14 May 1961 he died at home with his wife and daughter beside him.

Cooper, who had become a Roman Catholic in 1959, was buried at the Grotto of Our Lady of Lourdes at Holy Cross Cemetery, Los Angeles, after a solemn Requiem Mass at the Church of the Good Shepherd in Beverly Hills.

Crane, Hart (1899–1932).

The brilliant young U.S. poet was for much of his life a hard-drinking homosexual. While in Mexico on a Guggenheim Fellowship he fell in love with Peggy Cowley. He was much excited about it and marched into a bar in Taxco and announced to a small crowd of Americans, "Boys—I did it!" and then launched into a graphic account of the delights of heterosexual love.

April 1932 was a bad month and ended in death for Hart Crane. He was perpetually short of money, would torture himself about what his friends and critics thought of him, then go off on a riotous drinking spree. One night, after a day of hard drinking, he tried to commit suicide, first with iodine and then with Mercurochrome. A doctor cleaned out his stomach and gave him a heavy dose of morphine.

Peggy thought it would be better to return to the United States and the two booked passage on the *Orizaba*. Peggy, who had burned her arm badly when a box of matches exploded, lay in her cabin, heavily sedated, while Crane, who had been drinking heavily, rampaged over the boat. The purser locked him in his cabin and nailed the door shut but the poet managed to escape. The next morning, 27 April 1932, he seemed sober enough, though distressed by the loss of his wallet and ring. Peggy coaxed him to have some breakfast and later tried to talk him into getting dressed. About noon the boat suddenly stopped; Peggy screamed, "Hart!" He had been seen to come on deck in his pajamas, climb the rail and jump over into the Caribbean. Life preservers were thrown and four lifeboats were lowered. The search continued for two hours, but the body was never found. *See* J. Unterecker (1969).

Cranmer, Thomas (1489–1556).

The first Protestant Archbishop of Canterbury actively promoted the English Reformation during the reign of Henry VIII and supported the king in his efforts to check the power of the Pope. When Mary I, a Roman Catholic, assumed the throne, however, she soon became known as Bloody Mary for her persecution of the Protestants for heresy as she tried to restore Catholic worship in the realm. Cranmer was condemned as a traitor and imprisoned in the Tower of London toward the end of 1553. In March 1554 he was taken to Bocardo prison in the Corn Market, Oxford, and charged with heresy. He languished there for a year and a half. In 1556 he was removed to pleasanter quarters in the Deanery of Christ Church, Oxford, where he had a garden at his disposal and good food. There he began to write out recantations, each one more drastic than the last. On 21 March 1556 he was taken to St. Mary's, Oxford, to learn whether or not he was to be burned at the stake.

The rain beat heavily against the windows while Cranmer heard the Provost of Eton declare that never had evils so enormous been excused nor a man continuing in them so long pardoned. Cranmer, seeing all hope for life gone, bravely stated that he now renounced his recantations: "And as for the Pope, I refuse him as Christ's enemy and Antichrist, with all his false doctrines. And as for the Sacrament——" He got no further. The crowd rose up in anger, "Stop the heretic's mouth!" they shouted, but Cranmer escaped them. Through the pouring rain ran the little old man with the crowd at his heels, down narrow Brasenose Lane and out of the gate by St. Michael's.

There stood the stake with its pile of one hundred and fifty faggots of furze and one hundred faggots of wood. The archbishop quickly doffed his outer garment and stood in his long shirt. After being bound to the stake with an iron girdle, he was called upon to repent. He answered, "This hand hath offended and therefore it shall suffer first punishment," and he steadfastly held in the flames the hand that had written the recantations. As the fire rose about him he made no cry. No movement betrayed his pain, save that once with his unburned hand he wiped his forehead. The flames might scorch and consume his flesh but his spirit had found repose.

Crockett, David (1786–1836).

The U.S. frontiersman undoubtedly fell at the Alamo on 6 March 1836, but exactly how he died is unknown. John S.C. Abbott in his 1874 book tells us that the Battle of the Alamo was fought with the utmost desperation until daylight, when only six of the garrison remained alive. They were surrounded and surrendered. Davy Crockett stood like a lion at bay; his eyes flashed fire, a shattered rifle in his right hand and a gleaming Bowie knife streaming with blood in his left. His face was covered with blood from a deep gash in his forehead. General Castrillon wished to spare the lives of the six, but when he marched his prisoners before the president, Santa Anna was much annoyed. "Have I not already told you how to dispose of them? Why do you bring them to me?" Immediately, several Mexicans began plunging their swords into the men. Davy Crockett sprang at the throat of Santa Anna, but before he could reach the president he was dead with a dozen swords sheathed in his heart; a smile of defiance and scorn curled his lips and he fell without a groan.

In contrast, James Shackford in his 1956 book quotes the ancient Candelaria Villanueva (who may not even have been present) as stating that a volley from the Mexicans killed Crockett when he was walking unarmed in the stockade early in the siege.

Walter Lord in *A Time to Stand* (1961) gives us a Mexican account from Sgt. Felix Nuñez:

> This man apparently had a charmed life. Of the many soldiers who took deliberate aim at him and fired, not one ever hit him. On the contrary, he never missed a shot. He killed at least eight of our men, besides wounding several others. This being observed by a lieutenant who had come in over the wall, he sprang at him and dealt him a deadly blow with his sword just above the right eye, which felled him to the ground, and in an instant he was pierced by not less than twenty bayonets.

José Enrique de la Peña, whose diary was translated by Carmen Perry and published in 1975, covers the Battle of the Alamo. In it he describes the fate of seven prisoners (including one whom he identifies as "the naturalist David Crockett") brought before Santa Anna. Several officers, hoping to flatter him,

> fell upon these unfortunate, defenseless men just as a tiger leaps upon his prey. Though tortured before they were killed, these unfortunates died without complaining and without humiliating themselves before their torturers.... I turned away horrified in order not to witness such a barbarous scene.

However Davy Crockett met his end, it is certain he lived up to his legend as an American hero who died bravely and gallantly.

Cromwell, Oliver (1599–1658).

The Lord Protector of Great Britain for nearly five years suffered from a type of malaria (*Plasmodium vivax*) which he acquired in the swamps of Ireland during his campaign there. It caused chronic anemia, which made him more susceptible to a severe case of septicemia brought on by 'the stone', which had set off an infection in his bladder and kidneys. On 17 August 1658 he suffered severe pains in his bowels and back, and was obviously extremely ill. He was begged to name his successor but refused to do so, saying he would most certainly recover. His strong will kept him alive until the afternoon of 3 September 1658 when he died at Whitehall Palace. The postmortem showed that his spleen was suppurating and "a mass of disease." Embalmment was unsuccessful and the body had to be buried immediately. For the impressive lying-in-state in Somerset House, and the subsequent procession to Westminster Abbey on 23 November, a wax effigy was dressed in the protector's richest clothes. At one point in the proceedings the effigy was sat upright and crowned. On 29 January 1661 Cromwell and two other men who took part in the execution of Charles I were exhumed and hanged in their grave clothes on a triple gibbet at Tyburn. After six hours the corpses were taken down and beheaded. The bodies were thrown into a deep pit below the gibbet; the heads were stuck on poles and left at Westminster Hall until at least 1684. Cromwell's head was passed from hand to hand until 25 March 1960 when it was finally interred by his alma mater, Sidney Sussex College, Cambridge, in a secret spot close to the chapel. *See* A. Fraser (1973).

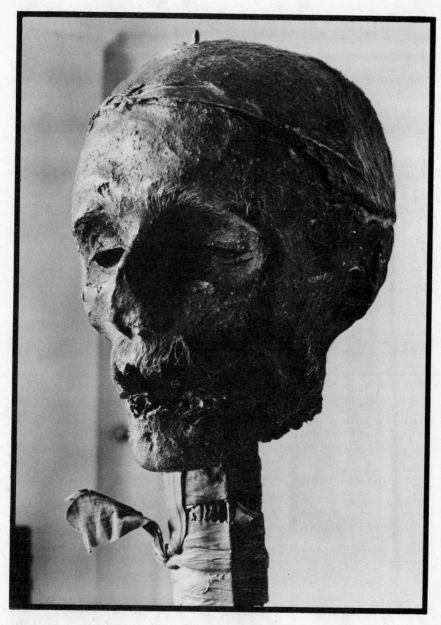

The mummified head of Oliver Cromwell before burial at a secret spot near Sidney Sussex College, Cambridge, England. Photo by Edwin Smith.

Curie, Marie Sklodowska
(1867–1934).

The Polish-born chemist who, with her husband, Pierre, disco-vered radium in 1898, was still working a sixteen-hour day in her Paris laboratory early in 1934. Occasionally she would murmur "Ah, how tired I am." She had contended with bad eyesight (she had double cataracts removed), her ears rang continuously, and after handling radium for thirty-five years her blood count was abnormal. In May of that year severe chills and fever threatened her life. In a desperate attempt to save her she was taken to the Sanatorium Sancellemoz at Saint Gervais. She fought death hard, but at dawn on 4 July 1934 her heart finally stopped. The cause was "an aplastic pernicious anemia of rapid, feverish de-velopment": she was a victim of the radioactivity she and her husband had discovered. Curie is buried beside her husband at Sceaux, in the southern outskirts of Paris.

Curie, Pierre (1859–1906).

It was raining hard. The narrow rue Dauphine in Old Paris was crowded with noisy traffic. Pierre Curie, hunched under his large umbrella, walked absentmindedly behind a closed cab. With a sudden movement he turned left to cross the street, directly into the path of a heavy dray pulled by two enormous horses. Shocked, he raised his hands as though attempting to hold on to the chest of the rearing animal. His feet slipped and, amid shouts of horror, Pierre fell beneath the hooves as the driver hauled in vain on the reins. Curie was untouched by the hooves or by the dray's front two wheels, which passed on either side of him. But the left rear wheel of the wagon, which was laden with military uniforms, passed over his head and crushed his skull with ease. The cranium was shattered and the brain of Pierre Curie trickled in the mud. It was 2:30 P.M. on 19 April 1906.

At the police station his wallet revealed him to be the famous Nobel Prize-winning scientist, codiscoverer of radium. Shouts of anger broke out against Louis Manin, the driver, and the gen-darmes had to intervene. As a doctor counted sixteen bony fragments of what had once been the cranium, outside the rain slowly washed the blood from the wagon wheel. Curie was buried in his mother's tomb at Sceaux. *See* E. Curie (1938)

Custer, George Armstrong
(1839–1876).

At 10:30 A.M. on 25 June 1876, when the 7th Cavalry joined Custer and his scouts at the Little Bighorn River, Montana, the general was informed that the Indians were aware of their presence. Though the men had marched ten miles that morning and were tired and hot, he felt they had no alternative but to attack. His scout, Bloody Knife, thought it would be a suicide mission as there were thousands of Indians waiting and watching them under the command of Sitting Bull and Crazy Horse. To Custer's question as to the outcome of the battle he replied with one word, "*Death!*" Custer divided the regiment into three squadrons; two would cut off Sitting Bull's escape while the general himself took 267 men to make the central attack.

At 3:30 P.M. Custer, at the head of his cheering, bellowing horsemen, thundered toward the river. Several hundred yards from the ford they ran into an ambush. Custer and his men galloped up an escarpment, tailed by a "hurricane" of Indians. Trapped between hordes of Sioux and Cheyennes they were forced higher into the maze of hills that offered no escape but death. At 4:15 P.M. Custer ordered his men to dismount and, facing the river, prepared to fight to the last man. By 4:45 there was only a ragged band of fifty in the dreadful heat around Custer's flag; hundreds upon hundreds of feathered heads bobbed around them. Custer ordered his men to shoot the horses and pile them around for a breastwork. The smell was sickening and though the carcasses formed some protection against the constant hail of bullets and arrows it was not enough.

The last glimpse of Custer showed him on his feet firing his pearl-handled bulldogs. By 5:00 P.M. nearly all the men had bled to death. Waterman, an Arapaho mercenary, described seeing "Yellowhair" (Custer) on his hands and knees. He had been shot through the side and was bleeding from the mouth. As the sun was setting, Meyotzi (Custer's Indian "wife") and her six-year-old boy Yellow Bird (presumed to be his only child) came up the

General Custer was killed with all his men at the Battle of the Little Big Horn. These monuments stand on the battlefield in Montana. Photo by H.R. Locke, 1894.

LIBRARY OF CONGRESS

slope. When the thirty-six-year-old Custer's naked body was found he had been washed clean, probably by Meyotzi, and unlike the others his body had not been mutilated. There was a wound in the left temple and it is thought that he had saved his last bullet for himself, because an Indian will not touch the body of a suicide. Only the horse "Comanche" survived the massacre and for years thereafter appeared at 7th Cavalry parades, saddled but riderless. Custer is buried at the U.S. Military Academy at West Point, N.Y. *See* D.A. Kinsley (1968).

Czolgosz, Leon F. (1873?–1901).

The assassin of President McKinley (q.v.) was a fair-haired, slender man with a pleasant but somewhat vacant expression. He was born in Detroit and brought up in northern Michigan. He had suffered a breakdown in 1898, after he had moved with his parents to the Cleveland area, and thereafter attended Anarchist meetings. He had been in Buffalo for several weeks when McKinley arrived in the city. He attended the president's speech at the Pan-American exposition on 5 September 1901. On the

Photographs of Leon Czolgosz, assassin of President McKinley in Buffalo, 1901, taken just after his arrest.

LIBRARY OF CONGRESS

6th he shot and mortally wounded the president. Just four days after McKinley's burial in Canton, Ohio, Czolgosz was brought to trial in Buffalo. The following day he was found guilty. He listened to the death sentence impassively and was electrocuted at Auburn State Prison, N.Y., at 7:12 A.M. on 29 October 1901. As he was strapped in the chair he said, "I killed the president because he was the enemy of the good people—the good working people. I am not sorry for my crime."

No abnormality of the brain was observable at autopsy. Because experiments with raw meat showed quicklime to be an ineffective agent for destruction of the body, a carboy of sulfuric acid was poured into the black-stained pine coffin after it had been lowered into its grave in the prison burial ground. The assassin's clothes and other effects were burned.

Damien, Father (*Joseph*) (1840–1889).

When the sturdy young Belgian was only twenty-three years old,

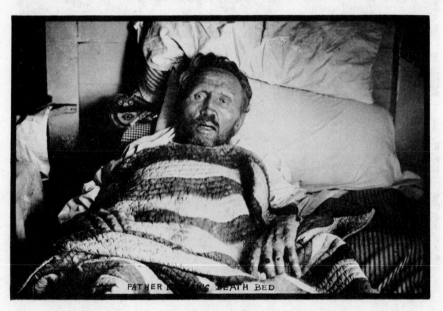

Father Damien as he lay dying of leprosy.

LIBRARY OF CONGRESS

Father Damien's funeral procession on the island of Molokai.

LIBRARY OF CONGRESS

he volunteered to take the place of his critically ill brother as a missionary in the Sandwich (now Hawaiian) Islands. Saddened by the dreadful plight of the lepers that were deported to Molokai (the island just south of Honolulu), he took spiritual charge of the settlement in May 1873. There, he was appalled by the living conditions of the pitiably grotesque lepers and immediately began—with many urgent appeals to the Hawaiian government—to improve these conditions.

On the first Sunday of June 1885 there was a shocked stir when, in celebrating early Mass, Father Damien addressed his listeners not by the usual "my brethren" but "we lepers." The signs of disease soon became evident, but he remained undisturbed, simply increasing the pace of his work as he realized his time was short. A farmer from the nonleprous side of the island gave him a ramshackle horse-drawn conveyance, which enabled him to get around the island after the leprosy had crippled his legs. He clung stubbornly to life. "There is so much left to do," he said, and drove his emaciated body to further endeavor. He was totally blind in one eye and losing sight in the other; his fingers merged with his knuckles in great ulcerated sores. Violent diarrhea, severe coughing and difficult breathing disturbed his rest.

Just after his forty-ninth birthday Father Damien began to prepare for death. "I would like to be put by the side of my church under the stout old tree where I used to rest so many nights before I had other shelter." He liked to be carried on his mattress to the grass patch in front of his house at Kalawao so that each day the lepers ("my people") could visit him. Noting that his sores were healing over with a black crust, he realized that death was not far off.

On the eve of Palm Sunday in 1889 he was given Holy Communion for the last time. He was unconscious most of Sunday though occasionally his eyes would flicker open and he would try to smile at those who watched by his bed. In the early morning of 15 April 1889 he died peacefully in the arms of Brother James. "All signs of leprosy disappeared from the face," his colleague reported in a letter dated the same day. Father Damien was dressed in his cassock and laid in a coffin lined with white silk. The outside was covered with a black cloth on which was sewn a white cross. His grave was dug in the cool shadow of the pandanus tree he had chosen. In 1936, amid great pomp, Damien's remains were reburied in Louvain, Belgium, near his birthplace.

Danton, Georges Jacques (1759–1794).

In March 1794 the thirty-four-year-old French statesman refused to flee the country (or even become unduly disturbed) when told that his arrest had been ordered by Saint-Just and Robespierre. Danton planned to use the dock to attack his enemies, but the jury had been carefully selected; Danton was not allowed to call witnesses and a verdict of guilty was brought against him and the fourteen men arrested with him. Fear of what Danton would say caused the president to read the verdict on 5 April 1794 to empty benches.

On 6 April the condemned men had to undergo the ordeal of the *toilette du condamné*. One by one they were forced to sit on a small stool which had become rounded and worn by much use. Their shirts were torn open at the collar, their hands bound behind them and all the hair that grew over their necks was cut off—the chill of the scissors a small foretaste of what was to come. The fifteen men were then hoisted into three tumbrels and jolted through the Paris streets past the waiting crowds. When Danton heard the mob and saw the *lécheuses de la guillotine*, those terrible women who were paid by the Committee of General Security to infect the crowd with their frenzy as each head tumbled down, he shouted "Stupid clods! They'll shout 'Long live the Republic!' when the Republic no longer has a head!"

There were fifteen necks to be sliced through; the knife had to be positioned fifteen times, each operation taking two minutes—or a mere half hour altogether—but it must have seemed an eternity for those waiting their turn. Danton was the last. As he slipped on the blood of those guillotined before him, the executioners heard him murmur of his sixteen-year-old wife, Louise, "I shall never see you again, my darling——" Then, "Come, Danton, no weakness!" To the executioner he remarked, "Sanson, show my head to the people; it is worth it." Then the knife fell. *See* R. Christophe (1967).

Darwin, Charles (1809–1882).

The English biologist recovered from a mild heart attack in 1881; another attack while he was walking alone on the "sand walk" at his home at Down, Kent, in March 1882 caused him to take to his bed, to be nursed by his devoted wife, Emma. ("I'm not the least afraid of death," he told her.) He was up answering his mail on 18 April but suffered a severe heart attack just before midnight. He died, surrounded by his family, shortly before 4:00 P.M. on 19 April 1882, and was buried in Westminster Abbey.

Though his death was straightforward, Darwin's medical history remains a great puzzle. For fifty years or more he suffered frequently from palpitations, vomiting, lassitude, headache, eczema, boils, shivering, trembling, flatulence and insomnia. Saul Adler in a letter to the magazine *Nature* in 1959 suggested Darwin's ailment was Chagas' disease (South American trypanosomiasis). Darwin records "an attack (for it deserves no less a name) of the Benchuca, a species of Reduvius," while at Luxan, Argentina, in 1835. This bug is the principal vector of the parasite that causes Chagas' disease, which it transmits to humans, not by its bite (as a mosquito transmits malaria) but by infecting open wounds with its droppings. Whether the insects that fed on Darwin's blood were infected is not known, but a principal legacy of the disease is chronic weakness of the heart muscle.

In a 1965 study, A.W. Woodruff rejected Adler's proposal on several grounds:

1. Darwin's ill health predates his foreign travels. His two months at Plymouth waiting, at the age of twenty-two, for the *Beagle* to set sail were, according to Darwin's diary, "the most miserable I have ever spent," and he mentions palpitation and pain about the heart at that time.
2. During his lifetime he was examined by the most eminent specialists, none of whom could ever detect signs of *any* organic disease.
3. Darwin's "weakness" was not a true physical weakness. It did not, for example, prevent his geological expedition into the mountains in 1838. In later life he regularly walked with energetic stride several times around his sand walk, one circuit of which, with the walk to and from home, amounted to nearly a mile. Again, during a six-month period he limited his use of snuff by keeping his snuffbox in the cellar and the key in the garret, up narrow stairs which the present-day occupants of his house dread to climb.
4. Darwin's ill health is linked significantly to periods of emotional stress aroused by his father's disapproval of his *Beagle* appointment; by publication of his masterpiece, *The Origin of Species,* delayed for over a quarter of a century and, once published, provoking sharp attacks by religious leaders ("I felt like a murderer," said the author); and by his father's death, when "weakness" prevented him from attending the funeral. In his later life, when such stresses became less frequent, his health improved markedly.

Taken together, the facts suggest that Darwin was the victim of a functional illness (one without a physical cause). The tendency to psychogenic disorders (nervous breakdowns and emotional problems) was present in both his mother's and his father's families, and Woodruff cites evidence that four of Darwin's children were likewise afflicted. A 1977 book by R. Colp, Jr., entirely devoted to Darwin's illness, also discusses other "solutions," including chronic arsenic poisoning and allergy to pigeons.

Davis, Adelle (1904–1974).

The U.S. nutritionist, whose best-selling books claimed good health came from proper nutrition, was shocked when she was told she had cancer of the bone marrow. "I thought this was for people who drink soft drinks, who eat white bread, who eat refined sugar and so on," she was quoted as saying, and added overcritically, "I have been a failure."

Miss Davis, who possessed a master's degree in biochemistry, had a sound academic and practical background to support her theories. But she was often attacked for seemingly wild statements. For example, she claimed that the Germans conquered the French in the Second World War because German black bread and beer were nutritionally superior to French white bread and wine.

In spite of chemotherapy she lived barely a year after the diagnosis was made, and died on 31 May 1974 at her home in Palos Verdes Estates, California.

Dean, James (1931–1955).

The young actor and his friend, Rolf Wuetherich, left Los Angeles early on 30 September 1955 in Jimmy's new silver Porsche Spyder to race it at Salinas. The day was hot and the road (Route 466) to Paso Robles monotonously straight and narrow. Jimmy had already received a speeding ticket, but he was still driving at eighty-five miles per hour when they noticed that an oncoming car appeared to be moving over into their lane. The car, driven by Donald Gene Turnupseed, who had not seen the Porsche, was actually taking a left fork toward Tulare. The two cars crashed. The Porsche was almost flattened, Rolf was thrown clear with a smashed jaw and a broken leg, but Jimmy was draped bloody and limp over the driver's door. His neck was broken. A coroner's jury brought back a verdict of accidental death and no charges were lodged against Turnupseed, who escaped with minor injuries. Dean was buried in Park Cemetery, Fairmont, Ind. *See* V. Herndon (1974).

De Quincey, Thomas (1785–1859).

The English essayist, best known for his *Confessions of an English Opium-Eater*, began his habit quite innocently in 1804 at Oxford University when he was advised to use the drug for a toothache. He was overjoyed by its effect of stimulating his imagination while quieting his nervous irritation. At first he took opium only about once every three weeks, but by 1812 he was a confirmed opium "eater," imbibing as much as 8,000 drops of laudanum a day (equivalent to 320 grains of opium in alcoholic solution). The consequence was severe irritation of the stomach and frightful nightmares. A frail man, he several times fought a courageous and agonizing battle to decrease his consumption of the drug but failed in the attempt. Finally, in 1848, fear of losing his mind forced him to limit his consumption to five or six grains of opium, or a hundred and fifty drops of laudanum, a day.

In spite of the hardships of his youth and his addiction to opium, De Quincey lived until he was seventy-four. He was confined to bed for two months at his daughter Margaret's cottage near Lasswade, seven miles from Edinburgh, before finally dying from the infirmities of old age on 8 December 1859. His last words were "Sister! sister! sister!" apparently addressed to a vision of his sister Elizabeth, who had died seventy years before. De Quincey lies beside his wife in St. Cuthbert's Churchyard, Edinburgh, in the shadow of the great castle.

Dickens, Charles (1812–1870).

The English novelist accelerated his death by the dramatic readings he gave publicly in the U.S. and Britain during his last few years. In 1869 he collapsed more than once when on tour. His foot became lame, he had effusions of blood from the bowels and he suffered some paralysis of his left side. In particular, the reading and acting out of Nancy's murder in *Oliver Twist* left him prostrated for hours after each performance. At the time of his death he was halfway through *The Mystery of Edwin Drood*, which was being issued in monthly parts as the installments were written.

On 8 June 1870 Dickens worked all day on his novel, a mystery story of great psychological profundity. His workroom was the upper chamber of a small, two-story Swiss chalet that had been erected in his garden at Gad's Hill, near Rochester in Kent. He worked later than usual that day and before dinner had time only to write a few letters. Since his separation from his wife, the household had been run by his devoted sister-in-law, Georgina Hogarth. As they dined, Dickens told her he had been feeling very ill for an hour and, after a few inconsequential remarks, pushed back his chair and staggered to his feet. Georgina raced around the table to offer support and help him toward the sofa. "On the ground," he gasped, and she lowered him to the carpet. He had suffered a massive stroke and these were his last words. He was lifted onto the sofa by the servants and died there exactly twenty-four hours later at 6:10 P.M. on 9 June 1870.

Ellen Ternan, the young actress with whom he had lived clandestinely for a period, was one of those who visited the house on Dickens' last day. *Edwin Drood*, of all his works the most in need of completion, has given rise to a shelf of speculations, dramatizations and sequels. Dickens is buried in Poet's Corner in Westminster Abbey.

Dickinson, Emily (1830–1886).

The U.S. poet, always withdrawn, became even more reclusive in her last two decades, seldom going far from her brother's house in Amherst, Mass. She was stricken by nervous prostration when her eight-year-old nephew, Gilbert (Gib), died of typhoid. "I was making a loaf of cake with Maggie [a servant] when I saw a great darkness coming and knew no more until late at night." In 1884 her health was set back further by the death of her friend, Otis Lord, and by late in 1885 she was often too ill to leave her room. Stricken by Bright's disease, a type of kidney inflammation, she became unconscious on 13 May 1886 and, after two days of "that terrible breathing," as her brother described it in his diary, she died at 6:00 P.M. on the 15th. She was carried in a simple white coffin across the fields to Amherst Cemetery. During her lifetime only seven of her poems were published, and these anonymously. After her death, her sister Lavinia discovered a treasure trove of her work in a locked box. These poems were published gradually between 1890 and 1945.

Disney, Walt (1901–1966).

In his last months, the U.S. cartoonist and film producer, who had developed a kidney ailment, had a premonition he would die soon. He pushed himself to accomplish more and more, but pain from a sinus condition and an old polo injury made him irritable. Shortness of breath and pain from his leg forced him into St. Joseph's Hospital, Los Angeles, on 2 November 1966. Tests revealed a spot the size of a walnut on Disney's left lung; surgery was imperative. The growth was found to be cancerous and was removed, but his lymph nodes were oversized and the surgeons gave him only six months to two years to live. After two weeks in the hospital, Disney was bored and eager to get back to work, but at home he grew weaker and on 30 November returned to St. Joseph's. Cobalt treatments diminished his strength and he sometimes became confused.

On Disney's sixty-fifth birthday, 5 December 1966, he was too ill for any observances. On 14 December when his wife, Lilly, visited him he got out of bed and hugged her fiercely. She was elated. Surely, she thought, he was going to get well. But he died the next morning at 9:35 A.M. of an acute circulatory collapse. The funeral was private, as Disney had requested. He was cremated and interred in Forest Lawn Memorial Park, Glendale, Cal.

Dostoyevsky, Fyodor (1821–1881).

In the fall of 1880 as the Russian author was finishing *The Brothers Karamazov*, he knew his life was coming to an end. At fifty-nine he looked many years older. Epilepsy and emphysema had taken their toll and he suffered from terrible bouts of nervous prostration. After long nights at his desk he was pale and gaunt with great circles under his deep-set, gray eyes, but he was worried that he might not be able to leave enough to take care of his "three golden heads": his wife, Anna, who was twenty-four years his junior; eleven-year-old Lyubov; and nine-year-old Fyodor.

Dostoyevsky had been warned against physical effort, but on 26 January 1881 he pushed aside a heavy bookcase to retrieve a favorite penholder. The effort caused an artery in his lung to

Dostoyevsky in his last years.　　　　　LIBRARY OF CONGRESS

break open and he hemorrhaged. When the doctor began his examination the novelist hemorrhaged again and this time fainted. A priest was sent for and Dostoyevsky made confession and received communion. The next day he felt better, but on the

Dostoyevsky's funeral in St. Petersburg. From a woodcut by A. Baldinger, 1881.

LIBRARY OF CONGRESS

28th, Anna awoke at about 7:00 A.M. and saw her husband watching her. He said he had been awake for three hours and had realized that this was the day he was going to die. When Anna pleaded with him he told her that in the Bible the Decembrists had given him it stated, "Do not hold me back." Anna wept and he tried to console her. At 11:00 A.M. he had a bad hemorrhage and became very weak; he asked for the children. At about 7:00 P.M. he suddenly raised himself slightly and the blood began to flow again; Anna gave him slivers of ice but to no avail. The children knelt at the head of his bed while Anna, holding her husband's hand, felt his pulse growing steadily weaker. Finally at 8:38 P.M. on 28 January 1881 in their shabby little apartment at No. 5 Kuznechny Pereulok, an unfashionable part of St. Petersburg, Dostoevsky died. He was buried in Tikhvin Cemetery after funeral services at St. Isaac's Cathedral.

Doyle, Sir Arthur Conan
(1859–1930).

Sir Arthur resented the "Sherlock Holmes" stories which had made his fortune because he felt that writing them interfered with more worthy activities. In 1917 he declared himself a spiritualist and from that time until his death he spent enormous amounts of time and money carrying this new cause to audiences all over the world. Angina pectoris troubled him in his last year; in the fall of 1929 he collapsed on his way home from a Scandinavian speaking tour but recovered sufficiently to address two large Armistice Day gatherings in London. By the summer of 1930 he was confined to bed at his home, Windlesham, in Crowborough, Sussex, with a failing heart and kidneys. On 7 July he was helped into a basket chair at 7:30 A.M. to look north through

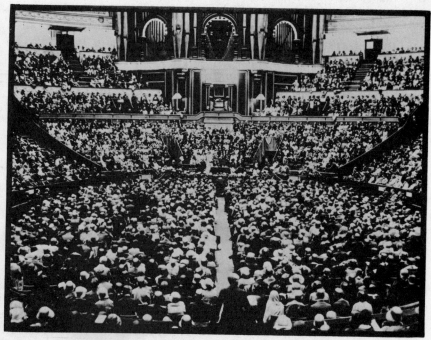

Conan Doyle's memorial service, held by spiritualists in the Royal Albert Hall, London.

the open windows across the rose garden to the distant downs. Barely able to speak, he sat holding the hands of his son Adrian and his wife Jean until he died about an hour later. He was buried in his garden, where Lady Conan Doyle joined him ten years later.

A crowd of eight thousand spiritualists and others filled the Albert Hall, London, a few days after Doyle's death. An empty chair had been left for the disembodied spirit's use and the medium, Estelle Roberts, was able to assure his widow that she had seen him enter and sit down beside her. A séance held in the Bronx, N.Y., to receive messages from Doyle proved to be a hoax, and at another, in England, the medium George Valiantine produced Sir Arthur's purported thumbprint only to have it shown to be an impression of Valiantine's big toe. Until her death, Doyle's widow believed he sent her messages to guide the family's health and business affairs. When the remaining family moved from Windlesham in 1955 to Bignell House, near Minstead, Hampshire, the bodies were reinterred in Minstead churchyard. A laundry van was employed to mislead reporters, and the reburial was done at dead of night. Curiously, when the Doyles moved out of Bignell House shortly afterward, the new owner thought the house was haunted. After the spirits were exorcised in 1961 there were no more disturbances. *See* C. Higham (1976).

Drake, Sir Francis (1540?–1596).

In a modern atlas the waters between the island of Escudo de Varaguas and Portobello (Puerto Bello) on the east coast of Panama are called the Golfo de los Mosquitos. The great English explorer and adventurer, hunting for treasure in the region, described them as "the sickliest place of the Indies." Countless men of his fleet were dying from dysentery; the deck above the ballast, the only sick bay in those days, stank with sickness. But Drake, feverish himself, still tortured himself with the thought of the unattainable gold of Peru. On 23 January 1596 he was too ill to leave his cabin on the *Defiance*. He ordered the fleet to weigh anchor and sail out of the fever-ridden place. After several days of illness he knew he was dying and on the 27th had his will witnessed by six of his friends. During the night Sir Francis became delirious and insisted he should don his armor so that he might die like a soldier. He raved in words that no one cared to record but a little later quieted down and was persuaded to go back to bed.

As the sun slowly rose at about 4:00 A.M. on 28 January 1596 Sir Francis Drake died. It seemed fitting that this intrepid man should die in a ship of war off Puerto Bello rather than at home in bed. His body was enclosed in a coffin of lead and the next day, to the thunder of guns and trumpets "lamenting in a doleful manner," his body was committed to the sea. Sir Thomas Baskerville took command of the fleet and burned the half-finished city of Puerto Bello for a funeral pyre.

Dreiser, Theodore (1871–1945).

On 24 December 1945 the U.S. author, noted for his realistic novels, told his friend, Mrs. Estelle Manning, "I am the loneliest man in the world." Then he wept terribly. When she suggested that he might marry Helen Richardson—the woman with whom he had lived for twenty-five years—he ranted. He had done many things for her, he said, but that was one of the things he would never do. Rather, he hoped she would leave. (In fact, he had secretly married her several months earlier.) On the 27th he and Helen walked along the Pacific beach near Venice, Cal., watched a beautiful sunset, had coffee and hot dogs and were home by 7:30. Dreiser went immediately to bed complaining of "kidney aches." Helen was aroused from the twin bed next to his by his shout around 3:00 A.M., "Helen! I have an *intense* pain." The doctor put Dreiser on oxygen and he seemed to rally. On Friday a nurse was in attendance but he insisted that Helen stay with him; she gave him a feeling of security. A friend visited him. "He looked gray and tired," she recalled. "Whenever he was sick he had a very helpless look." Dropping his oxygen mask for a moment, he told her he felt "bum."

A cold thick fog rolled in, obliterating the bright sunny day. Dreiser asked Helen to kiss him; his hands were cold, his breathing shallow, and as she held him he died. "There was something magnificent in the dignity of his departure, as though every atom of his body was in complete repose." He was pronounced dead of a heart attack at 6:50 P.M., 28 December 1945 in his home at 1015 North Kings Road, Hollywood. After a funeral service in the Church of the Recessional, at which Charlie Chaplin read "The Road I Came," Dreiser was buried in the Whispering Pines section of Forest Lawn Memorial Park, Los Angeles. *See* W.A. Swanberg (1965).

Duncan, Isadora (1878–1927).

The world-famous dancer was fascinated by the small Bugatti sports car that she often saw outside the restaurant La Mère Tetu's. The car became an obsession and she thought about buying it—though, as usual, she was penniless. Benoit Falchetto, the garage proprietor who owned the car, agreed to call at Isadora's Nice studio on Wednesday evening 14 September 1927 and take her for a trial drive. As she was lightly clad, her friend Mary Desti suggested that she should wear her cloak instead of the heavy silk-fringed red shawl that was tossed over her shoulders, but Isadora said she would be quite warm. Falchetto protested that his car was not very clean and offered her his leather coat. Again Isadora declined. As she was about to step into the car she turned and waved gaily to Mary and another friend, calling to them, "Adieu, mes amis, je vais à la gloire!" ["Goodbye, my friends, I am off to glory!"]

Isadora was seen to throw the long fringed end of the shawl, which she had wound twice round her neck, over her left shoulder. As the car started the shawl trailed alongside and Mary shouted to her to pick it up. The car stopped and, thinking it was to enable Isadora to gather up the ends of the shawl, the friends ran toward it, but the driver was getting out of the car shouting in Italian, "Madonna mia! I've killed the Madonna!" The fringe of the shawl and part of the fabric itself were wound around the hub and spokes of the wheel. Death had been instantaneous; Isadora's neck was broken and a blood vessel ruptured. The thick silk of the scarf was cut and torn away from the car and the dancer was rushed to St. Roch's Hospital, where the doctors pronounced her dead.

The coffin, covered by Isadora's purple cape, was taken from Nice to Paris. There it was placed in her brother Raymond's studio until it was taken, on Monday 19 September, to the Père-Lachaise crematorium. Her ashes were placed in the crypt where

Funeral of Isadora Duncan's children in Paris in 1917. Her ashes lie in their crypt.

BAIN COLLECTION, LIBRARY OF CONGRESS

her children lay. On the evening before her death she had been distressed by the sight of a little girl who reminded her of her own children, five-year-old Deirdre and three-year-old Patrick, who had drowned in the Seine. She had wept all night, crying to Mary Desti, "I cannot go on like this. For fourteen years I have had the pain in my heart.... I cannot continue to live in a world where there are beautiful blue-eyed, golden-haired children; I cannot, I cannot...."

Earhart, Amelia (1898–1938?).

The U.S. aviatrix who emulated Charles Lindbergh and, in her boyish figure, somewhat resembled him, was the first woman to fly the Atlantic (as a passenger in 1928, solo in 1932). After crashing in Hawaii in March 1937 during an attempted westward flight around the world, she reversed direction and, leaving Oakland, Cal., on 20 May and Miami on 1 June 1937, flew her repaired Lockheed Electra 10-E via South America, Africa, India and Australia (Darwin) to Lae, New Guinea. From there she set out on the longest, most hazardous leg of her journey, to tiny Howland Island in the Pacific, 2556 miles away to the east–northeast. Amelia and her navigator, forty-four-year-old Fred J. Noonan, never reached the island. The Coast Guard cutter *Itasca*, anchored at Howland to provide aid, had difficulty making radio contact throughout the flight. In the last message, received at 8:55 A.M. local time, 2 July 1937, Amelia's voice was heard anxiously repeating, "We are in line of position 157-337.... We are running north and south." No point of reference was mentioned, and the ambiguous message has been variously interpreted. The greatest air-sea rescue operation of the century failed to locate the fliers, and no wreckage was ever spotted. Officially, Earhart and Noonan are still "lost at sea."

In 1960 a California resident, Mrs. Josephine Blanco Akiyama, was quoted in a newspaper article as having witnessed, when an eleven-year-old schoolgirl on Saipan in the Mariana Islands, the crash landing of a large silver-colored, twin-engined plane in Tanapag harbor. The island was secretly fortified by the Japanese during that period, and Mrs. Akiyama had seen two fliers, said to be American, in Japanese custody a few minutes later. "They were both thin and looked tired. The woman had short-cut hair like a man and she was dressed like a man. The man, I think I remember, had his head hurt in some way." The witness identified them from photographs in 1960 as Earhart and Noonan. She had told the same story to a U.S. Navy dentist on Saipan in 1945, years before she could have heard of the missing U.S. pair. (The dentist was located in 1960 and confirmed this fact.)

After interviewing her, Fred Goerner, a San Francisco broadcaster, backed by CBS and various newspapers, began the six-year investigation described in his book *The Search for Amelia Earhart* (1966). Many witnesses on Saipan confirmed the 1937 crash landing. Mrs. Matilde Shoda San Nicholas, who as a child had lived next door to the Saipanese hotel the Japanese maintained as a prison, recalled that for many months in 1937 and 1938 she had frequently seen a tall, thin woman with short hair whom the Japanese described as a spy; the woman, according to Mrs. San Nicholas, wore men's clothes until provided with a dress. They would meet in the yard and exchange friendly gestures and gifts of fruit. Soon after seeing her looking sicker and sadder than usual, Mrs. San Nicholas heard that the woman had died of dysentery. This testimony was given with evident reluctance and in the presence of her priest. Nothing definite could be learned about Noonan, though he seems to have been imprisoned for a time; he may have been executed at the time of Amelia's death.

Saipan lies due north of Lae, almost at right angles to the announced course to Howland Island and at about the same distance. Goerner reports that more powerful engines were fitted to the Electra prior to the takeoff from Lae, doubling Amelia's maximum speed. She may have been engaged in reconnaissance of the Japanese-mandated islands at the time of her capture. Fleet Admiral Chester W. Nimitz, commander of the U.S. Pacific fleet in World War II, told Goerner the aviators had come down in the Marshall Islands (800 miles northwest of Howland). If so, it must have been their transfer as prisoners to the Japanese headquarters on Saipan that the Tanapag witnesses described. Goerner's book leaves little doubt that the U.S. authorities are still withholding information about the ill-starred flight.

A separate investigation by U.S. Air Force Major Joe Gervais, described in *Amelia Earhart Lives* (1970) by Joe Klaas, corroborates Goerner's work in many respects. It even makes a case for the Electra having been replaced by the new, powerful XC-35. However, Gervais advances the incredible conclusion that after the war Earhart returned to the U.S. with a new identity and was still alive in 1970.

Edison, Thomas Alva (1847–1931).

The U.S. inventor of the electric light and the phonograph became increasingly deaf after the age of twelve. Legendary accounts blame the affliction on a train conductor who boxed the boy's ears, but the facts seem to trace its origin to recurrent middle-ear infections that followed upon scarlet fever. Edison blamed its advent on an incident that may well have exacerbated it. Rushing out to a railroad train one day with his arms full of newspapers, he found the train already in motion and had

Mr. and Mrs. Thomas Edison in their garden in 1930, the year before the great inventor's death.

difficulty lifting himself aboard. A trainman reached down and pulled him up by the ears. "I felt something snap inside my head," the inventor recalled years afterward, "and the deafness started from that time and has progressed ever since."

In later life Edison suffered from diabetes, Bright's disease and a gastric ulcer. In October 1929, at the fiftieth anniversary of the birth of electric light, celebrated at Henry Ford's Greenfield Village in Dearborn, Mich., the old man collapsed after President Hoover's banquet speech. Back home at his mansion, Glenmont, in West Orange, N.J., Edison grew steadily weaker from uremic poisoning. Until early October 1931, when his mind began to cloud, he insisted on measuring his medicine himself, interpreting his clinical charts and peering through a microscope at specimens of his blood.

On the 17th he spoke his last audible words: "It is very beautiful over there," he told his wife, Mina, perhaps with reference to the view through the window. Reporters waiting on the lawn saw his bedroom lights come on brightly at 3:24 A.M. on 18 October 1931, a fitting signal for the inventor's passing. Suggestions were made that electric power across the U.S. be turned off briefly on the day of the funeral, but even by that date loss of Edison's creation for even a moment would have been disastrous for the nation's well-being. Instead, many citizens observed a voluntary dim-out at 10:00 P.M. Edison was buried in Rosedale Cemetery, West Orange. N.J.

Einstein, Albert (1879–1955).

The German-born physicist joined the Institute for Advanced Study at Princeton, N.J., in 1933 and became a U.S. citizen seven years later. The simplicity of his nature, the lucidity of his expressed thoughts and his humanitarian ideals caused him to be increasingly sought after as a speaker and signatory. He was offered the presidency of Israel in 1952, but, though deeply moved, declined the honor. Estranged from the mainstream of contemporary physics, he spent his last years working, with only partial success, on a unified field theory that would account for electromagnetic and nuclear forces purely in terms of the space-time continuum by which he had satisfactorily explained gravitation in his revolutionary theories of relativity.

Einstein's second wife had died in 1936; after the death of his sister in 1951 he shared his two-story home at 112 Mercer Street, Princeton with his stepdaughter, Margot, and his housekeeper-secretary, Helen Dukas. He gave up the violin in the last few years of his life but enjoyed playing Bach and Mozart on his Bechstein grand piano.

On 13 April 1955 Einstein was at home drafting a statement for Israel's Independence Day when he was overcome by nausea caused by a gallbladder infection. Later he collapsed. On the 15th he was admitted to Princeton Hospital where Margot, also a patient there at the time, failed to recognize him, "so changed was he by the pain and the lack of blood in his face." He made no complaint, but joked with her and waited for death "as if for a natural phenomenon." He had long known he had an aortic aneurysm that could burst at any time, causing death by hemorrhage, and this was indeed what killed him. At about 1:15 A.M. on 18 April 1955 his nurse heard him muttering in German, a language she did not understand. She went outside his room for a moment to seek a doctor and returned to find him dead. Einstein's brain was preserved for medical research; his body was cremated and his ashes were quietly tipped into a New Jersey river by a friend, Otto Nathan.

Eisenhower, Dwight David (1890–1969).

The thirty-fourth president of the U.S. (1953–1960) suffered sporadic abdominal pain throughout his life. During his presidency his health became a matter of grave national concern. He suffered a coronary thrombosis in Denver on 24 September 1955; this was announced as a digestive upset. After experiencing acute abdominal pain at the White House on 8 June 1956 he was operated on at Walter Reed Army Hospital for a diseased ileum (the last part of the small intestine). An ileotransverse colostomy was performed, whereby the defective tract was bypassed. Eisenhower's gallbladder, which was found to contain 16 stones, was removed in 1966. Partial bowel obstruction beginning the following year led to a second operation for ileitis in February 1969. By this time his terminal cardiac condition was well advanced.

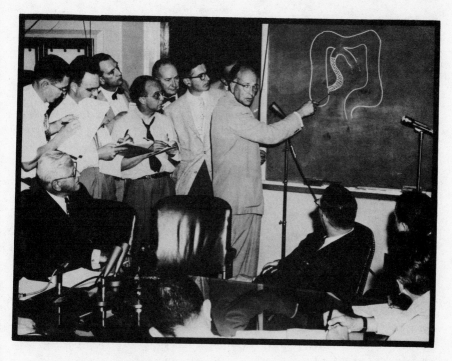

Eisenhower's ileitis operation: the commandant of Walter Reed Army Hospital, Maj. Gen. L.D. Heaton, explains on 9 June 1956 how the President's diseased ileum was bypassed.

LIBRARY OF CONGRESS

The final phase can be considered to have begun 29 April 1968 when Eisenhower suffered his fourth coronary thrombosis at his Palm Desert, Cal., home. Back at Walter Reed further heart attacks followed. Beginning with the seventh episode on 16 August 1968, ventricular fibrillations had to be controlled by application of electrodes fourteen times in eight days, four times on one day alone. Defibrillation ceased to be necessary after 24 August, but soon after the second abdominal operation his cardiac condition rapidly worsened. Though he was frequently unconscious, the patient never lost his memory or his keen interest in current events. Eisenhower died in Walter Reed Army Hospital, Washington, D.C., at 12:25 P.M. 28 March 1969 and was buried in Abilene, Kan. Following his death, his doctors received much criticism for the heroic measures used to lengthen the former president's life.

Elizabeth I (1533–1603).

England's "Virgin Queen" is considered by some to be the most effective monarch who ever ruled any country. She was only two years old when her father, Henry VIII, had her mother, Anne Boleyn, beheaded, and then married again the following day. By the time Elizabeth was ten her father had married three more wives and had executed one of them as well. It could well have been these experiences—and the shameless attentions paid to her a few years later by Thomas Seymour, who was married to her stepmother, Catherine Parr—that turned her permanently against marriage. Though Elizabeth has often been suspected of liaisons with her favorite ministers, F.C. Chamberlin in a 1922 book comes close to proving that she did indeed die a virgin.

With the aid of eminent British physicians he also investigated Elizabeth's medical history. Beginning at puberty, her health was always poor; she suffered from headaches, edema, pyorrhea and irregularities of the menstrual cycle. Like her father, she had a persistent leg ulcer, but in her case it is unlikely to have been syphilitic in origin. Probably her sex drive was feeble. But despite her disabilities she was an attractive woman and a shrewd and forceful ruler.

In January 1603 the queen caught a cold and moved from Whitehall to Richmond, the warmest of her palaces. At sixty-nine she was weary and lacked the patience to take her medicine. Her pyorrhea supplied a potent reservoir of infection; she endured a perpetual sore throat and thirst, accompanied by fever, restlessness and insomnia. She would walk about the palace until worn out, then recline on floor cushions, silent and apparently lost in meditation. For four days she lay on the floor with her finger in her mouth. Later a throat abscess burst and gave her some relief, but pneumonia was probably then present. Asked whether she wished James VI of Scotland to succeed her, she could respond only with a vague gesture of assent. While the Archbishop of Canterbury, Whitgift, prayed over her, she drifted into unconsciousness and died, her head resting on her right arm, at 2:45 A.M., 24 March 1603. She had lived longer than any English sovereign up to that date. Elizabeth I was buried in Westminster Abbey.

Faulkner, William (1897–1962).

The U.S. novelist's heavy indulgence in whiskey sent him to a hospital in Memphis in 1956 with a stomach hemorrhage. He also loved to hunt, and had several falls from horses. A fractured collarbone in 1959 caused him little inconvenience, but a concussion and facial injuries suffered in January 1962, when he was ill with pleurisy or pneumonitis, weakened him considerably. His last novel, *The Reivers*, was published on 4 June of that year. On the 17th he was thrown during an early morning ride near his home, Rowan Oak in Oxford, Miss., and an old back injury became painful again. He swallowed all the pain pills he could find around the house and washed them down with bourbon. By 4 July his wife, Estelle, was gravely concerned and persuaded him to go to a hospital. As he left his mansion the following day a servant spoke to him: "Mr. Bill, do you want to go to the hospital?" "I want to go home, Chrissie," he replied.

At Wright's Sanatorium, a private hospital at Byhalia, fifty miles north of Oxford, which he had first visited after a drinking bout in 1935, Faulkner complained of pains in the chest as well as the back, but cardiac signs were normal. Vitamins were administered during the evening, but no analgesics. The oppressive heat of the day continued after dark. The hospital was quiet except for the humming of fans. A few minutes after 1:30 A.M., 6 July 1962, Faulkner sat up and moved over to the edge of the bed. Before the nurse could reach him he groaned and fell over. Dr. Leonard Wright, who arrived within five minutes, could find no pulse, and external heart massage and mouth-to-mouth resuscitation were fruitless. Death was caused by coronary thrombosis. After services at Rowan Oak, Faulkner was buried in St. Peter's Cemetery, Oxford, Miss.

Fields, W.C. (*Claude William Dukenfield*) (1879–1946).

Taken ill during the filming of *Poppy* in 1935, the U.S. movie comedian spent much of his time in a sanatorium during the next two years while he did a weekly radio show. His convalescence was complicated by the effects of heavy drinking. Following a period of improved health his liquor consumption again increased during the filming of four eccentric movies for Universal Studios, ending with *Never Give a Sucker an Even Break*. When, in the summer of 1946, he was evicted from his large Spanish-style house on De Mille Drive, Hollywood, after refusing to pay an increased rent, Fields' secretary, Magda Michael, asked if he'd look for another house. "No, no," he replied, "I think it's back to the sanitarium for the nonce." His sleep by that time was shallow and fragmentary, his walk was unsteady and his old juggling skills had left him.

At Las Encinas Sanitarium, Pasadena, Fields made a series of records about the calamities that befell him after drinking a glass of water by accident. Visited regularly by Miss Michael and by the young companion of his final fourteen years, Carlotta Monti, he would sleep until ten and then, after a massage, drink orange juice followed by martinis—if he could get them. His cirrhosis of the liver and cardiac edema steadily worsened. Shortly before midnight on Christmas Eve, with anxious doctors and nurses filling the room, Miss Monti took his hand and begged him to respond. He opened his eyes, surveyed his visitors, raised a finger to his lips, and winked. A few minutes later, as church bells ushered in Christmas Day 1946, blood bubbled from his lips and, after several long sighs, Fields died; he had suffered a massive stomach hemorrhage.

His will stipulated cremation and no religious service, but his estranged wife, a Catholic, vetoed the cremation and had Fields entombed in a mausoleum at Forest Lawn Memorial Park, Los Angeles. He was given three burial services: Edgar Bergen, the ventriloquist, presided at the first, a nonsectarian ceremony; Mrs. Fields arranged a second, Catholic service; Miss Monti, prevented from entering the crypt until after the burial, then contrived to have a Spiritualist reading. *See* R.L. Taylor (1949).

Fitzgerald, F. Scott (1896–1940).

The U.S. novelist, chronicler of the "jazz age," suffered an eclipse in popularity toward the end of his life. Although nine of his books were in print in 1939, his total royalties that year amounted to only $33. His wife, Zelda Sayre Fitzgerald (1900–1948), suffered her first mental breakdown in 1930 and was under treatment for schizophrenia at Highland Hospital, Asheville, N.C., from 1936 to 1939. Scott would travel from California to visit her occasionally, but their meetings were disappointing. Their last trip together, to Havana in 1939, began and ended in drunken bouts on his part and, when he attempted to stop a cock fight, he was beaten up. Nevertheless, the old feelings of happier days were not entirely gone. "You were a peach throughout the whole trip," he wrote soon after. "You are the loveliest, tenderest, most beautiful person I have ever known." But living with her, he knew, would have been impossible.

After the Cuban trip a tuberculous lesion was found in his lung, and Fitzgerald spent two months in bed. In 1937 he had met the young British gossip columnist Sheilah Graham; they became lovers and in his last year were living on neighboring streets in Hollywood. After a script-writing stint for MGM, Fitzgerald was trying to support himself, Zelda and their daughter Scottie (a Vassar student) by writing short stories for the slick magazines. Sheilah, for whom he had prescribed a course of reading, helped keep him away from alcohol during his final year.

A mild heart attack suffered in a neighborhood drugstore in November 1940 left him pale and shaken. ("I almost fainted in Schwab's," he told Sheilah. "Everything started to fade.") Ordered to rest, he moved from his third-floor place on North Laurel to a ground-floor bedroom in Sheilah's apartment on Hayworth Avenue. There he worked on his novel *The Last Tycoon* at an improvised desk slung across his bed or armchair. He suffered another cardiac seizure as the pair left the Pantages Theater after a movie preview on 20 December. The following day, after lunch, Sheilah was settled on the sofa of her living room, reading a biography of Beethoven (part of her study program) and listening to the "Eroica" symphony on the phonograph. The sun streamed through the windows. Scott, off the bottle now, was sitting in a green armchair a few feet away. He wanted something sweet to chew and she fetched him a Hershey chocolate bar. He munched happily and scribbled nicknames of old classmates in the margin of a football article in the latest *Princeton Alumni Weekly*. They were waiting for the doctor to make his regular visit. Suddenly, Scott jerked to his feet and clutched the mantelpiece. A moment later he fell to the floor and lay spreadeagled on his back, unconscious and breathing heavily. Sheilah rushed to the kitchen for the bottle of brandy she had hidden away and tried to pour a little into his mouth. By the time help arrived he was dead.

Zelda had not seen Scott for eighteen months, but she missed him badly—his weekly letters, the knowledge he was there, caring about her. He was always planning happiness for her and Scottie. "Books to read—places to go....Life seemed so promissory when he was around." She was able to live with her mother in Montgomery, Ala., most of the time after 1939, but her mental health was always precarious. She worked on her second novel, *Caesar's Things*, never completed, and took daily five-mile walks. In November 1947 she returned to Asheville for treatment. A fire started in the diet kitchen of the Highland Hospital around midnight on 10 March 1948. Nine women died, burned to death behind locked doors. Zelda was identified by a slipper that lay protected from the flames under her body.

Scott had wanted to be buried in his father's family plot, surrounded by Fitzgerald tombstones, in the Catholic cemetery in Rockville, Md. But church authorities judged that Scott had not died a good Catholic, so permission was denied. Investigation revealed that the nearby Rockville Union Cemetery had a single plot left, even though it had been officially closed for fifty years with no burials there since the nineteenth century. So Scott was buried there. Contrary to some reports, Zelda was not later buried beside Scott; there was no room beside him. Consequently, when Zelda died, Scott's coffin was dug up, the grave made deeper, his coffin resunk, and Zelda was buried on top of him—an image that both of them would have appreciated.

Flaubert, Gustave (1821–1880).

The French novelist, author of *Madame Bovary*, lacked the funds to spend his last winters in Paris; for years he had impoverished himself in a vain attempt to save his son-in-law, the shady Ernest Commanville, from bankruptcy. Hence he secluded himself at his home at Croisset, near Rouen, working on the cynical novel *Bouvard et Pécuchet*. On 6 May 1880 he wrote to a friend in Paris that he would meet him in the capital shortly, but within two days Flaubert was dead. Only the housekeeper and a physician, Dr.

Tourneaux, were with him when he died on Saturday, 8 May 1880, and many rumors were circulated afterward, including one that he had somehow strangled himself in the bathtub. There is no reason to doubt the eyewitness accounts, however; according to these, Flaubert had just stepped out of a hot bath when he collapsed, presumably from a stroke.

The funeral procession wound its way from the writer's home to the little parish church at Canteleu. The graveside ceremony, attended by many of France's most illustrious men of letters, including Daudet, Zola and Maupassant, was marred by unseemly incidents. As the Goncourt brothers, who were present, recount the events, the grave had been dug too short, so that the coffin became wedged when halfway in and could be neither pushed down nor pulled up. "Enough, enough," called out the embarrassed mourners. "Wait until later." Journalists in the group talked loudly of the meal they expected to enjoy afterwards, even of the neighborhood bawdy houses they intended to visit. But at least the volley fired by the Garde Nationale, a tribute to the dead member of the Légion d'Honneur, added a touch of dignity to the proceedings.

Foster, Stephen (1826–1864).

The U.S. composer of "Old Folks at Home," "My Old Kentucky Home" and "Beautiful Dreamer" earned a comfortable income from song writing—about $1200 a year—during most of his short career. He was a gentle, impractical man who lived alone in New York during his last three years while his wife, Jane, supported herself and their daughter as a railroad telegrapher at Greensburg, Pa. More than once, Foster, overdrawing his account with his publisher, sold his copyrights for a lump sum. In New York, shabbily dressed in his brother's cast-off clothing, he slept in a cheap room at the New England Hotel at the corner of Bayard Street and the Bowery. During the day he could usually be found in a barroom behind a grocery at Hester and Christie Streets in lower Manhattan, where he fortified himself with cheap rum concocted by the barkeeper from French spirits and brown sugar. He was frequently reduced to dining on apples and raw turnips and, for want of music paper, to writing his songs on wrapping material. Though his musical invention was running

Stephen Foster's shabby purse. Found after his death, it contained only a few cents and a scribbled word or two, perhaps the idea for a song.

FOSTER HALL COLLECTION, UNIVERSITY OF PITTSBURGH

low, he could still readily convert the latest ballad into a ten- or twenty-dollar bill, for his popularity was undiminished. But his health was poor; reports of fever and ague may signify not malaria but tuberculosis.

On Saturday night, 9 January 1864, Foster retired early to his room, feeling unwell. The next morning a maid, bringing him towels, discovered him lying naked on the floor in a pool of blood. Evidently he had fainted while washing himself and the bowl had broken, gashing his throat and bruising his forehead. A friend, George Cooper, was summoned; he describes Foster whispering, "I'm done for," and asking for a drink. A physician, who was sewing up the neck wound with black thread, forbade alcohol but was overruled. "I decided the doctor was not much good," Cooper writes, "and I went down stairs and got Steve a big drink of rum, which I gave him and which seemed to help him a lot." The injured man was taken to Bellevue Hospital, where he told Cooper a day or two later that nothing had been done for him and he was unable to eat the food. No friend or relative was with Foster when he died on 13 January 1864. Cooper had to search for the body in the hospital morgue. Foster's shabby purse contained only about seventy cents in coin and paper scrip, and a few words on a scrap of paper, probably an idea for a song: "Dear friends and gentle hearts." Foster was buried in Allegheny Cemetery in the Lawrenceville section of Pittsburgh, not far from his birthplace.

Franklin, Benjamin (1706–1790).

On his return from France in 1785, Franklin was elected to three annual terms as president of the Pennsylvania executive council, and was also an important voice in the Federal Constitutional Convention. Though he had a good appetite and slept well, stone of the bladder was an increasingly grievous affliction and gout troubled him frequently. In January 1788 he slipped on the steps leading to the garden of his large house in Philadelphia and injured his right arm. Toward the end of his life Franklin was forced to resort to opium. Warned by James Madison of the undermining effects of this narcotic, he admitted to being well aware of them, but the pain of the stone was becoming unbearable and, Madison recorded, he thought "the best terms he could make with his complaint was to give up a part of his remaining life, for the greater ease of the rest." Answering a minister's inquiry a month before his death, Franklin expressed doubt in Christ's divinity, but believed "that the soul of Man is immortal, and will be treated with Justice in another Life respecting his Conduct in this."

At the beginning of April 1790 Franklin came down with a fever and pain in the left side of the chest, apparently caused by pleurisy. Eleven days later the pain and breathing difficulty left him, and a few hours later an abscess of the lung burst. As his strength declined, he sank into a calm, lethargic state and died between 10:00 and 11:00 P.M., 17 April 1790. He was buried beside his wife in Christ Church Cemetery, Philadelphia.

Freud, Sigmund (1856–1939).

On 15 March 1938, following the Nazi invasion of Austria, stormtroopers ransacked Freud's Vienna home at Berggasse 19. With difficulty the eighty-two-year-old Jewish psychiatrist obtained permission to leave his native country with his wife in June. Their savings and property were confiscated. But in England, they were treated as honored guests and customs and immigration formalities were waived for them. They joined three of their children in London and settled finally at 20 Maresfield Gardens in Hampstead. In the fall, Freud underwent an operation, the most serious since those of 1923 when a malignancy of the right side of the upper jaw and palate was removed and a large, ungainly prosthesis fitted to separate the oral and nasal cavities. This, and the removal of part of the tongue, made speaking difficult for Freud and his speech hard to understand. Yet the heavy smoking that caused his disease was never discontinued, even when his mouth needed to be forced open with a clothes pin.

Freud's last months were harrowing; daily x-ray therapy did nothing to ease the continuous pain in the jaw, yet he denied himself analgesics until the final heavy sedation of his last few days. "I prefer to think in torment, rather than not to be able to think clearly," he once said. He continued to work on his last book, *The Outline of Psychoanalysis*, and to conduct four analyses a day through much of 1939. By the time he died, uncomplainingly, just before midnight on 23 September 1939, his body was visibly wasted. The manner of his dying, wrote his friend and regular visitor Stefan Zweig, "was no less a moral feat than his life." Freud's body was cremated at Golders Green and the ashes were preserved in a Grecian urn. *See* G. Costigan (1965).

Frost, Robert (1874–1963).

The U.S. poet was a troubled, often angry man, given to feelings of guilt and suicidal depression, afraid that he had tuberculosis and that he would die, like his sister, in a mental institution. To balance this, his forty-three-year marriage was a stabilizing influence, and public recognition, when it did arrive, was complete. Frost's participation in J.F. Kennedy's inauguration ceremonies was the high point of his life. Early in 1962 he was in a Florida hospital with pneumonia, but later in the year, at the age of eighty-eight, he visited the U.S.S.R. under State Department auspices and succeeded in meeting Premier Khrushchev at Gagra in the Crimea. Tired and ill, he was sitting half dressed on the edge of his bed when the Russian leader called on him early in September. He caused a stir later when, putting words into Khrushchev's mouth, he quoted the premier as saying that Americans were just too liberal to fight for their beliefs.

After a final lecture tour, Frost entered Peter Bent Brigham Hospital, Boston, on 3 December 1962 for investigation of his chronic prostate discomfort. On the 10th, cancerous tissue was excised from the prostate gland and bladder and thereafter he progressed satisfactorily until the first of a series of pulmonary embolisms on the 23rd. His visitors in January included three

Robert Frost early in 1962, a year before his death. Photo by David H. Rhinelander.

Soviet writers and Ezra Pound's daughter. Frost began to sink on 27 January and the following day was unable to eat. At about midnight, new blood clots reached his lungs and he died very early on 29 January 1963. After a private service at Harvard and a public one at Amherst College Frost's ashes were buried, when the ground had thawed, in the family plot at Old Bennington, Vt. *See* L. Thompson and R.H. Winnick (1977).

Gable, Clark (1901–1960).

The U.S. movie actor, Hollywood's quintessential masculine star, was warned against making *The Misfits*; his costar Marilyn Monroe, always unstable and unreliable, was on the verge of a divorce from Arthur Miller, author of the screenplay, and coming apart mentally. But the money proved irresistible; Gable made more than $800,000 from this, the most expensive of all black-and-white films. Throughout the summer and fall of 1960 he was kept waiting countless hours in the Nevada desert near Reno for Marilyn's appearance on the set. For her sake he exhibited unparalleled patience in the 100-degree heat, nursing the sick actress along, but his frustrations, which probably damaged his health, were so deep that he dispensed with stunt men and himself repeatedly acted out scenes in which he lassoed stallions and was dragged painfully on ropes behind a truck through the alkali flats. His fourth wife, Kathleen (Kay) Williams, whose two children by her former husband, Adolph Spreckels, lived with the Gables, had become pregnant at the age of forty-three, and the knowledge he might after all have a son of his own gave Clark deep satisfaction.

The movie was finished at Paramount studios on Friday 4 November. The next day, at his Encino ranch, Gable felt a chest pain while changing a tire on his Jeep. During the night he complained of a headache and "indigestion" and while dressing at 7:30 he doubled over, pale and sweating. He was taken the twelve miles to Hollywood Presbyterian Hospital by ambulance and was sufficiently recovered by Tuesday to vote by absentee ballot in the Kennedy-Nixon election. Kay stayed with him and a few days later, using a stethoscope, he was able to hear the heartbeat of the son he would not live to see. At 10:10 P.M. on 16 November Kay dined with him and then, feeling rather ill, retired to her own room across the hall. "I love you," she told him with a goodbye hug. At 10:50 P.M. his physician, Dr. Fred Cerini, opened Gable's door. Clark looked up from his magazine, flipped the page and slumped back against the pillow. He had died of a final cardiac thrombosis. Kay held him in her arms for two hours before being gently led away.

Gable was buried at Forest Lawn Memorial Park, Los Angeles, with full military honors (because of his Air Force service in World War II) beside his second wife, Carole Lombard, whose death in a Nevada air crash in January 1942 had been the inconsolable grief of his life. His son, John Clark Gable, was born 20 March 1961.

Galileo Galilei (1564–1642).

The Italian mathematician and physicist, maker of the first astronomical telescope, was a frail man of sixty-nine suffering from arthritis and a double hernia when, in 1633, he was brought before the Holy Inquisitors in Rome. For holding the Copernican view that the sun and not the earth was the center of the universe, Galileo was found guilty of heresy and, though spared a prison sentence, was condemned to spend his remaining years at his small estate near Arcetri. He continued his observations of the heavens until glaucoma destroyed his sight.

When Galileo became bedridden in November 1641 with a low fever, kidney pains and heart palpitations, two pupils kept him entertained almost to the last with scientific discussions. He died quietly on the night of 8 January 1642. Pope Urban VIII denied the request of the city of Florence to honor the astronomer with a monument in the Church of Santa Croce. For almost a century his body lay in the basement of the church. Not until 1734 did the Holy Office relent and allow a memorial, so long as care was exercised with the inscription. Only in 1822 were the forbidden works of Copernicus, Galileo and Kepler removed from the Index of Forbidden Books.

Gandhi, Mohandas (1869–1948).

At the age of seventy-eight the Hindu leader, known as Mahatma ("great soul"), began a five-day fast to protest strife between Hindus and Muslims. On 30 January 1948, still weak

from the effects of the fast and leaning on the shoulders of two
grandnieces, he walked in the cool of the evening in the gardens
of Birla House, New Delhi. The crowd rose up to pay him
homage. All was serene until a young man, bent as though in
reverence, stepped up to Gandhi, pushed aside the two young
girls and fired at point-blank range. The first bullet entered his
abdomen and the blood gushed; the next two hit him in the
chest. Gandhi stumbled, his glasses slipped and his sandals became loose. He called out, "Hai Rama, Hai Rama!" folded his
hands and lifted them in a gesture of prayer, then fell to the
ground doubled with pain. Thirty minutes later came the announcement that he was dead. The assassin was thirty-seven-
year-old Nathuram Vinayak Godse. He was a high-degree
Brahman, editor and publisher of a Hindu Mahasabha weekly in
Poona, who believed that Gandhi had made too many conces-
sions to the Muslims.

Gandhi's body was burned on a funeral pyre of sandalwood by
the banks of the river Jumna and the ashes were scattered at the
confluence of the Ganges, Jumna and Saraswati—the most sacred rivers in India. Godse and fellow conspirator Narayan Apte
were hanged on 15 November 1949 at Ambala Prison, 150 miles
north of Delhi. Their bodies were cremated and the ashes
thrown into the Ghaggar River. *See* R. Payne (1969).

García Lorca, Federico
(1898–1936).

The Spanish poet and dramatist was not a man of deep political
passions, yet when his native city, Granada, fell to the Nationalist
rebels in 1936, he was murdered along with hundreds of others
suspected of Republican sympathies. A Nationalist friend, Luis
Rosales Camacho, had been hiding the author when Ramón Luiz
Alonso, jealous of Rosales and eager to embarrass him, delivered
García Lorca to the Civil Government headquarters on 16 August. Two nights later he was taken with others to the mountain
slopes above Víznar and at about dawn on 19 August 1936 he
was shot near the bubbling spring called Fuente Grande. The
bodies were buried in a narrow trench at the execution site. *See* I.
Gibson (1973).

Garfield, James Abram
(1831–1881).

The twentieth president of the U.S. (1881) was fatally shot by
Charles J. Guiteau (q.v.) in the Baltimore and Potomac railroad
station, Washington, D.C., on 2 July 1881 after only four months
of office. He was on his way to Massachusetts to deliver the
commencement address at his alma mater, Williams College. As
the president passed through the ladies' waiting room at 9:20
A.M., accompanied by Secretary of State James G. Blaine and one
detective, Guiteau, black hat pulled low over his eyes, stepped
from behind a bench and followed them. Drawing his revolver,
he fired twice. One bullet went harmlessly through the president's clothing, but the other struck him in the back. "My God,
what is it?" he gasped as he staggered and fell to his knees. The
assassin was seized before any of the remaining three chambers
could be discharged.

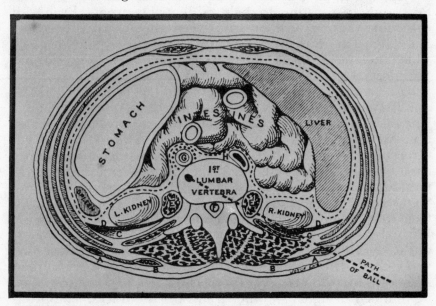

*A diagram of President Garfield's fatal wound, drawn by young Dr.
Frank Baker two days after the shooting. Baker's assumptions were
proven correct at the autopsy eleven weeks later.*

SURGERY, GYNECOLOGY AND OBSTETRICS

When Dr. Smith Townshend arrived a few minutes later he found the president lying on his back awaiting a stretcher. He was carried upstairs on a mattress and Dr. D.W. Bliss, a prominent Washington surgeon, was called. He observed the patient to be in deep shock, with respiration slow and sighing, the pulse feeble and rapid, with numbness of the legs and scrotum. Bliss probed for the bullet through the entrance hole, which was four inches to the right of the spinal column opposite the eleventh rib, and in so doing produced a false passage that baffled later investigators and probably introduced infection.

After Garfield was removed to the White House by horse-drawn ambulance, the hemorrhage stopped and his condition improved for several days, but infection thereafter became apparent. By mid-August inflammation of the right parotid gland led to suppuration in the mouth. A primitive but surprisingly efficient air-conditioning system was installed in the White House basement; it consisted of 3,000 feet of Turkish toweling cooled by dripping salted ice water, a charcoal-filled ice box, fans, and pipes leading to the presidential bedroom. Even with the windows open the temperature near the sick man's head was maintained at 75 degrees through a hot muggy spell (during which the outside temperature rose as high as 99 degrees), and his misery was considerably lessened.

By 23 August the patient's weight had fallen from 210 to 130 pounds and the infection had spread to the bronchi and lungs. The president begged to be taken to the seashore, and preparations were set afoot. A British subject, Charles G. Francklyn, offered his twenty-room residence at Elberon, on the New Jersey coast two miles south of Long Branch. Large numbers of workmen began laying extra track: 750 feet in Washington from the Sixth Street engine sheds to Pennsylvania Avenue, and 3,200 feet from a point near Elberon Station almost to the door of the Francklyn home. The president's bed was set on heavy springs; it was cooled by ice boxes and protected by screens against dust and cinders. During the six-hour trip on 6 September, railroad men were forbidden to use whistles and bells and a pilot engine went ahead to signal all other trains off the tracks. The president's transfer was one of the few successful aspects of his treatment. His spirits rose at Elberon, and hope revived for his recovery, but on 17 September he suffered a severe chill and chest pains. On the 19th he fell asleep a little before 10:00 P.M., to be awakened by a sharp pain in the chest that made him cry aloud. He died within a few minutes at 10:35 P.M. He had survived the assassin's bullet for seventy-nine days.

At the autopsy the next day it was discovered that the bullet had traveled, not downward to the right into the abdomen, as believed by the physicians, but to the left on a roughly level course through the first lumbar vertebra, causing temporary concussion of the spinal cord (and hence the numbness of the legs the president complained of after the shooting). The bullet had then torn the splenic artery, which had produced the massive hemorrhage, and finally lodged behind the pancreas where it was found encapsulated. The official cause of death, which has been generally accepted, was announced as rupture of the aneurysm of the splenic artery caused by the bullet. On the other hand, R.W. Prichard and A.L. Herring Jr. argued in a 1951 study that the amount of hemorrhage found at autopsy was insufficient to account for death, which was more likely due to myocardial infarction or—possibly—pulmonary embolism. In any case, it can be agreed that prolonged sepsis was the underlying cause. Garfield is buried in Lake View cemetery, Cleveland, Ohio.

After Garfield's death there was much criticism of the medical treatment he had received from Bliss and his colleagues, though it can be said that it would have been almost impossible, in the absence of radiography, blood transfusions, antibiotics and full knowledge of asepsis, to have saved the president.

Garibaldi, Giuseppe (1807–1882).

One of the greatest masters of revolutionary war, the Italian patriot was a gentle, courteous and lovable man in private life. After his last campaign at the end of 1871 he returned to his home on Caprera, a small, rugged island off the northern coast of Sardinia. His rheumatism and the pain from his old wounds grew increasingly worse until in 1878 he became confined to an iron wheelchair. By May 1882 he was unable to rise from his bed, which was pulled close to the window so that he could look out over the sea. He had bronchial catarrh and found it difficult to breathe and an effort to talk. On 2 June two finches fluttered onto the balcony; Garibaldi mused that they were the spirits of

Donna Francesca Garibaldi at her husband's tomb in 1921.
LIBRARY OF CONGRESS

his two dead baby daughters come to take him away. He asked for his little son, Manlio, but before the child could come his father died. Garibaldi had expressed a desire to be cremated on a fire of acacia, but his wishes were disregarded and he was buried near his house on Caprera. As though in protest the sky darkened, rain poured down and a vast block of granite nearby, which was later laid over his grave, cracked and broke.

Garland, Judy (1922–1969).

The U.S. movie actress' troubles seem to have started while she was filming *The Wizard of Oz*. She was made to fast on alternate days, then given, she reported later, "a lot of pills to sleep and a lot of pills to stay awake." She ultimately became dependent on them. In 1947, after sixteen years with MGM, Garland was dropped with no severance pay and no residuals from the twenty-eight pictures (grossing $80 million) she had made for them. Broke, she made a disastrous tour of the Middle East in May 1964. On her return to Hollywood a few days before Christmas, 1964, she was weak and depressed and weighed only seventy-eight pounds.

Her last concert was in the Falkoner Centret Theatre, Copenhagen, on 25 March 1969. On 22 June she was staying in her London home at 4 Cadogan Lane with her fifth husband, Michael ("Mickey Deans") De Vinko. Taking some capsules from a bottle containing 25 Nembutals, she went into the bathroom. In the morning, Deans pounded on the bathroom door. Then, fearing the worst, he climbed onto the roof where he could look through the window. "She was in a sitting position," writes Anne Edwards in her 1974 biography of the actress, "her head collapsed onto her breast, like a small sparrow with a broken neck." She had been dead for several hours. She had told John Gruen in an interview for the New York *Herald Tribune*, "If I'm a legend, then why am I so lonely?" Garland was buried in Ferncliff Cemetery, Hartsdale, N.Y.

Gauguin, Paul (1848–1903).

The French post-impressionist painter quit his employment with a Parisian banking firm to become an artist in 1881. Soon after, almost penniless, he separated from his Danish-born wife, Mette, and their children; hopes of a reunion in later years were not fulfilled. A year in Martinique (1887–88) gave him a taste for tropical life and in 1891 he went to Tahiti. In the capital, Papeete, he was laid up with heart trouble and the copious vomiting of blood, possibly (in his case) a sign of syphilis contracted years earlier. After two years of life in a cottage with a young native girl, he returned to France, lonely and depressed, with only four francs in his pocket. In Concarneau, Brittany, he broke his right leg in a brawl, and the compound fracture never healed.

Gauguin's return to the South Seas was postponed by an attack of widespread sores, apparently syphilitic, but he finally returned to Tahiti in August 1895 and built a house and studio at Punaauia, a few miles southwest of Papeete. His former lover was now married, but there was a steady supply of other carefree thirteen- and fourteen-year-old girls to meet his needs. His health was bad, though spells in Papeete's military hospital temporarily improved his eczematous, swollen legs. His house had to be pulled down when the land changed ownership. His wife wrote that his favorite daughter was dead of pneumonia at nineteen. In February 1898 he limped painfully up the mountainside and swallowed an arsenical preparation prescribed for his legs, but the overdose caused him to vomit, and instead of suicide he achieved only chronic indigestion. For a while he was forced to take a six-francs-a-day government job as a draftsman.

By the time Gauguin moved to his final home—on Hiva Oa in the Marquesas Islands—in August 1901, his financial position had been improved by the rise in real estate values and a contract to sell pictures regularly to French buyers. But his health continued to deteriorate. Erysipelas had infected his feet, his sight was failing and his stomach was ruined. In the village of Atuona he bought land from the Catholic mission, planning to build a sturdy home, but was soon feuding with Bishop Joseph Martin and the civil authorities over what he felt was their exploitation and corruption of the natives. The last of his young vahines, pregnant, left him in the summer of 1902.

Early on 8 May 1903 Paul Vernier, the Protestant pastor, found Gauguin lying on his bed, complaining of pains all over his body. At 11:00 A.M. old Tioka the carpenter discovered his friend lying motionless, one enormous leg slung over the side of the bed. A bottle that had contained laudanum stood on the bedside table. When he failed to rouse the painter by shaking, Tioka resorted to the Marquesan custom of biting Gauguin's scalp. Then he lifted up his voice in a shrill lament.

The next day, after a Catholic service, four native pallbearers carried the coffin up Hueakiki, the steep hill north of the village, to the cemetery on the summit. The administrator reported to the French authorities that the dead man's assets were negligible as "the few pictures left by the late painter, who belonged to the decadent school, have little prospect of being sold." The bishop, in a letter to his superiors, wrote: "The only noteworthy event here has been the sudden death of a contemptible individual named Gauguin, a reputed painter but an enemy of God and everything that is decent." The two old enemies now lie side by side beneath a forty-foot cross. *See* B. Danielsson (1966).

Gehrig, Lou (1903–1941).

The "Iron Man" of baseball had played 2,130 games in a row and now he couldn't get the top off a ketchup bottle. On 19 January 1939, Gehrig's thirty-sixth birthday, doctors at the Mayo Clinic diagnosed his illness as amyotrophic lateral sclerosis, a degeneration of certain nerve tracts in the spinal cord, and told his wife Eleanor that he had, at the outside, two and a half years to live. Lou was ever hopeful of a cure. On 4 July 1939 there was a "Lou Gehrig Appreciation Day" in Yankee Stadium, New York. Until his disease made it impossible, Lou performed his duties as a member of the New York City parole commission. For the last month of his life he was confined to his home, 5204 Delafield Avenue in the Fieldston section of the Bronx. As the paralysis progressed it affected his hands and arms and then his speech and ability to swallow. He lost weight steadily and was no longer able to leave his bed. On the evening of 2 June 1941, at 10:10 P.M., conscious to the end, he tightened his grip on Eleanor's hand, smiled and died.

Gehrig's body lay in state at the Church of the Divine Paternity at Central Park West and 76th Street during the afternoon of 3 June, and in the evening at Christ Protestant Episcopal Church in Riverdale, where 5,000 people paid their respects. After funeral services on the 4th at the Riverdale church he was cremated at Fresh Pond Cemetery in Middle Village, Queens. His ashes are in Kensico Cemetery, Valhalla, N.Y.

Genghis Khan (1162–1227).

The Mongol warlord who had slaughtered and plundered through half the world had not been well since his horse threw him, causing possible internal injuries, in 1226. He had long lain feverish and in pain but had insisted on continuing his campaign to conquer the Tanguts. In March 1227 he was increasingly weary but, aware that he was dying, became more determined than ever to capture the besieged capital, Ning-hsia, sixty-two miles north of the Yellow River. The defenders of the city were desperate and at the beginning of June the Tangut king Li Hsien came to the Mongol camp bearing magnificent gifts. The conquerer, extremely ill, did not give Li Hsien the audience he sought, but instead ordered that the man, the last of the Tangut sovereigns, be killed.

After hearing that his eldest son Jöchi had died about February 1227, Genghis Khan summoned his two favorite sons Ögödei and Toluy and, after reminding them of the enormous empire he had conquered ("so vast that from its center to its bounds is a year's riding"), he named Ögödei as his successor. On his deathbed he outlined plans for future victories and demanded that everyone in the fallen capital of Ning-hsia be exterminated to the last child. He died on 18 August 1227 in the mountains of Kansu where he had traveled in the hope that the cooler air would ease his pain.

Long before, as a young man, he had rested one day on a wooded slope in the mountain range, now named Kentei, sacred to the ancient Mongols, and had expressed a wish to be buried there. The funeral cortege began the journey in great secrecy; any stranger unlucky to happen upon it was slain without formality. When the funeral rites were over, the grave became taboo, the forest took over, and soon there was nothing to show where Genghis Khan was buried. *See* R. Grousset (1966).

George III (1738–1820).

During the reign (1760–1820) of "Farmer George," king of Great Britain and Ireland, both the American and French revolutions took place. The king suffered spells of mental derangement at ages fifty, sixty-two and sixty-six before lapsing into permanent insanity in October 1810. His son, the future George IV, became regent in 1811 and George III lingered on, blind and later deaf, until his death at eighty-one. Apart from his mad spells he was a conscientious ruler, a faithful husband and a good father to fifteen children. The loss of the American colonies was the result, not of kingly deficiencies, but of parliamentary policy supported by public opinion. In his last days the blind, mad, white-bearded old man spent much time playing, on the harpsichord and flute, music remembered from his youth. The end came rapidly from a terminal diarrhea at Windsor Castle at 8:35 P.M., 29 January 1820.

The day of the funeral, 16 February, was cold and foggy. The ceremonies went on until nightfall, when by the light of flickering torches and accompanied by tolling bells and muffled drums

King George III was taken from Windsor Castle to his final resting place at St. George's Chapel.

In an extensive study, reported in the *British Medical Journal* (1966, 1968) and in two books, Ida Macalpine and Richard Hunter present evidence that George suffered from porphyria, an uncommon hereditary metabolic disorder marked by excretion of porphyrins and resultant development of an intense color in urine that has been allowed to stand. They turned up four contemporary descriptions of this: In 1788, "urine" bilious; in 1811, "the water...leaves a pale blue ring upon the glass near the upper surface"; in 1812, "bluish"; and in 1819 "bloody water." They traced the genetic defect back to Mary, Queen of Scots, and forward to George III's granddaughter, Princess Charlotte.

There have, however, been many critics of the porphyria theory. Geoffrey Dean, an authority on the disease, considers it to be a mild, almost asymptomatic condition, so long as certain modern drugs are avoided. C.E. Dent has never found purple, still less blue, urine in porphyria; the usual color is reddish-brown to brownish-black. Others, willing to accept porphyria as the cause of the king's insanity, declare the matter to be of little significance. George III was mad nonetheless.

Geronimo (1829?–1909).

The courageous leader of the North American Apache Indians was finally settled about 1895 in Fort Sill, Okla., where he raised cattle and farmed. When he was nearly eighty years old his nimble fingers could still fashion bows and arrows, though he would occasionally forget where he had put his knife, only to find it still in his hand. One cold morning in early February 1909 he rode into nearby Lawton, sold some bows and arrows and, with the money, managed easily, but illegally, to get some liquor. He became intoxicated and on the ride home in the dark fell off his horse. He was found the next morning lying partly in a creek, his horse nearby. He had caught a very bad cold which by the 15th turned into pneumonia. His wife and the other old ladies who were caring for him would not let him go to the hospital where so many Apaches had died, but they were overriden by Lt. George A. Purington, who was in charge of Fort Sill.

Geronimo asked to see his son Robert and daughter Eva. They

The Apache chief Geronimo and his wife two years before his death. From a 1907 photograph by A.B. Canady.

were summoned from school at Chilocco, Okla., by letter instead of wire and arrived too late. During his last few hours Geronimo relived the tragedy of the long-ago massacre of his mother, first wife and children, and expressed his hatred of their assassins, the Mexicans. He longed to live until his son and daughter arrived but lost hope on the evening of the 16th. He died at 6:15 A.M. on 17 February 1909 and was buried the next day, after the arrival of Robert and Eva, in the Apache cemetery at Fort Sill.

Gershwin, George (1898–1937).

The U.S. jazz composer was a hypochondriac whose lifelong complaints about his health may have delayed recognition of his final illness. After the initial failure of *Porgy and Bess* he left New York in August 1936 for California, where he lived in an imposing Spanish-style house at 1019 North Roxbury Drive, Beverly Hills, while working for RKO on movie scores, beginning with the Fred Astaire film *Shall We Dance.* He also gave performances of his best known works when invited to do so, and it was during his playing of his Piano Concerto in F with the Los Angeles Philharmonic under Alexander Smallens on 11 February 1937 that the first hint of his fatal disease was picked up by a few in the audience, including the pianist Oscar Levant. "I noted he stumbled on the very easy passage in the first movement," recalled Levant. "Then, in the *andante*, in playing four simple octaves that conclude the movement above the sustained orchestral chords, he blundered again."

Gershwin could remember only that his mind went blank and he smelled burning rubber. A medical check later in the month gave him a clean bill of health. He kept busy in his remaining months, and found time to court Simone Simon and Paulette Goddard. By early June he was complaining of headaches and dizzy spells. Neurological tests revealed loss of the sense of smell on the right side, but he rejected the spinal tap that might have led to diagnosis of his brain tumor. He was placed under sedation and, to obtain greater privacy, was moved a short distance to the house of the lyricist E.Y. Harburg.

On the morning of 9 July Gershwin was able to play the piano at his doctor's request, but later in the day was taken in a coma to Cedars of Lebanon Hospital, Los Angeles. When the cerebrospinal fluid was found to indicate a brain tumor, a call went out via the Coast Guard to Dr. Walter Dandy of Baltimore, who was cruising on Chesapeake Bay. He was rushed to Newark for a transcontinental flight, but in a telephone consultation it was decided further delay would be dangerous. A craniotomy was performed late on Saturday night, 10 July 1937, and in a four-hour operation beginning at 3:00 A.M. on Sunday, Dr. Carl A. Rand partially removed an extensive cystic tumor (a highly malignant glioma) from the left temporal lobe of the brain. Gershwin died about five hours later at 10:35 A.M. Had he survived, the tumor would have rapidly recurred; the case was hopeless from the first. The body was taken to New York and, on the 15th, simultaneous funeral services were conducted in that city at Temple Emanu-El and in Hollywood at the B'nai B'rith Temple. Gershwin was buried in Mount Hope Cemetery, Hastings-on-Hudson, N.Y.

Gibbons, Euell (1911–1975).

The U.S. authority on wild, edible food began his career in sheer desperation in the 1920's. His family had moved to New Mexico where his father was forced to leave them to find work. When the food supply was down to a few pinto beans, Euell took a knapsack up into the mountains and returned with it full of puffball mushrooms, piñon nuts and the fruits of the yellow prickly pear. The family survived for a month wholly on what he provided.

Over the years Euell ranged from cowboy to beachcomber, once living exclusively on wild food for five years. When he was in his fifties a literary agent persuaded him to write his first book, *Stalking the Wild Asparagus*, and during the next ten years he published six books about the subject he knew so well. He warned amateurs to shun mushrooms and "start with raccoon pie and cattail salad. They never hurt anyone."

He indignantly denied that wild foods had caused the ulcer he developed in 1974, blaming it instead on the many aspirins he had taken to relieve arthritis.

Late on 29 December 1975 he was rushed from his farmhouse in Beavertown, Pa., where he lived with his wife, Freda, to the Sunbury Community Hospital. Upon arrival he was pronounced dead of a heart attack.

Gilbert, William Schwenk
(1836–1911).

The English playwright and humorist collaborated with Sir Arthur Sullivan (1842–1900) in a memorable series of comic operas that ended with *The Grand Duke* (1896). He was an irascible man, sensitive to criticism, his temper made all the shorter by attacks of gout. His last days, however, were among his most cheerful. On 29 May 1911 at the Junior Carlton Club in London, Gilbert, who had been knighted in 1907, amazed an actor with whom he had not been on speaking terms for years by insisting on joining him for lunch. Then he visited an actress who was lying ill in a darkened room. Her mother said, "I won't ask what you think of her appearance, for you can hardly see her." "Her appearance matters nothing," Sir William replied, "it is her disappearance we could not stand."

Returning home to Grim's Dyke, Harrow Weald, Middlesex, he changed into swimming trunks and walked down to his lake, where two pretty young guests, Ruby Preece and Winifred Emery, were already in the water. Ruby panicked when she ventured out of her depth. "It's not very deep, don't splash, you'll be all right," shouted the old man, who then dove in. "Put your hands on my shoulders and don't struggle," he told her. When she did so, her weight was too much for his weak heart and he sank. She struggled to the bank unaided; of her would-be rescuer there was no sign. A gardener with a boat retrieved the body and tried to revive it, but Gilbert was dead. He had succumbed to heart failure, not drowning. Gilbert was cremated, and his ashes were buried at Great Stanmore, Middlesex.

Goebbels, Paul Joseph (1897–1945).

One of the three leading Nazis (with Hitler and Goering) during World War II, Goebbels moved with his family into the Fuehrer's Berlin bunker on 22 April 1945; the end of the war was near and everyone knew it. Hitler was a physical wreck and apathetic most of the time. Goebbels played with his six children, aged four to fourteen, read them stories and kept his diary up to date. Magda Goebbels, a fanatic follower of Hitler, had decided

The charred remains of Paul Joseph Goebbels in the courtyard of the Reich Chancellery in Berlin, Germany.

THE BETTMANN ARCHIVE

that she and the children would die with Goebbels. On 30 April Hitler killed himself. The following day all six Goebbels children were put to death, possibly by a sleeping potion with their last meal and then a lethal injection. At 8:30 P.M. Goebbels went up to the coat rack, put on his coat, then his hat, and carefully drew on his gloves. Wordlessly, he gave his wife his arm, proceeded upstairs and into the courtyard. A shot was heard. They were both dead, Goebbels shot through the temple, his wife poisoned. An SS man fired a shot into Goebbels to make sure he was dead, then poured gasoline over the two corpses and set them on fire.

The next day Soviet troops found the corpses only partly burned. They are buried in Berlin in an undisclosed grave.

Goering, Hermann (1893–1946).

The Reich marshal was, after Hitler, the most powerful man in Nazi Germany. After the death of the Fuehrer, he became fear-

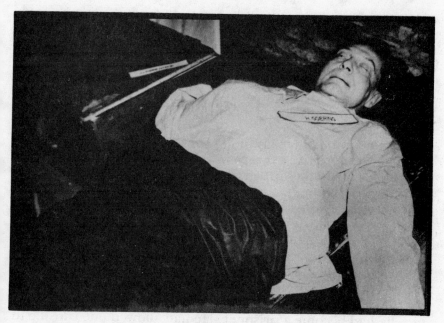

Herman Goering cheated the hangman by taking poison at the last moment.

U.S. NATIONAL ARCHIVES

ful of falling into the hands of the SS and left his temporary home at Mautendorf Castle near Salzburg to search the crowded roads for units of the advancing U.S. 7th Army. On 8 May 1945 he was taken prisoner by a search party who found him in a traffic jam on the road to Fischhorn. While undergoing interrogation at Mondorf, Luxembourg, he was cured of his dependence on dihydrocodeine and his weight was brought down from 280 to 200 pounds. After proceedings lasting more than eleven months, on 30 September 1946, Goering was the first of the war criminals to be sentenced by the International Military Tribunal at Nuremberg; found guilty on all four counts, he was to be hanged on an undisclosed date. His request to be shot was denied.

When his wife, Edda, visited him for the last time on 7 October, Goering assured her he would not hang. A buzz of excitement was evident in Nuremberg Prison on the evening of 15 October. Though the time of the executions was kept secret from the prisoners, they could hear the cars bringing news correspondents and a distant hammering from the gymnasium, where a triple gallows was being erected. The chaplain visited Goering in cell Number 9 at 7:30, after which the nightly inspection of his bedding and effects was carried out. When the doctor had come and gone at 9:30, the door was locked and the guard watched every movement of the prisoner, already in bed. At 10:30 the guard was changed and Pfc. H.F. Johnson continued the watch.

The condemned man lay on his back, his hands by his sides; at 10:40 he laced his fingers across his chest and turned his face to the wall. He no doubt slipped the glass ampule of cyanide into his mouth at that moment. At 10:44 he brought his hands down again. "About two or three minutes later," reported Johnson, "he seemed to stiffen and made a blowing, choking sound through his lips." The guard called the officers; the chaplain felt for a pulse in Goering's dangling wrist, but there was none.

Where had the Reich marshal obtained the poison? In a letter addressed to the commander of the prison and dated 11 October, he explained that he had had the capsules with him ever since he had become a prisoner. He had allowed one capsule to be found among his clothes at Mondorf; a second one was hidden in his high boots when in court and hidden under the clothes rack when he undressed; "the *third* capsule is *still* in my small suitcase in the round box of skin cream, hidden in the cream."

After the hangings, Goering's body was loaded with the others into a truck and taken under military escort to a crematory in Munich. The ashes were taken into the country by car and tipped into a ditch. *See* L. Mosley (1974).

Goethe, Johann Wolfgang von (1749–1832).

The brilliant German man of letters completed his greatest work, the second part of the poetic drama *Faust*, which had engaged his mind for sixty years, in 1831. His wide interest in all areas of human knowledge was maintained until his death. On 27 February 1832 he recorded in his diary that he was reading a pamphlet on the new railroad between Liverpool and Manchester. On 10 March he sent greetings through a friend to Sir

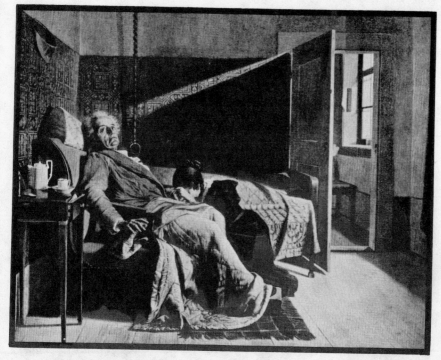

In his final moments anxiety caused Goethe to go from his bed to his armchair and back again. He eventually died sitting in his chair.

LIBRARY OF CONGRESS

Walter Scott and his daughter who, Goethe hoped, might soon visit him at his home in Weimar. He was now stooped with age. A cold, caught during his last drive, turned to pneumonia, which burdened his old heart.

Although Goethe's death is usually recorded as peaceful, it had its painful phases. Dr. Karl Vogel, his physician, records that the old man was gripped by an anxiety that drove him from bed to armchair and back again, constantly changing position to ease his chest pains, which were severe enough to cause groans and occasional screams. He died a few minutes before noon on 22 March 1832, sitting in his armchair, daydreaming in his last few minutes of a lovely woman's head against a dark background. Surrounded by relatives and friends, his daughter-in-law, Ottilie, holding his hand, Goethe talked until his energy was spent, then continued to trace patterns in the air with his free hand. His

A detail from a monument to Goethe in Rome depicting a scene from Faust.

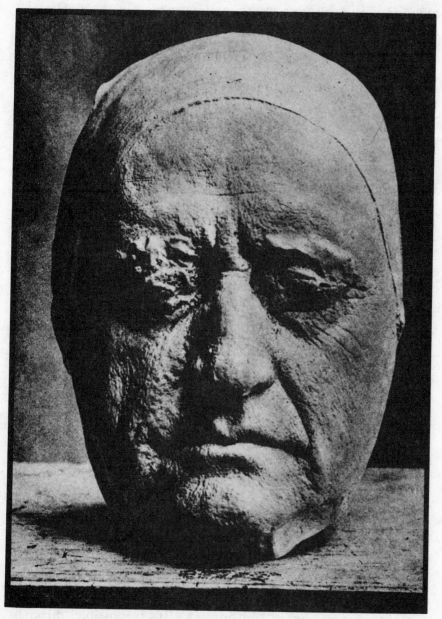

Life-mask of Goethe, cast by J.G. Schadow in 1816.

arm growing heavy, he traced words, always correctly punctuated, on the coverlet around his knees. His last spoken words were a request for more light, evidently a request that the window shutters be opened. His last movement was the tracing of the letter *W*. He was buried beside Schiller in the Princes' Vault, Weimar.

Gogh, Vincent van (1853–1890).

The Dutch artist, now considered one of the world's greatest painters, was virtually unrecognized during his lifetime. His mental illness, the nature of which still causes arguments among psychologists, led to the two great puzzles of his life: his self-mutilation in 1888 and his suicide two years later. Van Gogh persuaded Gauguin to join him in Arles in October 1888 but discord soon developed and Gauguin announced his intention of returning to Paris. This upset van Gogh, already unhappy at the news that his young brother and chief support, Théo, had become engaged. Gauguin's testimony that van Gogh brandished a razor at him in the street on Christmas Eve is suspect, but it is true that later that evening while at his lodgings the Dutch artist sliced away his own left ear, including the lobe. (In the self-portraits, which depict mirror images, it is of course the *right* ear that seems to be bandaged.) He delivered the grisly memento at a brothel for presentation to a prostitute named Rachel. Many psychological theories have been advanced for this act, drawing on castration, bull fighting symbolism and possible imitation of Jack the Ripper's activities in London. The fact is that there are too many possible explanations and no way of choosing among them (Van Gogh himself had no recollection of the incident.).

After the mutilation van Gogh was confined to a hospital and, in later months, to a sanatorium, where brief fits of insanity recurred. In May 1890 he took lodgings in Gustave Ravoux's café in Auvers-sur-Oise, northwest of Paris. On Sunday, 27 July he went out immediately after lunch in the heat of the day, a break in his usual routine. The town was deserted, except for a peasant who overheard him mutter, "It's impossible, impossible," as he passed. There was no reason to believe the artist was particularly depressed or disturbed, yet sometime that afternoon, perhaps in the fields (as the local newspaper reported) or in a farmyard on the rue Boucher, van Gogh shot himself in the chest, "level with the edge of the ribs on the left." He came back to the café later than usual that evening and went up to his room, where Ravoux found him curled up on the bed in pain. The bullet, directed toward the heart but deflected by the fifth rib, could not be extracted.

When Théo arrived from Paris, Vincent told him, "Do not grieve. I did it because it was best for us all." Throughout the following day Vincent sat propped up in bed, smoking his pipe and staring into space. His condition worsened at 11:00 P.M. and he died at 1:00 A.M. on 29 July 1890. The devoted Théo did not long survive him. In October his nephritis led to uremia with delirium; he died of a stroke at an asylum in Utrecht on 21 January 1891. His body was brought from Holland twenty-three years later and the two brothers now lie side by side in the little cemetery at Auvers.

Gogol, Nikolai (1809–1852).

The gloomy Russian novelist, whose realism—fantastic and distorted—is the antithesis of Pushkin's direct, poetic utterance, was an intolerable bore. A tormented, devious little man whose pathetic indecisiveness in the affairs of life was combined with an overweening egotism, he alienated many who met or corresponded with him. He was a hypochondriac whose maladies make distasteful reading: "nerves," "hemorrhoids," "heavy" or "lazy" stomach. In his last phase he came under the influence of the eloquent, bigoted Father Matthew Kostantinovsky, who criticized Gogol's *Dead Souls* and urged the author to renounce his art and follow God. "Deny Pushkin," he cried. "He was a sinner and a pagan." Appalled, Gogol resisted and then, within a day, characteristically changed his mind and submitted completely.

Already wasted and anemic, he began to fast. Count Alexander Tolstoy, at whose Moscow home on Nikitskaya Street (now 7 Suvarov Boulevard) Gogol was staying, called in medical aid. Late on the night of 11 February 1852, the tormented man crept through the dark house and, in a stove, burned the second part of *Dead Souls* and some other manuscripts. Lying across two armchairs in the ensuing days he was entreated and cajoled by physicians to take nourishment; even a hypnotist was called in by the count. In the dying man's last hours, bloodletting was perpetrated on his anemic body; he was placed in a hot bath while ice water was poured over his head; to his long, thin nose were applied half a dozen leeches, and his hands were tied as he tried hysterically to tear them away; blistering plasters were wrapped around his extremities; soap suppositories were inserted. His last visions were apparently of a ladder which, he had once written, was lowered from heaven to rescue suffering humanity. "The ladder! Quick, pass me the ladder," he shouted loudly. After a last attempt to regain his feet, he died quietly at 8:00 A.M., 21 February 1852, his chilled body surrounded by hot loaves of bread. Gogol was buried at St. Daniel's Monastery but in 1931 his remains were transferred to the Monastery of the New Virgins.

Gordon, Charles George (1833–1885).

"Chinese" Gordon was the nickname given to this British general during his life by reason of his heroic quelling of the Taiping Rebellion in 1863. He was in Palestine when trouble erupted in the Sudan, where he had been governor.

Mohammed Ahmed (1844–1885), a carpenter's son, declared himself the Mahdi (Islamic savior) in 1881 and led a revolt of his countrymen against their Egyptian overlords. After a force of 8,000 Egyptian soldiers under Sir William Hicks was annihilated in November 1883, the British Gladstone government declared a general withdrawal of forces from the Sudan.

In a newspaper interview, Gordon emphasized the grave peril to be faced by the soldiers and their families during the planned evacuation, and he was appointed to go to the Sudan to report and advise on the situation. En route, instructions from London and Cairo became confused—largely (it is to be suspected) owing to the idealistic, deeply religious Gordon's death wish—with a mandate for him to carry out the evacuation personally. There can be little doubt that Gordon sought martyrdom, preferably in a patriotic cause. "I feel so very much inclined to wish it His will might be my release," the bachelor-soldier wrote to his sister about this time. "Earth's joys grow very dim; its glories have faded."

Arriving in Khartoum, capital of the Sudan, on 18 February 1884, Gordon made approaches to the Mahdi and was able to send 2,600 Egyptians home before the situation worsened and a siege of the city began a month later. For ten months Gordon held out while the British government procrastinated. By January 1885 the food situation in the doomed city was critical; donkeys, horses, dogs, even rats, were killed to provide meat. Dysentery had weakened the soldiers and corpses filled the streets. After the fall of Omdurman, on the opposite bank of the Nile, the Mahdi turned his full attention to Khartoum. Instead of attacking immediately, he sent a friendly letter to "Gordon Pasha, may God protect him," offering to let him "rejoin the English." Gordon ignored the message, telling his men that help would surely arrive any day.

Early on 26 January, taking advantage of a gap left by the falling waters of the river, the Mahdist infantry swept into the city. At the top of the outside staircase of Khartoum's palace Gordon looked down scornfully on the advance party. Dressed in white uniform and tarboosh, one hand on his sheathed sword, the other holding a revolver, he made not the slightest gesture to defend himself. The Mahdi's orders to take him alive forgotten, the men thrust first one spear then several into his body. After he fell, Gordon's head was cut off and borne to the Mahdi, its blue eyes half-closed, its mouth "perfectly natural," the hair and whiskers almost white.

It was 10:00 A.M. before the massacre was ordered stopped. Gordon's desire for martyrdom had cost 4,000 lives and the slavery of countless women and children. His body was never recovered.

Gorky, Maxim (1868–1936).

The Russian writer's tuberculosis forced him to leave his native land in 1921 for southern Germany. In 1928, after a sojourn in Sorrento, Italy, he returned to Russia and, by way of petitions, increasingly opposed Stalin's reign of terror. In March 1936 he rested at Teseli in the Crimea but was back in his suburban Moscow home, "The Hillocks," in May. According to Moscow radio, he succumbed to influenza and died on 18 June. Gorky's funeral was a grand affair attended by Stalin, Molotov and other dignitaries, who watched the author's ashes being placed in the Kremlin wall.

At the Bukharin show trial in 1938, Yagoda, chief of the secret police, confessed to the murder of Gorky's son (in 1934) and, in due course, of the writer himself. The second crime was committed by means of repeated camphor injections and administration of digitalin and strychnine. Stalin later came under suspicion of being the prime mover in these acts. Although the trial testimony has never been officially repudiated, autopsy documents at the Gorky Museum in Moscow describe widespread tuberculous attrition of the lungs, only a third of the tissue being unaffected at the time of death. Complications of influenza could easily account for Gorky's demise, but that it was hastened for political reasons cannot be disproved. *See* G. Haberman (1971).

Gounod, Charles (1818–1893).

The doctors had forbidden the French composer to work. He had had a long siege with bronchitis, then heart trouble and a temporary paralysis of one side of his body. But he was determined to finish his last piece of music, a Requiem for his grandson. His eyesight was failing and he saw the manuscript as through a fog. On Sunday, 15 October 1893, he sat at the piano and sang through the Requiem for his wife, some friends and the organist who would perform the work. The effort tired him greatly. He sat down to read through the score again and collapsed. For two days he lay in a coma with his fingers tightly folded around a crucifix. He died at 6:25 A.M. on 17 October at his home at St. Cloud near Paris. After a funeral service in the Madeleine, Gounod was buried in the family vault in the Auteuil Cemetery.

Goya, Francisco (1746–1828).

At the age of forty-seven the Spanish painter was stricken with a mysterious illness which transformed his outlook and the content and style of his pictures. A boisterous youth, he narrowly escaped the death penalty for abducting a young nun. Later, he became an artist at the royal court, where his frank, happy portraits were widely popular. While in Seville with his mistress, the Duchess of Alba, early in 1793 he was struck down with giddiness, nausea, partial blindness and total deafness. The precipitating cause was evidently overexertion and exposure to cold while trying to repair the axle of their coach, but suspicions of a syphilitic origin were raised. Nevertheless, he recovered from most of the serious effects except the total deafness, and lived an active life for thirty-five more years with no reported recurrence of nervous or cardiovascular symptoms.

Sir Terence Cawthorne, in a 1962 study, suggests Goya suffered from a disorder of mysterious (possibly viral) origin first described by A. Vogt (1906) and further studied by V. Koyanagi (1929). Cawthorne himself had seen five cases of the Vogt-Koyanagi syndrome, in which the uveal tract of the eye is temporarily inflamed, the hearing is permanently destroyed and the patient is laid up for weeks with severe giddiness and nausea.

By the end of 1793 Goya was back at work, but brooding over his deafness transformed his artistic temperament. Many of his portraits after this date accentuate the grotesqueries of old age, and some, notably *Saturn Devouring His Son,* are downright gruesome. He left Spain when the autocratic Ferdinand VII returned to the throne in 1824, and died of a stroke in Bordeaux on 16 April 1838. His remains were transferred from the Cemetery of the Chartreuse in that city in 1899. Because his remains were jumbled together with those of a friend, Martin Goscoechea, whose tomb he shared, and because only one skull was found, the combined relics now lie in a single coffin in the Church of San Antonio de la Florida, Madrid, below a dome decorated with beautiful frescoes by Goya himself.

Grant, Ulysses Simpson
(1822–1885).

The eighteenth president of the U.S. (1869–1877) was elected following his victories in the Civil War. In office he was a complete failure but nevertheless gained a second term. In later years his partner in a New York investment business lost Grant's

President Grant's steel casket.

fortune, along with the savings of thousands of others. He was recovering from pleurisy when the scandal broke open in 1884. In October of that year Grant felt a sharp pain at the base of his tongue while eating a peach. After delaying several weeks he consulted a specialist, who diagnosed a carcinoma. In a race against time to provide for his family, the sick man began dictating his memoirs for publication by Mark Twain's publishing company; but speaking, and later swallowing, became difficult and the general was soon emaciated. He was reduced to sitting up day and night, his feet on a second chair. As he found the strength he would scribble a few lines. On 16 June 1885 Grant was taken to a friend's cottage at Mount McGregor near Saratoga Springs, N.Y.. His last word was "Water," when his son asked whether he wanted anything. At 8:07 A.M. on 23 July he took a deep breath, emitted a long sigh, and died. Mark Twain sold 300,000 copies of Grant's book, completed just a week before his death, from which his widow derived $450,000. Grant's Tomb, on Riverside Drive , New York City, is now a national memorial.

Grey, Lady Jane (1537–1554).

Queen of England for only nine days, Lady Jane, a short, slender girl, was executed for treason against Mary I when only sixteen years old. The moment Edward VI ascended the throne following the death of his father, Henry VIII, intrigues were set afoot to prevent his sister Mary from succeeding him. The unhappy Jane, granddaughter of Henry's sister, Princess Mary, was forced into marriage with the nineteen-year-old Guildford Dudley, son of the ambitious Duke of Northumberland, and the duke induced the young king to settle the succession on Jane. When Edward died in July 1553 Jane, much to her dismay, was proclaimed queen on the 10th and took up residence in the Tower of London. Mary's supporters soon won the day, however, and even Jane's father, the Duke of Suffolk, had to submit. Hurrying back to the Tower, he found his daughter sitting desolate in the council chamber beneath the canopy of state. "Come down from that, my child," said he, "that is no place for you." She did so gladly. "Can I go home?" she asked.

Northumberland died by the ax on 22 August, but Mary was in no haste to revenge herself on her young rival, and were it not that Suffolk foolishly allied himself with the Wyatt rebellion against Mary's marriage to Philip of Spain, Jane and Dudley might have been spared. Jane had been tried at the Guildhall in November, but her death warrant was not signed by Mary until February 1554. Guildford was beheaded on Tower Hill an hour before his wife died. By grisly mischance she saw his remains being returned to the Tower as she prepared to set out on her final short walk from her lodging in the gaoler's house to Tower Green. Preceded by two hundred Yeomen of the Guard, a tiny figure all in black, she walked to the scaffold with her gaze fixed on the prayer book open in her hands. Addressing the onlookers, she proclaimed herself always innocent of any treasonable intent, asked for their prayers and bade them a tearful goodbye. The masked executioner, enormous in his tight-fitting scarlet worsted, kneeled to beg Jane's pardon, which was freely granted.

Then a seemingly endless ordeal ensued as all waited in silence—and in vain—a full five minutes "for the Queen's mercy." "I pray you dispatch me quickly," she begged as she knelt in the straw and blindfolded herself with a handkerchief. Distressed, she could not find the block, "Where is it? What shall I do? Where is it?" Guided to the fatal object, she laid her neck upon it, stretched out her body and cried aloud, "Lord, into Thy hands I commend my spirit!" The ax flashed, a cannon boomed and it was over. Like Anne Boleyn (q.v.), Jane was left forgotten for several hours. Eventually, her bloody remains were placed in a deal coffin and deposited without religious ceremony in the vault below the Tower church of St. Peter ad Vincula, near the fresh corpse of her husband and between those of Anne Boleyn and Catherine Howard. Centuries later, the diminutive skeleton, reduced almost to dust, was placed in an urn under a plaque in the chancel above. *See* R. Davey (1909).

Guevara, Che (*Ernesto*) (1928–1967).

In the spring of 1966 Guevara, who had been one of Fidel Castro's most able commanders during the Cuban Revolution, went to Bolivia to establish a guerrilla movement in that country. The land was harsh to his band of forty-four, food was in short supply, maps were incomplete, mosquitoes vicious, support from the Bolivians nonexistent and the intense heat exhausting to the men. Many became ill with malaria, some died and Che's lifelong asthma was a constant source of discomfort. By September 1967 the situation of the seventeen survivors was desperate.

At about noon on Sunday, 8 October 1967, they were surrounded by a company of Rangers in charge of Capt. Gary Prado in the rugged ravine of Quebrado de Yuro. Che divided his force into two; his own group moved toward the closest exit from the ravine, but were caught in a rain of automatic weapon fire. Prado, through his field glasses, watched them run and put Sgt. Bernardino Huanca and his men in pursuit. The sergeant fired a machine gun burst at a guerrilla struggling through the thorn bushes. One bullet sent the man's black beret flying and two others tore into his left leg. The wounded man was Che Guevara. Another guerrilla, "Willie" (Simón Cuba Sarabia), rushed to him and helped him scramble up the side of the ravine. Four Bolivian soldiers, rifles cocked, ordered them to surrender. Che shouted, "Do not shoot; I am Che Guevara and worth more to you alive than dead!" He went into a violent attack of asthma and for a few moments could hardly breathe, but in answer to Capt. Prado's question, he said, "I am Che Guevara."

Prado was ordered to transfer Che and any other prisoners to La Higuera, about four miles away, where they were placed in the town's two-room schoolhouse. During the night of 8 October Guevara was interrogated by a number of army officers and a CIA agent who identified himself as Dr. Eduardo Gonzales. Che refused to answer any questions. In La Paz, President Barrientos and the high command of the Bolivian armed forces held an emergency meeting to decide what to do with Che. A trial would focus world attention and, if the revolutionary remained alive as a prisoner, sympathizers might try to rescue him. It was decided that he should be executed immediately and word given out that he had died from his wounds.

On Monday 9 October ranking officers at La Higuera received orders to execute Guevara. As no one was willing to kill him, lots were drawn and Sgt. Mario Terán drew the short straw. As the sergeant entered the classroom, trembling, Che asked him to wait until he stood upright. Terán turned and ran but was ordered back. Still trembling, he returned and, without looking at his victim's face, fired a burst from his carbine. The bullets slammed into Che's chest and side, passed through his body and made large holes in the wall. Willie and another guerrilla, Aniceto Reynaga Gordillo, were also executed.

Che's body, wrapped in canvas and strapped to the runner of a helicopter, was taken to Valle Grande, then to the Señor de Malta hospital where, after the blood had been washed from the body and fingerprints taken, it was placed on view in an adobe shack. Throughout the night the people filed silently by. Che was bare to the waist; he looked amazingly alive, his eyes open and a haunting smile on his lips. He was on view for twenty-four hours, then his hands were amputated for later identification. Che's brother Roberto was not allowed to see the body. Officials claimed first that it had been cremated, later that it had been buried in a secret place. Outsiders are now forbidden to travel in the La Higuera district; the schoolhouse has been torn down and no evidence remains of what took place on 9 October 1967.

Guiteau, Charles Jules
(1841–1882).

The assassin of U.S. President Garfield (q.v.) was born in Freeport, Ill., of Huguenot ancestry. Although his father believed himself to be immortal, he was otherwise respectable, but other family members were clearly psychotic. Charles's wife divorced him for cruelty and he had been in prison for defrauding a hotel before his capital offense. Claiming his pamphleteering had put Garfield in office, he demanded the Paris consulate, but was soon barred from the White House and other government buildings. His money almost gone, he bought a self-cocking .44-caliber British bulldog revolver, practiced shooting in a wooded area along the Potomac and began shadowing the president.

After firing the fatal shot at the railroad station, he shouted "I am a Stalwart; Arthur is president now," and ran out of the station into B Street. His greatest fear was of being lynched. "Be quiet, my friend," he told the policeman who collared him. "I *wish* to go to jail." Indeed, Guiteau had already looked the prison over and had a cab standing by to take him there. He told the presiding judge at his trial on 14 November, "I came here in the capacity of the Deity in this matter." At one point the judge threatened to gag him. There was universal detestation of the assassin, who survived two attempts on his life. He was found guilty and sane, and a reprieve was refused by President Arthur. Guiteau was hanged at the Old Capitol Prison, Washington, D.C., at 12:40 P.M., 30 June 1882. As he dropped he was reciting a poem he had written that morning: "I am going to the Lordy...."

T.N. Haviland reported in a 1973 study that Guiteau bequeathed his body to the Rev. W.W. Hicks, who relinquished it to Surgeon General C.H. Crane. After a burial service conducted by Mr. Hicks, an autopsy and a brief burial below the floor of the jail storeroom, the corpse was taken to the Army Medical Museum in the old Ford Theatre building and dissected. Plans to articulate and display the skeleton were dropped, and Crane disposed of the bones secretly. They are almost certainly still in the storage vaults of the present museum, possibly distributed among several trays.

Hamilton, Alexander (1755–1804).

In April 1804 a letter appeared in the Albany *Register* stating that at a dinner party the U.S. statesman Hamilton had been over-heard calling Aaron Burr "despicable." Two months later Burr used this letter as an excuse to provoke Hamilton to a duel. Hamilton had always abhorred dueling, especially since his brilliant young son, Philip, had been killed in 1801, and now he also had a strong religious feeling that he should not take a life. He resolved not to fire when the first exchange of shots was called, and mentioned this in letters written to his beloved wife Elizabeth, which were to be opened only if he died. It is strange that, feeling the way he did, he did not deny or explain the alleged statement.

The duel was set for 11 July at Weehawken on the New Jersey shore, the exact spot where Philip had died three years earlier. At 7:00 A.M. Burr and his second, William Van Ness, arrived, followed shortly by Hamilton, his second, Nathaniel Pendleton, and a physician, Dr. David Hosack. The two men took their positions and the seconds handed them their guns. Hamilton raised and lowered his several times, commenting that the direction of the light made it necessary; he then put on his spectacles. Burr's first bullet hit Hamilton in the abdomen. As he fell his pistol went off, though he was unaware of the fact and indeed cautioned Pendleton to take care "...it may go off and do harm." Pendleton and Hosack took him by boat across the Hudson to the home of William Bayard in Jane Street on Manhattan Island, and Mrs. Hamilton was sent for.

To spare her they tried to conceal the seriousness of the wound but it was soon evident that Hamilton was dying. Surgeons from a French frigate in New York harbor examined him, found that the bullet had penetrated the liver and lodged in the vertebrae and pronounced the case hopeless. In spite of the administration of laudanum the dying man was in great pain. He asked to be admitted to the Episcopal Church and to receive the Sacrament. Because of the prejudice against dueling, no clergyman could be found to accommodate him until the Rev. Benjamin Moore, Rector of Trinity Church and Episcopal Bishop of New York, finally consented. Shortly after receiving the Last Rites Alexander Hamilton, one of the most brilliant of America's founding fathers, died on 12 July 1804, leaving his wife and seven children in bad financial straits. He was buried in Trinity Churchyard.

Hammarskjöld, Dag (1905–1961).

When he died, the Swedish-born secretary general of the United Nations was engaged on a secret peacekeeping mission. It had been arranged that he meet Moise Tshombe, president of Katanga, the secessionist southern province of the Congo, at Ndola, a few miles over the Katangan border in what is now Zambia. A spurious flight plan was filed, but it is believed that the plane (a Douglas DC-6B) flew from Leopoldville due east to Lake Tanganyika and then south, skirting the Congolese border. Hammarskjöld spent the time calmly translating Martin Buber's *Ich und Du* into Swedish, covering a yellow legal pad with his neat handwriting.

At 10:10 P.M., GMT, 17 September 1961, ten minutes before the expected touchdown at Ndola, the plane acknowledged receipt of landing instructions. Its lights were sighted 2,000 feet up before it disappeared. Though there were eighteen military planes at the field, it took fifteen hours to find the crash site, only nine and a half miles away. Hammarskjöld, who is known to have had a strong aversion to seat belts, had been thrown clear of the wreckage; only he was unburned, but, with a fractured spine and massive internal bleeding, it is unlikely he lived long. He was lying on his back near a small shrub, his face extraordinarily peaceful, a hand clutching a tuft of grass. Hammarskjöld was awarded the 1961 Nobel Peace Prize a month later. The official report did not rule out sabotage, but concluded that the pilot had probably made too low an approach.

An interior view of the plane carrying the coffins of Dag Ham-marskjöld and the other staff members who died with him in the Congo.

UNITED NATIONS

After a state funeral in the Cathedral of Uppsala, Sweden, on 29 September, Hammarskjöld was taken by gun carriage to the seventeenth-century cemetery nearby and buried in the family plot.

Hammerstein, Oscar, II
(1895–1960).

The popular U.S. lyricist seemed to be in good health when he had his annual checkup with Dr. Ben Kean on 16 September 1959. Just as he was leaving the doctor's office, he stuck his head back around the door and mentioned that he was waking in the middle of the night hungry, but that a glass of milk helped. It didn't sound like much of a problem, but Dr. Kean ran out onto

Park Avenue and, catching up with Hammerstein, suggested that he come back in the morning for a test to determine whether he had an ulcer. X-rays showed that it was not an ulcer, but cancer of the stomach. Surgery was scheduled for the 19th at New York Hospital. His wife Dorothy and their five children waited anxiously while Dr. Frank Glenn, chief surgeon at the hospital, operated. Dr. Glenn and Dr. Harold Hyman, a friend of Hammerstein's since they were boys, broke the news to her that they had removed three-quarters of the stomach and that he would be dead in six months to a year. Chemotherapy was discussed briefly and rejected. Though Dorothy conspired to keep the facts from him, it is fairly certain Oscar knew he was a dying man.

Oscar remained in the hospital until 4 October and then went home for ten days. *The Sound of Music* was being tried out in New Haven and the reviews were predicting a smash hit. Oscar saw the production on the 14th in Boston and Dorothy stood in tears behind the scenery as she watched him talking to the company onstage. It was the forty-fourth show he had written and she knew it would be his last. In December, Oscar and Dorothy vacationed in Jamaica and the children joined them for Christmas. Oscar was feeling well; for the first time in many years he was not planning a show and he liked the idea of just being able to write as the mood took him.

On 7 July 1960 x-rays showed a recurrence of the carcinoma and Kean suggested a course of chemotherapy. Oscar gave it some careful thought and declined. He decided he would rather die at his home, Highland Farm, Doylestown, Pa., than in the hospital. The twelfth of July was his sixty-fifth birthday. He began to say his farewells, taking some time with each child. Jimmy, who was twenty-nine, burst into tears. Oscar yelled, "Goddamn it, I'm the one who's dying, not you!" Later he reminisced: "I've had a very happy childhood. I've had a good time as a young man. And I've had a terrific middle age. The only thing that I'm disappointed in is that I was looking forward to having a good old age, too." He talked to Dorothy about her future, helping her to plan a good life without him.

His great desire was to die with dignity. His friend, Harold Hyman, took care of him, sedating him against the increasing pain. On Monday night, 22 August 1960, Dorothy stayed with Oscar until just before midnight. Then Harold told her to leave the room. Ten minutes later he came out to say that Oscar was dead. After cremation his ashes were buried in Ferncliff Cemetery, Hartsdale, N.Y.

In spite of his long collaboration with Richard Rodgers, Oscar once remarked that he really didn't know Dick at all. Fifteen years after Oscar's death Rodgers said that though he was very fond of Oscar, he never knew whether Oscar liked him or not.

Handel, George Frederick
(1685–1759).

The German-born composer's left eye suddenly failed him on 13 February 1751 while he was composing his oratorio *Jephtha*, as a note in the score attests. The cause of this disability is difficult to determine. Handel had suffered a stroke in 1737; a less severe one followed six years later and there was some talk among his acquaintances about a disorder of the head in 1745; perhaps the loss of vision was due to yet another small stroke. At any rate, an examination at Guy's Hospital showed that, though he had incipient cataracts, they were not the cause of his sudden partial blindness, and no surgery was performed at that time. "Couching" (a tilting or displacement of the clouded lenses) was performed in 1752 with a temporary improvement, but in August of that year the *General Register* reported that the "celebrated composer of Musick" had been seized by "a paralytick disorder in the head which deprived him of his sight." This total blindness is confirmed by later news items.

On 6 April 1759 at Covent Garden Handel conducted his *Messiah* for the last time. After the sellout audience had left, the composer collapsed and was taken to his home at 57 Lower Brook Street. It was thought that he was merely exhausted after conducting ten concerts in little more than a month at the age of seventy-four; but he knew he was finished, and wished only to die on Good Friday. He said goodbye to each of his friends and then told his servant to admit no more, for he was done with the world. Good Friday came and went, and still Handel lay, breathing quietly. Some time early on the following day, 14 April 1759, he died. On the 20th he was buried at the foot of the Duke of Argyll's monument in Westminster Abbey; 3,000 people came to pay their respects.

Hannibal (247–?183 B.C.).

The Carthaginian warrior and statesman, best remembered for his feat of crossing the Alps with elephants in 216 B.C. fled to Asia when the Romans, alarmed by rumors that he plotted renewed war against them, demanded his surrender. He was living in a large house in Libyssa (present-day Gebze) in Bithynia (the ancient name for part of Turkey) on the shore of the Sea of Marmara. The house lacked comforts but had six doors for ease of escape and a secret passage through a cypress garden.

Flamininus, envoy of the Roman senate, demanded that Hannibal be given to him, but Prusias, King of Bithynia, refused and sent guards to protect the house at Libyssa. When Hannibal saw the armed men he thought he had been betrayed. He tried to escape through the cypress garden, but on seeing two soldiers outside the opening in the stone wall, he returned to the dining chamber, asked for wine, and with it took poison. "It is time now," he said, "to end the great anxiety of the Romans who have grown weary of waiting for the death of a hated old man." It is thought that Hannibal lies in a crypt above the modern Turkish village of Gebze overlooking the Gulf of Nicomedia. *See* H. Lamb (1958).

Harding, Warren Gamaliel (1865–1923).

The twenty-ninth president of the U.S. (1921–1923) was a handsome, easygoing man. Although he had fathered an illegitimate daughter the year before he was elected president and lived in daily fear of the fact leaking out, he continued to meet his mistress, Nan Britton, even in the White House. The senate had begun to investigate Harding's venal friends as early as February 1923, and the shadow of impeachment and disgrace loomed by the time he escaped Washington's heat on 30 June and headed for Alaska. A visit from Mrs. Albert B. Fall, wife of his corrupt interior secretary, in Kansas City left him visibly shaken, and a coded message sent to him in Alaska from Washington all but caused his physical collapse.

On the return journey at Seattle he suffered chest and abdom-

The bier on which President Harding lay in state in the U.S. Capitol.

inal pains early on 28 July. Surgeon General C.E. Sawyer diagnosed the illness as a gastric disturbance, and this view prevailed over that of a younger physician, Commander J.T. Boone, who concluded from the heart sounds and elevated blood pressure that it was a cardiac seizure. At the Palace Hotel, San Francisco on the 29th the chest pains and fever returned and the heart failure began to affect the brain and lungs. Bronchopneumonia with circulatory collapse was now diagnosed (the electrocardiograph, in use in the U.S. for five years, was never used in this case).

By 2 August Harding was feeling much better. At 7:30 that evening he was lying propped up in bed while his wife read a glowing report about him in the *Saturday Evening Post*; suddenly he shuddered and collapsed. Mrs. Harding rushed out to look for Sawyer and Boone; when they reached the patient he was dead. They declared that the cause was a stroke, and while this is a possibility, a massive hemorrhage from a ruptured cardiac infarct—heart tissue deprived of its blood supply by the recent episodes—is much more likely. He was taken to Washington by train and then to Marion, Ohio, where he was buried in Hillside Cemetery.

Hardy, Thomas (1840–1928).

There would have been no *Far From the Madding Crowd*, no *Tess of the d'Urbervilles*, if the nurse had not rescued the puny infant, firstborn of Jemima and Thomas Hardy, put aside by the doctor as dead. But the fragile child survived to become one of England's great old men. He and his first wife, Emma, moved to Max Gate near Dorchester in 1883. The marriage was not a happy one. In 1912 Emma died and two years later Hardy married Florence Dugdale, nearly forty years his junior, who collaborated with him in writing his biography.

The last years of his life were very quiet, though he received many distinguished visitors at Max Gate, including the Prince of Wales—later to be King Edward VIII. Even in the last year of his life, when he was eighty-seven, Hardy liked to take long walks by the Frome and reminisce with Florence in the evenings sitting beside the fire. Both mind and body grew weaker as Christmas 1927 approached and he was confined to bed. At dusk on 11 January he asked Florence to read him the verse from Omar Khayyam beginning:"Oh, Thou, who Man of baser Earth didst make."

Hardy died shortly after 9:00 P.M. on 11 January 1928. His heart was buried in Emma's grave at Stinsford; the remainder of the frail body was cremated and the ashes were deposited in Poet's Corner in Westminster Abbey.

Harrison, William Henry
(1773–1841).

The ninth president of the U.S. (1841) served only thirty-two days. As a youth he had been apprenticed to a surgeon, and later, as the first governor of Indiana, introduced smallpox inoculation and forbade the sale of liquor to the Indians. He seems to have been always subject to digestive upsets. Inauguration Day, 4 March 1841, dawned very cold, but the new president disdained to wear hat, coat or gloves as he addressed the crowd for fully a hundred minutes. He caught a cold and in weakened condition was obliged to interview the inevitable crowd of office-seekers.

Death of William Henry Harrison, ninth U.S. President, in 1841, after only thirty-two days in office. From a contemporary engraving by N. Currier.

Harrison's tomb at North Bend, Ohio.

He also insisted on taking his usual walks during cold, showery weather later in the month.

After dinner on 27 March Harrison sent for a physician, who diagnosed bilious pleurisy, complicated by congestion of the liver. The unfortunate man was cupped, blistered, bled, and dosed by more purgatives and other remedies of the time than even a hale man could have tolerated. An equivalent modern diagnosis would probably be virus pneumonia and hepatitis, aggravated by the loss of water and salts brought on by the medication. Harrison died on 4 April 1841 and was buried at North Bend, Ohio.

Harte, Bret (1836–1902).

The U.S. writer of western stories was not pleased when his wife, whom he had not seen for thirty years, arrived in England in 1898, disturbing his self-imposed exile. Anna hoped that if his relationship with Marguerite Van de Velde, a wealthy Belgian widow, was as innocent as Harte claimed, she could resume her rightful position. Harte, however, thought otherwise and instead Anna joined her daughter in Paris.

Harte's health was declining rapidly. He was crippled by neuralgia and suffered from a chronic painful throat which was not alleviated by the switch to a milder cigarette. In January 1902, gaunt and in constant pain, he sought the benefit of the sea air at Southsea, but it did no appreciable good. He returned to London in March for an operation on his throat that revealed deep-rooted, inoperable cancer. After leaving the hospital he spent a few weeks in his rooms at 74 Lancaster Gate, London, then went with Mrs. Van de Velde to her home, The Red House, Camberley, Surrey. There he rallied for a while and began to write what he said would be the best story he had ever done. He worked hard but was hindered by his weakness and the intolerable pain in his throat. He had completed only two paragraphs when his throat hemorrhaged and he collapsed. He died in the late afternoon of 5 May 1902 with Mrs. Van de Velde by his side. She and Anna met for the first time at his funeral in Frimley Churchyard in Surrey. Harte's red granite tombstone is inscribed:

IN FAITHFUL REMEMBRANCE
M.S. Van de Velde

Hawthorne, Nathaniel
(1804–1864).

In 1860, after seven years abroad, the U.S. author and his family returned home to Concord, Mass. During their stay in Italy their oldest daughter, fourteen-year-old Una, had become ill, at one time being very close to death. After their return to Concord she suffered a relapse which had an adverse effect on Hawthorne's already failing health.

In March 1864 Hawthorne went southward under the care of his old friend and publisher W.D. Ticknor. Driving in Fairmount Park, Philadelphia, Ticknor put his own coat over the old man's shoulders to protect him from the weather, which had turned suddenly cold and wet. A few days later Ticknor died of pneumonia and Hawthorne returned home to Concord, overcome by shock and fatigue.

His boyhood friend, former President Franklin Pierce, came

on 12 May to take him for another excursion to benefit his health. On 18 May 1864 they reached Plymouth, N.H., and stopped at the Pemigewasset Hotel. In a letter Pierce later wrote to their friend Horatio Bridge, he described how he could see Hawthorne in bed from his own bed in the adjoining room. Toward three or four in the morning he noticed that though Hawthorne appeared to be sleeping peacefully he had not moved his position in several hours. Suddenly apprehensive, he rose and touched Hawthorne's forehead and realized he was dead. Oliver Wendell Holmes, who saw the writer shortly before his trip to New Hampshire, stated "There were persistent local symptoms referred especially to the stomach—boring pain, distension, difficult digestion, with great wasting of flesh and strength."

On 23 May, an unusually beautiful day, Hawthorne was buried in Sleepy Hollow Cemetery, Concord. The officiating minister was the Rev. James Freeman Clarke, who had married Nathaniel and Sophia Hawthorne twenty-two years previously.

Haydn, Franz Joseph (1732–1809).

The Austrian composer's last years were marked by increasing weakness and bodily discomfort. His fame throughout Europe was such that rumors of his demise in 1805 caused special works to be written in his memory, and a performance of Mozart's *Requiem* to be arranged. Haydn, amused to hear of the premature commemoration, remarked that he would have been glad to go to Paris to conduct the *Requiem* himself. His public farewell occurred at a performance of his oratorio, *The Creation*, in Vienna fourteen months before his death. Carried in on a litter, he fainted at the intermission and, amid expressions of homage and affection by Beethoven and others, was taken back to his modest home at 73 Kleine Steingasse near Gumpendorf Church. Each day during the French bombardment of the city in May 1809 he was carried to his piano to play the Austrian imperial anthem. On 26 May the visit of a French soldier startled the household, but he wished only to pay his respects to "Papa" Haydn and to sing, with the composer accompanying him, an aria from *The Creation*. It was Haydn's last great pleasure; he died in his sleep at 12:40 A.M. on 31 May 1809 with his cook, Anna Kremnitzer, holding his hand.

He was buried in Hundsthurm Cemetery at the gate of Vienna with only one or two mourners present. In 1820 a remark by an English nobleman reminded Prince Nicolaus Esterházy, Haydn's one-time employer, that he had neglected to have the body buried at his Eisenstadt estate, thirty miles south of Vienna. Belatedly requesting the remains to be exhumed, the prince was astonished to learn that Haydn's head was missing. The police discovered that the dead composer's friend J.C. Rosenbaum, a student of the pseudoscience of phrenology, in league with a gravedigger and others, had had the corpse decapitated two days after the interment. Offered a bribe to produce the skull, Rosenbaum instead supplied a substitute which until 1954 shared a grave with Haydn's body and those of six other Esterházy servants in the Bergkirche at Eisenstadt. The genuine skull was later bequeathed to the Vienna Academy of Music, where it was displayed in a glass cabinet atop a piano. On 5 June 1954 the relic was blessed by the Archbishop of Vienna and reunited with Haydn's skeleton in a new copper coffin that was reinterred in the Bergkirche.

Hemingway, Ernest (1899–1961).

Although the U.S. writer and adventurer could fight high blood pressure, high cholesterol and a badly functioning liver, he was losing his battle against depression, and on 30 November 1960 he and his fourth wife, Mary, left their home in Ketchum, Idaho, for the Mayo Clinic in Rochester, Minn. His depression was severe enough for a course of electric shock treatments to be administered twice a week during December and early January. He tolerated them well enough except for headaches and temporary amnesia. On 12 January he received a telegram from President-elect John F. Kennedy inviting the Hemingways to the inauguration ceremonies on the 19th and 20th. Hemingway had to decline, but he and Mary watched on television. He was discharged on 22 January 1961 and flew back home to Ketchum, where he began a schedule of writing in the morning, hiking in the afternoons and in general following doctor's orders. Yet there was a feeling that all was not well. He was quiet and withdrawn and complained with tears running down his cheeks that he could not write.

One April morning Mary came downstairs and found him in

his red robe standing with a shotgun in his hand. Knowing that the doctor was due shortly, she played for time, talking to Ernest quietly for about 50 minutes until the doctor arrived, persuaded Hemingway to pass over the gun and took him to Sun Valley Hospital. It was arranged that he should return to the Mayo Clinic. When he came home briefly to pick up some clothes he again grabbed a shotgun and pointed the muzzle at his throat. It was wrestled from him.

They began the flight back to Rochester on 25 April. During a stop for refueling in Rapid City, Hemingway tried to walk into the whirling propellers of a taxiing plane. In Rochester he submitted to another series of shock treatments. Mary was very upset when she was told he was going to be discharged and tried to arrange his transfer to a psychiatric institute in Hartford; the Mayo Clinic advised against the move. Mary rented a Buick and on 26 June she and Hemingway began the journey back to Ketchum. It took them five difficult days to make the 1,700-mile trip.

On Saturday evening, 1 July, Hemingway prepared for bed in a cheerful mood, singing with Mary a gay Italian song, "Tutti mi Chiamano Bionda." Sunday was a beautiful sunny day. Hemingway woke early, put on his red robe and went downstairs. He took the keys for the basement from the window ledge behind the kitchen sink, tiptoed down the basement stairs and unlocked the storage room where Mary had put the guns. He chose a double-barrelled Boss shotgun, took a handful of shells, locked the door and came upstairs to the front foyer—a small entryway with oak-paneled walls and a linoleum-tiled floor. He inserted two shells, put the butt on the floor, leaned forward, pressed the twin barrels against his forehead just above the eyebrows and pulled both triggers.

His sons Jack, Pat and Gregory flew in for the services at Our Lady of the Snows Church and the burial in Ketchum cemetery.

Hendrix, Jimi (1942–1970).

The brilliant black guitarist and his road manager, Eric Barrett, arrived at Heathrow Airport, London, on 27 August 1970 for the Isle of Wight Festival at East Afton Farm. Hendrix then did some concerts in Europe, though one in Rotterdam on 14 September had to be cancelled because Billy Cox, the bass player, had had a nervous breakdown. While Jimi was in Germany he wrote to his girl-friend, Monika Danneman, asking her to find them an apartment in London; she found one in the fashionable Landsdowne Crescent in Notting Hill. He was due to meet lawyers on 16 September to discuss a settlement between two recording companies, but he did not show up. Instead, he went to the tiny apartment of twenty-one-year-old Lorraine James in the Fulham Road area; she later recalled he was "obviously high on drugs and he had a large quantity of cannabis on him. He was in a terrible state...one minute he was on top of the world and the next minute he was moaning about his backers and financial affairs."

After a night of partying and pot smoking Hendrix lay unconscious all day Thursday, 17 September, in an apartment in Redcliffe Gardens, Fulham. When he revived he returned to an orgy of drugs and girls, finally making his way in the evening to Monika's Notting Hill apartment. She cooked spaghetti bolognaise, and they drank a bottle of wine. He seemed happy, but at 1:30 A.M., 18 September, he left a puzzling message on the answering machine for Chas Chandler, his ex-manager, "I need help bad, man!" At 1:45 A.M. Monika took him to see some people, she picked him up again at 3:00 A.M. She made him a tuna fish sandwich and he worked on his last song, "The Story of Life." When Monika went into her bedroom she found Jimi with a handful of her sleeping pills; he said he was just counting them. He drank a glass of wine and went to sleep; she watched him until about 7:00 A.M. and then took a sleeping pill.

She awoke about 10:20 A.M., desperate for a cigarette; Jimi didn't like her to go out but he was safely asleep. Looking at him more closely she noticed there was vomit on his nose and mouth, but as she could hear him breathing, and his pulse, checked against her own, seemed normal, she put on her coat and shoes and ran quickly across the road. When she returned the door of the apartment was stuck and for a moment she was filled with apprehension. When she finally got the door open the room was deathly still. She tried to awaken Jimi; his face was cold, his parted lips purplish. She was scared to call a hospital because she knew he would hate the publicity; instead she telephoned a friend who insisted she call for help, regardless of the consequences. St. Mary Abbot's Hospital responded, but it was too late; Jimi was pronounced dead on arrival.

At the inquest Professor Donald Teare stated that the cause of death was suffocation from the inhalation of vomit due to barbiturate poisoning. Jimi had apparently swallowed nine of Monika's sleeping pills. The coroner could not determine whether it was suicide or accidental poisoning. Jimi had expressed a wish to be buried beside the Thames. "Don't bury me in Seattle," he had said, "it's too cold and damp there." But his wishes were ignored. Years before, when he was eight years old, he had been enchanted by the music and singing at the Dunlan Baptist Church in Seattle, but he was thrown out because he wasn't dressed suitably. He vowed never to go into that church again as long as he lived. His funeral services were held there and he was buried in Greenwood Cemetery in suburban Renton. *See* C. Knight (1974).

Henry, O. *(William Sydney Porter)* (1862–1910).

The career of this important U.S. short story writer was largely compressed into his final nine years. His adoption of the pen-name "O. Henry," like his refusal to allow his photograph to be published and his habit of giving out erroneous biographical information, was intended to hide from the world—and especially from his daughter Margaret—his criminal record, for he served over three years (1898–1901) in the Ohio Penitentiary for embezzlement of bank funds in Austin, Texas. Like many other American writers he shortened his life by heavy drinking; his average around 1902 was said to be two quarts of whiskey a day. His second marriage, in 1907, was not a success and his wife Sara soon returned to Asheville, N.C., while he resumed his bachelor life in New York City. He rejoined her in 1909 when his health began to fail and toyed with the idea of writing a novel, but nothing came of it.

In January 1910 O. Henry returned to New York, the scene of his best stories, with money advanced by a Broadway producer, George Tyler, for whom the writer promised to write a play. Nothing more was heard of this either. With ebbing strength he returned to the form he knew best. At last, unable even to sit up and hold a pencil, he had a fellow writer, H.M. Lyons, come over to the Caledonia Hotel and finish a story ("The Snow Man") for him. "His neck," said Lyons, who was shocked by O. Henry's appearance, "stood on his collar like a stick in a pond." On the evening of 3 June he was overcome by pain; a friend summoned a doctor, C.R. Hancock, who took him to Polyclinic Hospital on East Thirty-fourth Street by taxi. O. Henry, who insisted on walking in, gave the reception clerk the name "Will S. Parker." Emptying his pockets onto the desk, he said, "Here I am going to die and only worth twenty-three cents."

His diabetes and cirrhosis of the liver were both far advanced. "He had the most dilated heart I have ever seen," said Hancock later. At midnight on the 4th, when the lights in his room were turned down, he murmured. "Turn up the lights. I don't want to go home in the dark." When he died, at 7:06 A.M., Sunday, 5 June 1910, the morning light was streaming in at his window. The funeral scene might have come straight out of one of his stories. The solemn service at "The Little Church Around the Corner" on West Twenty-ninth street had as a lively counterpoint the happy voices of a wedding party waiting outside; somehow, both ceremonies had been scheduled for 11:00 A.M. on the 7th. O. Henry was buried at his native town, Asheville, N.C. The headstone does not even mention the name by which he is famous the world over; it says only: WILLIAM SYDNEY PORTER, 1862–1910. *See* R. O'Connor (1970).

Henry, Patrick (1736–1799).

The American patriot was a fearless and eloquent Virginian best known for a 1774 speech in which he cried, "Give me liberty or give me death!" After his retirement to Red Hill, his estate near Brookneal, Va., in the fall of 1799 he complained of feeling unwell. Dr. Cabell, a capable Edinburgh-trained physician, diagnosed intussusception (an infolding of one part of the intestine within another) but could offer no cure. After trying various remedies Dr. Cabell was driven on 6 June to a final desperate expedient—a dose of liquid mercury. "I suppose, doctor, this is your last resort?" Dr. Cabell admitted that it was and explained that acute inflammation of the intestines had already taken place. The medicine might give him relief, or—— Excusing himself, Henry drew his silken cap over his eyes and prayed a short prayer for his family, his country and his own soul. Then, calmly, he swallowed the liquid mercury. He said a few loving words to his family, then thanked God for allowing him to die without pain. Dr. Cabell left the house in tears; when he had regained control of himself he returned and found Henry quietly watching his fingernails turn blue. He lost consciousness and died a few minutes later. Henry was buried at the foot of his sloping garden at Red Hill. A large marble slab covers the grave, inscribed: HIS FAME HIS BEST EPITAPH.

Henry VIII (1491–1547).

The first of England's Tudor kings was a tall, red-haired youth, amiable, well-read, an able linguist and a practiced musician. His first wife, Catherine of Aragon (q.v.) (1485–1536), mother of Mary Tudor, was discarded in 1531 after twenty-two years of marriage and died of a coronary thrombosis; Anne Boleyn (q.v.) (1507?–1536), mother of Elizabeth, was executed in 1536 on dubious adultery charges; Jane Seymour (1509?–1537) died twelve days after giving birth to the future Edward VI, apparently of puerperal sepsis. Henry's marriage to Anne of Cleves (1515–1557) was probably not consummated; it was declared invalid after seven months in 1540. Catherine Howard (1521?–1542) wed the king a month later; he was twice her age, by this time an obese tyrant with a festering ulcer of the leg and an unprepossessing countenance from which tiny wicked eyes peered out. Catherine lasted a year and a half before being beheaded for prenuptial unchastity. Catherine Parr (1512–1548), a tactful, modest noblewoman of thirty, already twice widowed, took care of her unspeakable husband during his remaining three years.

By the summer of 1546, Henry's ulcer was painful and offensive. At the end of the year his dropsy was so far advanced that he weighed over 400 pounds and had to be lifted from place to place. On 27 January 1547 in his palace at Whitehall he dozed off, became comatose and, at two the next morning, ceased to breathe. "We infer," wrote P.M. Dale, "that Henry had cirrhosis of the liver with obstruction of the portal system of veins, so-called hepatic dropsy. Whether his dropsy was of the alcoholic or syphilitic type is anybody's guess. He had earned the right to both types."

Did Henry suffer life-long syphilis? In a 1956 study (reprinted in *Tenements of Clay*) the Danish physician Ove Brinch surveyed the medical history, much of it suggestive of the disease: at the age of twenty-two Henry suffered from a skin disease that was not smallpox (but it could have been furunculosis); for his final seventeen years his corpulence increased and his leg ulceration became a problem (but it may have been a common osteomyelitis); his character worsened dramatically in the latter part of his life as his egotism increased (but he may have been schizophrenic). The repeated stillbirths and miscarriages of his first wife are also suspicious, but syphilis is not the likeliest explanation for these. Only in the case of the malformation of the nose, observable in several of Henry's portraits and apparently a syphilitic gumma (rubbery tumor), is an alternative diagnosis hard to come by. He may well have contracted syphilis as a youth (the disease was rife throughout Europe), but in the absence of physical evidence the verdict must remain "not proven" until the skeleton lying in the royal vault beneath St. George's Chapel, Windsor, can be examined.

Hickok, Wild Bill (1837–1876).

James Butler Hickok was a tall handsome man who, as one of Custer's scouts, was praised by the general for his courage and skill in the use of rifle and pistol. Shortly before his death Hickok left his wife Agnes Lake, whom he had married in March 1876, in Cincinnati while he went off to make some money. His eyesight was failing but his target shooting at 25 paces was perfect. It was said that he appeared not to take aim but to bring the guns out of their holsters with a twist of the wrist and fire in one smooth action.

On 12 July Hickok reached the outlaw town, Deadwood, S.D. At every opportunity he gambled, losing more than he gained. But in a game on the evening of 1 August, Jack McCall lost all his money to Hickok; Wild Bill gave him enough money for his supper. He often talked of his premonition of death and insisted on keeping his back to the wall. On the following day he was persuaded to join a poker game at Nuttall and Mann's No. 10 saloon. He asked the man with the wall seat to change places with him but was ribbed good-naturedly and uneasily sat down again. At about 3:00 P.M. the front door swung open and Jack McCall

The original grave of Wild Bill Hickok at Deadwood, South Dakota, in 1876. His friend C.H. Utter is seen sitting on the right.
WESTERN HISTORY COLLECTIONS,
UNIVERSITY OF OKLAHOMA LIBRARY

slunk in. Facing him was Wild Bill, engrossed in the cards he held. McCall moved around until he was behind Hickok's stool. There was a friendly dispute going on between William R. Massey—a Missouri river pilot—and Hickok, who was heard to remark, "The old duffer—he broke me on the hand." Those were his last words. There was a loud bang and a shout from McCall: "Damn you, take that!" Hickok's head jerked forward and after a moment he toppled to the floor, the cards spilling from his nerveless fingers. McCall made his escape by a rear door.

A coroner's court determined that death was instantaneous, and resulted from a ball that entered the base of the brain a little to the right of center and exited through the right cheek. (It then lodged in Massey's left wrist and was still there for Massey to boast of as late as 1885.)

Before Hickok was laid in his coffin a lock of hair measuring about 14 inches in length was cut and is now in the Wilstach collection in the New York Public Library. He was buried at Inglenook but as the rapidly growing town of Deadwood encroached he was moved to Mount Moriah in 1879. At that time it was found that the body was petrified; the action of the water which had percolated through the coffin had performed a natural embalmment. Many markers and headstones were erected, but even the highest steel enclosure could not keep souvenir hunters from chipping away at them. The markers proved much less durable than the legend.

McCall, twenty-five years old, was tried for murder by an illegal miners' court and acquitted. He left town and was later arrested and tried legally for murder in Yankton, S.D., on 4–6 December 1876. He was found guilty and hanged on Thursday, 1 March 1877. *See* J.R. Rosa (1974).

Hitler, Adolf (1889–1945).

Toward the end of his life, and particularly after injuries suffered in the "bomb plot" of June 1944, the Austrian-born dictator of Germany showed marked signs of physical deterioration: bowed shoulders, a deeply lined face, a shuffling gait, a tremor of the left hand and a tendency to sweat and salivate excessively. After the failure of his Ardennes offensive, he and his mistress Eva Braun took up quarters in the chancellery in Berlin. Only in the last few days, when the Russian army entered the capital, did he abandon hopes of eventual victory. He then acceded to Eva's wish; the couple were married in a civil ceremony in the bunker under the chancellery early on 29 April 1945. Immediately afterward he dictated his will, in which he blamed the war and most other human woes on international Jewry. At 3:30 P.M. on 30 April he and his bride committed

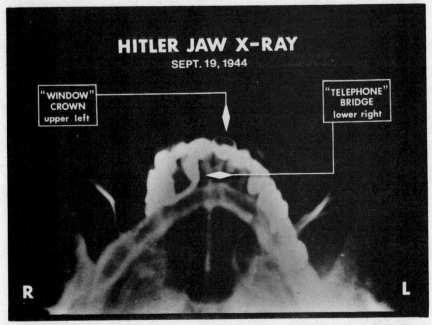

Adolf Hitler's jaw, x-rayed after the "bomb-plot" attempt on his life in 1944. This radiograph clinched the identification, by R.F. Sognnaes in 1972, of the remains found by the Russian Army in 1945.

R.F. SOGNNAES

suicide. The details, gleaned from available witnesses, were first reported by H.R. Trevor-Roper in *The Last Days of Hitler* (1947). He concluded that the dictator shot himself through the mouth, that Eva took poison and that the bodies were never found.

New evidence surfaced later. Hitler's valet Heinz Linge was released from a Russian prison camp in 1955. He reported that he was the first to enter Hitler's sitting room in the air raid shelter, which stank of gunpowder, to find the pair sitting side by side on the sofa, Hitler to Linge's left, Eva, her feet tucked under her, to her husband's left. Both were dead. The Fuehrer's head had flopped over toward the arm of the sofa, and blood trickled down his face from a large bullet wound, presumably the exit hole, in his right temple. Another hole was visible in the left temple. His hands rested on his knees or in his lap. Two Walther pistols lay nearby, but there is some confusion regarding their positions and which had been fired. Eva, who had swallowed cyanide, was unwounded. After crushing an ampule of the same poison between his teeth, Hitler had been finished off by a bullet, either self-inflicted or—to judge by the position of his hands when found and the known unreliability of his left hand—fired by Eva at her husband's request.

The bodies were carried up to the courtyard, doused with gasoline collected earlier for the purpose and set afire. Only about forty-five gallons of fuel had been found; this fact and the Russian barrage hampered the cremation. The same evening the remains were dumped into a shell hole and hastily covered with soil and refuse.

A few days later a search party unearthed the charred corpses and five Russian doctors performed autopsies. This became known in 1968 when a Soviet-authorized book by Lev Bezymensky was published in English and German. Finding glass shards in Hitler's mouth and no evidence of the reported gunshot wound (because the upper part of the head was missing), the pathologists reported that the German dictator had died a coward's death by poison. They also discovered the dead man had only one testicle, with no evidence to show he had ever possessed the usual complement. The identification was reportedly made by means of dental photographs and several gold crowns waiting to be fitted. The German dental technicians who supplied this evidence also recognized their late client's teeth, brought along by the Soviet team in a cheap jewel case.

Trevor-Roper and others challenged the belated Soviet revelations and, in the absence of a proper comparison with reliable antemortem data, the reported identification remained unconvincing to many Western authorities. Prompted by the Oslo dental professor Ferdinand Ström, his colleague Reidar F. Sognnaes of Los Angeles tracked down, at a U.S. National Archives depository at Suitland, Md., five x-ray films that had been made of Hitler's head after the bomb-plot. Using these and the detailed 1945 testimony of the Fuehrer's dentist and physician, Sognnaes constructed a model of the German dictator's dentition. A tooth-by-tooth comparison with the Soviet postmortem data (which includes photographs and diagrams) enabled Sognnaes and his colleagues to announce, at a forensic science meeting in Edinburgh in September 1972, that Hitler's remains had been conclusively identified.

Houdini, Harry (1874–1926).

The Budapest-born U.S. magician was being hoisted by his ankles for insertion, head first, into his "Water Torture Cell" at an Albany, N.Y., theater on 10 October 1926 when he felt a bone snap, but by means of splints and a brace he was able to continue his tour to Schenectady and Montreal. Before going on stage at the Princess Theatre, Montreal, for the matinee performance on Friday, 22 October, he was reclining on a sofa in his tiny dressing room, his injured ankle stretched out in front of him, reading his mail. A McGill University student, who had done a sketch of Houdini, had been invited to meet him again and had brought two friends. One of them, Joselyn Gordon Whitehead, reputed to be an amateur boxer, asked the magician whether he could, as claimed, withstand the heaviest punch to the midriff. Misunderstanding Houdini's casual, absentminded assent, Whitehead bent over him and dealt one, or possibly three, violent blows to

Houdini steps into his "casket" for one of his death-defying acts.
LIBRARY OF CONGRESS

A magnificent memorial to Houdini dominates the Weiss family plot at Machpelah Cemetery, Queens, N.Y. The original bust, vandalized in June 1975, has since been replaced. Photo by Betty Donaldson.

the left side of the reclining man's abdomen before being restrained. Houdini gasped and jumped to his feet, explaining that
it was necessary to brace his muscles first. Then, according to
some accounts, he invited a further punch, which caused him no
discomfort.

By Saturday night Houdini was feeling weak and feverish
during his performance. In agony on the train to Detroit, he was
medically examined on arrival but insisted on making his usual
appearance on stage on Monday evening. He collapsed during
his act and was found to have a ruptured appendix and streptococcal peritonitis. Before the introduction of sulfa drugs this
condition was invariably fatal, but he put up a good fight for
almost a week. To his wife Bess, who occupied a neighboring
room (she was recovering from a severe case of food poisoning),
he confided a secret message whereby she would recognize as
genuine any message sent by him from "beyond the veil." (No
message was ever received.) He died at 10:30 P.M., 31 October
1926, and was taken back to New York in the bronze casket he
had used for his "buried alive" stunt. After he had lain in state at
the Hippodrome Theatre, a service was held at the Elks Club,
where a rabbi delivered the eulogy. Burial was on Long Island at
Machpelah Cemetery, Cypress Hills, Queens. The bust, designed by Houdini himself, that surmounted the family plot was
probably the only graven image in any Jewish cemetery in the
U.S. It was smashed in April 1975 by unknown persons but was
later replaced.

Howard, Leslie (1893–1943).

The English actor, noted variously for quiet, emotional parts
and for his memorable portrait of the irascible Professor Higgins
in the first Shavian movie, *Pygmalion*, was asked by the British
Council in the spring of 1943 to tour Portugal and Spain as a
goodwill ambassador to aid the war effort. Reluctantly, he flew
by KLM to Lisbon at the end of April, taking Alfred Chenhalls,
his accountant, as traveling companion. The pilot of the Douglas
DC3 on which he was returning on 1 June 1943, at 12:45 P.M.
reported being followed across the Bay of Biscay by eight German fighter planes. Thirty minutes later his final message was
received: "We are being attacked." Then silence.

After the war, the Air Ministry in London, quoting Luftwaffe reports, explained that the German aircraft had been briefed to protect two U-boats. Failing to find them, they were apparently returning to base when they sighted the DC3. "There is no evidence to suggest that the crews were ordered to attack this particular aircraft." But one who was intimately concerned and who was also in an excellent position to know the facts had quite a different version. Winston Churchill had been attending a "Big Three" meeting in Algiers when the tragedy occurred. In *The Hinge of Fate* (1950) he wrote:

> [Anthony] Eden [the British Foreign Secretary] and I flew home together by Gibraltar. As my presence in North Africa had been fully reported, the Germans were exceptionally vigilant, and this led to a tragedy which much distressed me. The daily commercial aircraft was about to start from the Lisbon airfield when a thickset man [Chenhalls] smoking a cigar walked up and was thought to be a passenger on it. The German agents therefore signalled that I was on board. Although these neutral passenger planes had plied unmolested for many months between Portugal and England and had carried only civilian traffic, a German war plane was instantly ordered out, and the defenseless aircraft was ruthlessly shot down. Fourteen civilian passengers perished, and among them the well-known British film actor, Leslie Howard, whose grace and gifts are still preserved for us by the records of the many delightful films in which he took part. The brutality of the Germans was only matched by the stupidity of their agents. It is difficult to understand how anyone could imagine that with all the resources of Great Britain at my disposal I shoud have booked a passage in a neutral plane from Lisbon and flown home in broad daylight. We of course made a wide loop out by night from Gibraltar into the ocean, and arrived home without incident. It was a painful shock to me to learn what had happened to others in the inscrutable workings of fate.

Hughes, Howard R. (1905–1976).

During his final decade the U.S. billionaire isolated himself in a series of luxury hotels and then died miserably in his self-fashioned prison. Fleeing from Nicaragua to London after an earthquake struck in December 1972, he took up quarters at the Inn in the Park. There, while being helped to the bathroom early in the summer of 1973, he slipped and fractured his femur.

Under the pseudonym "Hugh Winston," he had a metal pin fitted at the London Clinic, but insisted on being spirited back to the hotel prematurely; he never walked again. For two years he lived at Freeport, Bahamas, in his usual blacked-out, top-floor hotel room until, inexplicably, he moved to the less convenient Acapulco Princess Hotel in Mexico.

There, in a darkened room in the twentieth-floor penthouse suite, Hughes spent his last seven weeks, totally cut off from the gay whirl of the luxury beach resort. At the foot of his bed stood his movie screen; behind him was his projector. Over and over he ran his favorites, particularly *Ice Station Zebra*, which he watched one hundred and fifty times. Nearby were boxes of the facial tissue and paper towels that he used to protect himself from infection from anything he touched or that might touch him. His six-foot-four-inch frame had shrunk three inches; dehydrated and without appetite, he weighed barely ninety pounds. His limbs were as fragile as matchsticks and almost as thin. On his back were two chronic bedsores. From time to time he would reach out listlessly for a hypodermic syringe and inject codeine or Valium, after which he would sleep for several hours.

Hughes had suffered from kidney insufficiency and constipation for many years. During the last few days, when he had stopped eating and drinking altogether, uremic poisoning set in. Though his entourage included four physicians, no blood or urine tests were done until the last few hours. A kidney dialysis machine could have saved Hughes, but there was none at the hotel, and moving him out into the world where people could see him was unthinkable. Furthermore, the old man couldn't be moved without an extensive grooming. In ten years his hair, beard and nails had been trimmed only twice—when he had to receive unavoidable visitors.

On the evening of 4 April 1976 an intravenous drip was begun; a local doctor, V.M. Montemayor, was called in. Even then, great efforts were made to preserve Hughes' anonymity; his admission to a Houston hospital was arranged under a false name. He was smuggled out of the hotel by the service elevator and died on a jet plane at 1:27 P.M., 5 April 1976, while still half an hour away from Houston airport. An official announcement from his Summa corporation gave the cause of death as a stroke, but the autopsy report stated it to be kidney failure. Though his personal living costs amounted to $5,000 a day, Hughes owned no clothes except drawstring shorts, pajamas and a couple of bathrobes. For his burial beside his parents in Glenwood Cemetery, Houston, his relatives had to buy him a dark blue suit. *See* J. Phelan (1976).

Hugo, Victor (1802–1885).

In 1855 the French poet and novelist, noted for his prodigious output, was exiled to Guernsey for fifteen years. In his last year on the island his wife and daughter left him; only Juliette Drouet, who was his mistress for fifty years, remained faithful. The two returned to Paris in September 1870. On 22 November 1882, Hugo's play *Le Roi s'amuse*, which had opened exactly fifty years earlier, was revived. Juliette and Victor occupied the royal box and received a tremendous ovation. Though Juliette managed to conceal the fact, she was in excruciating pain that night.

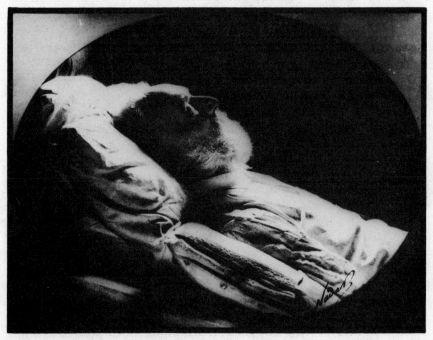

Victor Hugo on his deathbed, 1885. Photo by P. Nadar.
THE BETTMANN ARCHIVE

She had consulted a physician secretly and learned that she had cancer of the stomach. Friends noticed her increasingly gaunt appearance, but Victor was unaware of her illness until she was forced to take to her bed. Six weeks later, on 11 May 1883, she died in Victor's arms.

Hugo collapsed and never fully recovered, becoming a feeble old man, indifferent to life around him; he never wrote another line of prose or poetry. On 13 May 1885 he gave his last dinner party and seemed in relatively good health, but two days later he fell ill. The diagnosis was general debility of old age, complicated later by pneumonia. His condition was critical; bulletins were issued from his home at 130 Avenue d'Eylau, in the Champs Elysées quarter, to the European newspapers morning and night. His grandchildren were brought to him; he kissed them and murmured, "C'est ici le combat du jour et de la nuit!" He closed his eyes, lapsed into a coma and died at about 1:30 P.M. on 22 May 1885.

On the 24th Hugo lay under the Arc de Triomphe in the pauper's coffin he had requested. A million people followed him to his grave in an endless cortege while ten thousand soldiers struggled to control them. He was laid to rest beside Rousseau in the Panthéon. Ironically, in 1899 when the massive doors to the vault were opened Hugo's coffin was found to be still on trestles, with withered flowers and faded ribbons all around. No one had been concerned enough to have a tomb built for him.

Huxley, Aldous (1894–1963).

"For we, we can overcome all," wrote the English-born novelist and humanitarian when a child of thirteen. Valiantly he surmounted the problem of very poor vision (he was blind in one eye and had scar tissue on the other). At the end of May 1960 he underwent radium therapy for a malignant tumor at the back of his tongue, and though he described his convalescence as "unpleasant," he took part in a symposium in Mexico on 24 June. In May 1962 a malignant gland was removed from the side of his neck and he began a series of cobalt treatments, but a year and a half later more tumors appeared and it became apparent that in spite of intensive cobalt treatments the cancer had spread too far.

During the summer of 1963 Huxley traveled to Sweden, England and Italy, and at the end of August he returned to California with his second wife Laura. Though very weak and at times unable to speak he wrote his final article, "Shakespeare and Religion." He left the Cedars of Lebanon Hospital, Los Angeles, in November and returned to 6233 Mulholland Highway, the home of their friend Virginia Pfeiffer. A few hours before he died on 22 November 1963 he asked for his writing tablet and wrote, "Try LSD 100 mm [sic] intramuscular." With Dr. Cutler's consent, Laura gave him his first shot at 11:45 A.M. and a second one two hours later. The dying man became very quiet and, with Laura holding his hand and speaking to him gently, he died at 5:20 P.M., unaware that President Kennedy had died the same day. He was cremated; eight years later his ashes were taken to England and buried in his parents' grave in the hillside cemetery at Compton, Surrey.

Irving, Sir Henry (1838–1905).

The English actor, the first of his profession to be knighted (in 1895) got his feet wet in Edinburgh in October 1898 and then traveled to Glasgow in an unheated railway carriage. The consequences were pneumonia and pleurisy which, he told his manager Bram Stoker, caused "every breath to be like a sword stab." By December he was convalescing in Bournemouth, but the illness had aged him; his cheeks were hollow and his jaw cadaverous. It didn't help that his financial position was desperate; he had sold his collection of theatrical books and prints to pay off his immediate debts but ultimately he lost his London theater, the Lyceum. In May of 1899 his throat, which had been inflamed since his illness, was troubling him. A physician, while examining the actor, allowed a seven-inch instrument to slip down his gullet. Many hours later he coughed it up and returned it to the wretched doctor with a double fee and an understanding note asking him not to suffer undue remorse on his account. At about this time he moved from 15A Grafton Street, London, where he had lived for twenty-seven years, to a sunny flat at 17 Stratton Street. The condition of his heart was causing his doctors a great deal of concern in 1905 and they urged him to take life easier.

In October a series of six performances were given at the Theatre Royal in Bradford billed as a "Farewell to Henry Irving." On the last evening, Friday the thirteenth, the play was *Becket* by Tennyson, with the great actor taking the title role. It was Irving's practice never to vary his performance by so much as a hairsbreadth: every inflection, every action, had to be just so. Yet that night something was different and every member of the cast soon realized it. By a slight emphasis here, a deepened gesture there, they had an eerie awareness that Sir Henry was indeed making his farewell. He seemed dazed as he took his curtain calls. As Stoker left the theater, Irving made the unusual gesture of shaking hands with him and advising him to "muffle up your throat, old chap; it is a bitterly cold night." An assistant manager, J.W. Sheppard, accompanied him by cab to the Midland Hotel, where he was staying. As he entered he stumbled, but Sheppard caught him. "That chair...." he gasped, indicating the nearest one. A moment later Irving slipped from the chair to the floor; his tired heart had failed at last; it was 11:50 P.M.

The news traveled quickly. In Manchester, Ellen Terry, playing in *Alice Sit-by-the-Fire*, broke down and the curtain was lowered. Throughout the kingdom flags were flown at half-staff and the cabbies, to whom Irving had always been generous, tied a black bow on their whips. The Dean of St. Paul's refused to allow him to be buried there. The Dean of Westminster's sister, prejudiced against the theater, was pressing him to refuse also. But, threatened by blindness at the time, the dean gave permission at the special request of his oculist, Sir Anderson Critchett, to whom he owed a debt of gratitude. After cremation on 20 October 1905, Irving was buried in Poet's Corner beside the other great actor, David Garrick, and at the foot of Shakespeare's statue. It surprised no one that he died penniless.

Ivan the Terrible (1530–1584).

From an early age Ivan IV of Russia was surrounded by court intrigue and terror as his regents battled for power. When only three years old he became grand duke on the death of his father, Vasily III. He was crowned czar on 16 January 1547 and married Anastasia on 3 February. She was a beautiful and devout woman whom Ivan worshiped and who exercised a restraining influence on him. During an almost fatal illness in March 1553 he suspected treachery regarding the succession if he should die; this deepened his already distrustful and suspicious nature. Anastasia's death on 7 August 1560 drove him berserk. In his diseased and illogical mind he saw enemies everywhere and between 1563 and 1575 there were nine terrible periods of mass execution. Ivan often took an active role, looking for novel and ever more atrocious methods of slaughter. At other times he stood back to relish the dreadful scenes.

On 14 November 1581, in a fit of ungovernable fury, he struck his beloved son Ivan with a heavy, iron-pointed staff; five days later the young czarevitch, wounded in the temple, died. For weeks the czar raged through the corridors and rooms of the Kremlin, beating his head upon the floor. He had destroyed his heir; now only the younger son, the idiot Feodor, remained to succeed him.

The czar never fully recovered; he began to look like an old man, swollen with dropsy and riddled by disease. (Maclaurin believes he caught syphilis from the second of his seven wives—a coarse woman.) Early in 1584 from the Red Porch of the Kremlin he saw a comet shaped like a fiery cross and declared, "This sign foretells my death." Sixty magicians brought from Lapland, after casting spells, consulting oracles and studying the stars, foretold that 18 March would be the date of Ivan's death. No one dared tell this to the czar. His English friend Sir Jerome Horsey observed that he had begun "grievously to swell of the cods, with which he had most horribly offended above fifty years altogether, boasting of a thousand virgins he had deflowered...."

On 18 March 1584 Ivan's apothecary and physicians treated him as usual with potions for his various diseases, after which he took a bath. Evidently in high spirits, he could be heard singing. Wearing a loose gown he called for his chessboard, but had difficulty setting the king upright. Suddenly he fainted and fell back on his bed. Brandy was sent for and doctors and the apothecary summoned, but already, in Horsey's words, "He was strangled and stark dead." Maclaurin believes that an aortic valve damaged by syphilis had finally given way, causing a fatal derangement of the circulation. Feodosy Viatka, the czar's confessor, dressed the dead man in a monk's robe and cowl, performed the ceremony appropriate for a living man entering a community of monks and gave him the name Iona.

For two days Ivan lay in an open coffin which was then placed in a tomb beside his murdered son in the Cathedral of Michael the Archangel in Moscow. On 23 April 1953 his tomb was opened by the Soviet authorities. An examination of the skeleton indicated that he had suffered from a peculiarly painful form of arthritis. Traces of arsenic and quicksilver were found, the medicaments of his time. Movie cameras recorded the scene as he was replaced in the coffin and covered with sand. *See* R. Payne and N. Romanoff (1975).

Jackson, "Stonewall" (1824–1863).

Thomas Jonathan Jackson was the ablest of the Confederate generals serving under Robert E. Lee, and his early death was a severe blow to the Southern cause. On 2 May 1863, while Lee

Fellow soldiers of the Confederate hero, Stonewall Jackson, are shown gathered at the spot where he fell after accidentally being shot by his own men.

LIBRARY OF CONGRESS

1) *Jackson's raincoat worn on night of his shooting (note bullet hole in left shoulder).*
2) *Scalpel and needles used in emergency operation.*
3) *Canal boat "Marshall" carried Jackson's body to Lexington.*
4) *One of Jackson's kepis.*
5) *Jackson's handkerchief used to staunch flow of blood from his wounds.*
6) *Sheet music "Stonewall Jackson's Way," 1862.*
7) *Shawl in form of "Stars and Bars" made for Jackson by an admirer.*
8) *Mourning flag used by General Ewell at Jackson's funeral.*
9) *Kerosene lamp used by Jackson in camp.*
10) *"Death of Stonewall Jackson," engraving by Currier and Ives.*

This display commemorating Stonewall Jackson is on view in the Virginia Military Institute.

VIRGINIA MILITARY INSTITUTE,
LEXINGTON, VIRGINIA

sent ten thousand men to face the oncoming Federal forces under General Joseph Hooker at Chancellorsville, Va., Jackson's entire corps was sent around the Federal right flank. The maneuver was entirely successful, but in the moment of victory Jackson was fired on in the dusk by his own men and all but unhorsed. A round musket ball entered his right palm, breaking two bones. The left arm was destroyed by two bullets: the first entered below the shoulder, dividing the main artery and shattering the bone before passing out; the second struck the forearm and emerged above the wrist. The injured man was taken to the forward aid station four miles away; during the journey he fell from the litter when one of the bearers was hit. Early the next morning his arm was amputated under chloroform anesthesia and on the 5th he was conveyed by ambulance wagon twenty-seven miles to an office building at Guiney's Station.

All went well until the night of 6 May, when Jackson suffered nausea and pain in the right side. Chief Surgeon Hunter McGuire concluded that Jackson had contracted pleuropneumonia "attributable to the fall from the litter." Cups were applied, and mercury and antimony administered, along with opium. Jackson grew steadily weaker, but was able to greet his wife Anna when she arrived by train with their baby daughter. During his final delirium he shouted military orders, but when the end came at 3:15 P.M. on 10 May 1863, he became calm and smiled. "Let us cross over the river," he said, "and rest under the shade of the trees."

Amid scenes of widespread mourning, the Confederate hero was taken to lie in state in Richmond, then by rail and canal to Lexington, Va., to be buried in the hilltop cemetery.

In a 1963 study, L.W. Gorham questions McGuire's diagnosis. He also dismisses septicemia. A fat embolism arising from the marrow of the fractured long bones is a possibility, but most likely, Gorham believes, Jackson died of "a pulmonary embolism with pulmonary infarction followed by massive pulmonary thrombosis, with a slowly developing large laminated clot."

James, Henry (1843–1916).

In his last years the U.S. novelist depended heavily on nitroglycerin tablets for his heart condition, which was aggravated by the anesthetic used when most of his teeth were removed early in

1914. The grim days of the First World War depressed him, and the old bachelor anguished over the lists of bright young men who were killed in action. Many years previously he had bought the historic Lamb House in Rye, on the Sussex coast.

When, in 1915, he was forbidden to travel to that war-restricted zone because he was an alien he was greatly shocked, for he had lived in England nearly forty years. On 28 June Henry James became a British citizen; American reaction was sharp, many considering him disloyal. In October at Lamb House he burned vast quantities of papers and photographs. While there he had such difficulty in breathing that he had to sit up to sleep. The local doctor diagnosed intermittent tachycardia or auricular fibrillation, for which he prescribed digitalis; the diagnosis was later confirmed by Sir James Mackenzie, James' London physician.

In London he stayed at his sunny apartment overlooking the Thames, No. 21 Carlyle Mansions, Cheyne Walk, Chelsea. It was here that his maid, Minnie Kidd, found him lying on the floor of his bedroom on 2 December 1915. Minnie and his man, Burgess, managed with difficulty to get him back into his bed. A little later he calmly told his secretary, Miss Bosanquet, that he had had a stroke "in the most approved fashion." His sister-in-law Alice (Mrs. William James) cabled from America that she was sailing at once. The following day he had another stroke and the paralysis of his left side became more pronounced. His mind grew increasingly confused; he was never sure what town he was in, Edinburgh, Dublin or New York. The characters and situations in his books seemed more real than the life around him. One day he asked Burgess if his befuddled mind made people laugh. Alice James immediately replied, "Never, Henry...." to which he rejoined, "What is this voice from Boston, Massachusetts, breaking in with irrelevant remarks in my conversation with Burgess?" On New Year's Day, 1916, the Order of Merit, Britain's highest civilian award, was conferred upon the dying man.

James lingered on through January and into February; on the 23rd he told Alice that he would be "leaving" in two days. He lost consciousness on the 25th; on 28 February 1916 he began to sink rapidly. Two hours later, after three sighing breaths, he died. "He was gone," wrote Alice. "Not a shadow on his face, nor the contraction of a muscle." The funeral service was held in the Chelsea Old Church and he was cremated at Golders Green.

Alice smuggled the ashes into America and the urn was buried beside James' mother and sister in Cambridge, Mass. *See* L. Edel (1972).

James, Jesse (1847–1882).

The infamous U.S. bank robber and outlaw had been hunted in vain by the posses and the Pinkertons. Now a young fellow named Bob Ford, whose older brother Charlie was one of Jesse's band, decided the glory should be his. First he went to Kansas City and had himself appointed a detective so that the killing would be legal; then he had a secret meeting with the governor of Missouri to make sure he would get the offered reward. The Fords visited Jesse James, his wife Zerelda (Zee) and their two small children at 1318 Lafayette Street (known as the House on the Hill), St. Joseph, Mo., at the beginning of April 1882. The morning of Monday the 3rd was warm and sunny. "It's awfully hot today," grumbled Jesse, taking off his coat and vest. He picked up a feather duster and stood on a chair to dust the picture of a racehorse called Skyrocket, got down, unstrapped his holster and mounted the chair again. The watchful Fords quietly moved behind him. Bob drew his revolver and cocked it. The sound alerted Jesse and he started to turn around.

From about three feet away, Bob fired. Jesse, struck in the head, was knocked to the floor; the two men stood over him, guns in hand. Zee ran in. "What have you done?" she screamed. "Bob, have *you* done this?" "I swear to God I didn't," said Bob, and Charlie added, "A pistol went off accidentally." Zee held Jesse in her arms; he tried to speak but could not. The children came in and screamed. Zee ran for a cloth and tried to wipe away the blood but it was flowing too fast....

While the inquest was being held that afternoon, souvenir hunters ransacked the house. The body was turned over to the family and taken to the old James farm at Kearney, Mo., where it was buried seven feet down. Twenty years later James' mother gave orders for the body to be reburied in Mount Olivet Cemetery, Kearney. As the old coffin was lifted, it fell to pieces and the skull rolled out; behind the right ear was a hole almost as large as a quarter. Bob Ford, who seems to have received only about $1,200 of the $10,000 reward, was shot and killed on 8 July 1892 by Ed Kelly in Creede, Colo. Some years later, Charlie Ford shot himself through the heart. *See* H. Croy (1949).

The outlaw Jesse James, killed by treachery in Missouri. Photo by R. Uhlmann.

Jefferson, Thomas (1743–1826).

The third president of the U.S. (1801–1809) was tall (six feet two inches), slender and sinewy. His wide-ranging intelligence was matched by a fairly good health record, though he suffered several bouts of dysentery—probably of the bacillary type—and complained of severe headaches and "rheumatism" at various times. His attitudes toward medical practices are interesting. Jefferson disapproved of the indiscriminate bleeding of patients and the promiscuous use of calomel as a laxative. He had himself immunized against smallpox and also inoculated his family, friends and slaves against the disease. Once he stitched up a deep wound of the calf of a Negro boy. In France in 1786 he fractured his right wrist in a fall, which caused a permanent deformity, and in 1794 strained his back helping at the plow on his Monticello estate. Like Washington, he declined to serve a third term and retired to his Monticello mansion, which he had built years before on an eight-hundred-foot hill in Virginia.

Jefferson's last years were clouded by the threat of bankruptcy—caused by a friend's embezzling activities—and by severe rheumatic attacks. Dysentery and its effects hastened his death. After months of declining health, he fell into an intermittent stupor on 2 July 1826 at Monticello. On the evening of the following day he rallied to ask his doctor, "Is it the Fourth?" At four in the morning he spoke to the servants who, with his family, surrounded his bed. He sucked at a wet sponge offered him at eleven, and died a few minutes before 1:00 P.M. on the Fourth of July 1826 at the age of eighty-three years.

Joan of Arc (1412?–1431).

It is difficult to separate the story of Jeanne d'Arc, who was called Jeannette at home and whom we know as Saint Joan, from what Bernard Shaw called "the whitewash which disfigures her beyond recognition." Joan was born at Domrémy in the duchy of Bar. During the Hundred Years War, France was a kingdom of bits and pieces, occupied sporadically by the English, who had garrisons dotted here and there. The dauphin, later Charles VII (1403–1461), had become king in 1417, yet he was still unconsecrated in 1428 because Rheims, the traditional crowning site, was

Thomas Jefferson's self-designed tombstone in Charlottesville, Virginia.

LIBRARY OF CONGRESS

deep in English-held territory. The infant Henry VI of England was proclaimed sovereign of both countries in 1422 in Paris. Saints Michael, Catherine and Margaret, who had first appeared to Joan when she was thirteen, directed her in 1428 to go to Charles, four hundred miles away at Chinon. This she was finally able to accomplish, with the aid of kinsmen, in the spring of the following year. By then her dark hair was cropped above her ears and her stocky muscular figure was clothed in masculine garb. Persuading the hesitant king to accept her aid, by her presence and mystique she emboldened his army to lift the English siege of Orléans in May, and two months later was able to see him consecrated at Rheims.

On 22 May 1430, however, she was pulled off her horse, captured at Compiègne and sold to the English. Charles made no attempt to bargain for her release, and a few months later Joan leaped from a tower at Beaurevoir in a vain attempt to escape. She suffered a concussion, having possibly fallen into the moat of the fortress. The theologians at the University of Paris, English loyalists to a man, demanded she be tried by the Church without delay; the English "lent" her to the Bishop of Beauvais, Pierre Cauchon, and his fellow-judge, Jean Lemaitre, Vicar of the Inquisition at Rouen, on the understanding that, should she be left uncondemned by the powers spiritual, they would make short shrift of her.

At her long trial Joan made a spirited defense until the horror of what lay in wait for her sank in. The seventy counts against her were consolidated into a dozen serious charges, including the "abomination" of wearing a man's clothing, shedding human blood and her alleged "suicide" attempt at Beaurevoir. The court repeatedly urged her to disavow her voices, to admit they came to her, not from Heaven but from Hell; but this, above all, she could not do. When allegiance to the Church was demanded of her, she agreed, but insisted, "God must be served first." Though Joan was quite ill at this time, the threat of torture did not weaken her resolve. "Go ahead," she said, "but I shall recant anything that you force from me."

At Saint Ouen cemetery on 24 May, where the death sentence was read, she faltered at the sight of the awaiting funeral pyre, and uttered the required recantation formula. The lascivious spectators, robbed of the spectacle of the maiden's clothing being burned off her body, hurled stones at the dignitaries as she was led back to her cell at Bouvreil. Within a few days, forced to wear a dress and have her hair shaved off, still denied Mass and confronted with the certainty of life in prison, Joan—not yet twenty years old—found a new resolve. On Sunday, 27 May she was discovered to be again wearing masculine clothing, perhaps because she was trapped into doing so, perhaps because she felt safer in leggings. She withdrew her recantation and was immediately condemned.

At about 8:00 A.M., 30 May 1431, wearing a long shirt and, on her shorn head, a kind of miter bearing a list of her sins (Heretic, Idolator, Apostate, Relapser) she was handed over to the secular power with a recitation by Cauchon of the usual hypocritical formula, "begging it to be merciful...and to treat you kindly, this side of loss of life or limb," for the Church, although not above torture, did not officially countenance killing. Yet no lay court ever delivered sentence against Joan. Cutting short her last desperate *mea culpas*, the executioner hoisted her up the ladder to the top of the scaffold—a tall clump of masonry piled high with faggots and cordwood—and chained her arms behind her. She had begged for a crucifix and, when an English soldier handed her one hastily constructed from two twigs and thread, she had thrust it down against her bosom. Now, no longer able to touch it, she shouted for someone to hold up a cross. A monk ran to fetch one from a nearby chapel and held it high during her last moments. As the flames licked upward she coughed in the smoke and in the last seconds of consciousness she yelled at the top of her lungs: "Jesus!" When her clothing was entirely consumed, the burning wood was pulled back so that the crowd would be in no doubt that the sentence was carried out. "They saw her quite naked," said a contemporary account, "revealing all the secrets of a woman, and when this vision had lasted long enough, the executioner rekindled the fire high around the poor corpse." Her remains were thrown into the Seine.

In 1455, after a rehabilitation trial with carefully selected testimony, Joan was recertified as a good Catholic, thereby removing the shadow that lay over Charles VII's consecration. In 1909 she was declared "blessed" (her beatification had been delayed by political differences between Rome and France) and in 1920 she became Saint Joan. But she is not strictly a Catholic martyr, because it was a properly constituted court of that Church which put her to death.

Johnson, Samuel (1709–1784).

The English writer and conversationalist was a hodgepodge of disabilities. His stepdaughter described him as "very ill-favoured, tall and stout but stoops terribly.... His mouth is constantly opening and shutting...twirling his fingers and twisting his hands. His body is in constant agitation, see-sawing up and down; his feet are never a moment quiet and, in short, his whole person is in perpetual motion." "When he walked," wrote James Boswell, prince of biographers, "it was like the struggling gait of one in fetters; when he rode he had no command or direction of his horse, but was carried as if in a balloon." An obsessional habit caused him to touch certain posts as he walked along the street, turning back if he missed one.

The first child of a forty-year-old mother, Johnson was made to breathe only with difficulty. At two years of age, suffering from scrofula (tuberculous lymph glands of the neck), he was taken to be touched by Queen Anne. This malady, once the common sequel to drinking milk from infected cows, was called the King's Evil because it was believed to be curable only by the monarch. (Anne was the last British Sovereign to perform this ceremony.) The journey to London resulted only in a bad cold for Sam; the infected glands were incised a few years later, but not before he had lost the sight of his left eye and the use of his left ear. These defects, and the deficiency of his remaining eye, were of less moment to him than his fits of severe mental depression, of which he said, "I would consent to have a limb amputated to recover my spirits." The drinking of wine helped him, but he found it necessary to abandon alcohol for years at a time. "Abstinence is as easy for me, as temperance would be difficult." Asthma and dropsy troubled him in later life, both conditions reaching a crisis in February 1784 before a sudden urinary flow of twenty pints effected a dramatic recovery.

Having been confined to his London home at 8, Bolt Court, Fleet Street, for over four months, Johnson was glad of the chance to visit Oxford and his native Lichfield. Back home, the dropsy returned. One of his physicians, hoping the author was better, was greeted characteristically: "No, Sir; you cannot conceive with what acceleration I advance towards death." Friends sat by his bed continuously; one of them, placing a pillow for Dr. Johnson's greater comfort, was thanked: "That will do—all that

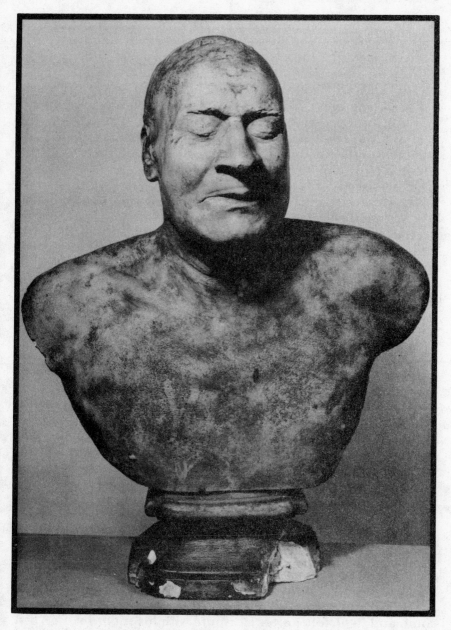

Samuel Johnson's bust incorporating his death mask.
NATIONAL PORTRAIT GALLERY, LONDON

a pillow can do." Begging to be told the truth, and learning that recovery was out of the question, he forswore further drugs, "for I have prayed that I may render up my soul to God unclouded." In bleeding him, his doctors were repeatedly urged to cut deeper. On 11 December he had his Negro servant, Francis Barber, bring him a lancet, with which, feeling himself inflated by fluid, he deepened the doctors' incisions. Later, while his friends watched in alarm, he snatched the scissors from a bed-side table and jabbed the points into both calves, thereby losing ten ounces of blood.

On his last day, 13 December 1784, a Miss Morris, daughter of a friend, called to ask for his blessing. "The Doctor turned on his bed," wrote Boswell, "and said, 'God bless you, my dear!' These were the last words he spoke. His difficulty of breathing increased till about seven o'clock in the evening, when Mr. Barber and Mrs. Desmoulins, who were sitting in the room, observing that the noise he made in breathing had ceased, went to the bed and found he was dead." But according to another biographer, Sir John Hawkins, Johnson's last words were a murmured "Jam moriturus" ("I am dying now").

At autopsy, deemed necessary to dispel rumors of suicide, Johnson's lungs bore signs of emphysema; his heart was "exceedingly large and strong," with the valves of the aorta beginning to ossify; the gallbladder yielded a stone "the size of a common gooseberry"; the pancreas was remarkably enlarged, and the right kidney almost entirely destroyed. Death was evidently caused, then, by high blood pressure and renal disease (chronic interstitial nephritis). Dr. Johnson was buried in Westminster Abbey beside his old Lichfield friend, the actor David Garrick.

Jones, John Paul (1747–1792).

The Scottish-born U.S. naval officer, foremost sea captain of the American Revolution, served in Catherine the Great's Black Sea fleet for several months of 1788 when, with the U.S. at peace, his adopted country no longer needed him. He was relieved of command in October after a dispute with his superior. In April 1789 he was falsely accused of raping a young girl in St. Petersburg; when he returned to Paris in 1790 he was an embittered man in physical decline. He died in his apartment on the

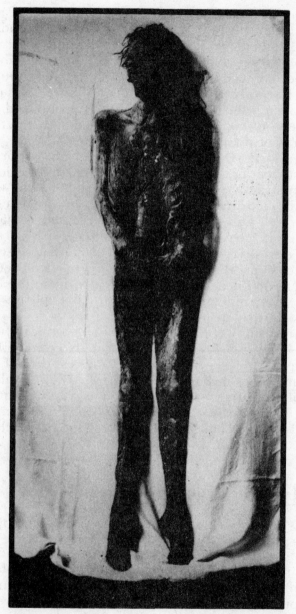

The body of John Paul Jones, exhumed 113 years after his burial in Paris.

U.S. NATIONAL ARCHIVES

third floor of No. 52 (now No. 19) rue de Tournon, Paris, late on 18 July 1792. For two months he had been jaundiced, with dropsy extending ultimately from his legs into his abdomen. It was bronchial pneumonia that finished him off; he had walked to his bed, lay face down with his feet touching the floor and expired. His body, wrapped in a winding sheet, was placed in a leaden coffin, which was then filled with alcohol and sealed. He was buried on the 20th in the cemetery designated for foreign Protestants near the great Hôpital St. Louis.

In 1899, Gen. Horace Porter, the U.S. Ambassador to France, began a search for the hero's grave, by that time hidden by sheds and other structures. Shafts were sunk in 1905 and lateral tunnels made. The third leaden coffin to be opened proved to contain a well-preserved body easily identified as that of Jones. An autopsy in Paris revealed glomerular nephritis in addition to the expected bronchial pneumonia. P.M. Dale, discussing the report, considers the dead man's dropsy to have been "due to a decompensated heart which had resulted from the high blood pressure incidental to chronic glomerular nephritis. Clinically, he died a cardiac death."

Jones' remains were carried across the Atlantic in July 1905 by a cruiser, the U.S.S. *Brooklyn*, and escorted to Annapolis by seven battleships. For seven years, while Congress dallied, the coffin rested on trestles in Bancroft Hall at the U.S. Naval Academy. Not until 26 January 1913, after public resentment had been aroused, did John Paul Jones finally come to rest in a specially designed tomb below the academy chapel. *See* S.E. Morison (1959).

Joplin, Janis (1943–1970).

Janis was an overweight, unhappy youngster, who by the 1960s was expressing her resentment in wild living, drink and drugs. Though she made it big as a rock singer, she found it hard to break completely from drugs. On the afternoon of 3 October 1970 someone had apparently come by her room in the Landmark Hotel, Los Angeles, and left her a supply of heroin that was probably unusually pure. Just after midnight on 4 October she went to her room and picked up her needle. Her biographer, Myra Friedman (1973), writes: "The rush could only have been jolting as she sent the smack through her vein with the jab of that needle."

Janis then walked into the hotel lobby and asked the clerk to change a five-dollar bill. Going back to her room, she closed the door, walked a step or two and fell heavily, cutting her lip. The autopsy report stated that Joplin had died of an accidental overdose of heroin. After a service at Westwood Village Mortuary, Los Angeles County, she was cremated and her ashes scattered by air along the coastline of Marin County, Cal.

Josephine (1763–1814).

The future empress of France and the Viscount Alexandre Beauharnais were married in December 1779; they had two children, Eugène and Hortense. Alexandre was guillotined after the fall of Robespierre. On 9 March 1796 Josephine and Napoleon were married by civil law; nearly nine years later a religious wedding took place at Pope Pius VII's insistence. However, with the help of a clever lawyer, Napoleon succeeded in divorcing Josephine in 1809 when he wanted an heir.

Josephine retired to her estate, Malmaison, near Paris. A chill caught on 14 May 1814 grew steadily worse, though she continued to receive guests. Her throat was painful and plasters were applied. She brooded over the news that the body of Hortense's little son had been exhumed from Notre Dame and buried in a parish cemetery. "They dare interfere with graves," she moaned; "it is just like the Revolution." When on 27 May Sir James Wylie, surgeon to the czar, visited Malmaison to announce that his employer would visit the next day, he was gravely concerned by Josephine's condition and told Hortense, "I think her Majesty is very ill." Specialists summoned by Hortense diagnosed a purulent sore throat; despite their best efforts they could not save her. During her last delirious night Josephine murmured, "Bonaparte...the island of Elba...the King of Rome." These were her last words, for though she later held out her arms to her children she was not able to speak.

Josephine died at about noon on 29 May 1814. An autopsy found her death to have been caused by pneumonia and a "gangrenous sore throat." (H. Cole in his 1962 biography suggests she may have had diphtheria.) Her heart and other organs, in a silver-gilt box, preceded the coffin as it was taken from Malmaison for burial in the church at Rueil.

Joyce, James (1882–1941).

The Irish novelist had undergone about twenty-five ophthalmic operations by 1930; for much of his career, although he wrote in large script, he was often unable to read the result. His father had contracted syphilis while a medical student and treated it inadequately with a topical application of phenol; this disease, if passed on to James, could explain his bad eyes and some of his other health problems. In the summer of 1940 Joyce was living near Vichy when the Germans invaded France. Many bureaucratic obstacles had to be surmounted before he was permitted to travel to Switzerland. At last, after receiving the endorsement of the Swiss Society of Authors and a financial guarantee from friends, Joyce, his wife Nora Barnacle, his mentally ill daughter Lucia, his son George and his eight-year-old grandson Stephen were able to travel by train across the occupied zone in mid-December. For lack of funds to pay the duty, the family had to abandon the boy's bicycle at the border. Lucia was placed in a cheap mental home and the others took two rooms at the Hotel Delphin, Zurich, the city in which Joyce's masterpiece *Ulysses* had been written during the previous World War.

A happy Christmas was spent with friends, but on 10 January 1941, after returning home from an art show, Joyce was taken ill with stomach cramps. At 2:00 A.M. a local physician gave him morphine and at daybreak he was taken by ambulance to the Red Cross Hospital. Stephen watched in awe as his grandfather, "writhing like a fish" despite the restraining straps, was carried in on a stretcher. X-rays indicated a perforated duodenal ulcer, and an immediate operation was urged on the reluctant patient.

"Is it cancer?" he asked. "No," said George. "You've never lied to me; tell me the truth now," Joyce persisted. "It is not cancer." "All right then," said Joyce, satisfied. But a moment later, "How are you going to pay for this?" "Never mind," said his son, "we'll manage somehow or other." After surgery the patient progressed well for a short time, but the next day, Sunday the 12th, he needed blood. Two Swiss soldiers from Neuchâtel were the donors. "A good omen," Joyce called this. "I like Neuchâtel wine." He sank into a coma on Sunday afternoon, coming around at 1:00 A.M. to ask for his wife and son, who had been urged to go home. At 2:15 A.M. on 13 January 1941, before they could arrive, he died of peritonitis.

Joyce, who years earlier had renounced Catholicism along with his allegiance to his native country, was buried at Fluntern Cemetery, Zurich, after a nonreligious ceremony at which a tenor sang a Monteverdi aria. A priest had offered to conduct a Mass, but "I couldn't do that to him," said Nora. The zoo adjoining the cemetery had always reminded the dead man of the one in Phoenix Park, Dublin. Until her own death ten years later, Nora would take visitors up the hill to see the grave, which was at first signified by a simple flat marker bearing his name and dates. Years later the Swiss erected a statue in the writer's honor. "He was awfully fond of the lions," Nora would recall. "I like to think of him lying there and listening to them roar." *See* R. Ellmann (1959).

Kafka, Franz (1883–1924).

The Prague-born Jewish writer's cultural environment was entirely German until late in his life. He was a slightly built man of great sensitivity and charm whose every personal relationship was neurotically disturbed: with his parents; with Felice Bauer, to whom he was twice engaged before the final rupture in 1917, the year his tuberculosis was diagnosed; and with other women, one of whom made him a father, though he never knew it. His last months were spent with Dora Dymant, a young Hassidic woman he met in July 1923. Later that year they were living in Berlin and studying Hebrew together. That winter, when ruinous inflation caused widespread poverty, Kafka would join the breadlines for no better reason than his sympathy for those he met there. By the end of the year he was suffering frequent attacks of the fever characteristic of his disease. Though his time with Dora, away from his parents, was one of great spiritual tranquillity, his physical deterioration accelerated.

Kafka was brought back to Prague in March 1924 and the following month, at a Vienna clinic, tuberculosis of the larynx was diagnosed. His last weeks, when he was unable to drink and could speak only in a whisper, were spent in a pleasant sanatorium room, full of flowers, at Kierling, just north of Vienna. His friend Dr. Robert Klopstock gave up his own work in order to help Dora nurse him. Until a few hours before his death Kafka worked on the proofs of his short story collection, *A Hunger Artist*, and showed his customary consideration for others.

But he became restless and impatient on the day of his death, 3 June 1924. Tearing off his ice pack and throwing it on the floor, he muttered, "Don't torture me any more; why prolong the agony?" Asking for increasing doses of morphine, he told Klopstock, "Kill me, or else you are a murderer." He was given Palopon (a mixture of opium alkaloids) and sank into a final stupor. His last words showed a return of selflessness. Imagining his sister, not Klopstock, to be holding his hand, and afraid of infecting her, he whispered, "Go away, Elli; not so near, not so near." His body was taken to Prague and buried in the Jewish cemetery at Straschnitz on 11 June 1924.

Karloff, Boris (1887–1969).

The famous monster was born an ordinary, rather endearing little boy named William Henry Pratt, the youngest of nine children in Dulwich, England. Though he had been rejected when he volunteered for service in the British Army in 1914 because of a heart condition (undoubtedly a mistake), his health was extremely good. His only problem was that the effort of acting encased in the weighty disguise of Frankenstein's Monster aggravated a slight back complaint and made spinal fusion necessary. Karloff's fifth wife Evie gave him loving encouragement during his last years, enabling him, as was his wish, to work to the last, even though he was far from well and usually in pain. His old back injury necessitated a leg brace, his severe arthritis frequently confined him to a wheelchair and emphysema, which left him with only part of a single lung, made it necessary for an oxygen cylinder to be kept near him at all times. Though not his final film, *Targets*, shot in 1967 when he was eighty, is described by Paul Jenson in his 1974 book on Karloff as the aesthetic climax of the actor's career.

Karloff caught a chill in Kennedy Airport while waiting for a flight to England. On his arrival he was taken to King Edward

VII Hospital at Midhurst near London. He was there for two months suffering from arthritis, emphysema and a heart condition. Just before he died he received a telephone call from his agent, Arthur Kennard, saying that Federico Fellini wanted him for a film. "It really set me up," wrote Boris in a note to Kennard. He died on 2 February 1969 and was cremated after a private service. Evie arranged for a commemorative plaque to be placed in St. Paul's Covent Garden, London, "the Actor's Church."

Kaufman, George S. (1889–1961).

The U.S. playwright was a hypochondriac. Alexander Woollcott claimed that he swooned at the sight of a stethoscope, an exaggeration perhaps, but Kaufman was afraid of every illness, physical and mental, and dreaded death night and day. He hated to touch people, yet he had dozens of affairs. He was afraid there might be germs on door handles, and when it was suggested that he could turn the handle through his coat pocket he followed that practice for the rest of his life. He was always under the care of doctors and specialists and demanded their full attention. He was furious with his physician, Dr. Greenspan, when he came to see him dressed in tennis whites. It was unthinkable that the doctor should be playing tennis while he, George S. Kaufman, might be stricken with a serious illness. He tested a new doctor by demanding his right to smoke, even though he was a nonsmoker, and was pleased by the doctor's adamant refusal. His wife Beatrice's sudden death from a cerebral hemorrhage on 6 October 1945 was a devastating blow to Kaufman and it was two years before he could resume his old pace.

Kaufman's first stroke occurred fourteen months after his marriage, on 26 May 1949, to Leueen McGrath. After several weeks in New York City's Mount Sinai Hospital he was discharged, but he had lost the sight of his left eye and his left arm and leg were also affected. He visited a psychiatrist for a while but left her because "she's asking too damn many personal questions." In his mid-sixties he tolerated three prostate operations well, but in 1958 he collapsed in the Royale Theater, New York, and a few months later he had a dizzy spell in the Oak Room of the Plaza Hotel; arteriosclerosis was causing a series of small strokes. Although a male nurse was hired to take care of him, Kaufman passed out one night in the bathroom and his arm became wedged between a hot radiator and the wall. It was two hours before he was found. The resulting burns were not severe but the traumatic experience caused him to become permanently bedridden.

One afternoon Kaufman said in a quiet voice to his daughter Anne, "I'm not afraid anymore; I love Leueen so much I'm not afraid anymore." On Friday morning, 2 June 1961, at his home at 1035 Park Avenue, New York, Kaufman sighed two deep sighs and was gone. After a short service at the Campbell Funeral Chapel in Manhattan, he was buried in an undisclosed cemetery.

Keats, John (1795–1821).

When the English poet discovered blood in his mouth on 3 February 1820, he remarked, "I know the color...; that drop of blood is my death-warrant." On 15 November Keats and a friend, Joseph Severn, went to Rome and settled in lodgings in the Piazza di Spagna in what is now the Keats-Shelley Memorial house. They were desperate for money and Keats was alarmed and depressed by the course of his illness. On 10 December he had a severe hemorrhage and his physician, Dr. Clark, bled him. He continued to cough up blood: he was in misery, suffering dreadfully and longing to die. For four days in February 1821 he hovered between life and death. At four o'clock on the fifth day Dr. Clark told him the end was near. Severn lifted Keats up in his arms to try to ease his labored breathing; the poet was covered with perspiration and in great distress but he murmured to his friend, "I am dying—I shall die easy—don't be frightened—be firm and thank God it has come." He died at 11:00 P.M. on 23 February 1821. It was a miracle he had lived as long as he did, because an autopsy revealed that little or no healthy lung tissue remained. He was only twenty-five years old. Keats was buried before daybreak on 26 February in the Protestant cemetery in Rome.

Kennedy, John Fitzgerald (1917–1963).

The thirty-fifth president of the U.S. was in pain for half his life.

Though his medical records were still unavailable when Joan and Clay Blair wrote *The Search for J.F.K.* (1976), they were able to establish that his unstable back dated from birth, not from a football injury or war service. In 1947 he collapsed in London with Addison's disease, caused by atrophy of the adrenal glands. The illness was disguised from the public as a recurrence of malaria. In later years Kennedy would admit to no more than a partial adrenal insufficiency, but some of his physicians (and his brother-in-law Sargent Shriver) now admit the facts. Until 1930 the disease had a mortality rate of 90 percent, and even in 1947, with regular administration of steroids to make up the hormonal deficiency, stress of any kind had to be avoided. Hence, the political consequences of disclosure were considered very serious.

On 22 November 1963 Kennedy was assassinated by Lee Harvey Oswald (q.v.) while riding through Dallas, Texas, in a limousine that also carried Texas Governor John B. Connally and the wives of the two men. At 12:30 P.M. (C.S.T.) shots were heard as the motorcade drove southwest past Dealey Plaza along Elm Street toward a railroad underpass. The president was shot twice from behind, first by a bullet that passed through his neck, grazing the knot of his necktie as it emerged, second by a bullet that blasted away much of the right rear part of his brain. Connally, sitting in front of Kennedy and apparently turned somewhat to the right, was wounded by a bullet that passed from behind through his chest from right to left, then through his right wrist, and finally stopped after penetrating his left thigh. The limousine speeded up and raced to Parkland Memorial Hospital where, after a tracheotomy that widened the neck wound, the president was given the Last Rights of the Church and pronounced dead at 1:00 P.M.

Because of echoing, there was great confusion regarding the origin and number of the shots, but a few onlookers had observed a rifle being fired from a southeast corner window of the sixth floor of the Texas School Book Depository building, which was behind the presidential limousine at a range of about 200 feet. Oswald, a twenty-four-year-old Depository employee and ardent supporter of Fidel Castro, Marxist president of Cuba, left the building within three minutes of the shooting and by bus and taxi reached his lodging at 1026 North Beckley Avenue in the Oak Cliff section of the city. He stayed there just long enough to pick up a revolver and don a zippered jacket. At 1:15 P.M. he was challenged by a police patrolman, J.D. Tippit, who was driving slowly and watching out for a man of Oswald's description. When the police officer left his car to question him, Oswald fired repeatedly; Tippit, shot four times, died instantly. A little later a shoe store manager, observing Oswald behaving suspiciously, followed him to the Texas Theatre, a cinema on West Jefferson, and had the cashier call the police. The assassin tried to draw his revolver as, with the house lights turned up at 1:50 P.M., he was overpowered and arrested. Two days later he was shot and killed by Jack Ruby.

A commission headed by the Chief Justice of the Supreme Court, Earl Warren, heard the testimony of more than five hundred witnesses; thousands more were interviewed (25,000 by the FBI alone) or gave affidavits. The commission reported in September 1964 that Oswald, firing an Italian-made Mannlicher Carcano 6.5 mm rifle, was the sole assassin of the president; that probably three shots were fired and that there was "very persuasive evidence" that the bullet which exited from Kennedy's neck went on to wound Connally; that Oswald also murdered Tippit; and that there was no evidence of a conspiracy or that the assassin was employed or influenced by any domestic or foreign organization, though it was impossible to prove this to a certainty. No definite conclusions were reached regarding Oswald's motives.

The commission's findings have been criticized in numerous books and articles, and many discrepancies discovered or alleged in the twenty-seven volumes of published evidence and additional material lodged in the National Archives. The critics generally attack defenders of the commission, including the *New York Times*, Time Inc., and CBS Television News; seldom do they challenge the overwhelming physical evidence (including palm prints) linking Oswald with the rifle found in the Depository building, or the rifle and revolver with the bullets and spent cartridges. Further, they seem unable to suggest a coherent alternative scenario for the events of 22 November 1963. The commission's work is not above criticism; for political reasons it was forced to conclude its activities in a hurry and, among other conclusions, those relating to the order and destination of the rifle shots are not convincing. In particular, it is still possible that Oswald may be found to have had co-conspirators. Revelations that the CIA made several attempts to kill Castro after he came to power in 1959 have made this more likely. On the other hand, 80,000 additional pages of FBI investigations released in 1977 have shown the great lengths to which the Bureau went in order to track down even trivial leads of this kind.

Many doubters of the Warren Commission report evidently have a subconscious need to believe the Dallas tragedy had a deep political significance. But the truth may well lie in the opposite direction. Oswald's motives, generally linked to his Marxist leanings and Castro sympathies, may have had a more personal and sordid basis. In her 1977 book, *Marina and Lee*, P.J. McMillan describes Mrs. Oswald as taunting her husband with his sexual inadequacies and arousing his jealousy by constantly talking of the president's attractiveness. "Would his bad back hinder him?" she would wonder in speculating about his prowess as a lover. Marina had bought a photograph of Kennedy, who resembled a former beau of hers in Russia, and admired it quite as much as Oswald admired his of Castro.

In December 1978 a House subcommittee accepted the testimony of acoustics experts that a second gunman probably fired a second shot, which evidently missed Kennedy, from the "grassy knoll" to the right front of the presidential limousine. Further evidence of any conspiracy was still lacking.

On 24 November 1963 President Kennedy's body was carried to the Capitol to lie in state. The following day, after a funeral service conducted by Richard Cardinal Cushing at St. Matthew's Cathedral, the president was buried in Arlington National Cemetery and his widow, Jacqueline, lighted an eternal flame at the grave.

Kennedy, Robert Francis
(1925–1968).

The younger brother of the assassinated U.S. president announced his candidacy for the same office in March 1968. After leading in the primary elections in Indiana and Nebraska, he lost to another senator, Eugene McCarthy, in Oregon. This made the result in California on 4 June especially crucial to his chances. A computer failure delayed the Los Angeles tally until long after television audiences in the east had retired to bed, but at midnight, Pacific time, Kennedy was able to come from his suite to the Embassy Room of the Ambassador Hotel, Los Angeles, and deliver a victory speech to a large crowd of his supporters. A few moments after he finished, at 12:15 A.M. on 5 June 1968, he was being escorted through a hotel pantry, shaking hands as he went, when he was shot three times and fell to the floor, bleeding from the head.

The assassin was a slightly built twenty-four-year-old Arab native of Jerusalem, Sirhan Bishara Sirhan, who had come to the United States in 1957 and who was later to give as his motive for the crime Kennedy's advocacy of weapons for Israel. Sirhan was wrestled to the floor and his gun, an 8-shot .22-caliber Iver-Johnson revolver, taken from him with difficulty. In addition to the mortally wounded senator, five others were hit by the eight bullets; all but Kennedy recovered.

The fatal shot entered behind Kennedy's right ear and fragmented in his brain; a second slug traveled forward through his right shoulder and is believed to have come to rest in the ceiling space (it was the only bullet not recovered); a third shot entered the same shoulder and traveled along the muscles to lodge in the base of the neck; a fourth shot passed through the shoulder pad of Kennedy's jacket without touching his body and struck another victim in the forehead. After a three-hour operation, Robert Kennedy died at 1:44 A.M. on 6 June 1968 at Good Samaritan Hospital, Los Angeles, having survived a little over twenty-four hours. He lay in state in St. Patrick's Cathedral, New York, where a burial service was conducted on 8 June; later the same day his body was taken by funeral train to Washington, D.C., and buried by candlelight at 10:30 P.M. near the grave of his brother John in Arlington National Cemetery.

Sirhan was found guilty of first-degree murder on 17 April 1969 and sentenced to death six days later; he was taken to San Quentin Prison to join over eighty others on death row. Though there were about a hundred witnesses to the assassination, doubts were raised long after the trial regarding a possible second assassin. A court-appointed panel of seven experts who studied the ballistics evidence reported in October 1975 that they could find no evidence of a second gun, but an article by A.K. Lowenstein (*Saturday Review*, 19 February 1977) indicates that the controversy continues.

Kern, Jerome (1885–1945).

Late in 1945 the U.S. composer, Jerome Kern, planned a trip to New York to coproduce, with Oscar Hammerstein II, a resplendent revival of *Show Boat*. En route to the train for New York, he realized he had forgotten to play a few bars from "Ol' Man River"—his good luck token—before he left the house. He and his wife Eva settled into the St. Regis Hotel, New York, on 2 November 1945. The following morning, after breakfast, he told his wife he had some chores to attend to. About noon he was outside the American Bible Society building at 57th Street and Park Avenue when he suddenly collapsed. He was carried gently inside the building and placed on a couch. He had had a stroke and was unconscious. A policeman identified Kern from his wallet, but in spite of that an ambulance took him to Welfare Island where he was put in a public ward with about fifty mental patients and alcoholic derelicts. Fortunately, someone noticed the ASCAP card in his wallet and eventually Hammerstein and Eva were notified.

Kern's condition was so critical that it was not possible to remove him from Welfare Island until 7 November, when he was transferred to Doctors Hospital. His wife, his daughter Betty and the Hammersteins took rooms there to be near him. Kern, who was in an oxygen tent, never regained consciousness, and on the 10th his condition deteriorated alarmingly. When he finally died at 1:10 P.M. on 11 November 1945, a cold wet day, only Oscar Hammerstein was with him. It was Hammerstein who delivered the eulogy at the funeral service in Ferncliff Cemetery Chapel, Ardsley, N.Y., after which Kern's ashes were interred in the Ferncliff Crematory.

King, Martin Luther, Jr. (1929–1968).

The black civil rights leader had reached the high point of his career at the time he delivered his "I have a dream" speech in Washington in 1963. By March 1968, when he came to Memphis, Tenn., to lead a peaceful march in support of striking sanitation workers, his control of increasingly fractious demonstrators was becoming uncertain, and he withdrew, shaken and unnerved, after violent confrontations between black teenagers and police in which sixty people were injured and one youth was killed. He returned to the troubled city on 3 April, staying at the Lorraine Motel, 406 Mulberry Street, with other members of his Southern Christian Leadership Conference. His room, Number 306, faced the rear of a cheap rooming house at 422½ South Main Street, about two hundred feet away. On the evening before his death he told supporters at the Mason Street Temple he had been "to the mountaintop. Like anybody else, I would like to live a long life. But I'm not concerned with that. I see the Promised Land. I may not get there with you, but mine eyes have seen the glory...." Despite his words, those around him sensed that he was obsessed by thoughts of imminent death.

As the sun set on the chilly evening of 4 April, several black ministers were passing in and out of Number 306, Ralph Abernathy, Hosea Williams, Jesse Jackson and Andrew Young among them. They were due to leave in a few minutes for dinner at a local preacher's house. Jackson walked down the steps from the balcony to join Ben Branch, a musician from Chicago. King, who had just finished shaving, emerged and walked over to the railing. "Ben," he shouted down, "make sure you play 'Precious Lord, Take My Hand.' Play it real pretty...for me." There was a loud crack, and King was thrown backwards, flat on his back, dead. It was 6:01 P.M. A heavy bullet had struck half an inch below the right side of the lower lip, shattering his jaw and continuing downward to the left, through the trachea and into the spine.

James Earl Ray, a small-time crook and escaped convict who had registered at the rooming house that afternoon under the name John Willard, hastily unlocked the bathroom door and retreated to his room, carrying his big 30.06-caliber Remington rifle. A minute later he was hurrying along the street; he dropped the hunting rifle (in a cardboard case) and a bag of personal effects in the doorway of a store before taking off in his white 1966 Mustang automobile. Ray returned to his room in Atlanta early the next morning before abandoning the car and making his escape by bus to Detroit, by cab across the Canadian border and by rail to Toronto. A travel agent obtained a Canadian passport for him; after flying to London and on to Lisbon in the hope of reaching a safe African country, he returned to Britain because of visa problems and a shortage of funds. He was arrested at Heathrow Airport on 8 June.

At his trial in Memphis Ray denied prior knowledge of the assassination. On instructions from a mysterious "Raoul," he said, he had waited in his car outside the rooming house; when he heard the shot, he decided to flee. His story was proved false by his finger and palm prints, found on the rifle and other abandoned articles, and on the windowsills of his room and the bathroom. Jim Bishop, a biographer of King, could find no trace of Raoul. W.B. Huie, who paid Ray large sums for his story, received remarkably accurate accounts of his travels to Canada, Alabama, Mexico, Los Angeles and New Orleans following his escape from the Missouri State Prison in April 1967. But Ray's account of his last days before the crime was evasive and erroneous; in particular, Huie proved the motel where Ray said he met Raoul shortly before the assassination to be nonexistent. Huie believes Ray, acting alone, hoped to become a successful, big-time criminal, one of what Ray himself called the FBI's "Top Ten."

Yet some questions remain: there were signs that someone else had been in Ray's car before it was abandoned and it is almost certain he was counseled on which type of rifle to buy. On 10 March 1969, to avoid the electric chair, he pleaded guilty and was sentenced to ninety-nine years' imprisonment. Immediately afterward, claiming undue pressure from his attorney, he demanded a new trial, but this was denied.

A House subcommittee in 1979 concluded that Ray had conspired with other family members. Martin Luther King, Jr., was pronounced dead at St. Joseph's Hospital, Memphis, and an autopsy was performed at John Gaston Hospital in the same city. On 9 April tens of thousands of mourners, black and white, followed King's coffin, borne on a farm wagon, from the Ebenezer Baptist Church in Atlanta, where the funeral service was held, to his grave in Southview Cemetery. His remains were later reinterred in Ebenezer Baptist Churchyard on Auburn Avenue, N.E. The inscription on the tombstone is derived from King's own words: FREE AT LAST, FREE AT LAST, THANK GOD ALMIGHTY I'M FREE AT LAST.

Lanza, Mario (1921–1959).

The Philadelphia-born tenor with the superb natural voice and amazing breath control loved success, but hated the discipline necessary to ensure it; "I feel like a guy in stir," he would protest. He loved the acclaim of rapturous audiences but would cancel appearances at short notice (of twenty-seven engagements in the spring of 1949, he honored only twelve). His gargantuan appetite (twenty eggs for breakfast) would send his weight soaring to 250 pounds; this would be followed by inevitable weeks of crash dieting and ill humor. Though warned that alcohol would kill him, he continually drank himself into violent fits. Within two years he nearly wrecked two houses and was being sued for over fifty thousand dollars.

Lanza was invited to London to sing at a Command Performance before the queen on 18 November 1957. He was thrilled to be met at Victoria Station on the 14th by a screaming throng carrying "Welcome Mario" banners. On reaching his suite at the Dorchester Hotel he had a glass of champagne, then another .... For three days he drank steadily; his friend and accompanist Constantine Callinicos found him surrounded by empty champagne magnums, red-faced, puffy and raspy-voiced. Fortunately, he fell asleep at 2:00 P.M. on Sunday the 17th and was able to sing the next evening; he was not at his best, but the audience responded with thunderous applause.

In July 1959 Mario, singing magnificently, began a recording session for RCA in Rome. In August he began drinking heavily again and the recording of *Desert Song* was suspended. Shortly afterward he fell on the marble walk outside his rented villa in Rome and lay all night unconscious in the rain. Desperately ill with pneumonia, he was rushed to the Valle Giulia Hospital. During his slow recovery he made promises to halt his drinking and overeating, to curb his temper and to complete the recording of *Desert Song*. On the 25th he was readmitted to the hospital suffering from intense pains on the left side of his chest and a high fever. Doctors found hypertensive heart disease with arteriosclerosis. He ranted and raged when told he must live more moderately and threatened to chase the doctor from the room. Lonely and afraid, he wanted to go home, but was strongly advised against it.

On the morning of 7 October 1959 Lanza talked on the phone to his wife Betty, then moved from his bed toward the couch to read the newspapers. Suddenly he was doubled over with pain. As a nurse rushed to help him he whispered, "I love you, Betty...Betty...." A few minutes later, as a physician attempted resuscitation, Lanza died. One thousand five hundred people attended the Requiem Mass at the Blessed Sacrament Church in Hollywood. Zsa Zsa Gabor accompanied Betty Lanza to the church. Mario was buried at Calvary Mausoleum, Los Angeles. *See* C. Callinicos (1960).

Laughton, Charles (1899–1962).

That the English-born U.S. stage and screen actor was homosexual came as a severe shock to Elsa Lanchester two years after their wedding in 1929. A badly shaken Charles made the confession after they had come upon a young man, to whom he had promised money, being picked up by the police for loitering outside their London flat in Percy Street and when a courtroom scandal seemed inevitable. Their sexual life soon withered away, but their marriage, despite some estrangement after 1949, endured as a strong emotional and intellectual bond for thirty-three years, until Charles's death.

The year 1960 saw Laughton's health decline alarmingly. He spent several weeks in Cedars of Lebanon Hospital, Los Angeles, with a severe gallbladder condition; in May he suffered a heart attack. Late in the year Elsa was forced to slap his face to bring him out of an hysterical, suicidal mood. Making his last movie, *Advise and Consent*, in steamy Washington was an enervating ordeal. In January 1962 Laughton set off on a final series of dramatic readings with his road manager Bob Halter and his lover Bruce Ashe, a young photographer's model whom he had met in London three years earlier. He slipped and fell in a bathtub in Flint, Michigan, and fractured his collarbone. Under treatment in New York, he was found to have bone cancer. Elsa, Bruce, Bob and a male nurse took him home, four seats on the plane being made up as a bed for him.

Laughton died on the night of 15 December 1962 in the schoolroom of their house on North Curson Avenue in Hollywood, the room in which, after they had moved there in 1949, he taught his craft to a group of young actors. His death was lingering, prolonged by the latest advances in chemotherapy. His brother Tom, visiting from England, took advantage of Elsa's absence to invite a priest to give him Extreme Unction. But the funeral service at Forest Lawn Memorial Park was conducted by the nondenominational chaplain from the University of Southern California. The eulogy was read by Christopher Isherwood. *See* C. Higham (1976).

Lawrence, D.H. *(David Herbert Lawrence)* (1885–1930).

The English author of *Lady Chatterley's Lover* was frail from birth and had twice nearly died of pneumonia. In Mexico in 1925 he was told he had tuberculosis and could not live long. He refused to accept this, but his wife, Frieda, lived with the fear of his death. In July 1927, at the Villa Mirenda in Tuscany, Lawrence had the first of what he chose to refer to as "bronchial hemorrhages." For the next two years the thin, red-bearded writer and his wife searched for a climate that would suit him. In October 1929 they rented the Villa Beau Soleil in Bandol on the French Riviera. Their house had large balcony windows overlooking the sea, and the plants in his room bloomed so luxuriously that Frieda would say, "Why, oh why, can't you flourish like those?"

Lawrence's nights were difficult; he told his wife when she bade him goodnight, "Now I shall have to fight several battles of Waterloo before the morning." The worst time was just before dawn when he coughed painfully, but after the sun rose he was glad another day had been given to him. His courage never faltered. An English physician, Dr. Morland, who thought that Lawrence had probably had pulmonary tuberculosis for ten or fifteen years and found him very ill and extremely emaciated, felt that Bandol was too exposed for him; he suggested that he go into a small sanatorium, Ad Astra, in Vence, an ancient little town a thousand feet up in the Maritime Alps. The five-hour journey by car and train on 6 February 1930 was very difficult for the sick man, but once he arrived he began to feel better. He enjoyed sitting out on his sunny balcony and wrote to Mrs. Aldous Huxley, "The mimosa is all out...and the almond blossom is very lovely."

A few weeks after his arrival Lawrence had an attack of pleurisy, for which he blamed the sanatorium, and insisted on being moved to the Villa Robermond (later the Villa Aurella), which Frieda had rented. Lawrence was so weak that he allowed his wife to put on his shoes. The short taxi drive to the villa on 1

The shrine of D.H. Lawrence and the grave of his wife Frieda, in Taos, New Mexico.

UNIVERSITY OF NEW MEXICO

March 1930 exhausted him. The following day, toward evening, he felt wretched. Seeing his tormented face Frieda began to cry. Aldous Huxley, who had come up from Cannes with his wife, went out to find a doctor to give Lawrence the morphine he was demanding. After the injection he grew calmer and murmured, "If only I could sweat I would be better." His breathing steadied for a time. Frieda held his left ankle. "It felt so full of life," she recalled later. "All my days I shall hold his ankle in my hand."

Toward 10:00 P.M. Lawrence's breathing became spasmodic and his chest heaved as he struggled for air. Then suddenly, like the snapping of a thread, he was gone. He was buried two days later, on 4 March 1930, in the small graveyard at Vence. His plain oak coffin, covered with golden mimosa, was interred without ritual or speeches. "Goodbye, Lorenzo," said Frieda as the earth was shoveled into the grave. Two young Italians were commissioned to make a mosaic phoenix for the headstone in pebbles of rose, white and gray. Lawrence, who had longed so often to return to New Mexico, where he had once been happy, was exhumed and cremated in 1935, and Frieda built the Lawrence Memorial Chapel for his ashes on a hill above her home, the Kiowa Ranch in Taos. Frieda herself, who died in August 1956, lies by the chapel door. The phoenix has an honored place in Lawrence's native town, Eastwood, Nottinghamshire.

Lawrence, Thomas Edward
(1888–1935).

The English adventurer and author was dubbed "Lawrence of Arabia" for his role, now generally regarded as exaggerated, in advising the Arabs in their revolt against the Turks. As a deliberate act of self-effacement after World War I Lawrence abdicated from all activities of national importance and served under assumed names in the ranks of the Royal Air Force and Army Tank Corps. In November 1917 he had been taken prisoner by the Turkish commander at Der'ā, Syria, and subjected to whipping and homosexual assault; his shame was deepened by the recognition of his own sexual fulfillment in the depths of pain. The effect on a nature sexually suppressed since childhood was profound. Press reports in 1968 revealed that in the Tank Corps in 1923 he arranged by means of an elaborate pretext to have himself whipped from time to time, while naked, by a fellow recruit. Lawrence spent his last months as T.E. Shaw, a designer and tester of boats for the RAF at Bridlington on the Yorkshire coast. On his retirement in February 1935 he bicycled in easy stages to his cottage at Clouds Hill, near Moreton, Dorset, a mile north of his old Tank Corps post, Bovington Camp. He had no plans; "I feel like a lost dog," he told a friend.

The day before his death Lawrence wrote, "At present I am sitting in my cottage and getting used to an empty life." There was never a better candidate for the accident syndrome. Next morning, 13 May 1935, he rode his Brough motorcycle to the camp to send a telegram concerning a friend's visit. Returning home at about 11:30 A.M., he topped a hill to find two fourteen-year-old cyclists just ahead of him riding in single file in the same direction. He swerved violently, struck the rear bicycle and was thrown over the handlebars. Lawrence, who was not wearing a

Lawrence of Arabia on his fatal motorcycle.
THE NATIONAL TRUST, LONDON

crash helmet, suffered a nine-inch-long fracture of the left side of the skull. He lingered in a coma for six days in the camp hospital while the authorities kept curious journalists away. He died shortly after 8:00 A.M. on 19 May 1935. Had he lived he would have been paralyzed.

The inquest on "T.E. Shaw, aircraftsman (retired)" was rather unsatisfactory; there was disagreement about whether a black car was traveling in the opposite direction past the accident site at about the same time. The damaged motorcycle was found jammed in second gear, putting the maximum speed at the time of the collision at thirty-eight miles per hour. The verdict was accidental death; the certificate, in the name of Shaw, forty-six years old, reported death as due to "congestion of the lungs and heart failure following a fracture of the skull and laceration of the brain sustained on being thrown from his motorcycle when colliding with a pedal cyclist." Probably Lawrence pulled well to the left on the narrow road to pass the "black car" (possibly a small black delivery van that regularly traveled that route) and then found himself, as he topped the rise, immediately behind the rear cyclist.

The funeral service at Moreton village church was attended by Thomas Hardy, who lived nearby, a weeping Winston Churchill and many other notables. Since the graveyard was full, the burial took place in a small adjoining plot.

Leigh, Vivien (1913–1967).

The British actress, who won two Academy Awards (for her roles in *Gone With the Wind* and *A Streetcar Named Desire*), spent several weeks in a London hospital in 1945 until a tuberculous patch on one lung cleared up. Beautiful, affectionate and genuinely considerate to others when in her normal state, she suffered for years from frightening spells of mental illness (manic-depressive psychosis). Depression would be followed by a mania in which she was almost impossible to subdue; she would rip off her clothes in claustrophobic terror, attack those she loved and use the vilest of language. A manic episode following location-work in Ceylon in 1953 caused her to be brought to Netherine Hospital, near Coulsdon, Surrey, for therapy that included ice packs (to lower her body temperature) and a diet of raw eggs. Thereafter, frequent electric shock treatments were necessary.

After her husband, Sir Laurence (now Lord) Olivier, left her in 1958, the young actor Jack Merivale became her lover. At the end of May 1967 Vivien was ordered to rest in her London flat at 53 Eaton Square after tuberculosis was found to have flared up in both lungs. Merivale called her as usual before appearing on stage at Guildford on Friday evening, 7 July 1967. Her sleepy, slurred speech seemed a little abnormal and after the play he drove to Eaton Square, arriving at about 11:10 P.M. He found her sleeping peacefully; relieved, he closed the bedroom door and fixed himself a snack in the kitchen. Fifteen minutes later, when he looked in again, he was shocked to find Vivien lying face down between door and bed. She was not breathing, and efforts at mouth-to-mouth resuscitation failed to revive her. A choking spasm probably woke her and fluid entering her lungs suffocated her as she staggered across the room.

Olivier came to the flat straight from his hospital bed, where he was recovering from surgery, and stayed all day with Merivale until the body was taken away. Vivien was never reconciled to losing her "Larry"; it was his portrait, not Jack's, that stood on the bedside table when she died. Theater lights throughout the West End were dimmed in tribute the following evening. After the Requiem Mass at St. Mary's, Cadogan Street, the body was cremated at Golders Green. *See* A. Edwards (1977).

Lenin (1870–1924).

Vladimir Ilyich Ulyanov, leader of the Russian revolution, adopted the name Lenin (sometimes with the initial "N") in 1907. On the evening of 30 August 1918 he was leaving the huge Michelson factory in southern Moscow after addressing the workers when he was shot and critically wounded. Fanya (sometimes called Dora) Kaplan, a twenty-eight-year-old Soviet revolutionary, approached him as he was about to enter his car in the courtyard and fired three shots with her Browning pistol. Two bullets struck the Bolshevik leader; one passed through his lower neck from left to right, piercing the apex of the left lung and lodging near the right collarbone; the other entered his left shoulder. A wave of terror immediately swept the country; more than eight hundred people were shot in Petrograd alone. Kaplan was executed on 3 September by a shot in the back of the head.

The fate of the revolutionary leader, treated in his Kremlin apartment, was in doubt for several days.

Lenin suffered his first stroke on 26 May 1922 after months of increasing fatigue. A luxurious manor house, formerly owned by a millionaire, was found for him at Gorki, a small woodland village twenty miles south of Moscow. He divided his time between the Kremlin and this retreat, where he was to die. With his second stroke in Moscow on 15 December, marked by three days of nausea and vomiting and by increased paralysis of the right side, Lenin was faced with the necessity of winding up his affairs. "From being an absolute dictator he was to become nothing," writes his 1964 biographer, Robert Payne, "and the thought was too terrible to be borne." Into brief sessions of bedside dictation he packed numerous letters to party colleagues, diary entries and, most important, his secret "testament," to be read only after his death. In it he warned against the power concentrated in the hands of the untrustworthy, "coarse" Stalin, the general secretary of the party; he also praised Trotsky and foresaw the devastating split between the two men.

Lenin must also have been aware that "dictatorship of the proletariat" was already degenerating into the intolerable tyranny of one unworthy individual whom he had been guilty of elevating to high office. An article by Lenin critical of Stalin appeared in *Pravda* on 4 March 1923 and the next day the invalid dictated a letter to the general secretary upbraiding him for intolerable rudeness to Krupskaya (Lenin's wife) on the telephone. These developments were interrupted on 9 March by a third stroke that completed the paralysis on the right side and affected the left. Though desperately ill for many weeks, Lenin was able to be taken to Gorki in May and by July was learning to walk with a cane; he could speak a few words and write with his left hand, but his mind was now reduced to an infantile level.

On 19 January 1924, Krupskaya read to him Jack London's gloomy "Love of Life," a tale he greatly enjoyed. On the 20th he complained of eye trouble, but a specialist could find nothing amiss. Lenin died on 21 January 1924. He did little that day but lie on his bed, drink tea and nibble a few morsels of food. Between 5:00 and 6:00 P.M. the servants reported him to be breathing with difficulty. Physicians were summoned as he went into violent convulsions. At 6:50 P.M., with Krupskaya holding his hand, Lenin expired.

Eleven doctors—and Stalin—were present at the lengthy autopsy, performed on the veranda at Gorki next day. The left cerebral hemisphere was found to be virtually destroyed by a recent hemorrhage and earlier degeneration; the immediate cause of death was paralysis of the respiratory organs. Cerebral arteriosclerosis was so far advanced that the dissected blood vessels emitted a clinking sound when tapped with forceps.

Rumors have persisted that Stalin poisoned Lenin. Payne believes this to be likely, though the medical history, the circumstances of death and the autopsy report clearly disprove it. No doubt Stalin was capable of killing his enemy and had every reason to accelerate his death, but that is quite a different matter.

Lenin's embalmed body lay in state for four days while 700,000 people filed through the Hall of Columns to pay their respects. The brain was removed and dissected into as many as 34,000 slices for study at a special institute headed by Prof. Oskar Vogt of Berlin. After a second embalmment, during which the decorticated remains were probably deeply cut in numerous places and steeped in a solution of glycerin, formalin and potassium acetate (a hygroscopic, or moisture-absorbing, salt), the body was put on display in a newly built mausoleum in Red Square, Moscow.

In 1927, to dispel rumors of fraud, officials invited a German physician to inspect the exhibit. There is little doubt that by 1928, when the mausoleum was closed for a month, a crisis had arisen. S.T. Possony, in his well-documented 1964 biography, reports the body to have seriously deteriorated. Apparently, abstraction of moisture from the cadaver and its replacement by paraffin wax was considered, perhaps even attempted. After the inevitable failure the remains were almost certainly replaced by skillful effigies of the head and hands. In the early 1930's it was observed that no protrusion marked the position of the feet; this oversight was later rectified. By then, Lenin displayed more hair than he had possessed at the age of thirty. After the exhibit's return from its wartime refuge in Kuybyshev, several other improvements were noticed. From 1953 to 1961 the mausoleum was shared by Lenin's arch-enemy Stalin (q.v.) Though he was demoted from this honored position, Stalin's present resting place in the Kremlin is at least known and properly marked; Lenin's final disposal can only be a matter of speculation.

Lincoln, Abraham (1809–1865).

The sixteenth president of the U.S. had been a strong, healthy man most of his life: the muscular development of his arms greatly impressed those who tended him as he lay dying. His major health problem was his tendency toward periods of intense, almost suicidal, depression, which, however, was balanced by his strong common sense.

Following Lee's surrender, victory celebrations were in full swing in Washington when the president visited Ford's Theatre on Good Friday, 14 April 1865. The party was completed by Major Henry Rathbone and his fiancee, Clara Harris. At about 10:00 P.M. the leading conspirator, John Wilkes Booth (q.v.), entered the theater unchallenged in the absence of the president's bodyguard, who had deserted his post. Lincoln's party sat in a box, or loge, to the right of and partly above the stage. The third act of a mediocre British comedy, *Our American Cousins*, was under way. Lincoln sat in a rocker near the back wall of the box,

President Lincoln's assassination: the pistol, ball, surgeon's probe, and skull fragments.

NATIONAL PARK SERVICE, WASHINGTON, D.C.

*A rare photograph of President Lincoln lying in state in New York's
City Hall.*

ILLINOIS STATE HISTORICAL LIBRARY

The chair in which Abraham Lincoln was sitting when he was shot in Ford's Theatre, Washington, D.C., on 14 April 1865. It is a rocker of black walnut with red silk damask upholstery.

GREENFIELD VILLAGE AND HENRY FORD
MUSEUM, DEARBORN, MICHIGAN

with a door behind him. Spying through a peephole he had made that afternoon, Booth chose a moment, probably about 10:13 P.M., when only one actor, Harry Hawkes, was onstage. He entered the box swiftly, moved past the other occupants and fired his derringer pistol at the back of Lincoln's head. At that moment the victim had turned his attention away from the stage and sharply downward into the auditorium. Thus it was that, though the assassin approached from the right, and was evidently right-handed, the half-inch Britannia-metal ball entered a little to the left of the midline and traveled slightly upward. Lincoln slumped in his chair while his wife leaped to his side and Major Rathbone grappled with Booth. The assassin slashed at the officer with a hunting knife, climbed backward over the rail of the box and jumped awkwardly to the stage, fracturing his left fibula. *"Sic semper tyrannis!"*—the motto of Virginia—he declaimed, as he limped across the stage to make his escape on horseback. Twelve days later he was surrounded by troops and fatally shot.

The first physician to Lincoln's aid was young Dr. Charles A. Leale of the U.S. Volunteers. Hearing the shot and Mrs. Lincoln's screams, he rushed to the box to find the president without perceptible pulse or respiration. He laid the body on the floor, searching first for a stab wound. Next he examined the eyes, saw evidence of brain injury and, passing his fingers through the president's thick hair, found the mortal wound behind the left ear. He applied artificial respiration, mouth-to-mouth resuscitation and even a form of closed-chest cardiac massage. After independent breathing had been restored, the president managed to swallow a little brandy and water. Within fifteen minutes he was carried across the street to a small, second-floor bedroom at the rear of William Petersen's boarding house, 453 10th Street, N.W., and, because of his great height, laid obliquely across the bed.

Other senior army surgeons had now arrived, but there was little more that could be done for the dying man except to keep him warm with large mustard plasters and to prevent the wound from being sealed by blood clots. Probing for the bullet was attempted but soon abandoned. For several hours the compassionate Leale held Lincoln's hand firmly in his own. At daybreak the president's breathing became slower and more labored and at 7:22 A.M. on Saturday 15 April 1865 he died.

The autopsy was conducted at noon in Lincoln's White House bedroom by an Army doctor, J.J. Woodward. He reported that the bullet made a path through the left side of the brain and lodged "just above the anterior portion of the left corpus striatum where it was found...." This agrees with evidence given at the conspirators' trial, but two surgeons who observed the autopsy reported the bullet to have moved across the brain's midline to a position behind the *right* orbit. The matter can never be resolved now. Lincoln's body was taken by a special train to various cities before being buried in Springfield, Ill.

Liszt, Franz (1811–1886).

In his last years the Hungarian pianist and composer suffered from dropsy, his eyesight was failing and only a few black stumps remained of his teeth. In spite of this, seated at the piano in his beautiful silk soutane with its broad violet sash, the candlelight making a halo of his snow-white hair, the Franciscan abbé cut a romantic figure. In April 1886 he was in London for celebrations honoring his seventy-fifth birthday. He had an audience with Queen Victoria, heard a performance of his oratorio *Saint Elizabeth* and astounded the Royal College of Music with the brilliance of his performance of his *Second Hungarian Rhapsody*.

Feverish and ill, Liszt traveled by train to Bayreuth for the Wagner celebrations on 21 July 1886. The carriage window was open and the young couple sharing the compartment refused his timid request to close it. His daughter Cosima, Richard Wagner's widow, did not offer the hospitality of her home, the Villa Wahnfried, but sent him to Frau Fröhlich's at No. 1 Siegfriedstrasse where, shaky and coughing incessantly, he took to his bed. It was a heroic effort for Liszt to leave his bed to attend a performance of *Parsifal*; the next day he was very sick and the local doctor did him no good by forbidding the brandy which had kept him going for years. To please Cosima he dragged himself to a performance of *Tristan* on 25 July. Between acts he acknowledged the applause of the audience; they were shocked to see him clinging to the rail of Wagner's box, gasping for breath, his face haggard and flushed. When the lights went down he crouched at the back of the box, vainly trying to stifle his coughing with a bloodstained handkerchief. He had to be taken

Liszt in his later years with his beloved piano.

LIBRARY OF CONGRESS

home early and helped to bed. The doctor diagnosed pneumonia. Cosima, too busy with the festival to spend much time with the old man, banned all visitors, so that he lay lonely and uncared for. Many who could have nursed him, including his two pupils, the devoted Lina Schmalhausen and Adelheid von Schorn, could only wait helplessly outside the door.

On the 27th Liszt was so ill that even Cosima was alarmed and another doctor was summoned. Still he was unattended; Cosima's fanatical belief that she must personally run the Wagner festival kept her away for lengthy periods. Liszt lay feverish and neglected, at times delirious, all day on the 30th. A third physician, called in on the 31st, warned Cosima that her father was sinking rapidly. She stayed at his bedside all day. At about 2:00 P.M. a great spasm shook him and he rose up in bed, uttering frightful cries. He was so strong his servant could not restrain him. He sank down again and lapsed into a coma. At about 10:30 P.M. he murmured the single word "Tristan" and died fifteen minutes later.

Although Liszt was an abbé of the Roman Catholic Church, Extreme Unction was not administered. Because the other guests in the lodging house objected, his body was hastily transferred to the Villa Wahnfried. The Wagner Festival continued; Liszt's friends and pupils were outraged at the lack of respect shown to him. He had requested in his will that he be buried in the habit of the Franciscan order and that a Requiem Mass be celebrated; neither request was honored. The parish minister, a Lutheran, pronounced the benediction. On 3 August Bayreuth, in festival spirit, watched the cortège go by to the cemetery. An onlooker, when asked who had died, replied, "Oh, Wagner's father-in-law."

Livingstone, David (1813–1873).

The Scottish medical missionary spent the last thirty years of his life exploring Africa. He discovered the Victoria Falls on the Zambezi and the source of the Congo River, but made only one convert, who later lapsed. His final journey, which lasted seven years, began in April 1866 and covered the largely unknown territory around Lakes Nyasa, Bangweulu and Tanganyika. His constant battle against fever was hampered by the theft of his medicine chest. In January 1869 he caught pneumonia at Lake Bangweulu and was carried by litter in excruciating pain to Ujiji where, to his great dismay, the long-hoped-for letters and medical supplies had been pilfered. Nearly three years later, again in Ujiji, he was greeted by the now famous words, "Dr. Livingstone, I presume?" H.M. Stanley of the New York *Herald* had reached him.

A half-share of Stanley's plentiful supplies enabled the sick, stubborn man to continue his travels. Almost dead from dysentery and heavy anal bleeding, Livingstone was carried on 29 April 1873 into a hut in Ilala on the Lulimala in northeastern present-day Zambia. Early on the morning of 1 May he was discovered kneeling by his bed; he had been dead for many hours. His body was embalmed by his African servants; when the internal organs were removed for immediate burial a large clot of blood several inches in diameter was found in the lower intestines. The cavity was packed with sand and the body slowly turned for fourteen days. It was wrapped in calico, then in bark, and sewn into sailcloth; finally the package was tarred to make it waterproof.

It took nine months to carry the body to Bagamoyo on the east coast of Tanzania, from where it was transported to Southampton on HMS *Vulture*. When examined in London the body was identified easily by the misshapen left humerus, which had been badly mauled by a lion thirty years previously. Livingstone lay in state in the Royal Geographical Society building on Savile Row in London for two days, and then was buried under a large black marble slab in the nave of Westminster Abbey on 18 April 1874.

London, Jack (1876–1916).

The U.S. author of *The Call of the Wild* (1903) became—ten years later—the most popular and highest paid writer in the world. He was a study in contrasts and frustrations: a racist who was uncertain of his father's identity; a socialist who became one of northern California's most prominent landowners; and a physical fitness cultist whose own body failed him in a dozen ways long before his early death. When he set sail across the Pacific in 1907 on his ketch, the *Snark*, with his second wife Charmian he was not only lame but was also losing his teeth because of pyorrhea. In addition, a rectal ulcer was giving him much discomfort when, on arrival in the Solomons, several tropical diseases caused him to abandon the cruise and continue on to Sydney by steamer. Malaria and yellow fever were debilitating enough, but yaws (a nonvenereal relative of syphilis) and a sloughing of the skin caused by either pellagra or psoriasis quite incapacitated him. His five months' treatment for yaws may have brought on the kidney disease that led directly or indirectly to his death. London tolerated poorly the arsenic preparations employed at that period, and by the time of a visit to Honolulu with Charmian in March 1916 he was in agony from kidney stones. Treatment was hindered by his alcoholism and insistence on a diet of raw fish (aku and bonito).

In August, back at his home, the Beauty Ranch, near Glen Ellen, southeast of Santa Rosa, London had lost much of his earlier zest and had become a bloated, gray-skinned figure with swollen ankles. Yet his restless mind still drove him to spend all day and much of the night writing stories and answering, with surprising patience, his considerable mail from young writers. His final dietary obsession was for undercooked wild duck. On 21 November he woke up vomiting, but in the afternoon took a drug-induced nap. After spending the evening with an exhausted, unsympathetic Charmian, he withdrew to his study and sleeping porch on one side of the house; she (after a stroll under the stars) retired to her bedroom on the other.

The following morning at seven the Japanese valet found London lying on his side, bent double, with face dark blue and constricted. Dr. Allan Milo Thomson, summoned from Sonoma, treated the comatose patient for morphine poisoning, using a stomach pump, stimulants and massage, and relays of ranch-hands walked him ceaselessly up and down. Later, two specialists from Oakland and San Francisco took over from the resentful local medico. Jack London lingered on throughout the day and died without recovering consciousness at 7:45 P.M., 22 November 1916, on the couch of Charmian's porch.

The press bulletin announced the cause of death as "a gastrointestinal type of uremia"; the death certificate records "uremia following renal colic." In 1937, Thomson charged (in a statement to London's biographer Irving Stone) that the specialists had concocted the cause of death to avoid an inquest and autopsy, and that the true cause was an overdose of morphine and atropine, as indicated by empty vials he found on the floor when he arrived, and by calculations for a lethal dose of morphine lying on the night table. That London injected a morphine overdose shortly before dawn is almost certain, but the motive is doubtful. Thomson's bias against the specialists and Charmian renders his testimony suspect. A planned suicide seems unlikely; the writer was on the eve of a trip to New York, where he planned to meet his former wife and his daughter, Joan. The alleged overdose calculations were never produced, and a search through London's many medical books has since failed to turn up relevant annotations. The sick man constantly injected drugs, including morphine, to which he had built up a fair tolerance. A sudden urge to self-extinction is not impossible, especially to one who was on record as favoring suicide and euthanasia in appropriate cases, but carelessness during fatigue and in the face of intense pain is at least as likely.

London was cremated in Oakland. His ashes, sealed in a copper cylinder, were buried on a knoll above his ranch among manzanita and white oaks. Concrete was poured into the grave and a red-brown boulder of volcanic rock rolled on top of it. It is now a tourist attraction within the Jack London State Historical Park, established in 1960. *See* A. Sinclair (1977).

Long, Huey (1893–1935).

The demagogic, flamboyant governor of Louisiana (1928–1932), who defeated impeachment in 1929, was a U.S. senator during his final three years. By 1935 his power in Louisiana was absolute. On 7 September his crony, Governor O.K. Allen, called a special session of the legislature to convene that night. One of the bills before it would gerrymander Benjamin H. Pavey, an anti-Long judge, out of office. The following evening, Sunday, 8 September 1935, only the house was in session in the Capitol in Baton Rouge. Long came down from his 24th-floor apartment in the same building to take part in the action. At about 9:00 P.M. he asked a protégé, Jimmie O'Connor, to get him some cigars from the basement restaurant. At 9:20, wanting to talk to a reporter who was in the governor's office, Long swept out of the chamber into the rotunda and turned right, down a corridor,

Huey P. Long, American lawyer and politician, lying in state.
THE BETTMANN ARCHIVE

with his bodyguards racing at his heels. He glanced into the governor's anteroom, then turned around and walked back into the middle of the passage, where his guards and associates had come to a standstill. A thin man in a white suit and dark-rimmed spectacles emerged from behind a pillar, walked to within a few feet of the senator, and, raising his right arm, fired his small pistol once.

"I'm shot," screamed Huey, who turned and ran toward the basement stairs. A bodyguard, Murphy Roden, grappled with the assailant and both fell to the floor. The man fired again, tearing off Roden's wristwatch, then broke away, crouching and facing the guards. Roden and another guard shot him as other policemen unholstered their guns. He fell face downward and Long's men stood over him and emptied their weapons into him. His body had sixty-one bullet wounds.

O'Connor, coming out of the restaurant, was startled to meet Long as he ran, swaying from side to side, through the basement corridor. "Kingfish, what's the matter?" "Jimmie, my boy, I've been shot." O'Connor half-carried the senator through the back door and, commandeering a car, had the driver take them to Our Lady of the Lake Hospital. Long had an entrance wound below his right rib cage with an exit wound directly behind it. Surgery revealed a small puncture of the colon, which was repaired, but a serious kidney wound was overlooked. In spite of several blood transfusions, Long died of an uncontrolled hemorrhage after less than thirty-one hours at 4:06 A.M., 10 September 1935. After lying in state he was buried in the State Capitol's sunken garden and a bronze statue was erected in his memory.

The assassin had already been interred at Roselawn Cemetery, two miles away. He was a twenty-nine-year-old physician, Carl Austin Weiss—an ear, nose and throat specialist for whom a brilliant future had been forecast. He and his wife, daughter of Judge Pavy, had a three-month-old son. Weiss had left home on the evening of the assassination after a happy day in the open air with his wife and parents. He took his gun—a .32-caliber automatic pistol he had purchased in Belgium—when he went off, as he explained, to make a sick call. Long's supporters charged he was a member of a conspiracy, but there is little evidence to support this.

A book by D. Zinman (1963) proposes that Weiss did not kill the senator, though he may have hit him, causing an otherwise unexplained lip wound Long was found to have sustained. According to Zinman's theory, a bullet fired by a bodyguard passed through Long's abdomen. This version presupposes perjury by a large number of witnesses and is unlikely on other grounds. It was nevertheless believed by, among others, J.F. Odom, an anti-Long attorney who conducted the inquest on Weiss. In his objective 1970 biography, T.H. Williams reports that Weiss had told at least one person he planned to kill Huey Long. The young physician was, Williams believes, a brooding and intense man who was appalled at Long's dictatorship and willing to become a martyr; he was the kind of man who could spend a happy day with his family and then, seeing an empty parking space as he drove past the Capitol, decide on impulse to carry out a plan long in his mind.

Louis XIV (1638–1715).

The Sun King reigned in France for seventy-two years, longer than any other recorded monarch. In his early seventies the king, though plagued by the maladies of old age, possessed a great zest for life. He was still so lusty that Madame de Maintenon, whom he had secretly married in 1684, had difficulty in responding to his needs.

On the night of 10 August 1715, in his room at Versailles, Louis was tormented by an unquenchable thirst. On the 13th he felt a stabbing pain in his left leg and a black spot was discovered. Though the leg was bathed in hot Burgundy spiced with aromatic herbs it became swollen, hot and painful. On the 24th the doctors began to suspect gangrene and the leg was wrapped in cloths soaked in camphorated brandy. Though now completely black it was less painful, but Louis was depressed and at 4:00 P.M. sent for his confessor. On the evening of the next day he received the Last Sacraments. The following morning he was very weak, and his heir, the Duke of Anjou, a charming little fellow with large dark eyes, was brought to him to receive the king's final words of advice.

That night George Maréchal, the king's first surgeon, probed the leg to find the seat of the gangrene but had to stop when the king cried out that the doctor was hurting him. The fact that they were causing pain in a gangrenous leg gave the surgeons hope. On 29 August a peasant arrived with some medicine which he claimed would cure the condition. As the royal doctors had just about given up hope, four drops were administered in a small glass of Burgundy followed by a second dose two hours later. The king appeared to revive a little but later relapsed. On the 31st prayers for the dying were recited. His last words are reported to have been, "Now and at the hour of my death, help me, oh God." Louis sank into a coma and died at 8:45 A.M. on 1 September 1715 without regaining consciousness.

After an autopsy and removal of the heart, which was taken to the Professed House of the Jesuits, the king's body was embalmed and placed in a lead coffin which was then encased in an oak coffin. After the solemn high funeral Mass the king was buried in the Bourbon vault of the Abbey of Saint-Denis where he remained until the royal tombs were desecrated by the Revolutionary mob seventy-five years later.

Louis XVI (1754–1793).

By August 1792 the royal family had been prisoners in the Tuileries Palace for nearly three years. On the tenth, Paris was restless: men were marching, noisy mobs filled the streets and there was the constant beat of drums and the ringing of the tocsin (alarm bells). The king and his family, told that the National Guard was no longer able to defend them, were persuaded to seek shelter in the Assembly. Everyone left behind, from the Swiss Guards to the maids and kitchen boys, were massacred when the Tuileries was overrun. The royal family was imprisoned in the Temple Tower in Paris, an awesome prison, massive as the Bastille, where they were deprived of all their possessions and subjected to constant scrutiny and harassment. On 21 September a proclamation was made that royalty was forthwith abolished. The king was brought to trial on 11 December and allowed to have as counsel the elderly M. de Malesherbes, who on 17 January 1793 brought him word of the verdict—death. Louis, not surprised, comforted the grieving old man.

On Sunday, 20 January at 2:00 P.M. a dozen or so men entered the king's chamber and read the Decrees of the National Convention, which had found Louis Capet guilty of conspiracy against the liberty of the Nation and condemned him to death. The king asked for three days to prepare himself, but was refused. However, his request that the Abbé Henry de Firmont should be allowed to attend him without "fear or uneasiness" was granted. Louis' final meeting with his family took place the same evening in the dining room, where he could be watched through the glazed doors. It was plain to the observers from the agitation of the queen and princesses that he was telling them of his condemnation. At 10:15 P.M. the king rose and, as he moved with his family to the door, only he was controlled. He once more embraced them tenderly and said, "Farewell! farewell!" With much difficulty the abbé obtained from the Church of the Capuchins of the Marais the articles necessary to perform Mass early the next morning. The king, asking to be called at 5:00 A.M., fell into a profound sleep.

As his valet Jean-Baptiste Cléry lighted the fire the next morning, Monday, 21 January 1793, the king awoke, remarking he was glad he had slept soundly, as the previous day had been fatiguing. After Cléry had dressed him, he heard Mass and received Communion. At 9:00 A.M. General Santerre, commander of the National Guard, came for Louis, who firmly told him to wait; he would be with him in a minute. "Tout est consommé," he said to the abbé, "Give me your last blessing and pray to God that he will uphold me to the end." Cléry offered him his greatcoat, but he declined it. During the two-hour coach journey the king and the abbé took turns reading aloud from de Firmont's breviary, their calm astonishing the two attendant gendarmes. The coach stopped in the middle of the Place Louis XV (now Place de la Concorde). The space was surrounded by canon and thousands of armed men. As one of the executioners opened the door, the king admonished the gendarmes to do no harm to the abbé. As soon as the king descended from the coach the executioners tried to remove his outer garments. He pushed them away and with great dignity removed his coat, collar and shirt. He was outraged when they tried to bind his hands, and for an agonizing moment the abbé was afraid that there was going to be violence.

Finally, Louis submitted and with great difficulty mounted the steep steps to the scaffold. With a glance he silenced the drummers and in a firm loud voice declared, "I die innocent of all the crimes of which I am charged. I forgive those who are guilty of my death, and I pray God that the blood which you are about to shed may never be required of France." Angrily, General Santerre ordered the drums to drown the king's voice. The executioners fitted his neck into the groove directly below the knife. In his final moment Louis shouted, "May my blood cement the happiness of Fr——" The executioner picked up the severed head, raised it on high, and showed it to the people on all four sides of the platform. A great roar went up: "Vive la république!" The mob fought wildly to dip their handkerchiefs in the king's blood. He was buried in the Madeleine Cemetery and the coffin covered with quicklime.

When the Bourbons, on being restored to the throne twenty-two years later, wished to give Louis XVI a decent burial, all that could be found of his remains was a handful of chalky mud. The queen went to the guillotine nine months after the king; the young prince is thought to have died when ten years old in the Temple prison. Only the king's young daughter escaped; she was exchanged for an Austrian prisoner. The Abbé de Firmont lived until 1807. See S. Scott (ed.), A Journal of the Terror (1955).

McKinley, William (1843–1901).

The twenty-fifth president of the U.S. (1897–1901) was six months into his second term when he was fatally shot by Leon Czolgosz (q.v.) at the Pan-American Exposition in Buffalo, N.Y., on Friday 6 September 1901. He died seven and a half days later.

The president's secretary, George Cortelyou, had tried in vain to have the reception cancelled for security reasons. McKinley and his companions stood in the garish Temple of Music at an angle of a corridor formed from cloth-draped chairs. Above them was a wooden frame decorated by flags: on either hand were potted palms and bay trees. Guards were posted inside and outside the building, perhaps fifty policemen and soldiers in all. The crowd was admitted in double file and brought into a single line as they neared the president. One man had his right hand bandaged; he was disabled and used his left to shake hands. Perhaps that explained why the appearance of a young, fair-haired man slightly farther back excited little comment. He had slipped his right hand into his pocket as he moved slowly forward and when he brought it out again it seemed, to one witness,

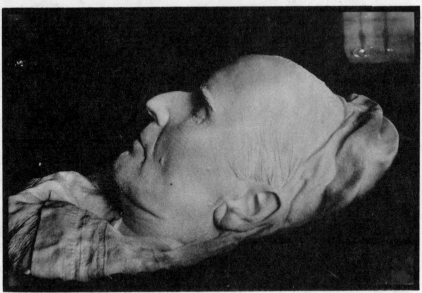

Death mask of President McKinley.

LIBRARY OF CONGRESS

that his sleeve hung loose. It was a handkerchief wrapped round his hand—and something else. Still, the day was warm; other handkerchiefs were in evidence as people in the line mopped their faces.

Ever nearer Leon Czolgosz advanced as organ music by Bach filled the air. The Secret Service agent beside the president looked into his eyes; the assassin looked calmly back. Not by as much as a flicker could his intentions be foreseen. "He looks like an engineer with a burned hand," thought the agent. Another Secret Service man, Samuel R. Ireland, was stationed beside the president urging each person forward as McKinley, with his well-known fifty-a-minute handshake, pumped away. The aisle was wider at that point and after greeting the president the public turned left toward the south exit. The time was about 4:07 P.M.; in three minutes the reception was due to end, and Cortelyou could breathe again. Ireland put his hand on Czolgosz's shoulder as he came abreast of the chief executive, pushing him gently forward. Like the disabled man a minute earlier, Czolgosz offered his left hand. McKinley reached for it. In an instant, with Ireland's hand still on his shoulder, the killer dashed the presi-

McKinley's casket being escorted from the train in Canton, Ohio, where he is buried.

LIBRARY OF CONGRESS

dent's hand aside and fired his short-barrelled .32-caliber Iver Johnson revolver twice in quick succession.

McKinley shuddered, stared at his murderer in astonishment, drew himself up to a full height and, murmuring "Cortelyou," fell into the arms of a guard. As he was led to a chair all hell broke loose. Czolgosz was thrown to the floor and attacked by a dozen people. On the floor nearby lay the blazing handkerchief through which the shots had passed. Excited soldiers began to pummel Czolgosz on the floor; one made as if to run him through with his bayonet. "Be easy with him, boys," called McKinley as the assassin was dragged away.

The wounded president was operated on by Matthew D. Mann, a Buffalo gynecologist, at a small exposition hospital without adequate lighting or suitable instruments. The anterior and posterior walls of the stomach were sutured, but the bullet, which had passed through this organ, could not be retrieved. (The other shot had struck the breastbone without penetrating.) McKinley was taken to 1168 Delaware Avenue, home of the exposition's director, where his condition remained stable for some days. Late on Thursday his pulse rate jumped and grew weaker; at 10:00 P.M. on Friday he lost consciousness and died a few hours later at 2:15 A.M., 14 September 1901. His tomb is adjacent to Westlawn Cemetery, Canton, Ohio.

At autopsy, considerable necrosis (tissue death) was found along the path of the bullet; in particular, the pancreas was largely destroyed, probably the cause of death. P.M. Dale writes regretfully that no physician had tested the patient's urine for sugar during the last few days; if diabetes had been demonstrated in the dying man, doctors might have discovered the role of the pancreas as the insulin-secreting organ, and the discovery of the hormone, not achieved until twenty years later, might have been accelerated.

Magellan, Ferdinand (1480?–1521).

Although the Portuguese explorer was wounded several times in the distinguished service of his country, in 1514 he fell out of favor with King Manuel of Portugal; he then renounced his nationality and offered his services to Charles I of Spain. On 10 August 1519 five vessels with a complement of about 275 men left Seville under Magellan's command to attempt the circumnavigation of the world. They sailed across the Atlantic and down the east coast of South America to Cape Virgins, where they discovered the entrance to what is now the Strait of Magellan. It took thirty-eight days to navigate the 260-mile-long, tortuous, narrow channel and reach the ocean which Magellan called "Pacific." For ninety-eight days they crossed that vast sea, suffering intensely from scurvy caused by the lack of fresh food. On 6 March 1521 they put into Guam, where they rested and took on food and water.

Continuing to sail westward, they reached Cebu in the Philippines on 7 April. In an excess of missionary zeal Magellan baptized the Sultan Humabon and all his people and had them swear allegiance to the king of Spain. But on the tiny nearby island of Mactan the powerful chief Lapulapu would not submit. Determined to punish him, Magellan ordered the capital town of Bulaia to be burned. Lapulapu was not intimidated and Magellan, against the advice of his officers decided to deal with him personally. He assembled a group of sixty volunteers to sail to the island in three boats; the sultan joined him with a thousand warriors and a fleet of war canoes. They left the ships at midnight. Instead of launching a surprise attack, Magellan sent an envoy to Lapulapu, again demanding his allegiance to the king of Spain. When this was refused he attempted to land, but the tide was not yet high enough and for several hours he and his men sat shivering in the predawn mist. Even then, the shallow, coral-strewn water forced them to leave the boats two hundred yards from the shore. The sultan suggested he send his warriors in first, but Magellan stubbornly refused.

As they landed at dawn on 27 April they were met by fifteen hundred islanders; Magellan's musketeers and crossbow men made a great noise but were too far away to be effective against the agile natives, who bombarded them with so many arrows and iron-tipped bamboo spears that the Spaniards could barely defend themselves. To create panic Magellan ordered the natives' huts to be set on fire, but this only angered Lapulapu's men further. Two of the incendiaries were stabbed to death and the captain suddenly realized his perilous position. The islanders charged; Magellan was shot through the right leg with a poisoned arrow. He called to his men to retreat slowly and in good order, but they fled in terror from the shrieking, leaping natives. Only a brave few remained to help their wounded captain. Stumbling through the shallow water they defended themselves for nearly an hour. An Indian threw a spear into Magellan's face; he responded with a thrust of his lance. It stuck in the man's body, and while he was struggling to unsheath his sword the natives fell on him. After being slashed in the left leg with a cutlass, Magellan fell face downward in the shallow water, and the attackers struck him again and again.

The waiting boats picked up the survivors and began to pull away. With their captain dead, the loyal few who had tried to defend him struggled after the boats. His body was never recovered. On 1 May the sultan invited the commanders of the ships to dine with him and receive some jewels for the king of Spain. Of the twenty-nine who went, two turned back; the rest were murdered. Only one ship completed the voyage; on 8 September 1522, the battered *Victoria* limped into Seville with eighteen men aboard. In 1869 Queen Isabella II of Spain had a monument to Magellan erected on the northern tip of Mactan where he was slain. The bay is now known as Magellan Bay.

Marlowe, Christopher
(1564–1593).

The English poet and dramatist, author of *Tamburlaine the Great* and *Dr. Faustus*, paved the way for Shakespeare. At the time of Marlowe's early death the plague had closed London's theaters and the playwright was living with a patron near Chislehurst, southeast of the city. On or about 19 May 1593 he was arrested on suspicion of writing atheistic opinions but was released on condition he make a daily appearance in London before the Privy Council's representative. His death a few days later saved him from a trial before the Star Chamber and possible torture.

For three centuries the details of Marlowe's violent end remained uncertain. One early account had him killed in a quarrel over a woman; another told of a street brawl. William Vaughan in his *Golden Grove* (1600), correctly described him as dying at "Detford," i.e. Deptford, near Greenwich on the south bank of the Thames, the victim of a dagger thrust "by one named Ingram." Investigation was foiled for a century by a misreading of the burial register at St. Nicholas Church, Deptford, as "Christopher Marlow slaine by ffrancis Archer the 1 of June." The correct reading, "ffrancis ffrezer," is also misleading; the wrong Christian name had been entered.

It was Dr. J. Leslie Hotson, searching in the Public Record Office, who solved the mystery and announced it in his slim 1925 book, *The Death of Christopher Marlowe*. In a quite unrelated document he saw the name "Ingram Frizar" and recalled the "Ingram" in Vaughan's work. Searching further, he found a queen's pardon dated 28 June 1593 granted to "Ingramo ffrizar" and finally a full account of a coroner's inquest which tells the tale of Marlowe's final day.

On 30 May 1593 Marlowe spent the day at the "house," possibly a tavern, of Eleanor Bull in Deptford Strand in the company of three dubious characters: Ingram Friser, a notorious confidence man; Nicholas Skeres, his accomplice; and Robert Poley, a disreputable government spy. They spent the day dining, walking in the garden and supping. After supper the poet lay on a bed while the other three sat at a table wth their backs toward him, playing backgammon. A dispute arose over "the reckoning"—payment for victuals consumed—and (according to those who lived to tell the tale) Marlowe snatched the dagger hanging from Friser's belt and inflicted head wounds on that gentleman, who was sitting on a bench between the others and unable to escape. The coroner's report continues: "In his own defense and for the saving of his life," he struggled for the weapon and with it dealt Marlowe "a mortal wound over his right eye of a depth of two inches and the width of one inch; of which wound the aforesaid Christopher Morley [*sic*] then and there died." There was a suspicious delay in reporting the death. On 1 June, Marlowe was buried in Deptford Church; the position of the grave is unknown, but in 1919 an unknown admirer had a brass tablet placed in the north wall of the church.

Dr. Hotson's discovery raises a host of questions. Few who read the testimony accept it at face value. Unless the wound is wrongly described and, in fact, entered the eye it could hardly have been instantly fatal. A complete mystery surrounds the nature of the all-day meeting at the tavern. The cause of the quarrel seems inadequate. If Marlowe indeed attacked Friser with the dagger, why were the latter's wounds so superficial? Were they inflicted afterward to corroborate a cooked-up self-defense story? What part did the other two men play in the affair? The pardon, coming so promptly, raises the question of whether the whole affair was arranged to rid the authorities of a nuisance. But if so, there must be many facts still hidden from modern investigators. Calvin Hoffman in a 1955 volume developed the argument that Marlowe was the true author of Shakespeare's plays, that the body in Deptford Church is bogus, and that the young poet escaped to the continent. The "Marlowe-as-Shakespeare" theory has received no support among scholars, but that Kit Marlowe plotted his own successful flight from justice remains an open question.

Marx, Karl (1818–1883).

The German-born Jewish philosopher, whose writings became the gospel of world communism, settled in London in 1849. Unable to support his family by journalism, and improvident by nature, he was reduced to living on an endless series of small loans. He was a prolific writer, but irregular working hours, cheap cigars and the highly seasoned food of which he was fond exacerbated his liver and gallbladder ailments. The strain of poverty was lifted from Marx and his wife, Jenny von Westphalen, in 1870 when his benefactor, Friedrich Engels, retired from manufacturing and supplied them with a regular income.

The first volume of *Das Kapital* appeared in 1867, but failing health and other preoccupations prevented publication of the remaining two volumes during Marx' lifetime. Late in 1881 he and his wife lay ill in adjoining rooms of their row house in Maitland Park Road, south of Hampstead Heath. Jenny was dying of liver cancer; her husband was stricken with "bronchitis." Marx never recovered from her death on 2 December. A spell in Algiers did nothing to improve his health. The death of a married daughter, Jenny, in Paris in January 1883 was a final blow. Through bitter February weather he sat with his feet in hot mustard baths, drawing sustenance from brandy and milk. When Engels called to see him on the morning of 13 March 1883 "the house was in tears; it seemed the end had come. There had been a small hemorrhage and a sudden deterioration had set in.... When we entered he sat there sleeping, but never to wake any more. In two minutes he had quietly and painlessly passed away."

Karl Marx's tomb in Highgate Cemetery, London. It contains also the bodies of his wife and mistress. Photo by Paul R. Lorch.

Marx died, intestate and stateless, of the cachexia (wasting) of tuberculosis. In 1956 a large marble block was placed over his grave in Highgate Cemetery; it is surmounted by a cast-iron likeness of Marx's bearded head. The tombstone bears the name of his wife, Marx himself, a four-year-old grandson who died the same week, his unmarried daughter Eleanor and his housekeeper, Helena Demuth, who secretly bore his son in 1851.

Mary I (1516–1558).

Mary Tudor, daughter of Henry VIII and Catherine of Aragon, ascended the English throne in 1553. She is remembered as "Bloody Mary" because, in the vain hope of persuading England to return to the Catholic faith, she revived laws for punishing heretics. Many Protestants were put to death: some, including Thomas Cranmer (q.v.), Archbishop of Canterbury, were burned at the stake. In addition, Mary's marriage to Philip, who was to become king of Spain in 1556, was unpopular, arousing fears that England might become dominated by Spain.

Mary had been a sickly child, suffering from indigestion, toothache, violent headaches and amenorrhea (absence of menstruation). It is possible that she became pregnant in 1555 and miscarried, but it could also have been that the amenorrhea, coupled with an edematous swelling and her great longing for a child, deluded her. In April 1555 she went to Hampton Court to await the birth of the child. As the months wore on it became apparent that the sumptuously trimmed cradle would not be needed. Mary, pale, sat for hours upon cushions, her knees drawn up to her chin. Her women, knowing how passionately she longed for a child, did not dare to tell her the truth. In 1877 Sir Spencer Wills hazarded a guess that she might have had "ovarian dropsy," which MacLauren terms a "parovarian cyst," a tumor that can cause immense swelling of the abdomen.

Shortly after the disastrous fall of Calais, the last British stronghold in France, in December 1557, the problem seems to have recurred, as Mary drew up a will making her husband regent if she should die in childbirth. All through the summer she was ill. In September she suffered a raging fever; at that time it was called "the new burning ague," now assumed to have been influenza. In 1558 the disease was epidemic in England, killing thousands. In November, realizing she was not pregnant, Mary agreed to name her half-sister Elizabeth as heir. She grew weaker and weaker, often lapsing into unconsciousness. One day, seeking to comfort her weeping women, she told them that she had such good dreams of little children singing like angels. On 16 November she heard Mass early in the morning, whispering the responses, "Miserere nobis, miserere nobis: dona nobis pacem." She died at 6:00 A.M. on 17 November 1558 in the Palace of St. James, London. MacLauren suggests she died from degeneration of the heart and arteries, possibly a late consequence of congenital syphilis.

Mary's body lay in state in the chapel of St. James for three weeks; on 12 December a tremendous procession escorted her coffin to Westminster Abbey; soldiers of the Royal Guard stood watch all night. The following day a Requiem Mass was sung; her coffin was buried on the north side of the Chapel of Henry VII in the abbey, her heart being interred separately. While the chief mourners were at dinner, servants and hired mourners tore up the flags, banners and wall hangings for souvenirs.

Mary, Queen of Scots (1542–1587).

When Mary Stuart married the Earl of Bothwell, who had murdered her husband, Lord Darnley, three months earlier, the Scottish lords rose in revolt, imprisoned Mary on an island in Loch Leven and forced her to abdicate in favor of her year-old son, James. After eleven months she escaped and fled to England, throwing herself on the mercy of Elizabeth I, who had her taken into custody. Mary spent much of her time at Tutbury Castle near Burton-on-Trent, a foul-smelling, cold and damp place where she suffered from fevers and aching limbs, precursors of the rheumatism that was to cripple her.

During Mary's eighteen-year imprisonment there were many unsuccessful attempts to free her. In 1585 the "Babington conspiracy" had the ostensible purpose of assassinating Elizabeth and putting her kinswoman Mary, a Roman Catholic, on the English throne. But this plot was the handiwork of Elizabeth's own minister, Walsingham. At her trial in 1586 Mary defended herself eloquently, but was found guilty of complicity in the conspiracy. Although Elizabeth wanted Mary dead she was reluctant to sign the death warrant. She asked Sir Amias Paulet, the Scottish queen's custodian, to murder her, but, fearful for his soul, he replied, "God forbid."

On 7 February 1587 a small deputation led by the Earl of Shrewsbury came to Mary's room at Fotheringhay Castle, near Peterborough. In a faltering voice the earl announced that she was to be executed at eight o'clock on the following morning. To Mary the news was welcome, for she was in continual pain and overjoyed to shed her blood for the Catholic church, but it was a serious blow to her when she was denied her own chaplain.

Mary spent the evening alone with her servants, making financial arrangements for their care and dividing up her possessions into little packets. She did not sleep that night; at six o'clock, long before it was light, she was dressed and in her little oratory, praying. A loud knocking at the door summoned her to the great hall, where a platform had been built and the executioner, Bull, awaited her. She was at first refused any of her ladies and, fearful that a rumor of suicide would be spread, she pleaded that Jane Kennedy and Elizabeth Curle might be with her. Three hundred spectators watched with awe as the tall, dignified woman, dressed in black, entered and mounted the

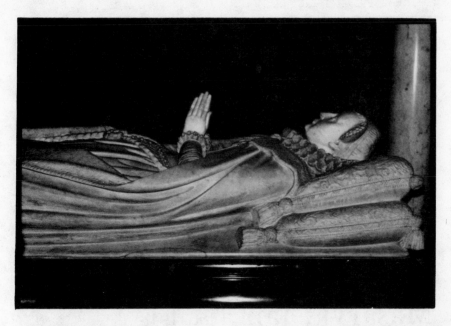

The effigy of Mary Queen of Scots above her tomb in Westminster Abbey. Photo by Paul R. Lorch.

three steps to the black-draped platform. She listened impassively while the commission for her execution was read, but when the Protestant dean of Peterborough began to pray in a forceful voice she turned aside and prayed aloud in Latin. The executioner, as was customary, asked her forgiveness. When her ladies removed her black garments, it was seen that she was wearing a red petticoat and, above it, a low-cut red satin bodice to which was added a pair of red sleeves. Jane Kennedy, weeping, kissed a white cloth embroidered with gold and tied it gently around her mistress's eyes. The queen, showing not the slightest sign of fear, knelt down and, feeling for the block, laid her head upon it. She cried, *"In manus tuas, Domine, confido spiritum meum"* three or four times. When she was motionless the headsman aimed his first blow; the ax missed her neck and cut into the back of her head. Her servants thought she whispered, "Sweet Jesus." The second blow severed the neck. Bull held the head high by the luxuriant auburn hair, crying out "God Save the Queen."

To the horror of the onlookers, the head tumbled to the floor; it was then seen that, under her wig, Mary's short hair was white.

When the executioner bent over the body to remove the adorn-
ments, Mary's little lap dog, a Skye terrier, was discovered
trembling piteously beneath her petticoat. Everything connected with the execution was burned so that nothing might
remain to become a holy relic. The body was examined and
found healthy. The heart and other organs were secretly buried
deep at Fotheringhay. The body, in its heavy lead coffin, was
given no burial but walled up within the castle where she had
died. The little dog pined away and died.

On 30 July 1587, in deference to her son James' feelings, the
body was taken by night from Fotheringhay to Peterborough
and, after a Protestant ceremony, interred in the cathedral.
After James ascended the English throne in 1603 he arranged
for his mother to be buried in Westminster Abbey beneath a
magnificent white marble tomb. A few years later the tomb
became a Catholic shrine.

Masaryk, Jan (1886–1948).

The son of Tomáš Masaryk, founder of an independent
Czechoslovakia, broadcast regularly to his countrymen from
London during World War II. He was perhaps the most popular
man in Prague from 1945, when he returned home, until 1948,
when a Communist tyranny replaced the Nazi one. In July 1947
Stalin summoned Masaryk to Moscow and virtually ordered him
to refuse American aid under the Marshall plan. "I went to
Moscow a free [Foreign] Minister," he told friends dejectedly; "I
came back as Stalin's puppet." The Communists, with thirty-
eight percent of the Czech vote in 1946, were the largest party,
but this was expected to drop sharply in the May 1948 elections.
When twelve non-Communists resigned from the cabinet early
in 1948 to permit the aged, sick President Eduard Beneš to call
an early ballot, the Communist Prime Minister, Klement
Gottwald, aided by bands of armed workers in the streets, forced
his own list of replacements on Beneš. Masaryk, normally a witty,
genial man, showed increasing strain.

The U.S. novelist Marcia Davenport, who was then in her
mid-forties, had known Masaryk since 1941 and they were now
in love. Early in 1948 she had come to live in Prague, and in her
memoirs, *Too Strong for Fantasy* (1968), she reports Jan's increas-

ing unhappiness and exhaustion during February. On the 25th Beneš caved in to Gottwald but did not resign; Masaryk, who owed allegiance to his father's old comrade, elected to stay in the government for the time being, but sent Marcia off to London on 7 March with a promise to follow her when he could; they planned to be married then. On the 9th he asked Beneš to release him from his pledge and burned his papers. Recovering from a recent bout of bronchitis, the foreign minister was settled in bed with a writing pad when his butler last saw him after dinner that night. Evidence showed he had finished writing a speech as planned and that he had taken two Seconal tablets as usual to help him sleep till morning.

At dawn two workmen descending from the roof of the Czernin Palace, Prague, saw Masaryk's pajama-clad body lying barefoot in the courtyard below his third-floor bathroom window. He lay face upward, his head toward the building, about four yards from the wall, with one arm outstretched. Both legs were fractured above the ankles and his heels were splintered; there was a narrow vertical scratch on his belly, and paint and plaster were found below his fingernails. He had died almost instantly from internal injuries, according to an irregularly performed, unsigned autopsy report. By noon the authorities had hastily announced death to be due to suicide and closed the case.

For twenty years all discussion of the case was stilled. In the 1968 "springtime" of liberalization under Alexander Dubček, no time was lost in reinvestigating Masaryk's death, and crowds began again to visit his grave in the village of Lány, near Prague. Claire Sterling, a courageous, persistent U.S. journalist living in Rome, was able to establish the extent of the 1948 cover-up. In *The Masaryk Case* (1969) she writes: "At least twenty-five Czechs with some information about Masaryk's death...went to prison afterward." Of these, ten were executed and one was murdered. None of the facts points directly to suicide; most point to murder. Masaryk had disapproved of a colleague's recent leap from a high window, which he had survived; it was "the way servant-girls choose to die," said Jan, who further felt it solved nothing. If he wanted to kill himself he had, according to his doctor, more than enough barbiturates to do the job, and there was a loaded revolver in his bedside table. His swallowing of sleeping tablets before settling down to sleep was an unlikely prelude to suicide. No farewell note was found. On the morning his body was found, Masaryk's bedroom and bathroom were in a state of wild disorder: furniture awry, drawers and cupboards open, glasses and bottles trampled underfoot, the contents of the medicine chest spilled all over the floor, a dirty pillow in the bathtub and another under the sink.

A messy but vital clue was the state of the bathroom windowsill and the dead man's body. Masaryk had lost control of his bowels in the last moments. Prof. F.E. Camps, Home Office pathologist, told Mrs. Sterling in London that this feature is never found in authentic suicide cases; on the other hand, it is regularly present in the last stages of suffocation. A leading Rome pathologist with forty years' experience, Prof. Gerin, confirmed both statements. That the bathroom window should have been used for the jump was also inexplicable; it had only half the effective height of the one in the bedroom; it was difficult to open, and unlike the other it was obstructed by a window seat, a screen and a radiator. How a 200-pound, six-foot-tall man could have eased himself through it and, necessarily from a sitting position, propelled himself several yards outward as he fell was just one more puzzle.

The police doctor, Teplý, who first inspected the body had grave doubts about the official verdict; he died in mysterious circumstances at police headquarters. Dr. Klinger, Masaryk's own physician, was convinced it was murder; he escaped to the U.S., where he died in 1973. The Dubček administration at first pursued the investigation energetically, but after the invasion of Prague by Soviet tanks in August 1968 the inquiry was stalled.

Claire Sterling believes the murder was planned in Moscow by NKVD agents who acted as soon as their sources passed on Masaryk's plans to leave the country and repudiate the government. The assassins, probably two Czech Communist agents, could easily have entered the Czernin Palace some time between midnight and 4:00 A.M. by the unguarded back door. Jan fought desperately—across the bedroom and into the bathroom. Finally the victim was subdued in the bathtub by the assassins' pressing a pillow over his face until he was almost gone; then he was hoisted up to the window by his legs until, from a sitting position, he could be given a hefty shove.

As though in answer to the Sterling book, the Prague government withdrew its suicide verdict. On 11 December 1969, with a straight face, it announced that the investigation, having "excluded the possibility of murder" would now be closed. The foreign minister had evidently died as the result of "an unfortunate accident." Apparently, he had been sitting on the bathroom windowsill, fighting insomnia by cooling off, when he slipped. The pillows found "near the window" were no doubt intended to keep warm certain parts of his body, such as his kidneys! By the inept substitution of this incredible version for the earlier, barely credible suicide story, the Communist government in effect gave official confirmation, almost twenty-two years after the event, of Jan Masaryk's political murder.

Maugham, William Somerset (1874–1965).

The English novelist and short story writer lived quietly at his Villa Mauresque on the Riviera during his last years. Situated on a twenty-acre estate on Cap Ferrat, near Nice, it had its own pool, which Maugham used regularly until well into his eighties. He employed six servants and four gardeners, and was looked after by his devoted companion and secretary, Alan Searle. In 1962 he shocked his friends by a bitter attack in his serialized memoirs, *Looking Back*, on his wife Syrie, who had died in 1955. It was, they knew, his prolonged homosexual affair with an American, Gerald Haxton, whom he had met before his marriage in 1916, that led to the couple's divorce eleven years later. Maugham, however, was determined that no hint of such matters would ever come to light. In 1958 he and Searle had a series of "bonfire nights," during which thousands of letters and other papers were destroyed, and he forbade his executors to allow publication of any documents that might turn up later. It was at about this period that a visitor found the atmosphere at the villa particularly tense; Maugham could not bear Alan out of his sight for a second, and the younger man's life was being made "positively hellish." There was a strong suspicion among those around him that the aged writer was going out of his mind, imagining people were skulking in the shadows, waiting to knife him in the back.

Physically, Maugham remained spry, a trim figure in his quilted smoking jacket, black trousers and black velvet slippers; to his nephew, Robin Maugham, he resembled a mandarin, "ancient, fragile, wise, benign." But, far from being benign, he was desperately unhappy. Even the reading of detective novels was becoming impossible as his eyes failed him, and he had long been deaf. In *The Summing Up*, written when he was sixty, Maugham explained how he had shaped his life to possess a certain design, but after he reached eighty that design had become misshapen. "I've been a horrible and evil man," he told Robin. "Every single one of the few people who have ever got to know me well has ended up by hating me." The advent of his ninetieth birthday, heralded by a flood of telegrams, presents and newspaper reporters, simply made Maugham's moods more intolerable. "If you believe in prayer," Robin's Uncle Willie said to him during that weekend, "then pray that I don't wake up in the morning."

In December 1965 Maugham was admitted, seriously ill, to the British-American Hospital at Nice. When it became clear no treatment could save him, Alan brought him home again; he died in his room at the Villa Mauresque on 16 December 1965, six weeks short of his ninety-second birthday. On the 22nd his ashes were interred, in the presence of his daughter, Liza (Lady Glendvon), near the Maugham Library at the King's School, Canterbury, where he had been so miserable as a boy.

Maupassant, Guy de (1850–1893).

Émile Zola described the French short story writer as one of the happiest, and one of the unhappiest, men the world has ever known. In the 1870s he was a happy, penniless civil servant, enjoying girls, fun-loving friends and boating on the Seine. He was a broad-shouldered, stocky fellow, with wiry chestnut hair and regular features. He loved dirty stories, the cruder the better. His sexual appetite was prodigious; inevitably he contracted syphilis, possibly in 1874. By 1878 his eyesight was badly affected; he was subject to fits of melancholia and violent migraines. Maupassant refused to acknowledge his syphilis, and blamed his symptoms on everything from overwork to the humid air of Normandy.

The poet Auguste Dorchain and his wife met Guy at the Hotel Beauséjour in Champal, Switzerland, in 1891. He would not leave them alone, but talked incessantly of his illnesses. He read to them the fifty pages he had written of his novel *L'Angélus*, often breaking into tears at particularly touching moments. One day he visited Geneva for a few hours and returned in high spirits. He told Dorchain that he had seduced a young girl. "I was brilliant; I am cured!" Nevertheless, he was aware of what was wrong with him and had said to a physician, "Don't you think that I am going insane?——If so, I should be told. Between madness and death, there is no question of hesitation; my choice is made." In a letter to a friend he said, "I don't want to survive myself."

Maupassant visited his mother in Nice on New Year's Day, 1892. She was shocked by his appearance and begged him on her knees not to return to Cannes, but to stay and rest. He refused and returned to his cottage, the Chalet de l'Isère on the Route de Grasse, where his valet François bled him and gave him chamomile tea. At 1:45 the next morning François was awakened by loud noises; Maupassant, frustrated by his failure to cut his throat with a paper knife, was pounding on the window shutters in an attempt to smash them and throw himself out. "Look what I have done, François," he said. "I have cut my throat...there is no doubt I am going insane."

On 7 January Maupassant was taken to a mental sanatorium in Paris established by Dr. Esprit Blanche. The luxurious asylum, in the Passy district, was surrounded by a beautiful park. François was allowed to remain with his master, who could receive male visitors (no women by order of his mother!). Sex continued to obsess him during his final eighteen months. In his madness he accused the faithful François of embezzling his money. On one occasion he refused to empty his bladder for thirty-six hours, stating that his urine was diamonds and belonged in a safe, not a pot. Howling like a dog he would lick the walls of his room. He was aware when a fit of madness was coming on and would ask for a straitjacket. In late June, after violent convulsions, he fell into a coma. Maupassant died at 11:45 A.M. on 6 July 1893. On the 8th, after a service at the Church of St. Pierre de Chaillot, Émile Zola gave the farewell tribute at the graveside in Montparnasse Cemetery.

Mencken, Henry Louis
(1880–1956).

The most colorful U.S. newspaperman since Poe was a hypochondriac who, beginning in 1940, described at his typewriter his own steady deterioration. At sixty he suffered his first mild stroke, but was still capable of supplying *The New Yorker* with autobiographical pieces and of working on a supplement to his most important work, *The American Language*, first published by Alfred Knopf in 1919. His active career ended with his reporting of the 1948 political conventions, all held in Philadelphia, at which Truman, Dewey and Wallace (the Progressive candidate) were nominated. He enjoyed himself as immensely as ever and, if his dispatches to the Baltimore *Sun* fell below his earlier level, they were still excellent.

Back in Baltimore on the evening of 23 November 1948 Mencken had taken his secretary Mrs. Rosalind Lohrfinck to dinner when he suffered a severe stroke. Complaining of a headache, he was handed a glass of water which slipped from his fingers. He began to pace the floor and shout incoherently until restrained. After five weeks in the hospital he was taken back to his beloved row house at 1524 Hollins Street, Baltimore, where he was to linger on for seven years. Unable to read or write or speak coherently and with his hearing impaired, he threatened to kill himself, but was reassured and cared for by his brother August, the guardian angel of his declining years.

All his life Mencken had lived at Number 1524 except during his brief, happy marriage (1930–1935) to Sara Haardt, who died of tuberculous meningitis at thirty-seven. After a five-month stay in the hospital following a heart attack in late 1950, he obtained the services of a young nurse, Lois Gentry. Though H.L.'s speech improved, his memory for the right word often failed him. In the morning he and Mrs. Lohrfinck would deal with his correspondence; after a nap and a formal lunch Miss Gentry would take him for a walk down the garden or around Union Square. Baltimore friends would sit with him. Knopf and his wife, Blanche, came down from New York when they could spare the time. Most literary work was beyond Mencken then, but he could still make editorial judgments on notes he had written years before and filed away if they were read to him. In this way his final book, *Minority Report*, published posthumously, was compiled.

On 28 January 1956 Mencken lay on the sofa in his study upstairs listening to the Saturday afternoon broadcast from the Metropolitan Opera House, New York. The work was *Die Meistersinger*, his favorite. In the evening a friend came to supper,

eaten near a cheerful fire tended by August. In spite of his
faltering speech, Henry enjoyed the conversation. He retired
soon after nine. In the early hours of 29 January he died peacefully of a coronary occlusion. A handful of friends gathered at a
funeral home a block from Hollins Street to wish Mencken
farewell; he had requested there be no ceremony of any sort.
The body was then cremated at Loudon Park Cemetery and the
ashes were buried there next to those of Sara. *See* C. Bode (1969).

Mendelssohn, Felix (1809–1847).

The German composer fulfilled his promise to make a tenth tour
of England in 1847. Though obviously ill and suffering from
constant headaches, he conducted between 16 and 30 April four
performances of his oratorio *Elijah* in London and single performances in Manchester and Birmingham. He was a great
success musically and socially, but friends noticed that when he
was not making music he looked haggard and weary. At the
frontier town of Herbesthal near Cologne on his way home on 9
May he was mistaken for another Dr. Mendelssohn, a political

*The funeral cortege of Felix Mendelssohn at Leipzig, preceding his
burial in Berlin. From a contemporary drawing.*

THE ILLUSTRATED LONDON NEWS

activist, taken off the train and questioned until he was prostrated with exhaustion. The day after his return home a letter
arrived from his brother Paul; after reading it he cried out and
fainted: his beloved sister Fanny was dead from a cerebral
hemorrhage, the disease that had killed so many Mendelssohns.
Felix was incapable of attending the funeral. In an attempt to
bring about some improvement in his health, Felix, his wife,
Cecile, and their four children traveled to Baden-Baden and
then to Interlaken, Switzerland. When the weather and his
headaches permitted, Felix and Cecile took long walks and
sketched. He composed, in Fanny's memory, the deeply moving
Quartet in F minor (opus 80) and was asked to write several other
works, including a new symphony for the London Philharmonic
Society.

Mendelssohn returned to Leipzig in September looking even
older and more feeble; a friend noted he seemed "much
changed in looks and...often sat dull and listless without moving
a finger." On 9 October he visited Ignaz Moscheles and his wife
Charlotte; Moscheles suggested they take a walk in Rosenthaler
Park and Charlotte wanted to accompany them. With a touch of
his old playfulness, Mendelssohn said to Moscheles, "What do
you say? Shall we take her?" Later that day an old friend, Livia
Frege, played and sang some of his songs, including the mourn-
ful *Nachtlied*, perhaps his last composition. When she returned to
the room after fetching a light she found Mendelssohn shivering
on the couch, complaining of a dreadful headache, his hands
cold and stiff. After a while he recovered sufficiently to walk to
his home in the Königstrasse and go to bed. All the doctors'
medicines, tonics, leechings and bleedings failed to help, though
occasionally a friend's visit would cheer him up. One day he
dressed and went for a walk with Cecile; when he returned he
had a stroke. A few days later a second seizure left him partly
paralyzed and in great pain.

On 3 November he suffered a third stroke and though unconscious emitted cries of pain. He later regained consciousness for
a few moments; Cecile asked him if he was in pain; he replied he
was not but, "I am tired, terrible tired." These were his last
words. Mendelssohn died at 9:24 P.M. on 4 November 1847.
After a service at St. Paul's church, Leipzig, he was taken by
funeral train to Berlin where he was buried beside Fanny near
the Halle Gate in the cemetery of Holy Trinity Church.

Michelangelo Buonarroti
(1475–1564).

The Italian Renaissance artist was not only a superb painter, sculptor and architect, but also in his later years a poet. In this final role he was inspired by the intelligence and beauty of Vittoria Colonna. He was a short man with broad shoulders, piercing brown eyes and a broken nose. His work was his life; he lived frugally, slept beside his unfinished painting or sculpture and rarely changed his clothes. In spite of the pain of kidney stones and the stiffness of his back and legs, he was a vigorous old man. He survived a severe stroke in 1561; in the fall of 1563 and the following winter he was far from well but stubbornly continued with his projects. He realized that much of his work would have to remain unfinished, but he had Pope Pius IV's assurance that the dome of St. Peter's would be completed in strict accordance with his plans and model.

On 12 February 1564 Daniele da Volterra reported that his master was chipping away at a marble Pietà, working late into the night with the aid of a candle in his cap, but two days later Michelangelo suffered another stroke. He was found wandering in the rain, his face congested and his speech impaired. His disciple Tiberio Calcagni coaxed him back to his house on the Macello dei Corvi and into bed, but he was restless. The following day Michelangelo had his chestnut pony saddled so that, though it was still raining and he was feverish, he might ride as usual through the streets of Rome. When it was suggested that he should not go out, he replied, "What would you have me do? I am ill and cannot find rest anywhere." But he was too weak to mount and in despair he returned to his chair by the fire. A moment later he slipped to the floor and Dr. Donato was sent for. Daniele moved into the studio until Michelangelo's nephew Lionardo could reach Rome from Florence. On 18 February 1564 it was clear the artist was dying. Daniele, Tomasso Cavalieri and other close friends gathered around his bed; Cardinal Salviati administered the Last Rites and late in the afternoon Michelangelo died.

Although Michelangelo had reiterated only two days before his death that he wished to be buried in Florence, his funeral was held in the church of the Holy Apostles in Rome and it was quite clear that Pius IV intended that the coffin should remain there. Lionardo arranged for the body of his uncle to be stolen and shipped to Florence disguised as freight. The secret leaked out and artists of the Academy took the coffin from the customs house and on 12 March, by torchlight, carried it, covered with a velvet pall, through the streets of Florence to the Gothic Church of Santa Croce. Michelangelo was in an unusually good state of preservation; the lid of the coffin was raised so that the Florentines might have a glimpse of the famous man. A memorial service was held at the Medici family church of San Lorenzo, and Michelangelo's pupil and friend, Vasari, designed the tomb to mark his final resting place in Santa Croce.

Milton, John (1608–1674).

The English poet, whose work is generally regarded as being surpassed only by Shakespeare, was of medium height, well-proportioned, with a handsome visage and ruddy complexion. Though his sight began to fail in his mid-thirties, his eyes never lost their original appearance; in a sonnet he wrote, "these eyes, though clear / To outward view, of blemish or of spot / Bereft of light, their seeing have forgot." In March or April 1652 at the age of forty-three his blindness was complete. Enemies of Milton ascribed his affliction to "the wrath of the Lord." Of more orthodox causes (glaucoma, detached retina, congenital syphilis, albinism) discussed in the medical literature, Arnold Sorsby in a 1930 study (reprinted in *Tenements of Clay*) favors abrupt detachment of the left retina and detachment of the right "following on progressive myopic changes in that eye." R. H. Major in two papers (1936, 1949) accounts for the blindness and other more general symptoms by postulating a suprasellar cyst that pressed on the chiasma (the spot where the optic nerves cross one another) and progressively destroyed Milton's sight; in a similar recent case, removal of such a tumor (a craniopharyngioma the size of a pigeon's egg) saved the forty-one-year-old patient's remaining vision.

Milton adapted well to his affliction, creating and polishing his lines within his head until he could be periodically "milked" of them by one or another member of his family taking dictation. Gout, on the other hand, was a torment to the poet, though never mentioned in his writings. He spent his last nine years in a brick and timber cottage (now a museum) at Chalfont St. Giles, twenty miles northwest of London, with his third wife, the young, sensible Elizabeth Minshull. He took to his bed when the gout "struck in" and died on 8 November 1674, so quietly that the time of his demise was not observed. He left no will, only oral requests that his small estate go entirely to his wife, with no share to his three ungrateful daughters. The prudent Betty, however, faced with a court action, gave 100 pounds to each of her step-daughters and retired to her native Cheshire with the remaining 700. Milton was buried in London near his father in the Church of St. Giles, Cripplegate.

Mitchell, Margaret (1900–1949).

The Atlanta author whose one book, *Gone With the Wind* (1936), broke all records (twelve million authorized copies sold by 1965), was a diminutive woman, less than five feet tall, with blue eyes, auburn hair and a modest, cheerful disposition. Her Civil War novel won a Pulitzer prize; the motion picture version received an Academy Award as the best picture of 1939. By the summer of 1949 the flood of readers' letters showed signs of abating, and Miss Mitchell ("Peggy" to her friends) began to hope that she might, after all, soon be able to begin another book.

When a cool breeze sprang up during the evening of 11 August, she and her husband, John R. Marsh, drove into downtown Atlanta, parked their car on the west side of Peachtree Street, and walked arm in arm across toward the Arts Theater, where they planned to see the British movie *A Canterbury Tale*. It was 8:20 P.M. When they were halfway across Peachtree Street, a northbound car traveling, according to John's testimony, at about fifty miles per hour, came around the curve and braked violently. Margaret pulled away from John and ran back the way she had come. The automobile, while skidding sixty-seven feet, swerved toward her, striking her near the curb. She fell unconscious, blood-stained fluid trickling from the left ear. At Grady Memorial Hospital she lingered for almost five days without fully regaining consciousness. She had sustained a fracture of the skull extending from the crown to the top of the spine and two pelvic fractures. She died at 11:59 A.M., 16

August 1949. After a private Protestant service at the Spring Hill funeral home she was interred in the old Oakland Cemetery, Atlanta.

Hugh D. Gravitt, a twenty-nine-year-old off-duty taxicab driver, had been at the wheel of the speeding automobile. In ten years he had been cited twenty-eight times in traffic court and convicted eight times. In November 1949 he was sentenced to eighteen months imprisonment for involuntary manslaughter. Why was he exceeding the twenty-five miles per hour limit? "Everybody does it," he said. The day after sentencing and before beginning his term, he and his wife were injured when he crashed his car into a truck in Atlanta's outskirts. *See* F. Farr (1965).

Monroe, Marilyn (1926–1962).

The U.S. movie actress combined a sexual allure with an image of defenseless innocence many found irresistible. In private life she was an emotionally disturbed woman, insecure and given to fits of depression; her waywardness was the despair of a series of husbands and close friends. She was late or absent much of the time during the shooting of *The Misfits* in 1960 (see Gable, Clark). When, after treatment in New York psychiatric hospitals, the same pattern recurred in the making of *Something's Got to Give* in the summer of 1962, she was fired by Twentieth-Century Fox. A few months earlier she had bought her first house, a modest three-bedroom villa at the end of a cul-de-sac at 12305 Fifth Helena Drive in the Brentwood section of Los Angeles.

A month before her death, her friend, Robert F. Slatzer, reported her as being badly shaken by the termination of an affair with Robert Kennedy, Attorney General of the U.S., when he abruptly cut off all communication with her. Yet she showed no despondency, still less suicidal intent, during her last days and hours. The studio had rehired her to complete the stalled movie, other offers were coming in, and the body beautiful had never looked better. Accompanied by her companion-housekeeper, Mrs. Eunice Murray, during her final week she searched through the local stores for items needed for her house and garden.

On Saturday, 4 August, Marilyn stayed in all day, eating

nothing, puttering around the house in a terry cloth robe. At 4:30 P.M. her psychiatrist, Dr. Ralph Greenson, visited her and stayed until after six. A little later Mrs. Murray heard her laughing during a light-hearted call from Joe DiMaggio, Jr., son of her former husband, after which she phoned her psychiatrist to tell him about it. Peter Lawford, brother-in-law of the Kennedys, also called Marilyn that evening, according to his own account, and invited her to dinner, but she begged off because she was "sleepy." Mrs. Murray did not overhear this call, which may have come through after she saw Marilyn carry her personal telephone, attached to its long cord, into her bedroom and close the door.

"Sometime after midnight," as she put it in a 1973 interview, the housekeeper awoke, left her room, and found the telephone cord still under the actress' bedroom door. This was alarming; she knew Miss Monroe always removed the phone from her room before inserting earplugs, donning an eyeshade and settling to sleep. She went outside and, with the aid of a poker, drew aside the bedroom drapes enough to see Marilyn's naked body lying face down on the bed with the telephone hidden beneath her. She had already talked to Greenson on the household phone; he came over, broke a window and climbed into the bedroom. "We've lost her," he told Mrs. Murray. "Rigor mortis has set in." Marilyn had evidently died well before midnight on 4 August 1962.

Later, there were arguments about the time these events took place. Even if the body was not discovered until 3:30, as the official reports state, there was still considerable delay before the police were called at 4:25. The autopsy on "the 36-year-old, well-nourished Caucasian female weighing 117 pounds and measuring 65½ inches in length," was conducted by Dr. Thomas Noguchi. The stomach was almost empty, containing less than an ounce of brownish mucoid fluid. There was no trace of sleeping capsules or even of dyes from their brightly colored coatings in the stomach or colon. Yet, in addition to chloral hydrate (8.0 mg. percent), a drug the dead woman was known to have been taking as a sedative, the blood contained 4.5 mg. percent of barbiturates. This is astonishing. A New York professor of forensic pathology, Dr. S.S. Weinberg, comments, "These findings are certainly not characteristic of an oral ingestion of large amounts of barbiturates," and adds, "one must seriously consider the possibility of an injection or the use of a suppository to account for the toxicological findings." No drinking glass is mentioned in the reports either, making the supposed swallowing of a large number of capsules (forty-seven is the number mentioned) barely credible. Weinberg also observes that it is almost unknown for a woman to commit suicide in the nude; the absence of a note, too, is not without significance.

The first policeman on the scene, Sgt. Jack Clemmons, sensed the death scene and position of the body to be unnatural—"arranged"—and later complained that statements made to him were subsequently revised; he and others charge his chief with suppressing evidence obtained from the telephone company.

In his 1969 biography, F.L. Guiles concludes that Marilyn, aware that she had taken an overdose, called fruitlessly for assistance until she lost consciousness, but this does not explain the postmortem findings. Slatzer (whose 1974 biography includes copies of the autopsy report and other documents) unconvincingly raises the possibility of a murder conspiracy. Information necessary for a final conclusion is lacking. An inquest, omitted in 1962, could still be conducted on the remains resting in a crypt at Westwood Cemetery, Los Angeles. In the meantime, it is clear that the common belief that Marilyn Monroe deliberately took her own life has not been adequately demonstrated.

Mozart, Wolfgang Amadeus
(1756–1791).

The Austrian composer, sometimes regarded as the greatest genius in all the arts, did not cut an impressive figure; he was below average height, with small, plump hands, near-sighted blue eyes, a rather large head and an aquiline nose. But he took pride in his full head of hair. That his increasing fame as a composer brought little change in his impoverished existence was partly due to his lack of business sense and his wife Constanze's poor household management. Suffering from malnutrition and overwork, by 1791 Mozart was moody and depressed, though no hint of this is discernible in his last works. He reluctantly accepted the commission to write music for *The Magic Flute*, but later developed great enthusiasm for the project, even singing Papageno's opening aria on his deathbed. While en-

Artist's impression of Mozart performing his final requiem with friends.

gaged on the opera he received a mysterious request to write a Requiem Mass, an occurrence that oppressed him thereafter.

On 18 November, two days after conducting his last completed work, a Masonic cantata, he took to his bed. His modest apartment was on the second floor of the Klein-Kaiserstein House in Vienna's Rauhensteingasse; the building was demolished in 1844 and is now the site of the "Mozarthof." The cause of his symptoms—splitting headaches, fever, swelling of the extremities—remains the subject of lively controversy. "Thank goodness you have come, Sophie," he greeted Constanze's sister. "You shall see me die." He was sure he would not recover. "I have the taste of death in my mouth," he said more than once. The score of the Requiem lay before him on the bed as he instructed his pupil Franz Süssmayr on how it should be completed. He took the alto part in performances, with visiting friends, of the completed sections; in a sense, he participated in his own funeral, for at his actual obsequies no music was played.

During his last conscious hours his thoughts were with *The Magic Flute*.

Late on 4 December Mozart's physician, T.F. Closset, was summoned from the theater, but would not come until the play was over. When he directed cold compresses to be applied to the dying man's fevered brow, Mozart lapsed into a coma and died at about 1:00 A.M. on the 5th. The following day the remains were consecrated in a chapel on the north side of St. Stephen's Cathedral. Only a few friends were present; Constanze, prostrated with grief, did not attend. For reasons now obscure, only a small dog followed the cart bearing the coffin to the mortuary chapel of St. Marx' Cemetery outside the city wall. Reports of snow and rainstorms are inaccurate; the weather was mild, with a slight mist. On 7 December 1791 Mozart's body was lowered, with others, into a common unmarked grave. A monument was erected at the approximate spot in 1859. Constanze married a Danish diplomat a few years later and survived her first husband by over half a century.

The belief that Mozart was poisoned is still held by some today. The most likely perpetrator, it is said, was his rival Antonio Salieri, a lesser composer but a more successful musician. Mozart, overcome by morbid fancies, suspected he had been poisoned; Salieri is said to have made a confession, but this was denied during his lifetime. Beethoven seems never to have believed the rumors and Constanze in due course entrusted her son's musical education to Salieri, who was one of the very few who attended Mozart's funeral. Other versions of the poisoning theory mention Masonic plots and the toxic effect of mercury salts used in the treatment of syphilis, a disease from which the composer almost certainly never suffered.

What can be described as the orthodox modern belief, that Mozart died of uremic poisoning, dates from a 1905 study by the French physician J. Barraud. But the buildup of waste products caused by progressive failure of kidney function would be expected to result in a lengthy period of physical and mental incapacity. The attending physicians, Closset and Sallaba, described the illness as *hitziges Frieselfieber* ("a high fever with rash")—not an illuminating diagnosis. A friend of Constanze's, Dr. G. von Lobes, first suggested a rheumatic origin, using the term *febbre reumatica infiammatoria*. Carl Baer in his *Mozart: Krankheit–Tod–Begraebnis*, published by the Mozarteum,

Salzberg (2nd enlarged edition, 1972) has developed this idea in a painstaking study of Mozart's early medical history. What may have been the primary attack of rheumatic fever occurred in October 1762 when the six-year-old prodigy complained of pain in the buttocks and legs, with a rash and sweats; further episodes can be traced to 1766 and the following year. Baer makes a persuasive case for Mozart having died from the effects of carditis of rheumatic origin ending in congestive heart failure, a not uncommon cause of death in young adults even now. This diagnosis has the support of the Mozarteum and of the Friends of Mozart, Inc. (Erna Schwerin, president), of New York.

Mussolini, Benito (1883–1945).

The leader (*Il Duce*) of the Fascist movement, dictator of Italy from 1925 until imminent military defeat by the Allies caused his downfall, was repudiated by the grand council in July 1943 and arrested. In a brilliant parachute operation ordered by his ally Adolf Hitler he was freed from imprisonment at the 7,000-foot-high Campo Imperatore in the Abruzzese Mountains on 12 September and later, under German supervision, he set up the puppet Republic of Salò in northern Italy on the shore of Lake Garda. But Mussolini was now a broken man, yellow and emaciated, with a large duodenal ulcer. As the Allies advanced, and with Italian partisans active within the borders, the new republic began to crumble and Mussolini moved to Milan. News of Germany's surrender reached him on 25 April 1945 as the first U.S. columns entered the city and he retreated north to Como near the Swiss border with the hope of fighting in the mountains. His wife, Rachele, was also in Como, but they made contact only by telephone. His mistress, Claretta Petacci, joined him at Menaggio as, with his Italian supporters dwindling in numbers, he joined a German motorized column on its way home. The Italian members, including Claretta, were turned back by partisans, but Mussolini, disguised in a German topcoat and with his hat pulled low over his face, reached the village of Dongo before being recognized and arrested.

At three o'clock the next morning, after some sleep at a partisan frontier post, Mussolini was driven to a small peasant dwelling. On the way they met Claretta, who had been searching for

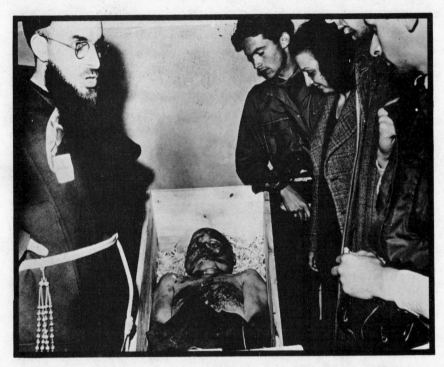

Italian patriots and a priest view the mutilated body of Mussolini in a plain wooden casket in Milan, 1945.

THE BETTMANN ARCHIVE

him. In Dongo a partisan officer, "Colonel Valerio" (real name: Walter Andisio, an accountant) convened a military court which swiftly condemned Mussolini to death along with seventeen other high-ranking Fascisti who had been taken prisoner. Valerio came for Mussolini and his companion at 4:00 P.M. the same day, 28 April 1945. They were taken by car to a place called Giulino di Mezzegra and made to stand against a low wall. Claretta murmured to Mussolini, "Aren't you glad I followed you to the end?" Valerio read the death sentence aloud; then he and his comrades fired. The following day the bodies, along with four others, were exhibited head downward at a gas station in the Piazzale Loreto, Milan. Mussolini wore black boots, black riding breeches and T-shirt; his head was close-shaven and disfigured by bullet wounds and bruises. Claretta, with trim figure

The remains of Mussolini are restored to his family at Predappio, twelve years after his death.

LIBRARY OF CONGRESS

and short curly hair, wore a gray suit, lacy blouse and blue high-heeled shoes.

The two were buried in unmarked graves at Musocco Cemetery, Milan. The following year Mussolini's remains were removed by a Neo-Fascist group and later found beneath the altar at the Franciscan monastery of the Angelicum in Padua. The Italian government hid them in a Capuchin monastery at Cerro Maggiore, fifteen miles north of Milan, and did not pass them over to Donna Rachele until eleven years later. On 1 September 1957 she laid her husband permanently to rest at his birthplace, Predappio, 160 miles north of Rome, in the family vault in the cemetery of San Casciano. In a gesture of defiance, she declined to employ a coffin; the square zinc box handed over by the government was placed in the stone sarcophagus. *See* L. Fermi (1961).

Napoleon (1769–1821).

Napoleon Bonaparte, the Emperor Napoleon I of France (1805–1814), was short (five feet two and a half inches) in stature, tuberculous during part of his life and tormented by many ailments, including malaria and cystitis. After his defeat at Waterloo in 1815 he was exiled on the small, isolated South Atlantic island of St. Helena, then governed by the autocratic Hudson Lowe. Napoleon lived, with a retinue of twenty-six but without his wife, at Longwood, a mansion converted to his needs. In 1817 he suffered from swollen legs, the recurrence of an old complaint; more serious was a pain below the ribs on the right side. When his physician, Barry O'Meara, concurred with French suspicions that the prisoner had contracted tropical hepatitis, the physician was ordered home by Lowe, who forbade

Napoleon's death mask, attributed to his physician, F. Antommarchi.

THE NEW YORK PUBLIC LIBRARY

For nineteen years, until they were transferred to Les Invalides in Paris, Napoleon's remains lay in this simple grave on St. Helena, where he had died in exile.

LIBRARY OF CONGRESS

any talk of the island not being salubrious to the highest degree. A naval physician, Dr. Stokoe, was court-martialed and ousted from the service for repeating the diagnosis in 1819.

Napoleon's final care was provided by the young anatomist Francisco Antommarchi, sent out from Corsica by the family. Antommarchi found his patient to be hard of hearing, with a yellow corpulent body and with the left lobe of the liver tender and painful to the touch. Beginning on 22 March 1821, the emperor vomited frequently; Antommarchi was giving him tartar emetic, a poisonous antimony compound, in lemonade without his knowledge. After a period of remission the symptoms resumed on 24 April. On 3 May a military surgeon, Dr. A. Arnott, administered ten grains of the mercurial laxative calomel (over three times the recommended maximum dose).

Within a few hours the patient was prostrated by tarry diarrhea and signs of internal bleeding. Napoleon died at 5:50 P.M., 5 May 1821.

The body was laid on the billiard table in the drawing room at Longwood for an autopsy the following afternoon. The conditions were less than ideal: seventeen observers, including eight physicians, were crowded into the stuffy, ill-lighted room. The atmosphere was tense and suspicious, the French and British both apprehensive of what would be discovered. The official report, evidently a political document, is highly unsatisfactory. It describes a cancerous stomach and implies no abnormality in the liver or any other organ. The report produced by Antommarchi, who conducted the examination, has generally been judged the most complete and objective. He noted the liver to be enlarged but otherwise normal, inflamed patches on the external surface of the intestines, and "a cancerous ulcer which had its center at the superior part along the lesser curvature of the stomach communicating with the liver." However, he later expressed doubts about the cancerous nature of the lesion. His request that the stomach be preserved was refused; the silver vessel containing it was placed in the coffin. He claimed to have abstracted small specimens of the intestine, which still exist and which have been declared by Lord Moynihan to show clear signs of amebic dysentery. In fact, A.P. Cawadias in a 1963 study goes further, concluding the entire clinical picture to be one of amebiasis (amebic infection) with liver involvement, which was endemic at that period in St. Helena; the ulcer might have originated in the stomach or it might have been a perforation from an abscess of the liver.

S. Forshufvud, H. Smith and A. Wassen in two reports in the magazine *Nature* (1961, 1962) found an arsenic concentration of 10.38 parts per million (about thirteen times the normal amount) in a specimen of Napoleon's hair. Though the presence of arsenic, determined by the sensitive neutron-irradiation method, can scarcely be doubted, interpretation of this finding is far from easy. Medical writers and recent biographers alike have tended to discount the suggestion that Napoleon was systematically poisoned either by someone on his staff or by his British captors. What we know of the circumstances during his last years is quite at variance with this theory. Many modern historians would probably agree with D.C. Wallace, who wrote in an Australian medical journal in 1964: "The only possible conclusion is that although he received arsenic, he did not die of its administration...." Probably, Wallace believes, arsenic was present in "one of the multitude of imprecisely described medicines administered during his last illness." Napoleon's fatal disease was a perforated stomach ulcer, probably cancerous. The immediate cause of death was calomel poisoning. Other diseases, including a long-standing amebic dysentery, probably afflicted the exiled emperor, further confusing the diagnosis.

Napoleon's body, in its four coffins of tin, mahogany, lead and again mahogany, was buried on the island in a favorite spot beside a stream. When it was exhumed nineteen years later it was found to be remarkably well preserved. It now rests under the high dome of Les Invalides in Paris.

Nehru, Jawaharlal (1889–1964).

The first prime minister of independent India (1947–1964) suffered a slight stroke in 1963 and a much more severe one on 7 January 1964 while attending the congress session in Bhubaneswar, about 250 miles southwest of Calcutta. He recovered, but his left side was slightly paralyzed, affecting his speech and forcing him to drag his leg. His colleagues, perturbed about his health, requested he choose a successor; he refused, believing it would be unfair to indicate a preference. On 16 and 17 May, while attending the All-India Congress Committee session in Bombay, he seemed to have regained some of his zest for life, but on his return to Delhi the following day he complained of feeling unwell. A three-day break at Dehra Dun in the highlands north of the capital again restored his spirits.

At his Delhi residence, the palatial Teen Murti House, the prime minister spent the evening of May 26 in his usual manner: he attended to some official business in his study after dinner and retired to his bedroom at 11:00 P.M. His male attendant slept close by. His only child, Indira, the First Lady (Nehru's wife Kamala had died in 1936) occupied rooms at the opposite end of the house. He had a restless night, twice awakening and taking a sedative. At about six in the morning he was roused by severe pains in his abdomen and lower back. Doctors who reached him half an hour later diagnosed a ruptured aorta. By then Nehru had lapsed into a coma. Though a transfusion of Indira's blood was given, his condition was hopeless from the outset. He died at 1:44 P.M. on 27 May 1964.

On the 28th nearly six thousand people lined the six-mile funeral route to a place on the bank of the River Yamuna near where Gandhi's body had been cremated in 1948. At 4:30 P.M. Nehru's grandson, Sanjay, lighted the pyre while Hindu and Buddhist priests chanted. A volley of small arms was fired three times and twenty-four buglers sounded taps. On 9 June, as Nehru had requested, a portion of his ashes was thrown into the River Ganges; the remainder was scattered by airplane over the fields of India. *See* B.N. Pandey (1976).

Nelson, Horatio (1758–1805).

The British admiral began his life at sea as a delicate, undersized, twelve-year-old midshipman. He suffered many attacks of malaria and nearly died from yellow fever. As late as 1801 he wrote of being "sick to death" of seasickness. He lost the sight of his right eye during the siege of Calvi, Corsica, on 10 July 1794 and his right arm at Santa Cruz de Tenerife, on 25 July 1797. He was a frail man with an indomitable spirit. It is commonly thought he wore a patch over his blind eye, but the eye was not disfigured and he wore instead a green shade over his good eye to protect it from the glare of sun and sea.

The Battle of Trafalgar was fought off the southwest coast of Spain on 21 October 1805. At dawn Nelson was already pacing the quarter-deck of the *Victory* with Captain Thomas Hardy. His officers, noticing that his four Orders of Knighthood would make an excellent target, wished he would cover them, but no one dared suggest it. The admiral had flags hoisted reading ENGLAND EXPECTS THAT EVERY MAN WILL DO HIS DUTY, and a great cheer rose from every ship; with flags still flying they went into action. The *Victory* was hit several times, and at 1:15 P.M. Nelson was struck by a bullet fired by a sharpshooter stationed high on the French ship *Redoutable*. He collapsed to his knees, steadying himself with the fingers of his left hand. Sergeant-Major Secker and two seamen ran to his aid. He murmured to Hardy, "They have done for me at last" and, when the other demurred, insisted, "Yes, my backbone is shot through." As he

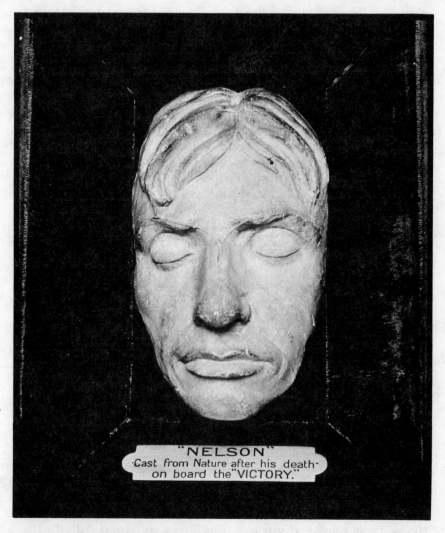

Death mask of Horatio Nelson, taken after he had been preserved in a cask of brandy for several weeks.

PORTSMOUTH ROYAL NAVAL MUSEUM,
PORTSMOUTH, ENGLAND

was carried below he drew a handkerchief over his face so that the men would not know that their admiral had been wounded and become dispirited. Hardy remained on the quarter-deck of the *Victory*, which would remain the flagship as long as Nelson lived.

The wounded man was laid on a pallet, undressed and examined by the surgeon, Mr. Beatty, who thought that the ball had penetrated deep into the chest and was probably lodged in the spine. Later evidence at autopsy was to show that it had entered through Nelson's left epaulette (taking some of the cloth and gold with it), broken two ribs, severed the main trunk of the left pulmonary artery and fractured the sixth and seventh dorsal vertebrae. Nelson had no sensation in the lower parts of his body but he was aware of a gush of blood every minute within his chest and he was in great pain. He reminded his chaplain Dr. Scott that he had left Lady Hamilton and their daughter, Horatia, to the care of his country. When his captain was at last able to come below Nelson asked anxiously, "Well, Hardy, how goes the battle? How goes the day for us?" Hardy gave him the good news that twelve or fourteen of the enemy ships were in British hands. "I am a dead man, Hardy. I am going fast; it will be all over with me soon. Come nearer to me...." Hardy bent over the frail admiral, who was supported by Dr. Scott and the purser, Mr. Burke. "Pray let dear Lady Hamilton have my hair, and all other things belonging to me." The severe internal bleeding was making him very thirsty. It was hot and airless in the foul-smelling cockpit. "I wish I had not left the deck, for I shall soon be gone."

Dr. Scott gently rubbed Nelson's body in an attempt to ease the pain while others gave the admiral sips of lemonade or stirred the fetid air with paper fans. Hardy returned with the news that victory was complete. Nelson, close to death, said, "Don't throw me overboard, Hardy," to which the unhappy captain stammered, "Oh, no, certainly not." After Nelson reminded him once more of Lady Hamilton, he said, "Kiss me, Hardy." The tall captain bent down and kissed his cheek. "Now I am satisfied; thank God I have done my duty." Hardy stood quietly for a moment or so, then knelt and kissed his forehead. "Who is that?" asked Nelson, almost gone. "It is Hardy." "God bless you, Hardy." He spoke little more, only asking to be fanned or rubbed. The log of the *Victory* records: "Partial firing continued until 4:30, when a victory having been reported to the Right Honourable Lord Viscount Nelson, K.B., and Commander-in-Chief, he died of his wounds."

After Nelson's hair had been cut off, his body was placed in a large cask which was then filled with brandy. When the *Victory* reached England in December, Mr. Beatty had the cask opened. The body was found to be perfectly preserved, and death masks were made. The body lay in state in the Painted Hall at Greenwich before being taken by funeral barge up the river to Whitehall. Thousands of people crowded into London for Lord Nelson's funeral on 9 January 1806. His remains, in a coffin made from the mainmast of the former French flagship *L'Orient*, were lowered into a black marble sarcophagus under the cupola of St. Paul's Cathedral. It is surmounted by a viscount's coronet and inscribed only with his name and dates of birth and death.

Nero A.D. (37–68).

The Emperor of Rome (A.D. 54–68) reached the throne when his mother Agrippina (q.v.) murdered her husband, his stepfather the Emperor Claudius. Nero, in turn, put to death anyone who constituted a threat, however remote. He has been described as "a satyr with a swollen belly, spindly legs, tangled yellow hair, and lusterless gray eyes." A man of varied and depraved tastes, his sex partners ranged from men of all ages to his own mother.

After the fire of Rome on 18 July 64, Nero imposed heavy taxes to rebuild the city and construct the famous palace, "The Golden House." Support for the emperor dwindled. The upper class, whose ranks had been decimated by his assassinations, turned aginst him. The soldiers had not been paid for a long time and the people were hungry; ships which should have brought grain held sand for a court performance of wrestlers. On 8 June 68 Nero fled his palace with the idea of taking refuge in Egypt but had traveled only as far as his mansion in the Servilian Gardens, still within the gates of Rome, when he stopped to rest. On awakening he found that the Praetorian Guard had deserted him. The senate proclaimed Galba, the seventy-three-year-old governor of Nearer Spain (Hispania Tarraconensis), as emperor and passed sentence of death on Nero. His first thoughts were of suicide, but he put it off. His freedman Phaon offered him the use of his house, about four miles outside the city. For a few hours he hid in the storeroom there, but was persuaded by his attendants that suicide would be preferable to inevitable discovery and ignominious death. He ordered a grave to be dug, measuring it with his own body, weeping and repeating over and over again, "What a loss I shall be to the arts!"

A runner brought a letter from Phaon, announcing that Nero had been declared a public enemy by the senate and would be punished in "ancient style" when caught. This, it was explained to him, meant he would be stripped naked and, with his head thrust into a wooden fork, flogged to death with rods. Terrified, Nero snatched up two daggers and felt their points. When none of his companions would agree to commit suicide first, he hesitated, moaning about his cowardice and the ugliness of his life. In Greek he mumbled, "This certainly is no credit to Nero, no credit at all—one should be tough in such situations—come, pull yourself together, man!" As the sound of horses' hooves signaled the arrival of the cavalry, he stabbed himself in the throat with the help of his minister Epaphroditus. When a centurion entered, affecting concern and stanching the bleeding with his cloak, Nero murmured wryly, "Too late; how *loyal* you are!"

Nero's death on 9 June 68 ended the Caesarian line. Acte, the woman he had loved but never married, gave him an expensive funeral. His ashes, placed in a porphyry urn, were taken to the burial place of the Domitian family beneath the Pincian Hill. On the site of the tomb now stands the church of Santa Maria del Popolo. *See* M. Grant (1970).

Nicholas II (*Nikolai Alexandrovich*) (1868–1918).

The last of the Russian czars, a man of great personal charm, was a devoted husband and father but a weak emperor. The czarina, German-born Alexandra Feodorovna, supplied the strength of character he lacked, but she was willful and reserved, and the Russian people, especially after war with Germany broke out in 1914, suspected her loyalty. An added source of distrust was the degree to which she came under the influence of the debauched monk Rasputin (q.v.). Following the Petrograd riots in March 1917 the government resigned and the czar's abdication was requested. In August the imperial family was moved to Tobolsk, a river town in West Siberia where Bolshevik influence had not yet become predominant. In April 1918 the czar was ordered to Moscow; at Ekaterinburg (now Sverdlovsk) in the Urals the progress of the party, which included the czarina and one daughter, Maria, was interrupted by the local Bolsheviks. The remainder of the family and a small number of retainers soon rejoined them in captivity there. Their prison was five upper rooms of a private residence, the Ipatiev house on Voznesensky Street.

The accepted account of the imperial family's massacre derives from a book by N. Sokolov, a monarchist who conducted an investigation shortly after their disappearance. According to Sokolov, a decision was made in Moscow to liquidate the czar's entire family when Ekaterinburg became threatened by anti-Bolshevik forces advancing from the east. At midnight on 16 July (new style) 1918 the prisoners were awakened and ordered downstairs to a semibasement room. There they were shot and bayoneted to death by Yakov Yurovsky, the secret police chief, and his squad. With the family members died their physician, cook, valet and parlormaid—eleven persons all told. The bodies were taken to a disused mine near the village of Koptyaki, dismembered and cremated, and the ashes treated with sulfuric acid. The residues were tipped down a mine shaft.

Until recently, the only serious challenge to this version was that of "Anna Anderson," who surfaced in Berlin in 1920, claiming to be Anastasia, the youngest of the czar's daughters. In *The File of the Tsar* (1976), A. Summers and T. Mangold describe their four-year investigation, beginning with work on a 1971 BBC television documentary. They discovered suppressed evidence in Sokolov's files and brought to light other material, from which they conclude that (a) the complete lack of human remains at the mine (except part of a finger) suggests that eleven bodies could hardly have been destroyed there (teeth in particular are almost impossible to destroy by the treatment described); (b) there is good evidence, including eyewitness accounts, that the czarina and her four girls were living as prisoners in the town of Perm, 200 miles west of Ekaterinburg, as late as Christmas Eve 1918 (they had evidently been moved there by train at about the date of their supposed massacre); (c) Anastasia was roughly handled during her recapture after an attempted escape from Perm, as testified by a physician who treated her injuries; (d) Anna Anderson (Mrs. John Manahan), who was living in Charlottesville, Va., when the investigators interviewed her in 1974, is quite likely to be the genuine Anastasia; (e) the czar himself does appear to have been shot by a firing squad, possibly near the notorious mine area, on 16 July 1918, and his body taken away by car (the invalid czarevitch Alexis—a hemophiliac—was probably also killed by the Bolsheviks). Summers and Mangold have no evidence regarding the ultimate fate of the Romanov women.

Nightingale, Florence (1820–1910).

The English nurse and hospital administrator who raised her profession to a place of honor became a national heroine when her achievements in the Crimean campaign (1854–1856) became known at home. Her first achievement was to bring the bare, filthy, ill-equipped hospital at Scutari up to a reasonable standard and reduce the appalling death rate from disease. The enlisted men came to worship "The Lady with the Lamp." Back in England she obtained a commission in 1857 to investigate sanitary conditions in military hospitals, and later she extended her inquiries into civilian establishments, which were often not much better. She established the first nursing school (at St. Thomas's Hospital, London) in 1860, and her shrewd, compassionate *Notes on Nursing* became a bestseller. Late in life, when the tall willowy girl had become a stout, pleasant-faced old lady confined to her room at 10 South Street, Park Lane, her advice was in constant demand by government ministers on various topics, including India, which she had never visited. She had a forthright way of expressing herself; never satisfied to hear what had been achieved, she would ask, "How many things still remain to be done?"

By 1902, when Florence's sight was quite gone and her mind had begun to weaken, a companion had to be tactfully brought into her home. Books were read aloud to her (a favorite was Theodore Roosevelt's *Strenuous Life*) and she enjoyed reciting poetry and singing operatic arias in a voice that had kept its sweetness. Only in 1906 was the India office told not to send more papers for Miss Nightingale's attention. In 1907 she became the first woman to have the Order of Merit conferred on her; reading of this honor in the newspapers, many were surprised to learn the heroine of half a century ago was still alive. Her nursing school's jubilee was celebrated in Carnegie Hall, New York, in May 1910. Gradually Florence Nightingale's strength faded. On 13 August 1910 she fell asleep at about noon and died at 2:30 P.M.

Her will, like her official reports, was exceedingly long. She requested no memorial; her body was "to be carried to the nearest convenient burial ground accompanied by not more than two persons without trappings." This was not done, but burial in Westminster Abbey was declined and she was carried by six sergeants of the Guards regiments into the churchyard at East Wellow, west of Romsey, Hampshire, and laid to rest with her parents. To the plain four-sided tombstone were added a cross and the simple inscription: "F.N. BORN 1820. DIED 1910."

Nijinsky, Vaslav (1890–1950).

At his debut in Paris in May 1909 the Russian dancer stunned the audience with his incredible performance. His relationship with Diaghilev, who had brought the Ballet Russe to Paris, was more than mere friendship. When Nijinsky married Romola de Pulszky in 1913, Diaghilev, livid with jealousy, dismissed him.

Nijinsky opened his final performance at Suvretta House, St. Moritz, on 19 January 1919 in aid of the Red Cross by bringing out a chair and sitting motionless, staring at the increasingly nervous audience for half an hour. Rising at last, he made a cross on the floor from black and white velvet and, standing like a living cross, announced, "Now I will dance you the war, with its suffering, with its destruction, with its death." And dance he did, brilliantly, terrifyingly and tragically. In Zurich, the famous psychiatrist Professor Bleuler diagnosed Nijinsky as a schizophrenic, a word he had coined himself in 1911. Romola tried to keep her husband with her as much as possible. As they traveled over the years in Switzerland, France and England, she took him to leading psychiatrists and attempted to stimulate his mind at the theater and ballet. At a performance in 1928 a friend barely recognized him. "I was thunderstruck. His face, so often radiant as a young god's, for thousands an imperishable memory, was now grey, hung slackly, and void of expression....Nijinsky, who formerly seemed able to leap over roof-tops, now feels his way, uncertainly, anxiously, from step to step."

In August 1938 Dr. Sakel began an experimental treatment at Kreuzlingen Sanatorium in Switzerland. Nijinsky was given insulin shock therapy; each treatment was a great strain on his heart and for hours he lay in a deep coma. On regaining consciousness he was able to answer questions—a great improvement, because he had been mute for years—and hopes for recovery were high. But war intervened. The Nijinskys traveled from one European country to another seeking shelter. Romola placed Vaslav in a hospital in Sopron on the Austrian-Hungarian border. One evening in March 1945 she answered a knock at the door to find Vaslav with an attendant who told her, "I had to bring Mr. Nijinsky home. We have received orders to exterminate our mental patients by tomorrow morning."

In November 1947 permission was granted for them to live in England. They moved from house to house "Kak Tsigane" ("like gypsies") commented Vaslav. On Tuesday 4 April 1950, in spite of a headache, he was at the BBC's Alexandra Palace studios watching with keen interest the Paris Opera Ballet being televised. The following day, back at the Welbeck Hotel, he lay listless, with a rapid pulse, refusing to eat. On Thursday he was taken to a clinic and on Good Friday he lapsed into a coma, moaning constantly. Doctors began to treat him with streptomycin and told Romola that if they could bring him out of the coma within twenty-four hours he would be saved; however, another consultant said he was "beyond human help; his kidneys are gone." On Saturday, 8 April 1950, Nijinsky opened his eyes and was able to sit up and be fed some breakfast. Everyone felt optimistic, but suddenly Vaslav's expression changed; "Mamasha," he cried, and fell back on the pillows, dead.

A Mass was held at St. James's Spanish Place, on Friday, 14 April. He was buried in St. Marylebone Cemetery, Finchley Road, London. In June 1953 his body was moved to the Montmartre Cemetery, Paris. *See* R. Buckle (1971).

Onassis, Aristotle (1906–1975).

The Greek shipping and airline tycoon felt tired and dejected after his son, Alexander, was killed in a 1973 airplane crash. The following spring he was told he suffered from myasthenia gravis, a defect of nerve-muscle transmission; unable to keep his eyes open, he had his eyelids taped behind his dark glasses. His marriage to Jacqueline Bouvier Kennedy had been in trouble at least since 1972, and divorce plans were being discussed. In the last of a series of business reverses, his bankrupt Olympic Airways was taken over by the Greek government in December 1974. Two months later Mrs. Onassis in New York received word that her husband was ill in Greece with pneumonia and gallbladder disease, the outcome of cortisone therapy for his other health problems. She flew over in time to accompany him to Paris for an operation; on 10 February his gallbladder was removed at the American Hospital at Neuilly. He was only semiconscious during the next five weeks, his breathing aided by a respirator. His daughter, Christina, refused to share the Onassis apartment on the rue Foch with her stepmother. Jacqueline, for her part, put in a daily appearance at the hospital, but otherwise left the bedside watch to the blood relatives and at the end of the month flew back to the U.S.

Onassis died on 15 March 1975 of bronchial pneumonia, which had defied all antibiotics. His wife returned to Paris the following day with Edward Kennedy to escort the body to the millionaire's private island, Skorpios, for burial. Seven large wreaths were in evidence, one of them bearing the inscription: TO ARI FROM JACKIE. As the coffin was laid to rest near Alexander's grave, the Onassis yacht *Christina* rode at anchor in the harbor below, its flag at half-mast. *See* N. Fraser et al. (1977).

O'Neill, Eugene (1888–1953).

The first important U.S. dramatist determined on his future career while in a sanatorium in 1913. Until that date he lived among the bums on waterfronts around the world. His first marriage had already ended in divorce and he had tried, perhaps not very seriously, to kill himself with barbiturates. By September 1950, when his elder son, Eugene Jr., committed suicide at Woodstock, N.Y., by slashing his wrist and ankle, the playwright's writing career had come to an end; he could no longer hold a pencil in his palsied hands, and even his legs and feet were affected by the tremor. He would sit for hours on the porch of his house at the tip of Marblehead Neck, twenty miles north of Boston, looking dejectedly out to sea. Cut off by his own wish from the two children of his second marriage, Shane and Oona (Mrs. Charles Chaplin), he lived with his third wife, Carlotta Monterey (born Hazel Tharsing in 1888) in a state of exasperation that sometimes erupted into mutual hatred and violence.

Both he and his wife, a former actress, had an instinct for self-dramatization. On 5 February 1951 the playwright was found, late on a chilly evening, lying in his front yard with his right kneecap fractured; he had hurried out of the house, ill clad and without his cane, during one of their flare-ups. At Salem Hospital she made a scene and was taken to a mental institution at Belmont. Soon O'Neill, weighing only eighty-four pounds, was in Doctors Hospital, New York, reunited with old friends previously kept from him by his wife. He signed a petition charging her with being mentally incapable; she, released after treatment for accidental bromide overdose, countercharged him with cruelty and abuse. But in May it was time for sad farewells; he admitted to his New York friends his need for Carlotta and was reunited with her at the Shelton Hotel, Boston, where they lived thereafter in the two rooms of Suite 401. He was insolvent and dependent on the annuity settled on her by a former lover, a Wall Street banker. A nurse was engaged, but Mrs. O'Neill cared for him herself most of the time, bathing him and half-carrying him to the window, from which he could view the Charles River. The hotel employees often heard angry voices; sometimes, Carlotta later said, he was insisting noisily on more Nembutal. Certainly he was sedated much of the time. During the last year she helped him tear up and burn at least six plays of his projected cycle.

On 24 November 1953 O'Neill stopped eating and his temperature shot up; he had pneumonia and little strength or will to put up a fight. Shortly before sinking into a final coma he raised himself from the pillow, stared wildly around the room, and cried, "I knew it, I knew it! Born in a hotel room—goddamn it—and dying in a hotel room!" He died a few minutes after 4:30 P.M., 27 November 1953.

According to Dr. R.S. Schwab, an expert on Parkinson's disease who once examined O'Neill at Marblehead, the autopsy revealed that he had "suffered chiefly from a familial tremor inherited from his mother and only to a minor degree from Parkinson's."

Carlotta, carrying out (she said) "every wish of Gene's to the letter," kept his funeral arrangements secret, changing taxi cabs on the way to and from the funeral parlor and hiring strong-arm agents to keep out reporters who besieged the hotel. In an effort to foil the press burial was deferred so long that the health department made inquiries. The cortege on 2 December consisted only of the hearse and a single limousine carrying the widow, the nurse and the physician. It was followed at a distance by two cars bearing curious onlookers: O'Neill's barber and an admirer of his plays. A few days later, because the coffin extended six inches beyond its allotted space in Forest Hill Cemetery, Boston, it was dug up and reburied. Carlotta died in 1970. *See* L. Shaeffer (1973).

Orwell, George (1903–1950).

The English libertarian writer, whose works are noted for their great power and honesty, lived in poverty for much of his life. He achieved fame in 1945 when his anti-Stalinist novel *Animal Farm* was published after several rejection slips. He was a very tall, thin man with cadaverous features, sad eyes and a voice weakened by a throat wound in the Spanish civil war. After the death of his wife, Eileen, under anesthesia during a minor operation, he went to live in the wilds of Jura, off the west coast of Scotland, in the winter of 1946–47. For a man in his precarious health to go so far from adequate medical facilities was ill advised, and the primitive conditions under which his household lived may well have shortened his life. He began his last book, *1984*, in August 1946 and completed it with difficulty in November 1948. By that time his worsening tuberculosis, first diagnosed in 1938, had driven him to sanatoriums on the mainland, first near Glasgow and later at the little village of Cranham, Gloucestershire. The novel, which expresses the writer's equal distrust of political power of the left and right, introduces many autobiographical touches, including his hospital experiences. Though powerful, it is marred by an absence of hope or personal heroism, and therefore of suspense. Orwell himself admitted that it would have been less gloomy if he had not been so ill.

Orwell spent his last weeks in London, at University College Hospital. There his mood brightened remarkably, and he began to plan future work. His financial worries were over, and the beautiful Sonia Brownell, assistant editor of *Horizon*, had consented to marry him. For the hospital wedding, his fellow author

Plaque at the corner of Pond Street and South End Road in Hampstead, London, commemorating George Orwell. Photo by Paul R. Lorch.

Anthony Powell bought him a mauve velvet smoking jacket which he wore over his pajamas. A plane had been chartered to take the bride and groom to Switzerland, where he hoped to convalesce. Malcolm Muggeridge, another of his regular visitors, records that his fishing rod lay ready at the foot of the bed.

The end was sudden; after a massive hemorrhage of the lungs Orwell died on 21 January 1950. "Sonia came to see us the same evening," wrote Muggeridge. "She cried and cried. I shall always love her for her true tears on that occasion." Orwell, who had no time for religious sentiment during his life, in his will asked for a church funeral and burial in a country churchyard. His friends had little trouble arranging a Protestant service at Christ Church, Albany Street, on the 26th, but the country churchyard was more of a problem. At last, the Astor family arranged for Orwell to be laid to rest at All Saints, Sutton Courtenay, near Abingdon, Berkshire.

Oswald, Lee Harvey (1939–1963).

The assassin of President John F. Kennedy, a habitual truant from school, underwent psychiatric study in New York at the age of twelve. In the U.S. Marine Corps in 1956 he was rated as a sharpshooter and also became a Marxist about that time. He defected to the U.S.S.R. in 1959 and married Marina Prusakova in 1961. Discontented in Russia, he was permitted to return to the U.S. with his wife and baby daughter in June 1962 and at that time became an ardent supporter of Cuba's Marxist president, Fidel Castro. He talked to Marina of killing Richard Nixon and other notables. With his mail-order rifle he shot at and barely missed retired Maj.-Gen. Edwin Walker, a right-wing spokesman, at Walker's home on 6 April 1963.

After the assassination of President Kennedy (q.v.) on 22 November, Oswald was arrested and charged with the murder of Police Patrolman J.D. Tippit. At 1:30 A.M. on Saturday, the 23rd, he was charged with the murder of the President. At 11:20 A.M. on the following day, Oswald was escorted through the basement of Dallas police headquarters to a vehicle for transfer to the county jail. Jack Ruby (1911-1967; born Jacob Rubenstein), operator of the local Carousel nightclub, pushed forward out of the crowd of reporters and onlookers and fired one shot into Oswald's left lower chest with the Colt .38 revolver he habitually carried. Like Kennedy forty-seven hours earlier, Oswald was rushed to Parkland Memorial Hospital. Dr. George T. Shires later testified to the Warren Commission that there was never any hope of Oswald's survival. Major blood vessels, including the aorta and inferior vena cava, had been punctured, and the loss of blood was rapid and extensive. After a tracheotomy and surgery to control the bleeding, Oswald was declared dead at 1:07 P.M. He was buried in an isolated section of Rose Hill Cemetery, Fort Worth, with only his widow, mother and brother present. The cemetery manager was not happy; it would be bad for business, he complained. Already one man had called, threatening to remove the coffins of family members.

Ruby was convicted of murder on 14 March 1964. The verdict was overturned in October 1966 on the grounds that Judge Joe B. Brown had permitted inadmissible evidence to be introduced into the trial. A second trial was pending two months later when Ruby was transferred from Dallas County Jail to Parkland Memorial Hospital and found to have cancer; the primary site was evidently the lungs, but by the time of his death the disease had spread to the lymph nodes with tentative involvement of the liver. However, the cause of Ruby's sudden death at 10:30 A.M. on 3 January 1967 was a blood clot that traveled from his leg to his lungs. He was buried in Westlawn Cemetery, Chicago.

Paganini, Niccolò (1782–1840).

The Italian violinist and musical showman was aided by the abnormal flexibility of the connective tissue that allowed his fingers, wrists and shoulders unusual freedom of movement. M.R. Shoenfeld in a 1978 medical study concludes that the musician suffered from Marfan's syndrome, a hereditary disorder in which a tall, thin stature, spidery fingers and hyperextensible joints are linked with various cardiovascular and ocular defects. But there is a lack of evidence for this diagnosis; an earlier medical study by R.D. Smith and J.W. Worthington (1967) makes alternative suggestions to account for the virtuoso's remarkable technique. He was indeed tall and very thin, but his hands, as proved by plaster casts, were normal in size and shape.

Paganini suffered from a legion of ailments: a stubborn (probably tuberculous) cough; an irritable bowel; throat ulceration and pains of the abdomen and legs caused by syphilis, the treatment of which by mercury compounds led to inflammation of the mouth and loss of all teeth at an early age; and prostatism, with bladder infection, urinary retention and orchitis. He lost his voice in his last two years. He died at his home, a third-floor apartment on the Grande Rue in Nice (at that time in Italy) at 5:00 P.M. on 27 May 1840 after a long period of weakness, trembling limbs and sunken cheeks. It is said he expired in an armchair, no doubt after a final pulmonary hemorrhage, while attempting to swallow a sopped crust.

The body was embalmed—a new procedure at that date—but the bishop of Nice, antagonized by the dead man's refusal to receive the abbé, by his private reputation and no doubt by his failure to mention the church as his beneficiary, refused to permit burial in consecrated ground. For two months the corpse remained in the apartment, after which the health department had it moved to the basement of the house. In September 1841 it

Paganini in his heyday!   LIBRARY OF CONGRESS

was transferred to a leper house in Villefranche, later to a disused concrete vat in an olive oil factory, then to an estate at the seaward end of Cap Ferrat. In April 1844 the government had the body moved by sea to Genoa and buried at the Villa Paganini at Polcevera. A year later the remains were reburied at the Villa Gaione in Parma. Only in 1876, when the bishop's provisions were revoked, did the maestro achieve a resting place in consecrated ground in the cemetery of Parma. Even then he was denied rest: the Czech violinist Ondricek, moved only by idle curiosity, had the corpse resurrected during a visit in 1893. When it was finally inspected (upon the opening of a new burial ground in 1896) the features were still recognizable, but the lower body had been reduced to a skeleton. *See* G.I.C. de Courcy (1957).

Paine, Thomas (1737–1809).

The English-born author of the pamphlet *Common Sense*, which had a vast influence on public opinion during the American Revolution, was a man of wide interests, ranging from investigation into the cause of yellow fever to building bridges. Paine traveled to Paris in 1787; he deplored the terror of the French Revolution and attempted to gain a reprieve from the guillotine for Louis XVI. When Robespierre came to power, Paine in December 1793 was thrown into Luxembourg prison in Paris. The cold and the strain of months in prison caused him to become ill with a fever which he later said "nearly terminated my existence." An abscess that formed in his side was to trouble him long after his release in November 1794.

Paine returned to America in 1804 to find himself the center of controversy because of his outspoken writings and opinions. He was a bulbous-nosed old man, his face bloated by excessive drinking, none too clean in his habits. Articulate, outspoken and an excellent raconteur, he was either hated or loved. He lived frugally at his farm in New Rochelle, which had been given to him by New York State, or in New York City. William Carver found him drunk in a tavern in New Rochelle in the spring of 1806 and after washing him all over several times and cutting his nails, which resembled bird claws, he took him to his home in New York where he was struck with a fit of apoplexy in July and bed-ridden for many weeks.

Paine changed his New York lodgings many times during the

last few years of his life, until finally it was arranged that he should stay with a man named Ryder at what is now 309 Bleecker Street for ten dollars a week. He had lost the use of his legs and was forced to spend the days in a chair with a table pushed against it; yet he was not sorry for himself and was witty and cheerful when the occasional visitor came by. By January 1809 he required total care and Ryder was paid twenty dollars a week. On the 18th Paine wrote his third will, leaving most of his money to his old friend Mme. Bonneville for the education of her sons. Paine grew weaker, ulcerous sores appeared on his feet and his abdomen swelled, indicating, said his physician Dr. James R. Manly, "dropsy, and that of the worst description." He suffered from bedsores exacerbated by the water he passed in bed, yet he never complained. His request to be buried in Quaker ground was denied, the reason given being that Paine's friends might wish to erect a monument, which would be contrary to the Quakers' rules. Mme. Bonneville promised to have him buried on the farm. "I have no objection to that," said Paine, "but the farm will be sold, and they will dig my bones up before they be half-rotten." He told Dr. Manly bitterly, "I think I can say what *they* made Jesus Christ to say—'My God, my God, why hast thou forsaken me!'"

Paine persuaded Mme. Bonneville to take him to her house at 59 Grove Street and was carried there on 4 May in an armchair. His body, according to Dr. Manly, had "assumed a gangrenous appearance" and become "excessively fetid and discolored." The doctor observed that his belly had diminished and received a terse reply, "And yours augments!" Paine died in his sleep at 8:00 A.M. on 8 June 1809 and was buried on his farm. A headstone was erected with the inscription: THOMAS PAINE AUTHOR OF 'COMMON SENSE' DIED ON THE EIGHTH OF JUNE, 1809, AGED 72 YEARS.

In 1819 William Cobbett had Paine's bones dug up and taken back to England, intending to raise a monument to his memory, but this was never done. After Cobbett's death in 1835 the bones were lost.

Pasternak, Boris (1890–1960).

The Soviet writer was less a novelist than a poet; his *Doctor Zhivago* (1957), still denied publication in his own country, is not so much a novel as a prose poem. It is permeated by the author's sense of disillusionment with the Soviet system and by strong religious feelings (Pasternak, a Sephardic Jew, became a baptized Christian). For these reasons the government of the U.S.S.R. regarded the award of the 1958 Nobel Prize in literature to the writer as a political provocation and forced him to decline it. The model for Lara in the novel was Olga Ivinskaya, whom Pasternak had met in 1946. She was a widow, twenty-two years his junior, with two children. Though she was imprisoned for four years (1949–1953) because of her relationship with him, Pasternak could never bring himself to leave his second wife, the strong-willed Zinaida, and marry her. Deprived of this protection, on his death she was left vulnerable to further punishment.

Pasternak took time from his growing correspondence in his last fall and winter to begin writing *The Blind Beauty*, a play about Russian serfdom. When he turned seventy in February 1960, his health was beginning to fail. He had suffered a heart attack ten years earlier. In April he was troubled by angina pectoris and suspended his regular visits to Olga's apartment near his home in the artists' and writers' village of Peredelkino, eleven miles southwest of Moscow. When he took to his bed at the end of that month he was in effect imprisoned within the bosom of his family. Olga waited anxiously for his penciled notes. In an early one he wrote, "Don't take any active steps to see me....Z in her foolishness would not have the wit to spare me. I have already taken soundings on the subject." Early in May he had a severe heart attack; soon afterward lung cancer was detected.

On his last day, Pasternak summoned his two sons and charged them with Olga's care. That evening, as he fought for breath, he gasped, "I can't hear very well. And there's a mist in front of my eyes. But it will go away, won't it? Don't forget to open the window tomorrow." He died at 11:20 P.M. on 30 May 1960. Early on the 31st Olga heard the news and walked into the house unchallenged. The body seemed still warm.

Pasternak was buried at Peredelkino on 2 June 1960 after a civil funeral ceremony. Later, Olga was sentenced to eight years' hard labor, her twenty-two-year-old daughter Irina, who had once been an innocent conveyer of royalties to Pasternak, to three years'.

Pepys, Samuel (1633–1703).

The English diarist (1660–1669) and naval administrator was "cut for the stone"—an operation which, at that time, had a high mortality rate—at the age of twenty-two. The calculus removed from his bladder (said to be the size of a tennis ball) he preserved in a bottle, and on each anniversary of the surgery he celebrated his deliverance. The operation, however, left him sterile; his wife Elizabeth never became pregnant during almost fifteen years of marriage. She died, probably of typhoid fever, in 1669 when only twenty-nine. Pepys, during the last two years of his retirement, lived at Clapham, four miles south of St. Paul's, in a house belonging to his friend and former servant, Will Hewer. His final illness was evidently caused by degenerative arterial disease aggravated by his life-long kidney and urinary tract ailments. At post-mortem his kidneys were said to contain numerous stones, and senile arteriosclerosis is mentioned. Despite considerable pain he exhibited great tranquility of mind at the last; he died at 3:47 A.M., 26 May 1703, and was buried beside Elizabeth in front of the altar of St. Olave's Church in the City, just around the corner from his old home in Seething Lane.

Peter the Great (1672–1725).

Czar Peter I, founder of the Russian empire, was six feet seven inches tall, powerfully built, with regular features and a ruddy complexion; he was also epileptic, but less mentally incapacitated than his half-brother and half-sister. The attacks appear to have been aggravated by alcoholism and hysteria, the latter arising from the bloody scenes the ten-year-old Peter witnessed at the palace during a coup. He was sexually promiscuous and, according to P.M. Dale, probably suffered late syphilitic involvement of the spinal cord in middle life. His last decade was marked by attacks of bronchitis, and his constant grimacing and shaking of the head became more noticeable. He passed a large bladder stone in 1724, after which his urinary function was improved for a time. Early in November 1724 he caught a chill while helping in the rescue of shipwrecked sailors in the Gulf of Finland and during the New Year's festivities a drinking bout sent him to bed for the last time. His bladder was greatly distended and had to be tapped. His sufferings continued for many days as the infection spread to his thighs and produced suppurating sores.

On 22 January Peter made his last confession and received the Eucharist. His trembling hand failed him as he tried to write a short will, and he was never, even orally, able to name his successor. While his advisers hotly disputed the question, the illiterate, shrewd czarina surrounded the St. Petersburg palace with troops. Peter had had her latest lover, William Mons, executed a few weeks earlier, and the relations of the royal pair had greatly worsened. When Peter, after lying unconscious for many hours with staring eyes, died early on 28 January 1725, the succession of Catherine I was a *fait accompli*.

The czar's embalmed body lay in state in the palace until 10 February, when it was moved to a central position in the Cathedral of Saints Peter and Paul and covered with an imperial mantle. Not until 1 June 1731 was it consigned to the vault below, where it still reposes.

Piaf, Edith (1915–1963).

At 3:00 A.M. on 19 December 1915 Edith Gassion was born in freezing weather on a policeman's cape under a lamppost at 72 rue de Belleville, Paris. The youngster had to fend for herself almost from birth and by the time she got her first break at Gerny's in Paris with Louis Leplée she was a seasoned street singer. Leplée gave her the name "*la môme Piaf*" (literally, "Kid Sparrow"). She was an indefatigable worker and drove herself to perform even when her tiny body was racked with pain. She was generous—too generous—because however much money she earned she was often completely broke.

Piaf had always abused her body with drugs and alcohol in an effort to drive herself even harder, but in the years between 1951 and 1963, as her sister, Simone Berteaut, writes in her 1969 book *Piaf*, "Edith Piaf had undergone four automobile accidents, one attempted suicide, four drug cures, one sleep treatment, two fits of delirium tremens, seven operations, three hepatic comas, one spell of madness, two bouts with bronchial pneumonia and one with pulmonary edema." In 1962 she met and married Theophanis Lamboukas, whom she promptly renamed Théo Sarapo ("I love you" in Greek). He was twenty years younger than Piaf, but gentle and loving. In June and August 1963 she suffered her second and third hepatic comas. Doctors considered her case hopeless, but Piaf still talked of tours. In September when she was released from the hospital, Théo took her to a secluded little house in Plascassier, near Grasse. She weighed a mere seventy pounds; only her violet eyes reminded one of "*la môme Piaf*."

On 9 October, her first wedding anniversary, Edith asked Simone to come to her; Simone took a plane immediately and, though she was shocked at Edith's appearance, the two sisters, to Théo's great delight, talked and laughed until nearly 4:00 A.M., reliving their youthful years. The nurse finally intervened and gave Edith a shot; she suddenly said in a loud voice—like a cry—"I can die now; I've lived twice." Cold-shouldered by the servants, and tired and hungry, Simone left in the early morning hours for Paris. By the time she had reached home, Edith Piaf was dead. She was buried on 14 October 1963 at the Père-Lachaise Cemetery in Paris.

Plath, Sylvia (1932–1963).

The Boston-born poet, suffering severe depression, attempted suicide at the age of twenty during her summer vacation from Smith College. Leaving a note to explain her absence, she lay behind a cinder-block wall in her mother's basement at Wellesley, Mass., and swallowed forty sleeping tablets. She had made headlines in the Boston *Globe* and the surrounding woodlands had been searched before her moans were heard two days later and she was revived.

In 1956 she married the English poet Ted Hughes and was the mother of two small children when, on the advent of another woman, she left their Devon cottage and took the children to London. By the time she had found a flat, at 23 Fitzroy Road near Primrose Hill, it was Christmas 1962. The worst winter weather in over a century froze the pipes and made pushing a pram in the streets impossible. Her last months had been a period of intense literary activity; many of her poems reflected her sense of betrayal. In the New Year her autobiographical novel *The Bell Jar* (published under a pseudonym, Victoria Lucas) received disappointing reviews. Her doctor, aware of her deepening exhaustion and depression, vainly attempted to have her admitted to the hospital. He arranged for a nurse to come to her flat on the following Monday, but by then his patient was dead.

Sylvia spent part of the weekend with friends but left on Sunday evening. At about 6:00 A.M. the following morning, 11 February 1963, she took bread and butter and mugs of milk up to the children's room. Sealing the door and windows of the kitchen with towels, she turned on the gas taps and, kneeling, laid her head in the oven. When the nurse arrived later in the morning, artificial respiration was useless; Sylvia Plath Hughes was declared dead on arrival at St. Pancras University College Hospital. She was buried in Heptonstall churchyard in Yorkshire. *See* E. Butscher (1976).

Pocahontas (c. 1595–1617).

The favorite daughter of the Indian chief Powhatan, who befriended the Jamestown settlers, took the name Rebecca on becoming a Christian. In April 1614 she married John Rolfe, a widowed settler then in his late twenties, who had introduced tobacco cultivation into Virginia. Two years after their marriage they traveled to England with their infant son Thomas and a dozen Indians, including a sister and a brother-in-law of Pocahontas. The Indian princess aroused great interest in London social circles, and was graciously received at the court of James I, although her husband was persona non grata with the dour, tobacco-hating sovereign. Most of the Indians, who possessed no natural immunity to Old-World diseases, were soon ill, and only about half of them survived their visit.

Pocahontas was an early victim of respiratory ailments. By the time the party was ready to set sail for Virginia in a convoy of three ships in March 1617 she was probably tuberculous and may also have had pneumonia. Her sister and young Thomas were also ailing. As they sailed down the Thames estuary Lady Rebecca's condition suddenly worsened, and the vessel bearing the Rolfes put in at Gravesend, just twenty miles from London on the south bank. She died in the third week of March at an unrecorded inn (or cottage) in the river port. Though no more than twenty-two years old, she faced her end with the stoicism of her forebears, attempting to cheer her husband by saying, "All men must die," and "Tis enough that the childe liveth." The register of St. George's Church, Gravesend, gives the date of her burial though it misspells her name and misstates her husband's name: *March 21–Rebecca Wrolfe wyffe of Thomas Wrolfe gent. A Virginia Lady borne was buried in the Chauncel.*

Interment in the chancel was evidently an honor attributable to her rank and eminence. The original church and much of the town were destroyed by fire in 1727. In 1923 a search was made for the grave of Pocahontas but no recognizable Indian remains were found. In 1957 the churchyard was converted into a garden, a plaque was unveiled and a statue of the Indian princess—a replica of the one that stands in Jamestown—was presented by the State of Virginia and erected on the site.

Two-year-old Thomas had to be put ashore at Plymouth; later he was commissioned in the colonial militia at Fort James, Va. John Rolfe married a third time and had a daughter; he died in Virginia in 1622. *See* F. Mossiker (1976).

Poe, Edgar Allan (1809–1849).

The U.S. poet, critic and author of macabre tales, whose short story "The Murders in the Rue Morgue" (1841) is the foundation stone of modern detective fiction, was a manic depressive of apparently weak sexuality. It is probably untrue that he was ever addicted to opium or other narcotics, but his dependence on alcohol was great and more than once cost him his job. His relationship to Virginia Clemm, only thirteen years old at the time of their marriage in May 1836, was platonic, at least for some years, but her devotion was absolute. She was tuberculous, and every downturn in her illness, until her death in January 1847, sent her husband to the bottle. "I became insane," he wrote, "with long intervals of horrible sanity. During these fits of absolute unconsciousness I drank, God knows how often or how much." Thereafter, he courted two widows with settled incomes, but in a vacillating, uncertain manner that, his 1953 biographer P. Lindsay believes, reveals his hidden dread of a true marriage relationship. Flight from it may be the real cause of his death.

Traveling south on a lecture tour in July 1849, he arrived in Philadelphia in a state of fear and suicidal depression after imagining he had overheard enemies on the train whispering their plans to kill him. In Richmond the income from his lectures on "the poetic principle" barely covered expenses, but when he left for Baltimore early on 27 September (taking with him a friend's handsome Malacca cane) he seemed to be in normal spirits. The boat was due in on the 28th; how Poe spent the next few days is a mystery. It is possible he went on to Philadelphia and made a social call before confusing trains and returning to Baltimore by mistake; or he may have gone on a five-day binge. On Wednesday, 3 October, his former friend, Dr. J.E. Snodgrass, received the following note:

Dear Sir——
    There is a gentleman, rather the worse for wear, at Ryan's 4th ward polls, who goes under the cognomen of Edgar A. Poe, and who appears in great distress, & he says he is acquainted with you, and I assure you, he is in need of immediate assistance.

Yours, in haste
Jos. W. Walker

The polling place to which Walker, a newspaper compositor, directed Snodgrass was a public house at 44 Lombard Street, a few blocks from the physician's residence. The poet's clothing had been replaced by an old suit of threadbare alpaca; he had lost his vest and neckcloth but still grasped the Malacca cane, hence he had evidently not been robbed. In a second-floor room of Washington College Hospital (now part of a stairwell in the Church Home and Infirmary), Poe partially regained consciousness early the next morning without being able to explain his adventures. A period of despair and self-reproach gave way to wild delirium. On Saturday night he called out loudly for "Reynolds," perhaps an echo of his early tale, "A Manuscript Found in a Bottle." He died on Sunday, 7 October 1849 at 5:00 A.M. with no friend or relative at his side; his last words were "Lord help my poor soul."

The apparent cause of death was cerebral edema caused by alcohol. On the 9th, four friends accompanied the body to the Presbyterian Cemetery at Fayette and Green Streets, Baltimore, present site of the Westminster Church. In 1875 the remains were moved a short distance to the southeast corner of the burial ground, and a monument was erected; at that time the body of

Mrs. Maria Clemm was placed beside him. In 1885 a small bronze box containing all that remained of her daughter, Poe's young wife, was buried in the same plot. Poe's original coffin, a gift from the hospital's young resident, J.J. Moran, was found split at the time of his exhumation and the skeleton could be seen; hair still clung to the skull, the broad brow of which was instantly recognizable, and the teeth were pearly white.

Pollock, Jackson (1912–1956).

The leading U.S. abstract painter of his generation gained an international reputation by his "action painting," whereby colors are dripped onto canvases laid on the floor. Late in 1952 he completed three outstanding works, most notably his explosive *Number 12*. Thereafter, exhaustion and frustration crippled him, his heavy drinking became even heavier and sessions with psychoanalysts seemed to do little for him. He and his wife, Lee Krasner, had moved into a nineteenth-century farmhouse at the far end of Long Island after their marriage in 1945. Behind the house, on Fireplace Road in Springs, a few miles beyond East Hampton, was the converted barn Pollock used as a studio. Each morning he would still light the stove there in the hope that he would be able to work in earnest again. "Painting is no problem," he told Lee, "the problem is what to do when you're not painting." What he did was drink; and when drunk he became foulmouthed and unpredictable. He was overweight and had grown a straggly beard.

The last of Pollock's series of extramarital relationships was with Ruth Klingman, a twenty-five-year-old model, plump and dark-haired, from Newark, N.J. Lee went off to Europe for a few weeks in the summer of 1956. Ruth came down for the weekend as usual on Saturday morning, 11 August. This time she brought a friend, Edith Metzger, a twenty-six-year-old beautician from the Bronx. Pollock met them at the station but wasn't much company for them. He drank beer all day and ate nothing; he seemed exhausted. He took the girls to a wayside sandwich place in the evening. At 10:15 P.M. they were speeding north toward his home in his 1950 Oldsmobile convertible when he lost control of the wheel at a curve. The car ran off Springs Road to the right, rebounded from an embankment, swerved to the other side of the road and ran through underbrush until it collided with a clump of young oaks. The car turned end over end and landed upside down.

Pollock was thrown clear but his head hit a tree and he died instantly. The certificate reads: Compound fracture of skull, laceration of brain, laceration both lungs. Hemothorax—shock. Ruth was also thrown clear; she recovered from her injuries, including a fractured pelvis, and later married a painter. Edith, the innocent guest, was rammed backward with great force into the trunk, where her body was found, her neck broken.

Jackson Pollock was buried nearby at Green River Cemetery. He had always liked boulders; Lee arranged to have a huge one hauled in by tractor and set sideways at the foot of the grave. It bears a bronze plaque; on it is the dead artist's signature and two dates. *See* B.H. Friedman (1972).

Pompadour, Madame de
(1721-1764).

Jeanne Antoinette Poisson, usually called "Reinette" was a married woman with an infant daughter when she achieved her ambition of becoming the French king's mistress in 1744. Her beauty was then at its peak, but she was sexually unresponsive and physically far from robust, so that Louis XV's demands and her frequent miscarriages soon began to undermine her health. Her great achievement was to manage, with great finesse, the transition—after four or five years—from bedmate to daytime companion and entertainer and finally to trusted friend and counsellor. So pervading did her influence in matters of state become that it may be said of her she was mistress not of Louis but of France.

Madame de Pompadour's health suffered a setback in 1754 when her daughter Alexandrine and then her father died within two weeks. Dilatation of the right atrium, associated kidney trouble and digestive upsets prostrated her. It was while the Court was at Choisy in February 1764 that she suffered a lung hemorrhage that marked the beginning of her last decline. Lung inflammation returned at Versailles on 7 April during a spell of wet, cold weather. Though rouge could no longer disguise her ravaged cheeks, her eyes retained their alertness and she played out her role of trained courtesan to the end. Louis, easily bored by invalids, was not allowed to see signs of illness; his attention was constantly engaged by amusing or telling remarks. He paid his final visit on the 14th, after the priest had administered the Last Rites. She spent her final night propped up in a chair, gasping for breath. On the evening of Palm Sunday, 15 April 1764, her confessor, who had spent a little time with her, rose to go. Madame de Pompadour made her last gesture. "One moment, Monsieur le Curé," she said with a smile, "and we will leave together." Upon which she died.

On Tuesday evening Louis stood in tears in a heavy downpour as the funeral cortege passed his balcony on its way to Paris. Madame de Pompadour was laid beside Alexandrine in the Capuchin Church in the Place Vendôme. In 1806 the church was demolished and the bones were transferred to a private ossuary in the Catacombs. *See* D.M. Smythe (1953).

Porter, Cole (1893–1964).

The leading sophisticate among U.S. songwriters wrote both the music and the lyrics of his numerous hits, which include "Begin the Beguine," "Let's Do It," and "Night and Day." In October 1937 his life was tragically affected by a riding accident at the Piping Rock Club in Locust Valley, Long Island. His skittish mount, frightened by a clump of bushes, reared and fell backwards. As the horse rolled to one side, Porter's leg was crushed; before fully regaining its feet, it fell again, this time on its other flank, and compound fractures of the rider's other leg resulted. His wife, the wealthy Linda Lee Thomas, returned from her Paris home to plead successfully with the surgeons not to amputate. The accident ended the Porters' only estrangement, and their close, curious marriage was restored. They occupied adjoining apartments at the Waldorf when in New York. Cole was openly homosexual; Linda seems to have had no interest in sex, but she was a potent influence in advancing Cole's career.

Porter's remaining twenty-seven years were spent in almost continuous pain, only partly relieved by drugs and alcohol. He showed remarkable stoicism, enduring more than thirty operations on his legs, which had become infected with osteomyelitis. His life was further diminished when Linda died in 1954. She left him almost $2 million and his gross estate at his death amounted to $6 million, yet he maintained a tough working schedule until 1958, when he wrote the songs for the television feature *Aladdin*.

In 1957 Porter was operated on for gastric ulcer; the following year, at the Harkness Pavilion of the Columbia-Presbyterian Medical Center, New York, his right leg had to be amputated at the hip after the infection could no longer be controlled by antibiotics. The blow to his self-esteem was severe, and his debonair appearance was undermined by a growing lack of concern even with personal hygiene. Debilitated and reduced to eighty pounds, he entered the hospital in November 1960 and grew so accustomed to the routine that he stayed there for seven months. He was back there with severe burns in April 1963 after falling asleep while smoking at his Williamstown, Mass., home.

Porter was accustomed to spending part of each year at his California home on North Rockingham in Los Angeles. He was living there in September 1964 when he entered St. John's Hospital, Santa Monica, with a bowel obstruction. He developed pneumonia and a bladder infection recurred. A kidney stone lodged in the ureter was removed by surgery on 13 Ocrober; thereafter he remained unconscious, still suffering from pneumonia. A nurse was turning him two days after the operation when his heart stopped, and the usual resuscitative measures were unavailing. He was pronounced dead at 11:05 P.M. on 15 October 1964.

Cole Porter was taken back to his native town, Peru, Ind., where the simple service he had asked for—a reading of one Biblical passage ("I am the resurrection and the life....") and the Lord's Prayer—was performed. He was buried in Mount Hope Cemetery between his father and Linda; the graves are marked by small, simple stones.

Presley, Elvis (1935–1977).

The U.S. rock singer's last years were spent in an uneasy alternation of monthly concert tours and rest periods—passed largely in isolation in a private upstairs suite—at his luxurious estate, Graceland, in Memphis. When his wife, Priscilla Beaulieu, left him for a karate instructor, Mike Stone, Presley asked one of his bodyguards to have Stone killed. He enjoyed handling guns, shooting at his television set or at doors and walls without bothering to check first who might be behind them. His rages may have been triggered by overmedication. Several physicians supplied Presley with drugs for dieting, for sleeping, for waking up, and for hypertension; the prescriptions, which included pain killers, were sometimes made out in the names of his employees and the medical bills are said to have amounted to as much as three thousand dollars in a single month. More and more frequently he would forget the lyrics and the order of songs on his programs and descend to talking to the audience instead of singing.

According to his father, Vernon, Presley's last checkup showed his problems to include a disorder of the colon, some "liver damage" and high blood pressure. He also had trouble with one eye and 70 pounds above his normal weight of 180 pounds. Vernon Presley says that Elvis had a disturbed final night. Evidently unable to sleep, he was known to have been playing racquet ball at 4:00 or 5:00 A.M. What happened next is uncertain. His current girl friend Ginger Alden, uneasy at his absence when she awoke late, went looking for him at 2:30 P.M. on 16 August 1977. She found him lying on the floor of his bathroom-dressing room, wearing blue pajama tops and yellow bottoms. His personal physician Dr. Nichopoulos went to work on him without result. At Baptist Hospital a cardiac arrest unit attempted resuscitation for twenty-five minutes before pronouncing Presley dead at 3:30 P.M.

By the following day a line of admirers, fifteen to twenty deep, extended a mile from the gate of Graceland, waiting to glimpse the body in its copper coffin in the foyer of the mansion. At one time, thirty people, overcome by emotion and exhaustion, could be seen lying prostrate. At 4:00 A.M. on the 18th a car driven by an intoxicated eighteen-year-old Memphis youth drove into the crowd, killing two young women from Louisiana.

After a short service at the Woodland Church of Christ, the cortege of sixteen cream-colored Cadillacs traveled four miles along Elvis Presley Boulevard to Forest Hills Cemetery, where the singer was interred in a mausoleum near his mother's grave. There were plans for Elvis' twin brother, Jesse—born dead—to join him later. The final autopsy report disclosed that the blood contained some ten prescription drugs, including Demerol, Valium, an antihistamine, and codeine.

In September 1979 Dr. Nichopoulos was indicted on charges of recklessly prescribing narcotics to several patients, notably

Presley, to whom he had allegedly supplied 5,000 tablets during his final eight months. The codeine and other central nervous system depressants swallowed by the singer in his last hours were probably sufficient to have caused his death.

Three months after his funeral the bodies of Presley and his mother were reinterred on the Graceland estate south of the mansion.

Puccini, Giacomo (1858–1924).

For four long years the Italian composer used all his superb talents on the music for *Turandot*; it was to be his greatest work. Toward the end of those years he was uneasy that he might not be able to finish the opera. He constantly harassed and cajoled the two librettists, Giuseppe Adami and Renato Simoni, to "come to grips." "If they wait much longer," he wrote to his British friend Sybil Seligman, "I shall have to get them to put paper, pen, and inkpot in my tomb." By 25 April 1924 he was pleased with his progress and played part of it for Arturo Toscanini, who declared it to be a fine work.

Puccini's throat, however, was giving him much trouble, and in October it was so painful he was easily persuaded by his wife, Elvira, to seek medical help. One doctor said he should stop smoking, but a specialist in Florence noticed a small spot of inflammation and suggested he return in two weeks. Puccini, frightened, consulted another specialist who told him he had a "papilloma." Afterwards, it was explained to Tonio Puccini that his father had advanced cancer of the throat and that the only hope was radium treatment.

On 4 November Puccini and Tonio left for the Institute de la Couronne, run by Dr. Ledoux in Brussels; Elvira was too ill to travel. The composer took with him thirty-six pages of *Turandot* which he had yet to orchestrate. On the train he bled from the nose and mouth and arrived in Brussels weary and feeling unclean. A biopsy confirmed the Florentine doctor's diagnosis. At first, external application of radium by means of a "Columbia" collar was tried. On 20 November Dr. Ledoux told Tonio that the cancer was spreading rapidly and surgery was now imperative. On 24 November Puccini was given an injection of morphine to minimize the pain and make him drowsy. General anesthesia was inadvisable because of his weak heart; so he was bound to the table and for three hours and forty minutes endured the operation with heroic composure. When his beloved stepdaughter, Fosca, arrived with Tonio they were shocked by his pallor, the seven radium needles protruding from his throat and the silver tube through which his breath whistled. His only nourishment was given by a tube through his nose and he could communicate only by pencil and pad. After three days his fever abated, he was able to move around the room and there was even talk of his returning home.

At about 6:00 P.M. on 28 November, after a good day, Puccini scribbled on his pad, "I am worse than yesterday—Hell in my throat—I am going to faint—fresh water!" The radium had proved too much for his heart. Dr. Ledoux took out the needles but it was too late. He fought a losing battle all night; early in the morning the Papal Nuncio pronounced the last benediction. Puccini was quite tranquil. At about 4:00 A.M. he took two deep breaths, the handsome head fell to one side and Giacomo Puccini died. He was brought back to his home in Viareggio near Pisa, and his coffin lies in a small chapel specially constructed between his study and his bedroom.

When *Turandot* was performed for the first time on 25 April 1926, Toscanini laid down his baton during the lament over the body of Liù and said in a trembling voice: "Here ends the Master's work."

Pushkin, Alexander (1799–1837).

Russia's national poet was short in stature, ugly in a way that attracted many women and proud of a pedigree that included a Negro grandfather who had been an Ethiopian noble. In 1831 he married the beautiful Natalia Nikolaevna Goncharova, who by 1836 had borne him four children. In 1834 the Pushkins met George Charles d'Anthès, a tall, handsome cavalry officer, just twenty-two years old, who had recently quit his native Alsace to enter the Russian imperial service, and who had been legally adopted by the Netherlands ambassador in St. Petersburg, Baron Louis van Heeckeren. D'Anthès was soon head-over-heels in love with Madame Pushkina; she, for her part, was indiscreet in her encouragement of his attentions. Though these evidently never went beyond stolen kisses, by 1836 she was under heavy pressure to become his mistress and before the end of the year the affair was the talk of the capital.

Pushkin, who never doubted his wife's fidelity, might have let the matter run its course had he and several friends not received an anonymous letter that mockingly announced his election to the "Most Serene Order of Cuckolds." Furious at last, Pushkin challenged d'Anthès to a duel. Heeckeren intercepted the message and pleaded with the poet for a postponement; with some difficulty the challenger was placated by the engagement of the young officer to Natalia's sister Ekaterina. But dissatisfaction was keenly felt on both sides, and the antagonists remained at odds even after the wedding on 10 January 1837. Moreover, d'Anthès persisted in pursuing Natalia and craved, under threat of suicide for a private rendezvous with her. When another unsigned letter apprised her husband of the meeting he was beside himself. He sent off a grossly abusive letter, not to d'Anthès himself, but to the adoptive father, whom Pushkin all along (but mistakenly) suspected of sending the "cuckold" letter.

A duel was now inevitable. Pushkin had difficulty finding a second but on the afternoon of 27 January 1837 he was able to introduce Constantin Danzas, an officer in the corps of engineers, to the Vicomte August d'Archiac, the French diplomat who represented d'Anthès. Toward dusk the same day the parties traveled in separate sleighs to Chernaya Rechka, outside St. Petersburg, and walked to a spot three hundred yards from the road. The knee-high snow was trampled down and greatcoats were laid ten paces apart, from behind which the two duelists would fire. Danzas waved his hat, Pushkin walked forward and d'Anthès did the same, firing before reaching his barrier, as he was entitled to do. The poet fell, mortally wounded in the abdomen, but was sufficiently recovered a moment later to demand his shot. Danzas handed him a pistol to replace the one that was now stuffed with snow and, while his adversary with great fortitude stood sideways, arm slung across his chest, Pushkin took aim very carefully; some accounts say this required all of two minutes. At last he fired and d'Anthès fell; the ball had passed through his right arm and fractured two ribs, but the wound was not serious.

Pushkin was taken home in a carriage supplied by Heeckeren and was laid on the sofa in his study. "Don't worry," he told his wife, "you are innocent of my death." An ill-advised enema brought him great agony, and he tried to obtain a weapon to kill himself. He accepted the Last Rites of the church; the czar sent his forgiveness and promised to take care of his family; the children were carried in one by one to be blessed. His last wish was for a taste of blackberries in syrup. At 2:45 P.M. on 29 January 1837 Pushkin died. A hasty autopsy revealed gangrenous changes in the small intestine and much coagulated blood from the perforated femoral artery; the ball had shattered the sacrum before lodging nearby.

To discourage crowds of admirers the funeral was conducted in an obscure church, after which a convoy of three troikas hurried the body across the frozen plains south via Pskov and Trigorskoye to the Holy Mountain Monastery near Mikhailovskoe, the dead man's family home. There Pushkin was laid to rest beside his mother. D'Anthès, after his recovery, was demoted and deported; he died in 1895. Heeckeren became ambassador in Vienna; he died in 1884. Natalia Pushkina went into mourning for two years; she married a cavalry captain in 1844 and died in 1863.

Quisling, Vidkun (1887–1945).

The Norwegian politician, whose name was to become synonymous with "traitor," was a dour-faced, ex-Army officer who founded the fascist Nasjonal Samling (National Unity) party in 1933. Visiting Germany in December 1939, he persuaded his hero, Adolf Hitler, to invade Norway. The invasion was poorly planned, and King Haakon VII and the Labor government were able to escape to Hamar and then to Elverum. Quisling sealed his fate when, aided by a telephone call from the German embassy, he gained access to the radio station and broadcast to the nation that he was seizing power. "By virtue of circumstances and of the national aims of our movement, we are the only ones who can do this and thereby save the country from the desperate situation brought upon us by the party politicians." The Germans soon learned of the revulsion felt by nearly all Norwegians at this usurpation of power by a party without a single member in the Storting (Parliament). Within a week he was pushed out and his place taken by a Reichskommissar, J. Terboven.

But Quisling was reinstated as sole political head in September and made premier or "minister-president" in February 1942. He showed little independence in the face of Hitler's demands. He failed to protest when ten prominent citizens of Trondheim were shot by the Gestapo in October 1942 in reprisal for an act of sabotage, and he persecuted the small community (eight hundred) of Norwegian Jews, many of whom later died in Polish and German concentration camps.

On the liberation of Norway in May 1945, Quisling was arrested. His trial and execution can be criticized on strict legal grounds. The constitutionality of the government itself was suspect, and the prewar peace code had no provisions for a death penalty. Moreover, several of Quisling's enemies were allowed to take part in his trial (20 August–7 September 1945). He was found guilty of treason and other charges under a 1902 military law as made applicable retroactively to Quisling by the Norwegian government in exile in October 1941. After his appeal had been dismissed by the Supreme Court, he was taken to the condemned cell, Number 34, at Mollergaten 19. He spent his last hours reading the Bible. At 2:00 A.M. on 24 October 1945, he was driven to the old Akershus castle outside Oslo. Before being bound to the stake he shook hands with the ten members of the firing squad, but his request to dispense with a blindfold was denied. He was declared dead at 2:40 A.M. His ashes were returned to his widow many years later and buried beside his mother at Gjerpen in his native Telemark.

Raleigh, Sir Walter (1554?–1618).

The Elizabethan adventurer and author was a leading favorite at the court of England's Virgin Queen, but on the accession of James I in 1603 his fortunes quickly declined. Late that year he was sentenced to the ax for treason (he was accused of plotting to make peace with Spain, to relax the restrictions on Catholics and to place James' cousin Arabella Stuart on the throne). From his own testimony it is evident that he at least knew of the conspiracy and failed to apprise the Privy Council of it. Reprieved at the last moment, he spent many years in the Tower of London, where he wrote his *History of the World* (1614). He was released in 1617 without a pardon to make good his promise to bring gold from Guiana without giving "just cause" of offense to Spain, whatever that might mean. The gamble failed; no gold mines were found. With Sir Walter lying ill off the coast, his devoted supporter Laurance Kemys led a party of 400 into the interior, where they attacked and burned the Spanish city of St. Thomé. Raleigh's elder son, Wat, and 250 other Englishmen were killed. Kemys, met on his return by Raleigh's icy disapproval, killed himself in his cabin.

When Sir Walter returned to Plymouth on 21 June 1618 his wife, Bess, begged him to escape abroad, but he vacillated too long. Convincing new charges against him being hard to find,

At midnight before the day of his execution Raleigh bid his wife farewell, then composed a love poem to her on the flyleaf of his Bible.

LIBRARY OF CONGRESS

James in effect had him condemned on the old counts of treason. After his final hearing in Westminster Palace on 28 October 1618, the unkempt prisoner was lodged in the Abbey Gatehouse overnight while a scaffold was erected in Old Palace Yard. Now that his destiny was certain, Sir Walter underwent a surprising change of mood. He bade his wife farewell at midnight, set his affairs in order, made written answers to charges against him regarding the Guiana expedition and other matters, and wrote out a love poem for Bess on the flyleaf of his Bible. After Communion he ate a hearty breakfast and enjoyed a final pipe of tobacco. It was Lord Mayor's Day, and the king had hoped other attractions would keep the populace away from Sir Walter's execution. On the contrary, a crowd had gathered and various noblemen came to shake his hand; to a degree the affair became an anti-Stuart demonstration. In his final speech, Raleigh, immaculately turned out in black with a velvet gown and cap, answered his critics in masterly fashion and ended: "So I take leave of you all, making my peace with God. I have a long journey to take and must bid the company farewell."

Directing the executioner to let him see the ax, he ran his thumb across the blade with evident approval. "This is sharp medicine," he said with a smile, "but it is a sure cure for all diseases." As he knelt on the executioner's cloak, which had been laid for him before the block, he was asked whether he would not prefer to face the east. "So the heart be right," he replied, "it is no matter which way the head lieth." After a short silent prayer he stretched out his hands in the prearranged signal, but nothing happened. "What dost thou fear?" he cried. "Strike man, strike." After a long pause, the ax fell and fell again. Though the executioner lifted the head by its silvery hair, he did not repeat the time-honored formula: "Behold the head of a traitor."

The body was buried south of the altar in St. Margaret's, Westminster. The head, in a red velvet bag, was conveyed to Bess, who had it embalmed and kept on view. It was to have been buried in due course with Sir Walter's surviving son, Carew, but it disappeared during his lifetime.

Rasputin, Grigory (1872?–1916).

The "Mad Monk" from Siberia was an unkempt muzhik whose great influence over Russia's last imperial family led to his own death and indirectly to theirs. The first four children of the Czar Nicholas II (q.v.) and his wife Alexandra (Princess Alix of Hesse-Darmstadt) were girls, but in 1904 a male heir was born. Alas, the czarevitch was only six months old when uncontrollable bleeding from the navel showed him to be suffering from hemophilia, a genetic blood-clotting deficiency inherited through his mother from Queen Victoria of England. Alexandra despaired until, after vainly seeking orthodox medical aid, Rasputin's healing powers were recommended to her and she found them capable of halting the bleeding and restoring little Alexis to health. The monk, whose most notable feature was his large, brilliant blue eyes, undoubtedly exercised a hypnotic effect on most of those who met him. In the case of the young invalid, whom he continued to visit throughout the boy's childhood, it may have been the reassuring effect of his skill in narrating folk tales that reduced the anxiety, and thereby the blood pressure, of the patient. This is known to be a beneficial factor in treating hemophiliacs. But, assuming the effects of Rasputin's therapy to have been correctly reported, it cannot be said they have yet been adequately explained.

At court, at Tsarskoye Selo (now renamed Pushkin), fourteen miles south of St. Petersburg, the holy man was careful to keep up appearances, but at home in the capital he frequently showed himself to be a debauchee and a satyr. Many women, even of the nobility, submitted eagerly to him; others, on at least one occasion a nun, he would attempt to take by force. But Alexandra would believe no such reports; on the contrary, she passed on his advice in matters of state to the amiable, weak Nicholas, and in this way such nonentities as Rasputin favored were appointed to high positions. By resisting any compromise in the czar's autocratic rule, he undoubtedly increased the public unrest.

The ardent monarchist V.M. Purishkevich received a standing ovation in the Duma (elected legislature) on 2 December (new style) 1916 after denouncing the role of the "obscure muzhik" in government. The wealthy young Prince Felix Yussupov, husband of the czar's niece, eagerly volunteered to kill Rasputin, and conspired with Purishekevich and three others to lure him to his home, the Moika Palace in St. Petersburg, on the evening of 29 December. While a phonograph manufactured sounds of gaiety upstairs, the prince entertained the evil holy man in the basement. Offered small cakes laced with cyanide, Rasputin gobbled two with no ill effect. A glass of poisoned Madeira did not even slow him down. "Play for me," he demanded, and the wretched host plucked his guitar and sang one song after another to his grinning visitor. The other conspirators listened with increasing anxiety at the top of the stairs; one of them passed out under the strain. In desperation, the prince directed Rasputin's attention to an ornate crucifix, then fired into his back with a Browning revolver. With a scream, the monk fell back onto a white bearskin.

The other assassins rushed in; one of them, Dr. Lazovert, felt the debauchee's pulse and pronounced him dead. A minute later the corpse opened one evil eye, sprang up, and gripped Yussopov by the throat. In terror the prince raced for the stairs, followed by his roaring victim. Out into the courtyard ran the poisoned, wounded man, heading for the gate. Twice Purishkevich fired and twice missed; a third shot entered Rasputin's shoulder, a fourth probably his head. He fell, then attempted to rise but could only grind his teeth. The body was wrapped in a curtain, roped and borne to the frozen Neva, where it was pushed through a hole in the ice; it was found three days later. Incredibly, the dying man had freed one arm, which was raised above the head as though in a final benediction. The lungs were full of water, showing that Rasputin's death came by drowning.

He was buried secretly in a small chapel in the imperial park at Tsarskoye Selo with a goodbye message from the czarina on his breast. After midnight on 22 March 1917 revolutionary bands broke in, exhumed the body, cremated it on a pyre of pine logs and dispersed the ashes. *See* R.K. Massie: *Nicholas and Alexandra* (1968).

Ravel, Maurice (1875–1937).

The French composer, probably best known for his *Bolero*, was injured in Paris when the taxi cab carrying him from the theater to his hotel at 21 rue d'Athènes collided with another cab on 10 October 1932. Ravel had two teeth knocked out, suffered severe facial injuries and bruised his chest; he joked about the latter, saying that the bruises forced him to cough in a "crooked way." The accident was generally discounted as the cause of his years of aphasia and ataxia; yet, apart from a cycle of three songs, *Don Quichotte à Dulcinée*, which he finished while convalescing, he composed no more.

The following year while swimming at Saint-Jean-de-Luz he found himself incapable of coordinating his movements. His physicians, who also observed speech difficulties and partial loss of memory, advised complete rest. He understood what was said to him but had difficulty in speaking and writing. He could think musically but was unable to express his ideas in either writing or performance. If a certain score was requested he could unerringly select it; he could play the piano from memory but could not sight-read. His inability to express his musical thoughts caused him grief; "I've still so much to say, so many ideas in my head," he lamented. Ravel tried every suggested cure, from electric treatments to re-education, but the disease progressed inexorably. In 1936 he visited the writer Colette, who lived nearby. She described him as "thin, gray-white as fog....as though he was in danger of falling apart."

Ravel's last year, 1937, was long and painful. Needing peace, he went to Le Belvédère at Montfort-l'Amaury, about twenty miles west of Paris, where his friends frequently visited him. On good days he enjoyed showing them his garden and the Japanese dwarf trees that grew there; but he was often found just sitting. "I'm waiting," he would reply, if anyone asked him what he was doing. His friends helped whenever they could, but in spite of their devotion and the tender care of his long-time housekeeper, Madame Revelot, his condition worsened.

On 18 December 1937 he entered the Centre Français de Médecine et de Chirurgie at 12 rue de Boileau in Auteuil, where Professor Clovis Vincent performed brain surgery the following day. Ravel's neurologist, Dr. T. Alajouanine, who was not consulted, did not know why Dr. Vincent operated in such a hurry. Several hours after the operation Ravel called for his brother Edouard; he lapsed into a coma and died on the morning of 28 December 1937. No autopsy was performed. Ravel was buried on 30 December beside his parents in the cemetery at Levallois.

Richard III (1452–1485).

Richard, of the House of York, the last of the Plantagenet kings of England, is a mysterious figure. It was Sir Thomas More, writing from hearsay, who first painted him as a villain and a monster, and Shakespeare who made this characterization immortal. Neither Richard's portraits nor contemporary accounts depict the dark-complexioned, slightly-built sovereign as a hunchback; at the most, one of his shoulders may have been higher than the other. That his young rivals, the "Princes in the Tower," were murdered on his order is also doubtful; no accusations were made against him until 1502, after the death of the alleged murderer, Tyrell. Nevertheless, two small skeletons were unearthed in the Tower of London in 1674; in 1933 expert testimony showed them to have been roughly of the correct age to have been killed during Richard's reign.

Richard III was killed at the Battle of Bosworth Field on 22 August 1485 after a reign of only two years. The previous day he had ridden westward from Leicester to meet the advancing forces of Henry Tudor, brought up in France and now claiming the crown in the Lancastrian interest. The pretender landed in Wales at Milford Haven early in the month and gathered support on his westward march through Shrewsbury and Tamworth. That night the opposing armies pitched camp within sight of each other three miles south of Market Bosworth. Early the next morning Richard hastened to occupy a slight eminence, Ambien Hill. In the van, on the slope below him, were the Duke of Norfolk's forces. Away across the valley a sharp-eyed soldier spotted Henry near his standard, a red dragon. Richard elected to make a surprise foray with only his four-score of Household cavalrymen. The move was full of hazard. Sir William Stanley's large force stood in an ambiguous position to the north; Stanley had been declared a traitor by Richard, who at this moment held his son hostage. But if Henry could be swiftly dispatched, support might well switch to the Plantagenet cause.

Shouting peremptory orders to his small band, he pulled down his visor and raced his white charger down to the northwest, around the right end of his battle line, across the valley and up the gentle incline on the other side, a royal crown perched on his helmet. With his flashing ax he felled the gigantic Sir John Cheyney, and after him the standard-bearer, William Brandon. But by now Sir William's men had joined the fray against him. Within moments, Richard was cut off from his men, and a hundred weapons surrounded him. A dozen blows beat him lifeless to the ground. The narrow circlet of gold fell from his helmet, to be placed a few minutes later on the head of Henry VII. The dynasty that was to include Henry VIII and Elizabeth I had begun.

Richard's naked body was slung across a horse and carried the twelve miles to Leicester. Two days later it was unceremoniously buried at the house of the Grey Friars. A few years later Henry VII disbursed ten pounds for a tomb of sorts, but this was destroyed at the dissolution of the monasteries and Richard's remains were thrown into the River Soar.

Richthofen, Manfred, Baron von (1892–1918).

Germany's flying ace, nicknamed the "Red Baron," shot down eighty Allied aircraft between 17 September 1916 and 20 April 1918. The following day his bright red Fokker triplane crashed near the Somme, close by the Bray-Corbie road. Richthofen had been fatally shot by a single bullet that passed upward and forward from right to left through his chest. The bullet was kept as a memento by a medical orderly and was never examined by ballistics experts. The death was credited for many years to Capt. A.R. Brown (died 1944) of the Royal Air Force, who had been pursuing Richthofen in a Sopwith Camel.

P.J. Carisella and J.W. Ryan in a 1969 book conclude that the Red Baron fell victim to ground fire from a Vickers machine gun manned by two Australians, C.B. Popkin (died 1968) and R.F. Weston. Richthofen was buried at Bertangles, near Amiens, but in 1925 his remains were reputedly transferred to the Invaliden cemetery in what is now East Berlin. Carisella reports that only the skull was reinterred there and that in 1969 he discovered the rest of the skeleton in the original coffin at the Bertangles gravesite. He handed it over to Germany's military air-attaché in Paris.

Rodale, Jerome Irving (1898–1971).

Shortly before his death the outspoken U.S. advocate of organic food declared "I'm going to live to be a hundred unless I am run down by a sugar-crazed taxi driver." J.I., as his friends called him, grew up on Manhattan's Lower East Side, a near-sighted youth, plagued by ill health, who worked hard to improve his health and physique.

During the Depression he began a publishing firm in Emmaus, Pa. Among other publications, he nursed along a magazine called *Organic Gardening and Farming* for sixteen years until growing public awareness of health food caused the magazine's circulation to rocket. Until his death he and his wife, Anna, lived in a large, sprawling Pennsylvania Dutch house close to his sixty-three acre Rodale Experimental Organic farm, Emmaus. J.I. was not a vegetarian but even his meat had to be produced without chemicals or growth-spurring drugs. In spite of this J.I. and his wife each took seventy food-supplement tablets every day.

On 8 June 1971 the vigorous, articulate seventy-two year old, taping a segment of ABC's "Dick Cavett Show," was inveighing vehemently against wheat, milk, and in particular sugar when he slumped in his chair—dead of a heart attack.

Rommel, Erwin (1891–1944).

The German field marshal who was nicknamed "The Desert Fox" first became disillusioned with his commander-in-chief, Adolf Hitler, early in 1943. During his long retreat in North Africa before the superior forces of the British Eighth Army under Montgomery, he appealed to his Fuehrer to sacrifice the remaining materiel and pull his men out in readiness for the coming battles in Italy. Hitler, in one of his notorious rages, denied the request and told Rommel his Afrika Korps was of no importance. Later, Rommel's candid reports on the state of the Atlantic Wall must have enraged Hitler, as did his face-to-face protest against SS brutalities in France. On 17 July 1944, while commander of German forces from the Netherlands to the Loire, he was critically injured when his staff car was hit by Allied dive bombers. He was still convalescing from multiple skull fractures and eye injuries when, on Hitler's orders, he killed himself.

Since February 1944, months before the D-Day invasion, Rommel had realized it would succeed and was secretly pledged to seek, at the proper time, an armistice with Generals Eisenhower and Montgomery. The leaders in the plot against

Rommel's funeral at Ulm "with full military honors" after his enforced suicide.

MANFRED ROMMEL

Hitler were Dr. Goerdeler, mayor of Leipzig, and Col.-Gen. Beck, former chief of the general staff. They had successfully sought the support of Rommel, probably the most respected and charismatic of Germany's military men; but he knew nothing of the bomb plot of 20 July until afterward, his understanding being that the Fuehrer would be arrested and forced to abdicate. He later told a confidant, "The man is a devil incarnate, but why try to make a hero and a martyr out of him?" Rommel's home at the village of Herrlingen west of Ulm in south Germany was being watched by the Gestapo, but at first no moves were made against him. On 7 October he was ordered to Berlin by special train, but declined on medical grounds. At noon on 14 October 1944 Gen. Burgdorf, head of the Army Personnel department, arrived in Herrlingen with two aides and a driver and asked to speak with Rommel privately. Frau Rommel, waiting anxiously upstairs, was shocked by her husband's "strange and terrible expression" when he came up to see her. "I have come to say goodbye," he told her. "In a quarter of an hour I shall be dead.... They suspect me of having taken part in the attempt to kill Hitler; it seems my name was on Goerdeler's list to be President of the Reich.... I have never seen Goerdeler in my life.... The Fuehrer has given me the choice of taking poison or being dragged before the People's Court. They have brought the poison."

Rommel's wife pleaded with him to take the second course but he refused. He would not reach Berlin alive, he said. He must, he told his longtime aide, Capt. Aldinger, consider the fate of his wife and his son Manfred. If he took poison (no doubt a quick-acting cyanide ampule) a pension would be paid, he would be given a state funeral and he would be buried at home. Furthermore, he concluded, "I will never allow myself to be hanged by that man Hitler."

Rommel was driven away in the back seat of the general's small green car. Burgdorf ordered it to stop a few hundred yards away on the Blaubeuren road. The aides walked to a distance and saw Burgdorf pacing up and down beside the car. When next seen, Rommel was doubled up, sobbing and almost unconscious. The driver sat him up and replaced his cap before driving the party to Ulm. Aldinger received the expected telephone call from one of Burgdorf's men a few minutes later. The field marshal had had "a hemorrhage, a brain-storm in the car. He is dead." His body was taken to the hospital at Ulm at 1:25 P.M.

At the funeral on 18 October 1944 in the town hall at Ulm, Field Marshal von Rundstedt delivered the oration and placed a gigantic wreath from Hitler at the foot of the coffin. Rommel's body was cremated and the ashes were buried in the churchyard at Herrlingen. Later, Frau Rommel recalled being struck by the expression of deep contempt on her husband's dead face. "It was," she said, "an expression we had never seen on it in life." *See* D. Young (1950).

Burgdorf committed suicide in May 1945.

Roosevelt, Eleanor (1884–1962).

The wife of U.S. President Franklin Roosevelt did not, as many expected, fade from view after she became a widow in 1945. On the contrary, at the time of her death she was the most admired woman in America, and her popularity throughout the world was almost as high. In 1961 she earned over $100,000 from her writing and lectures; by plane, train, even bus, she met her commitments, finding it difficult to refuse any request made in a liberal or humanitarian cause.

Eleanor Roosevelt was taken ill in New York while her physician was away in July 1962. Another doctor, knowing that aplastic anemia had been diagnosed, ordered a blood transfusion; it was a disaster, and she was taken to the hospital with a temperature of 105.6 degrees. A recurrence of fever sent her back there in September. On returning to her apartment at 55 East 74th Street on 18 October, her spirits revived, but her mind from then on was confused. On the 25th it was discovered that Mrs. Roosevelt had a rare tuberculosis of the bone marrow. As her son-in-law, Dr. James Halsted, explained it, a tuberculous lesion dating from 1919 had been activated by the steroids prescribed to reduce the risk of internal bleeding. It was the rapidly spreading hemic (blood-borne) tuberculosis that caused her death at 6:15 P.M. on 7 November 1962. While she was conscious she resisted all attempts to prolong her life, refusing—even spitting out—any pills she was given. One of her final visitors was Adlai Stevenson.

Mrs. Roosevelt was buried beside Franklin in the rose garden at the old family estate at Hyde Park, N.Y., which is now a national historic site. She had requested her body be placed in a plain wooden coffin covered with pine boughs from the woods around her country cottage at Vall-Kill, Hyde Park. No embalming was done, but, because of her dread of live burial, she had asked that her veins be cut. *See* J.P. Lash (1972).

Roosevelt, Franklin Delano (1882–1945).

The thirty-second president of the U.S. (1933–1945) contracted poliomyelitis while at his seaside cottage at Campobello, New Brunswick, in August 1921, after which he lost the use of his legs. During his presidency he began suffering from hypertension, and by 1944 his health was seriously undermined. At the Yalta conference in February 1945 "an audible gasp of dismay" was heard from onlookers as FDR was lowered from his plane; he was clearly a dying man. Back in the U.S., at his cottage ("The Little White House") on the grounds of the Warm Springs Foundation in Georgia, his health improved.

On 12 April 1945 Roosevelt sat in his favorite leather chair in the main room of the cottage, wearing a dark gray suit and Harvard crimson tie, chatting with two cousins and his intimate companion Lucy Mercer Rutherfurd. Elizabeth Shoumatoff, a Russian-born artist, had come down from Long Island to paint the president's portrait. The Filipino houseboy began setting lunch at about 1:00 P.M., and FDR looked at his watch. "Now we've got just about fifteen minutes more," he said. A short while later he raised his left hand to his head, pressed his temple and ran his fingers around his forehead as though in severe pain. Then he slumped back. A woman screamed. Shoumatoff and a cousin ran out for help. The houseboy and the valet Arthur Prettyman approached FDR in time to hear his last murmured words: "I have a terrific headache." They carried him into the adjoining bedroom and got him into pajamas.

Roosevelt's physician, Commander Howard Bruenn, was swimming at the pool two miles away when he was summoned to the cottage. "It was apparent," writes Bruenn in a 1970 medical journal, "that the President had suffered a massive cerebral hemorrhage." Papaverine and amyl nitrite were administered and hot water bottles applied. As Bruenn and George Fox, FDR's masseur, watched anxiously, the blood pressure fell slowly from the first recorded reading at 1:30 (well over 300/190 mm Hg). Breathing stopped at 3:31 P.M. Central War Time. Artificial respiration and injected stimulants were unavailing. Bruenn declared Roosevelt dead at 3:35 (4:35 P.M. in Washington).

Roosevelt's wife, Eleanor, was called back to the White House from a tea party to be told the news. Shoumatoff and Rutherfurd, who had been hustled away, heard the news as they passed through Macon. When Churchill was told, just before midnight in London, he sat stunned and silent. Ambassador Averell Harriman was awakened in Moscow at 2:00 A.M. to tell Stalin. In Berlin, an exultant Goebbels called Hitler in his deep Berlin bunker: "My Fuehrer, I congratulate you; Roosevelt is dead!"

"A cloud of grief...descended on the country and the world," wrote John Gunther. "Citizens saw the headlines and burst into tears on the street." FDR was buried at his Hyde Park, N.Y., estate.

Roosevelt, Theodore (1858–1919).

The U.S. president (1901–1909), severely afflicted by bronchial asthma until the age of seventeen, built up his puny frame by long hours of exercise. He was injured several times when thrown from his horse and once when the presidential carriage collided with a trolley car in 1902, hurling him forty feet and killing a Secret Service agent. During his unsuccessful "Bull Moose" campaign, on 14 October 1912 in Milwaukee, he was shot in the chest by John F. Schrank, but his life was saved by a metal spectacle case in his breast pocket. The bullet, which penetrated four inches, was never removed. He was crippled during his last years by an infected thigh bone, the result of an ill-starred Amazonian expedition in 1913; in 1918 he contracted mastoiditis which led to permanent deafness of the left ear. He developed erysipelas, a streptococcal infection, during his last year, and late in 1918 spent a month in the hospital with inflammatory rheumatism.

President Theodore Roosevelt's grave at Oyster Bay, Long Island.
LIBRARY OF CONGRESS

Roosevelt asked to go home to Sagamore Hill, near Oyster Bay, Long Island, for Christmas, where he spent ten happy days. On 5 January 1919 he wrote an editorial for a newspaper and retired at 11:00 P.M. At four the next morning the attendant in the next room thought Roosevelt's breathing sounded unusual. He called the day nurse, but by the time she arrived the ex-president was dead, apparently of a coronary embolism; there was no autopsy. Roosevelt was buried at Sagamore Hill, near the bird refuge.

Rossini, Gioacchino (1792–1868).

The Italian composer wrote twenty operas, notably *The Barber of Seville*, between 1815 and 1823, but with *William Tell* (1829) his career as an active composer ended abruptly, and for the rest of his life—almost forty years—he remained in semiretirement. For some years his chronic urethritis required almost daily use of a catheter to permit urination, and gross hemorrhoids were a constant burden. But these physical ailments alone can hardly explain Rossini's abandonment of his career. Bruno Riboli in a 1954 study concludes that the composer had a cyclothymic personality, i.e., exhibiting wide swings in mood, and that his episodes of depression were of a magnitude typical of manic-depressive psychosis. After 1848 these episodes included auditory delusions, deep anguish and thoughts of suicide. However, Riboli's diagnosis fails to explain why Rossini, who composed innumerable works throughout his later years, notably the piano compositions which he termed *Sins of My Old Age*, refused to have them performed or published.

His Paris home, the Villa Rossini on the Bois de Boulogne in Passy, became a noted rendezvous for artists. In October 1868 he was enfeebled by bronchitis, and a "rectal fistula," probably cancerous, began to spread rapidly. By the time he reluctantly agreed to make his confession, erysipelas covered much of his body. At about 10:00 P.M. on Friday, 13 November 1868, the dying man murmured the name of his second wife, Olympe. At 11:15 P.M. the physician, Dr. D'Ancona, said to her, "Madame, Rossini has ceased to suffer." Olympe threw herself on her husband's body and could be pulled away only with difficulty.

The service at the Église de la Trinité was attended by five thousand; a large choir and many opera singers performed parts of Rossini's *Stabat Mater* and other works. In May 1887 his body was moved from the grave in Père-Lachaise Cemetery that he shared with Olympe, who had died in 1878, and transferred with much ceremony to the Church of Santa Croce in Florence. A monument was placed to his memory on the north side of the church in 1902. *See* H. Weinstock (1968).

Ruby, Jack. SEE OSWALD, L.H.

Ruth, Babe *(George Herman Ruth)* (1895–1948).

In his last years with the New York Yankees, the "home run king" (he hit 714 of them in major league play) was not in good physical condition; by 1931 he was overweight, and his weak ankles needed to be taped before each game. In his last three seasons, as his home run totals slipped from forty-one to thirty-four to twenty-two, his salary was cut from $72,000 to $35,000. After the Yankees let him go in February 1935 he played with the Boston Braves for a few weeks; in one memorable game at Forbes Field, Pittsburgh, he hit three home runs, the last of them clear over the right-field grandstand into a neighboring backyard. It was the Sultan of Swat's final blaze of glory; after twenty-eight games with a batting average of only .181, Boston fired him on 2 June.

In retirement, hopes of a management offer gradually faded. Ruth acted as coach of the Brooklyn Dodgers for a time in 1938 and played in a few exhibition games. During World War II he did some work for the Red Cross. The first sign of his fatal illness was a sharp pain over his left eye in the summer of 1946. A cancer that—according to the autopsy report—originated high up in the naso-pharynx, in the air passages under the skull, had by that time spread to the neck and encircled the left carotid artery. At French Hospital, New York, on 5 January 1947 doctors excised as much of the growth as they could. Ruth's larynx was affected; when he spoke at Yankee Stadium on Babe Ruth Day, 27 April 1947, his voice was heard to be a frightful croak.

On his final appearance at the stadium on 13 June 1948 his six foot two inch frame seemed shrunken and he used a baseball bat for support. Never told what he was suffering from, he paused as he walked up the steps to Memorial Hospital, New York, later that month and said, "Hey, isn't this a hospital for *cancer*?" Poker-faced, his nurse, Frank Dulaney, replied, "Cancer *and Allied Diseases*." Ruth went on a few outings from the hospital. After the Last Rites were given on 21 July he rallied enough to attend *The Babe Ruth Story*, a hurriedly made movie that starred William Bendix, who had to be coached in holding a bat. Ruth, in pain and no doubt disgusted, left before the end. After that he remained in the hospital. On the evening of 16 August 1948, George Herman Ruth said his prayers and drifted into unconsciousness. When he died at 8:00 P.M. his wife, Claire, his two adopted daughters and a few friends were at the bedside. Groups of youngsters who idolized Ruth had been waiting anxiously outside for as long as five days.

After a service at St. Patrick's Cathedral, the body was driven thirty miles north from Manhattan to Hawthorn, N.Y. The coffin remained in a receiving vault at the Gate of Heaven Cemetery until 25 October 1948, when it was buried in the hill section.

Sand, George *(Amandine Lucie Aurore Dupin)* (1804–1876).

The French novelist, who had been the mistress of Chopin, de Musset and Merimée, among others, lived quietly at her home in Nohant, near La Châtre in Berry, in the final years, organizing theatrical and puppet shows, educating her grandchildren and writing yet more novels. Each new book was received politely in the new age of realism as a specimen of an old-fashioned genre. For some years she had suffered from painful attacks of colic, when in mid-May 1876 these gave way to prolonged constipation. So much did she make light of her troubles that when, brightly smiling, she greeted her physician on the 29th while seated at her desk writing, it was with a shock that he observed her abdomen to be grossly distended. He prescribed castor oil and barley water. By the following afternoon she had acute gastric pain and began to vomit. The latter symptom was allayed

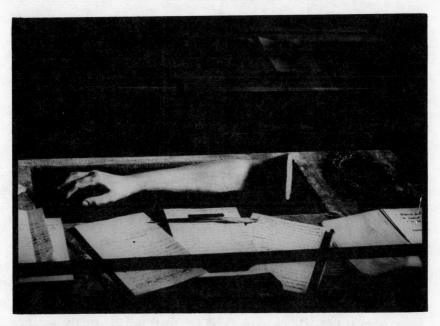

A cast of George Sand's arm among her writing things.

THE BETTMANN ARCHIVE

by warm baths and stomach massages, but the pains became so severe that her screams at night could be heard across the garden.

At Sand's request, a specialist named Favre was summoned from Paris. The local medicos, knowing him to be a charlatan, insisted that he bring a colleague, but he arrived alone and, even before seeing the patient, diagnosed the ailment to be dysentery or hernia. The author had, in fact, an intestinal obstruction that was probably inoperable at that date. Two minor operations relieved the gas pressure for a time. Thereafter, Mme. Sand developed a great thirst, but toward the end became more comfortable. Her last remark, "Leave the grass," was interpreted as a request to be buried under turf, not marble slabs. After her death, at 9:00 A.M. on 8 June 1876, the family thought it more prudent to arrange a religious burial; though the dead woman evidently preferred a civil one, no written instructions could be found. The lead coffin proved to be too small for the swollen body, and a wooden one was hastily constructed. After a Roman

Catholic service, George Sand was buried in the private graveyard behind the chapel at Nohant, near the graves of her grandmother, her parents and her adored granddaughter, Nini.

Savonarola, Girolamo (1452–1498).

The Italian prior of San Marco in Florence constantly exhorted both church and state to reform. Pope Alexander VI, whom the zealous monk had bitterly attacked, excommunicated him, but Savonarola declared the sentence null and void. On 6 April 1498 Savonarola had been undisputed master of the Florentine state; twenty-four hours later he and two other friars were prisoners. For two weeks, as authorities attempted to obtain a confession, Savonarola was tortured by having his hands tied behind his back, being hoisted by his wrists to a height of twenty feet, and dropped to within a few inches of the ground. His resolution remained unshaken though his arms were dislocated at the shoulders and elbows, and his legs at the hips and knee joints. Pope Alexander VI, who received a daily report from the torture chamber, complained of the lack of progress. On the 22nd, Savonarola and two disciples were condemned *in absentia*, ordered to be defrocked and handed over to the secular justices "as heretics and schismatics, and for having preached innovations." A scaffold was erected overnight in the Piazza della Signoria. Fagots were heaped to the height of a man's shoulder and sprinkled with gunpowder, resin and oil. The thirty-foot gibbet was in the center, its cross beams uneven so as not to resemble the cross of Christ.

The people fought ferociously to be as near as possible. The three friars were divested of their priestly garments. The two disciples were hanged first at the extremities of the cross beam; the center position was reserved for Savonarola. At the top of the ladder he turned, faced the crowd and seemed to try to raise a hand in blessing. At 3:30 P.M. the fire was lighted; as the flames leaped up they burned the rope around his wrists and a number of eyewitnesses claimed "that all at once the dead man's right hand, with two fingers uplifted in blessing, rose to the height of his shoulders." "Miracolo! Miracolo!" roared the crowd; pandemonium swept the piazza as onlookers stampeded and the smoke and flames leaped up, removing Savonarola finally from the eyes of man. At dusk the martyr's remains were thrown into the River Arno. *See* P. van Paassen (1960).

Schubert, Franz (1797–1828).

The chubby young Austrian composer with the thick glasses, curly hair and dimpled chin loved good friends and good times, and in spite of his constant poverty he had an abundance of both. However, when he was twenty-six he was hospitalized with syphilis; the treatment, probably mercury, left him completely bald for over a year and until his death five years later he suffered excruciating headaches and vertigo. On 1 September 1828 Franz went to live with his brother Ferdinand in his new home at No. 694 Firmiansgasse (now No. 6 Kettenbrückengasse) in the Neue Wieden suburb of Vienna. On the last day of Oc-

An invitation to Schubert's funeral sent by his father.

AUSTRIAN NATIONAL LIBRARY, VIENNA

tober the brothers had supper with some friends at a tavern, Zum Roten Kreuz, in the suburb of Lichtenthal. Franz ordered fish, but after tasting it declared he was poisoned. On 12 November he told his friend Franz Schober in a letter that he had neither eaten nor drunk for eleven days and that when he tried to eat anything he promptly brought it up again. He begged for more books by James Fenimore Cooper. He tried to correct the proofs of the *Winterreisse* songs but had not the strength to finish the task.

Toward the end Schubert became wildly delirious and had to be held in bed by force. He was sure that he was being buried alive. He murmured the name of Beethoven, whom he revered and who had said about him, "Truly in Schubert lives the divine fire!" It was obvious to those around him that he was dying, but when in a brief, lucid moment he begged to be told his condition, Ferdinand assured him he would soon recover. Schubert lay quietly for some time, then, just before he died at 3:00 P.M. on 19 November, speaking slowly and thoughtfully, he said, "Hier, hier ist mein Ende."

In a 1958 study D. Kerner observed that the originally announced cause of death ("nerve-fever," or typhoid) is not consistent with the symptoms; there was no evidence of somnolence, fever or diarrhea. The clinical picture (headache, giddiness, vomiting and lack of appetite, with terminal signs of confusion) points persuasively to occlusion of a cerebral artery, which may have been syphilitic in origin. Percy Scholes writes: "He left worldly property of the tiniest value and a huge mass of lovely music—more, perhaps, than the world will ever have time to know." Schubert was buried in the Währingerstrasse Cemetery, but in 1888 he was moved to the beautiful Central Cemetery in Vienna, where he lies near Beethoven.

Schumann, Robert (1810–1856).

The German composer showed signs of mental instability throughout much of his later life. He was a manic-depressive in whom the depressive state predominated. Signs that his sturdy common sense was being eroded occurred in the spring and summer of 1853 when he took a serious interest in table turning.

"The table knows all," he told a friend eagerly, his eyes widening and a fanatic look coming into his face. Auditory phenomena had disturbed him from time to time. One day in a café he put down his newspaper and told his companion, "I can't read any more. I keep hearing the note A." But until then his trouble had been temporary. In February 1854 a crisis approached. "Night is falling," he told his friend, the violinist Joachim, in a letter.

It is from his wife Clara's diary that much of the last phase of Schumann's life is best learned. By her piano playing she was the main support of the family, yet her maternal duties (eight children in thirteen years of marriage) and her inability to practice while Robert composed were great obstacles. In the middle of February she writes:

> My poor Robert suffers terribly. All sounds are transformed for him into music, and he says it is magnificent music, with instruments of splendid resonance, the like of which has never been heard on earth before. But of course it upsets him terribly....He has said several times that if it does not stop he'll go out of his mind.

During the night of the 17th Schumann wandered about their home in Düsseldorf, his eyes turned upward, listening to the magnificent music the angels were sending to him. But the heavenly voices later turned to diabolic sounds determined to drag him down to hell, and he became hysterical. On 21 February the sounds abated, to be replaced by a sense of guilt and an intolerable fear that he would do injury to Clara or his children. On the 27th he raced out of the house into the rain without shoes and, climbing the parapet of a bridge, jumped into the Rhine. He was fished out by the townspeople, who walked him home, his hands covering his face.

Schumann was placed in a small private asylum at Endenich, near Bonn, on 4 March. There was at first some hope of a recovery. Schumann was not locked away, and took walks and went on outings. He wrote sensible letters to Clara and to their great friends, Brahms and Joachim. But relapses occurred every few weeks, and Clara was advised not to visit him. However, a telegram summoned her to Endenich when her husband showed signs of sinking. She arrived there with Brahms on 27 July 1856 and went to Robert's room. "With a great effort he put his arm around me: not for all earthly treasure would I exchange that embrace." She could make out few of his words; much of his conversation was apparently directed at unseen spirits. On the following day he was tormented and convulsed and Clara was able to observe him only through a window. Mercifully, he at last sank into a deep sleep and died without waking on 29 July 1856.

At autopsy Schumann's brain, one of the smallest and lightest in the history of medicine, was found to have certain spicules of cranial bone impinging upon it and lacerating its membranes. No clear diagnosis has been offered, but in a 1977 study T.R. Payk concludes that Schumann's schizophrenic psychosis was combined with a cardiac and circulatory ailment. The composer was buried in the Old Cemetery in Bonn.

Schweitzer, Albert (1875–1965).

Orinase brought down his blood sugar, but the humanitarian from Alsace hated to be deprived of sweet things and would, when he could, snatch a piece of cake. At ninety he was growing tired; he realized with frustration that he did not have the time left to speak out against nuclear weapons. One evening, instead of the usual Bible reading, he outlined his hopes for the continuation of Lambaréné and signed a letter to the Strasbourg Association of the hospital indicating that his daughter Mme. Rhena Eckert-Schweitzer was to be director after his death.

From that moment Schweitzer began to fail. Four days later he walked through the hospital's orchard for the last time and looked over the grounds from the top of the hill. The following day, 28 August 1965, he took to his bed with cerebrovascular insufficiency, which resulted in a partial lack of consciousness and impairment of heart and lung functions. At first he was able to drink fluids, including beer, but by 3 September his coma had deepened, one lung had begun to fail and uremic poisoning had set in. He died at 11:30 P.M., 4 September 1965. Tom-toms mingled with church bells as he was buried under the palm trees beside the Ogowe River. Officials of the Gabonese government attended his funeral; so did the French, German, British, Israeli and U.S. ambassadors. But they were outnumbered by the natives, including lepers, who had come to see their "Grand Docteur" laid to rest.

Scott, Robert Falcon
(1868–1912).

When Capt. Scott's ill-fated party was within a few miles of the South Pole on 16 January 1912, their worst fears were confirmed; the British expedition had been beaten to their objective by a Norwegian party led by Roald Amundsen. "Many thoughts come and much discussion have we had." They visited the Pole on the 18th and began the weary eight-hundred-mile journey back across the plateau, down the Beardsmore Glacier to the frozen Ross Sea and on to the base camp at McMurdo Sound. Petty Officer Edgar Evans, a rugged, reliable man, was the first casualty. He began to act "stupidly" after a trivial fall and delayed his four companions repeatedly before his death thirteen days later, on 16 February, at the foot of the glacier. A.F. Rogers, in a 1974 study, concludes that Evans was suffering from scurvy, and that his fall, though insignificant in ordinary circumstances, led to continuing subdural and later brain stem hemorrhage. The party's rations contained no vitamin C at all.

The next to succumb was Capt. L.E.G. Oates, whose feet were terribly swollen, and who had asked the others, in vain, to go on without him. On 17 March Scott wrote in his diary, "He slept through the night before last hoping not to wake; but he woke in the morning—yesterday. It was blowing a blizzard. He said, 'I am just going outside and may be some time.' He went out into the blizzard and we have not seen him since."

The three survivors managed only a few more miles, pulling the heavy sled. Unusually low temperatures (about −40 degrees F.) and difficult surfaces slowed them badly, and supplies of fuel had been unexpectedly low at the previous depot. On 19 March they camped only eleven miles from the well-stocked One-Ton Depot, although one of Scott's feet would have needed amputation if they had made it through. But an endless blizzard set in and Scott and his companions (Dr. E.A. Wilson and Lt. H.R. Bowers) were doomed. Scott's last message reads:

Thursday 29 March: Since the 21st we have had a continuous gale from WSW and SW. We had fuel to make two cups of tea apiece and bare food for 2 days on the 20th. Every day we have been ready to start for our depot 11 *miles* away, but outside the door of the tent it remains a scene of whirling drift. I do not think we can

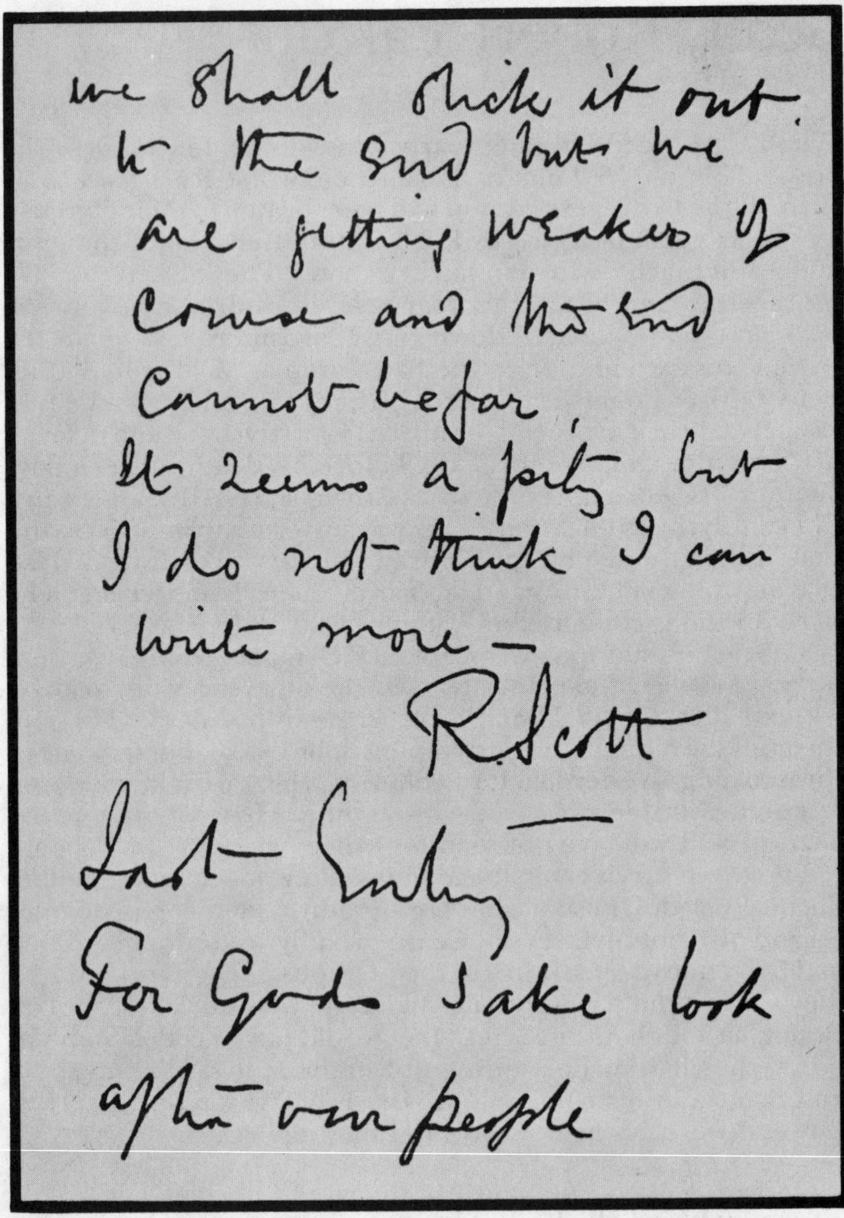

we shall stick it out
to the end but we
are getting weaker of
course and the end
cannot be far.
It seems a pity but
I do not think I can
write more —
                    R Scott

Last Entry —
For Gods sake look
after our people

The final entry made by Scott of the Antarctic as he and his two
companions froze to death.

SIR PETER SCOTT

hope for any better things now. We shall stick it out to the end, but we are getting weaker, of course, and the end cannot be far.

It seems a pity, but I do not think I can write more.

R. SCOTT

For God's sake look after our people.

Their bodies were found by a party led by E.L. Atkinson on 12 November 1912. Only the top of a ski stick could be seen. Under the drifted snow the tent was intact. Bowers and Wilson lay on each side of their leader with their sleeping bags closed. Scott, who probably died last, had thrown back the flaps of his bag and, in a last gesture, stretched out his left hand toward Wilson, his lifelong friend. The tent was lowered, a cairn built, a cross erected on it, and a burial service read. The search party failed to find Oates: they built a cairn where they thought his body might lie deep under the snow.

Scott, Sir Walter (1771–1832).

The Scottish novelist's childhood illness is probably the first recorded case of poliomyelitis in Britain or anywhere else:

> I showed every sign of health and strength until I was about eighteen months old. One night, I have been often told, I showed great reluctance to be caught and put to bed; and after being chased about the room was apprehended and consigned to my dormitory with some difficulty. It was the last time I was to show such personal agility. In the morning I was discovered to be affected with the fever which often accompanies the cutting of large teeth. It held me three days. On the fourth, when they went to bathe me as usual they discovered that I had lost the power of my right leg.

At his grandfather's farm in the Border country Scott was swathed in the still-warm skin of a newly flayed sheep, and during the next few years was subjected to various other unorthodox treatments. Though the leg remained "much shrunk and contracted," Scott battled against his lameness and in his teens was accustomed to walking upward of ten miles. In 1816 attacks of gallbladder colic caused him to resort to large quantities of opium in the form of laudanum, and it was under the

Sir Walter Scott's grave at Dryburgh Abbey.

influence of this narcotic that he wrote *The Bride of Lammermoor* and other works.

In 1822 he first feared the onset of apoplexy. On 5 January 1826 he described the onset of dysgraphia:

> [At twelve noon I] sat down to my work. To my horror and surprise I could neither write nor spell, but put down one word for another, and wrote nonsense....

In April 1829, his "thoughts will not be duly regulated; my pen declared for itself, will neither write nor spell, and goes under independent colours." A year later he suffered a more severe attack while working on his papers. He staggered to the drawing room and fell "at all his full length on the floor." He was speechless for ten minutes, by which time a physician had arrived and bled him. He recovered his faculties gradually, but symptoms of paralysis (including a strange fixity of facial expression), dysphasia (difficulty in speech) and—worst of all for a writer—dysgraphia persisted. It was under this great burden that Scott composed his later novels, the proceeds from which were already mortgaged to meet enormous debts.

During a Mediterranean cruise in 1832 he heard of Goethe's death and was impatient to return home. "Alas for Goethe," he exclaimed, "but he at least died at home—let us for Abbotsford [his small estate near Melrose]." He arrived there on 11 July more or less in a stupor. A week later Sir Walter made a pathetic last attempt to write. The pen was placed in his hand, but his fingers refused to grasp it, and he sank back into his pillows with tears rolling down his cheeks. He lapsed into a final coma on 17 September 1832 and died at 1:30 P.M. on the 21st, surrounded by his children. He was buried at Dryburgh Abbey.

A postmortem examination of his brain showed areas of disease on the left side. In a 1976 study, M. Anderson concludes that Scott was "arteriosclerotic and suffered cerebral ischemia [localized blood supply deficiencies] and numerous episodes of infarction [tissue necrosis] causing cerebral softening.... The overwhelming impression left by a study of Scott's medical history is of his outstanding courage and determination."

Shakespeare, William (1564–1616).

The greatest English poet and dramatist retired from London during his last three or four years to enjoy a quieter existence at his recently purchased house, New Place, in his native Stratford-on-Avon. His eldest child, Susanna, was married to a physician and had presented Shakespeare with a granddaughter. His only son, Hamnet, had died at the age of eleven, but Hamnet's twin sister, Judith, married a vintner of the town in February 1616. Shakespeare's will, made on 25 March when he was "in perfect health and memory, God be praised" left the property to Susanna and her heirs. His phrase "unto my wief my second best bed" has evoked amused comment, but Anne would be provided for by her widow's dower (one-third of the income from the estate) and would be living with Susanna and her husband, who would need the big double bed for themselves.

The poet's death on 23 April 1616, his fifty-second birthday, seems to have been sudden. John Ward, who became vicar of Stratford in 1662, wrote in his notebook:

> Shakespear, Drayton, and Ben Jhonson, had a merry meeting, and itt seems drank too hard, for Shakespear died of a feavour there contracted.

Ben Jonson was a great admirer of Shakespeare's, and the Warwickshire poet Michael Drayton is known to have been a frequent visitor to the district, so Ward's account may have some truth in it. On the other hand, Shakespeare was an abstemious man. Perhaps he had taken his friends for an after-dinner drink to a local hostelry, and caught a chill as they returned home in the cool of the late evening.

The stone slab over his grave in the chancel of Holy Trinity Church, Stratford, bears the verse:

Good Frend for Iesvs sake forbeare
To digg the dvst encloased heare:
Bleste be ye man yt spares thes stones
and cvrst be he yt moves my bones.

The doggerel curse, evidently intended by the poet as a warning to sextons of future generations not to throw his bones into the charnel house when new graves were dug, prevented Anne from joining him in 1623; she is buried separately nearby. It also robs Poet's Corner in Westminster Abbey of its greatest prize.

Shaw, George Bernard
(1856–1950).

The Irish dramatist, socialist pioneer and wit was lonely after his wife, Charlotte, died in 1943. He celebrated his ninety-fourth birthday quietly in July 1950 at his home, Shaw's Corner, in the tiny village of Ayot St. Lawrence, near Welwyn, Hertfordshire. His Scottish housekeeper, Mrs. Alice Laden, went off on vacation in September and Maggie Smith, his former parlormaid, returned to take care of him. On her first day back she was alarmed to hear a whistle. "He carried a whistle with him always, to blow if he fell over or anything like that....I ran out into the garden and found him on the ground." Shaw had been pruning his trees, a favorite task, and had slipped as he stepped back. "I had him sitting on my knee for fifteen minutes. 'Put me down and go and fetch someone,' he said, but I wouldn't put him on the wet grass, and blew at the whistle till my husband, who happened to be near, came to help Mr. Shaw into the house."

Shaw's broken thighbone was set by L.W. Plewes at the Luton and Dunstable General Hospital; a kidney operation was also performed, but the patient declined a second, vital one. "He might have lived to be a hundred if he had stayed in hospital a little longer," said Plewes later. "You won't be famous if I recover," Shaw told him. "Surgeons only become famous when their patients die." He was grossly anemic on admission, but a blood transfusion and meat extract—slipped into the aged vegetarian's soup without his knowledge—improved his condition.

Back home he knew he was finished, and told his housekeeper he wanted to die. His temperature rose to 108 degrees, and he became comatose; he died at 5:00 A.M. on 2 November 1950. "When he was dead he looked wonderful—quite different; clear of complexion and with a sort of whimsical smile on his face, as though he'd had the last laugh." In accordance with his wishes Shaw was cremated without religious ceremony (no cross or "any other instrument of torture or symbol of blood sacrifice" was to be in evidence). His ashes were mingled with his wife's, which had been kept at the crematory, and the local physician sprinkled them on Shaw's garden at Ayot. *See* A. Chappelow (1962).

Shelley, Percy Bysshe (1792–1822).

Although he died before he was thirty, Shelley, one of the leading poets of the Romantic movement in England, left a legacy of great poetry. His last residence was the Casa Magni on the Gulf of Spezia on the northwest coast of Italy. The poet and his friend Edward Williams had a small schooner, the *Don Juan*, which, with the help of their boat boy Charles Vivian, they sailed to Livorno on 1 July 1822, covering the distance of fifty miles in seven hours. They left at about 2:00 P.M. on 8 July for the return journey and were seen hoisting full sail. A storm came up rapidly from the southwest and broke about half-past six. The local feluccas ran for the safety of Livorno harbor. One of the captains said later that he had seen the *Don Juan* in heavy seas and had offered to take the men on board; when they declined, he told them at least to reef their sails or they would be lost. The *Don Juan* went down in the Gulf of Spezia, ten miles west of Viareggio, under full sail.

The bodies of Shelley, Williams and Vivian were washed up on the beach between Massa and Viareggio during a storm ten days later. Though the exposed flesh had been eaten away, Shelley was easily identified by the nankeen trousers and the copy of Keats' poems in his jacket pocket. The body was buried in the sand with quicklime until 15 August, when it was cremated on the beach in a portable iron furnace. At the last moment his friend Edward Trelawny snatched the heart from the flames with tongs. The poet's widow, Mary, kept it in her desk; ultimately it was buried with his son in 1889. Much later Shelley's ashes were buried in a tomb in the Protestant Cemetery in Rome. When salvaged, the *Don Juan* had the appearance of having been run down, perhaps by a felucca or fishing smack; the timbers on the starboard quarter were broken, and the boat had not capsized when it sank. A rumor, neither verified nor refuted, tells of an old Italian seaman who confessed that he had been one of the crew on a felucca that deliberately collided with the *Don Juan*, in the belief that there were valuables on board.

Siamese twins (1811–1874).

The most famous pair of congenitally united twins, Chang and Eng, were born near Bangkok to a Sino-Siamese mother by a

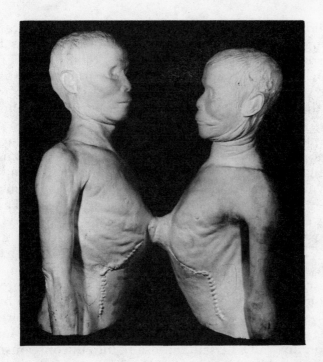

Plaster cast of the Bunker Siamese twins made after autopsy. The incisions are clearly visible. The family would not permit the band of union to be severed.

MÜTTER MUSEUM, COLLEGE OF
PHYSICIANS OF PHILADELPHIA

Chinese father. Although their lower chests were joined by a thick band of cartilage not exceeding six inches in length, the twins were able to stand side by side and, when young, run and swim with admirable coordination. During fourteen years of public exhibition they became world-famous.

In 1840 they borrowed the surname "Bunker" from a New York family of their acquaintance, married two young American sisters from Wilkesboro, N.C., and settled down just south of the Virginia border as farmers. Their established routine was to spend three days alternately in one another's homes, about one mile apart, at Mount Airy. The marriages resulted in twenty-one children.

The twins exhibited marked differences in later life. Chang was the more irritable and less healthy of the pair; his drinking bouts did not affect the abstemious Eng in the slightest, a fact that suggests the vascular and nervous connections between their bodies were not significant. During their tour of Europe in 1870, Dr. Rudolf Virchow declined to separate them, suspecting that their livers might be directly connected. On their way back across the Atlantic, Chang suffered a stroke and his health steadily deteriorated thereafter.

In January 1874 he developed a dry cough and chest pains. They moved to Eng's house as scheduled on the 15th, and on the following night Chang was restless and unable to breathe easily while lying down. At 4:00 A.M. on the 17th, Eng's son William looked in on them to see how his uncle was. Eng woke, feeling "mighty sick," and asked William, "How is your Uncle Chang?" The boy who had just turned up the lamp, cried out in alarm, "Uncle Chang is cold—Uncle Chang is *dead*." The entire household was now aroused. To his wife, Eng wailed in terror, "My last hour is come; I am dying." He said he needed to get to the bathroom, but this request had to be ignored. After a half-hour of panic-stricken movements, including raising and lowering his arms, he complained of a choking sensation. "May the Lord have mercy on my soul," he said, and sank into unconsciousness. He died an hour later, just before Dr. William Hollingsworth arrived, prepared to separate him from his dead brother.

Afraid of grave robbers, the families delayed the funeral. A tin coffin was hastily made, in which the double corpse was stored in the basement for two weeks. There was talk of selling the curiosity for a high price, but this idea was gradually abandoned. Meanwhile a commission of physicians from Philadelphia arrived to examine and embalm the corpses, but were forbidden to disfigure them or to cut the front of the band of union. On 10 February an autopsy was conducted by Dr. W.H. Pancoast in Philadelphia under the same restrictions as before. He concluded that because of an apparent connection between the twins' livers and diaphragms, their separation in life would probably have had a fatal outcome. However, a prompt dissection after Chang's death—when a cut could have been made at a distance from the union with Eng—would have had an improved chance of success. Though the brains could not be examined, Pancoast believed Chang had died of a cerebral thrombosis. As for Eng, he died—according to Harrison Allen's 1875 report of the autopsy—"in all probability in a state of syncope induced by fright—a view which the overdistended bladder and retraction of the right testicle would appear to corroborate." From a 1961 review of the documents, W.B. Daniels concludes that Chang died, not of a stroke but of congestive heart failure with pulmonary edema leading eventually to arrythmia (probably ventricular fibrillation), but he is in agreement that Eng, who had shown no sign of illness previously, had literally died of fright.

Sallie Bunker, Eng's wife, died in 1892 at the age of 70; Adelaide survived Chang by forty-three years. On her death in May 1917 the bodies of the twins were buried with her in the graveyard of White Plains Baptist Church, N.C., a church the twins helped to build. Their remains had been returned to Eng's cellar for a year, after which they had been interred under Chang's lawn. The tombstone bears the names of the two husbands and their wives, although for reasons unknown Sallie remains buried on Eng's farm. *See* I. and A. Wallace (1978).

Sitting Bull (1834?–1890).

The great Indian chief was causing so much unrest among the Sioux on Standing Rock reservation in North Dakota by his opposition to the sale of tribal lands and his promises of a coming Messiah that his arrest was ordered. When Major James McLaughlin received the order at Fort Yates he sent in a force of Indian police. Just before dawn on 15 December 1890 the men broke into Sitting Bull's cabin on Grand River. He awoke to find several men lifting him from his bed where he had been sleeping naked. His carbine, knife and revolver were snatched from his bed and the kerosene lamp was lit. Weasel Bear had hold of his right arm and Eagle Man his left. Red Tomahawk wound his arms around the naked, unarmed old man from behind. Lt. Bullhead laid his hand on the chief's shoulder and said, "I am holding you for arrest."

Most of the police were young and nervous and wanted to get Sitting Bull away before the whole camp was alerted. They rushed to get him dressed, roughly thrusting odd pieces of clothing on him until the chief was thoroughly disgusted and balky. It was obvious to him that this was not the customary ceremonial dressing to do him honor. As they lugged him to the door he spread his legs across the opening, but Eagle Man kicked his legs aside. Taunted and kicked, he was manhandled outside and urged forward, one policeman persistently prodding him in the back with a revolver. Angry supporters came running from their tents. The noise was terrible: women wailing, children crying and men shouting insults and threats at the Indian police. "Kill them, kill them—shoot the old policemen and the young ones will run!"

The chill dawn was breaking when, out of the corner of his eye, Lt. Bullhead saw someone in a gray blanket slink around the corner of a house carrying a Winchester rifle. It was Catch-the-Bear, who had previously made many threats against Bullhead. He screamed at the police, "Let him go!" and Sitting Bull knew that the fight he had been stalling for was about to take place. "Come on! Come on! Take action! Let's go!" he ordered, struggling vigorously in the arms of his captors. Bullhead, hit in the leg by Catch-the-Bear, shot at Sitting Bull as he fell. The bullet struck the chief in the back, on the left side between the tenth and eleventh ribs. As he staggered from the impact, Red Tomahawk shot him from behind. Sitting Bull, killed instantly, dropped like a stone as dawn rose on 15 December 1890.

He was buried at Fort Yates, N.D., but in April 1953 when Clarence Grey Eagle heard that the grave would be covered by the new Oahe Dam he asked the Mobridge, S.D., Chamber of Commerce whether it would build a memorial if Sitting Bull's remains were moved there. Mobridge agreed but North Dakota's governor refused to let the grave be opened. However, both sites were within the Standing Rock Indian Reservation and with the Secretary of the Interior's permission Grey Eagle, under cover of a blinding snowstorm, had the bones dug up, rushed to Mobridge, reburied and covered with twenty tons of cement. *See* S. Vestal, 1932.

Smith, Bessie (1898?–1937).

The great U.S. blues singer of the twenties and thirties was badly injured when her car, driven by her friend Richard Morgan, crashed into the back of a truck on Route 61 near Clarksdale, Miss. Dr. Hugh Smith was at the scene almost immediately and sent for an ambulance while doing what he could for the injured woman. In the poor light he was unable to determine whether or not she had suffered a head injury. She was obviously in excruciating pain, had a shattered left elbow and seemed to have crushed ribs and internal injuries. While they were waiting for the ambulance, a car driven by a partying white couple crashed into Bessie Smith's car; the woman became hysterical and the man probably fractured some ribs. The deputy sheriff and an ambulance arrived. Bessie and Morgan were taken to Clarksdale; a second ambulance arrived and took away the white couple.

Rumors spread later that Bessie Smith was refused admission to a white hospital and consequently bled to death. Dr. Smith refutes this rumor, stating that in Clarksdale (a town of 12–15,000 people) there were two hospitals, one for white patients and one for colored, and that in 1937 no ambulance driver would ever have taken a black person to a white hospital, especially when the hospitals, as in this case, were only half a mile apart. Bessie's right arm was amputated but her other injuries were severe and she died of shock a few hours after the accident at 11:30 A.M., 26 September 1937, in Ward 1 of the Afro-American Hospital, 615 Sunflower Avenue, Clarksdale. She is buried in Sharon Hill, Pa. In 1967 several people, including Janis Joplin and John Hammond of Columbia Records, contributed to the erection of a headstone. *See* C. Albertson (1973).

Smith, Joseph (1805–1844).

In the spring of 1844 the prophet of the Mormons was mayor, municipal judge and foremost merchant of the city of Nauvoo, Ill.; in addition, he was running for the U.S. presidency. Though the countryside around the Mormon city was distrustful of the Latter-Day Saints and jealous of their prosperity, it was Smith's own actions that precipitated violence and tragedy. One of his ablest advisers, William Law, had already become disillusioned by Smith's worldliness, his commercial sharpness and his political ambitions. Now he was incensed by Smith's secret marriages—he had perhaps fifty "celestial" brides in addition to his faithful (but suspicious) legal spouse, Emma. The attempted seduction of Law's own wife was the last straw. He begged Smith to confess his sins to the High Council of their church. But the

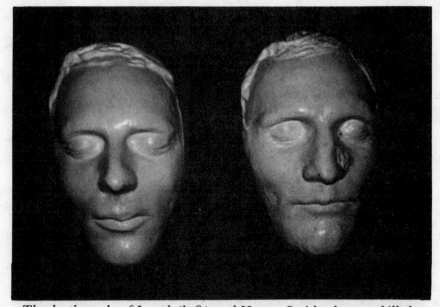

The death masks of Joseph (left) *and Hyrum Smith who were killed in a Carthage jail and now lie buried together in Nauvoo, Illinois.*

CHURCH OF JESUS CHRIST
OF LATTER DAY SAINTS

prophet could neither bring himself to do this nor to declare openly the "revelation" of polygamous marriage. Whereupon Law on 7 June published a scathing editorial in his new Nauvoo *Expositor* attacking these evils. The city council in a highly irregular "trial" denounced the newspaper as libelous and fit for destruction, and the city's militia (the Nauvoo Legion) wrecked Law's press and destroyed all the copies they could find.

After Illinois Governor Thomas Ford promised protection, Joseph Smith, his elder brother Hyrum and a few others surrendered for trial in nearby Carthage. They were released on bail, but the two brothers were immediately rearrested on a flimsy charge of treason (for declaring martial law and initially resisting arrest). When members of the disbanded militia from Warsaw, Ill., attached the two-story jail at Carthage on 27 June 1844, the Smiths were upstairs with two friends, Willard Richards and John Taylor. A six-shooter and a pistol had been smuggled in to them the previous day. Their door was forced open by the mob, and Hyrum was struck in the face and body. "I am a dead man," he called as he fell. Joseph emptied the six-shooter down the stairs, wounding several of the attackers, before leaping on the sill and, some say, giving the Masonic sign of distress. "Is there no help for the widow's son?" he shouted.

A shot fired from inside struck Smith in the back, and he was probably hit by another bullet from the crowd that had gathered outside. He fell to the ground but was immediately propped up against the well curb in the yard. Colonel Levi Williams, head of the Warsaw militia, ordered his men to fire on the wounded man, who then fell on his face, dead. As one of the murderers leaped forward with a knife to cut off Smith's head the storm clouds parted and a shaft of sunlight suddenly shone down. Unnerved, the mob broke up. Some time later, Richards, who was unhurt, carried the body inside and laid it beside Hyrum's. Taylor was seriously wounded but recovered. Several officers were tried for Joseph's murder but were found not guilty at a trial in which the prosecution was mishandled and the witnesses were uncooperative. No trial for Hyrum's murder was held.

Because desecration of the graves was feared, coffins filled with sand were interred at the public funeral and the brothers' bodies were hidden under the yet incomplete Nauvoo House. Emma later had the bodies reburied near her summer cottage. In January 1928 the remains were sought and found a hundred feet from the Mississippi on South Main Street, Nauvoo. They were reinterred nearby alongside Emma and a distinctive marker was erected.

Socrates (469–399 B.C.).

At seventy, the Athenian philosopher had a grotesque exterior; he was a stout man, below middle height, with prominent eyes, a wide mouth and a snub nose with broad nostrils. But his friends knew him to be "all glorious within." For complex reasons, indictments were brought against him of corrupting the young men of the city and of failing to worship its gods. The philosopher had been friendly with Critias, the most criminal of the "thirty tyrants" set over Athens by the victorious Sparta after the Peloponnesian War, and with Alcibiades, who had gone over to the Spartan side. Though he defended himself ably, Socrates

The death of Socrates. Painting by J.L. David 1787.

METROPOLITAN MUSEUM OF ART

would not debase himself before the court. Instead, he antagonized the 501 jurors by claiming a reward as a public benefactor. They responded by sentencing him to death. When his old friend Crito suggested a plan of escape, Socrates courteously declined, explaining that as a son of Athens he could not in good conscience disobey its laws.

As Plato recounts events in his *Phaedo*, Socrates began his final day in the company of his wife, Xanthippe, and his two young sons. Then, sending them away, he discussed with his friends the fate of the human soul, cheering them in their grief by arguing that death was a good, not an evil thing. In the afternoon he retired to bathe, so that the women "will not have the trouble of washing my body." "And how shall we bury you?" asked Crito. "In whatever way you wish in accordance with our customs. But remember, Crito, it shall not be me that you bury, only my body. I shall be gone."

When the potion of hemlock was brought, Socrates asked if he might make a libation—that is, sprinkle or pour some of it on the ground as an offering to the gods. Only a bare sufficiency had been prepared, he was told. "Very well, but I may and do pray that they bless me in my journey from this world to the next." Whereupon he cheerfully drank the entire draught while his friends, their composure lost, unrestrainedly began to weep. Socrates asked for peace while he died. Following the jailer's earlier instructions, he paced the prison floor until his legs began to feel heavy, then he lay down. The jailer pressed his feet, then his legs, to see if all feeling had left them. When the coldness had reached his groin Socrates uncovered his face, which he had hidden, and spoke his last words: "Crito, I owe a cock to Asclepius; will you repay him?" "The debt will be paid," was the reply. "Is there anything else?" But there was no answer, and in a little while Crito closed the eyes and mouth. The location of Socrates' grave is unknown.

W.B. Ober in a 1977 study reminds us that although poisoning by coniine (the alkaloid of hemlock) is chiefly marked by ascending motor paralysis, as in Plato's account, other symptoms are also present. These include nausea, vomiting and convulsions. If Plato suppressed these details it was no doubt because "he wanted to preserve the noble image of his friend and teacher, 'the wisest and justest and best.'"

Spinoza, Baruch (Benedict) (1632–1677).

The Dutch creator of one of the world's great metaphysical systems was of Portuguese-Jewish descent. He supported himself as a lens grinder and spent the last seven years of his life in a few bare rooms in the house of Hendrik van der Spyk in The Hague. Spinoza had been ill for twenty years with consumption, inherited from his mother but aggravated by the glass particles that floated in his workroom. Toward the end he had to combat great physical weakness to complete his daily work. On 21 February 1677 his friend and physician, Dr. Schuller, came to visit him and prescribed some broth for dinner, which Spinoza greatly enjoyed. The doctor remained, holding the philosopher's hand, while his voice grew weaker and his breath became even more gasping and labored, until he died quietly on Sunday afternoon, 21 February 1677. Many illustrious people attended his funeral on 25 February at the New Church on the

Spuy. All Spinoza's relatives had long ignored him. After the funeral they descended upon the little house with covetous eyes, but when they heard that after the payment of debts nothing would be left, they hastily renounced all claims.

Stalin, Joseph (1879–1953).

At 8:00 A.M. on 4 March 1953, Moscow radio announced "the misfortune which has overtaken our Party and the people—the serious illness of Comrade J.V. Stalin. During the night of March 1–2, while in his Moscow apartment, Comrade Stalin suffered a cerebral hemorrhage affecting vital areas of the brain. Comrade Stalin lost consciousness, and paralysis of the right arm and leg set in. Loss of speech followed. There appeared to be serious disturbances of the heart and breathing."

The initial shock was followed by suspicion regarding the delay and wording of the announcement and those that followed. The final bulletin came at 4:00 A.M. on 6 March: "The heart of Joseph Vissarionovich Stalin...has ceased to beat." Death had occurred at 9:50 P.M. on the 5th. Through the years rumors continued to circulate. It was not until Svetlana Alliluyeva fled to the U.S. and published her *Twenty Letters to a Friend* in 1967 that a trustworthy account of her father's death became available. Stalin had not died in Moscow. Svetlana was summoned on 2 March 1953 to her father's favorite dacha near Kuntsevo, some miles to the southwest of the capital. (This was the house to which he was sped every evening from the Kremlin by a convoy of armored linousines.) She was met in the driveway by Nikita Khrushchev and N.A. Bulganin who, as she hastened inside, told her that her father had been found at three that morning lying senseless on a rug. He had been carried to a sofa in the main room of the dacha, where she found him surrounded by a crowd of doctors, nurses and Politburo members.

During his final twelve hours, her father began to suffocate. "He literally choked to death as we watched. At what seemed like the very last moment he suddenly opened his eyes and cast a glance over everyone in the room. It was a terrible glance....Then something incomprehensible and awesome happened that to this day I can't forget and don't understand. He suddenly lifted his left hand as though he was pointing to something above and bringing down a curse on us all."

In 1956 Khrushchev denounced Stalin's reign of terror, and in 1961 the body was moved from the Lenin mausoleum to a less exalted place outside the Kremlin wall.

Stein, Gertrude (1874–1946).

The U.S. writer spent World War II in German-occupied France. Two war correspondents, Eric Sevareid and Frank Gervasi, were the first Americans to reach her during the liberation of September 1944. She and her companion, Alice B. Toklas, returned to their Paris house at 5 rue Christine in December, where Miss Stein became an instant celebrity. GIs "swarmed all over her" and addressed her as "Gerty." She loved it.

In November 1945, during a flight to Brussels to lecture to the GIs there, she suffered an attack of abdominal pain. The following July, during a drive into Indre-et-Loire, Gertrude was taken ill again. She returned to Paris by train and was driven to the American Hospital at Neuilly on the outskirts of the city. After several days of continued pain, the doctors were still reluctant to operate. A young surgeon was called in and the patient addressed him sternly: "I order you to operate; I was not born to suffer."

Before the orderlies wheeled her away on the afternoon of 27 July 1946, and under heavy sedation, she turned to Alice and murmured, "What is the answer?" Receiving no reply, she continued, "In that case, what is the question?" She was suffering from extensive abdominal cancer. After the operation she lapsed into unconsciousness and died an hour later at 6:30 P.M. Unaccountably, her burial at Père-Lachaise Cemetery was delayed until 22 October. Alice joined her there twenty-one years later, in March 1967, a month before her ninetieth birthday. *See* J.R. Mellow (1974).

Stevenson, Adlai (1900–1965).

Had he lived, Stevenson would probably have resigned the United Nations Ambassadorship by the end of 1965, for he was frustrated at having to defend policies, such as the bombing of North Vietnam, to which he was opposed. After making a speech to a U.N. body in Geneva in July, he flew to London for a few days. When he left New York he was fatigued, but in Britain as the guest of U.S. Ambassador and Mrs. David Bruce he seemed fit, eager to play tennis whenever he could find a partner. Still, he was overweight, suffered a heart "flutter" from time to time and had been warned to cut down on his drinking and smoking.

On his final day Stevenson had lunch at Claridge's as a guest of the *Encyclopaedia Britannica*, then recorded an interview at the U.S. Embassy in Grosvenor Square for broadcast by the BBC that evening. At four o'clock he suggested to Mrs. Marietta Tree, the tall, handsome U.N. delegate from New York, that they take a walk. They went first to see his 1945 mews home at 2 Mount Row, but discovered it had been torn down. "It makes me feel so old," said Stevenson. They talked briefly to a Jamaican diplomat who met them. Then, as they turned into Upper Grosvenor Street toward Hyde Park, "You're going too fast for me," he called, for Mrs. Tree is a notoriously fast walker. (He had retaliated in the past by dodging into an entry and hiding from her.) At a slower pace, they discussed various professions he might pursue in his post-U.N. years. "I have ten more years of working life," he told her.

As they approached a picket fence he stopped and said, "I feel terribly faint." "He looked ghastly," Mrs. Tree recalled in 1967. "I spotted a crate or something in a doorway and I rushed to get it for him to sit down on. As I moved toward it, I felt his hand hit hard against me as he went down....I ran into what I thought was a hotel but turned out to be a club [the International Sportsmen's Club]....People brought blankets. His eyes were open, but he was unconscious....A man came along, said he was a doctor, and began heart massage. He asked for someone to give mouth-to-mouth resuscitation, and I volunteered. He instructed me and then said I was going too fast. After a few minutes, Adlai began to breathe in long, shuddering gasps. Along came the doctor that had been called [from the club]. He gave injections after having trouble finding the great vein inside the elbow."

Stevenson was still breathing when the ambulance arrived. Mrs. Tree hurriedly collected the scattered papers from the sidewalk and traveled with her stricken friend to St. George's Hospital, Hyde Park Corner. A few minutes after they arrived a doctor came out and told her he was dead. "I asked to see him. They said, 'No, you'd rather remember him as he was in life.'"

Elie Abel of NBC happened to be at the embassy when the news came in; a few minutes later, Pauline Frederick, NBC's U.N. correspondent, was passing on the news. It was 1:00 P.M. in New York on 14 July 1965. The body of Stevenson was brought to Washington by the presidential plane. He lay in state in the National Cathedral, Washington, then in the Illinois Capitol at Springfield. He was buried in Evergreen Cemetery, Bloomington, Ill.

Stevenson, Robert Louis
(1850–1894).

Six years before his death, the Scottish novelist set out on his tour of the Pacific in search of a climate where his tuberculosis might be halted. Three miles from the town of Apia, on the island of Samoa, and six hundred feet up the slope of Vaea, he found the perfect spot to build a house, Vailima, on a wooded estate of three hundred acres. There he lived in greatly improved health with his wife Fanny, his mother, who had come over from Edinburgh, and his stepchildren, Lloyd and Belle Osbourne. His last Thanksgiving dinner on 29 November 1894 was a great success, though U.S.-born Fanny had to use red native berries with the roast turkey in place of the unobtainable cranberries.

Stevenson's last day, 3 December, was spent as usual in his small balcony workroom, dictating to Belle with great power and fluency his unfinished masterpiece, *The Weir of Hermiston*. Coming down for dinner at sunset he first went to the cellar for a bottle of Burgundy, then returned to the veranda to help Fanny make a salad of pineapple, guava, papaya and other local fruits. They stood with their heads close together, smiling and speaking softly. Fanny had been glum for two days with an awful presentiment of disaster, and Stevenson was intent on cheering her up. Belle saw him suddenly put down the cruet. Fanny says he raised his hands to his head for a moment and muttered, "What's that?" and then, "Look at me." Both heard his last words a second later: "Do I look strange?" He sagged at the knees as his body servant Sosimo rushed forward to support him.

Stevenson was laid, already unconscious, in a chair in the great hall, and later on a couch. Fanny paced in anguish up and down

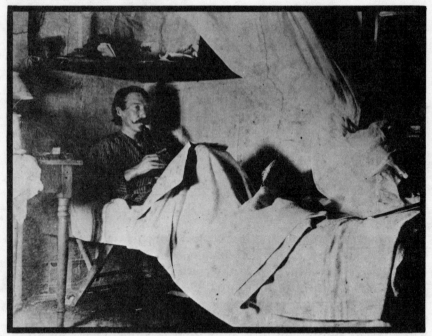

Robert Louis Stevenson before (above) *and after* (top, right) *death in his house on Samoa. He was buried a few hours later atop Mount Vaea* (bottom, right). *This temporary marker was replaced by a massive tomb bearing Stevenson's own words: "Under the wide and starry sky/ Dig the grave and let me lie/ Glad did I live and gladly die/ And I laid me down with a will/ This be the verse you grave for me/ Here he lies where he longed to be/ Home is the sailor, home from sea/ And the hunter home from the hill."*

TOP: LIBRARY OF CONGRESS; OPPOSITE: CITY
OF EDINBURGH MUSEUMS AND ART GALLERIES

the long room; his mother wept over him until the summoned physicians declared him dead (of a stroke) at 8:10 P.M. Two Samoans rubbed the body with perfumed coconut oil during the night while volunteers hacked a path up the mountain for the necessary quick burial. The hardwood coffin was taken by relay teams of Samoans to the chosen grave at the summit of 1,200-foot Vaea, where their beloved Tusitala ("teller of tales") was laid to rest with Presbyterian rites at 4:00 P.M. on 4 December 1894.

Strachey, Lytton (1880–1932).

The English critic and satiric biographer of Queen Victoria and others wickedly displayed both his wit and his homosexuality when he appeared as a conscientious objector before a tribunal in 1916. "What would you do if you saw a German soldier attempting to rape your sister?" asked a military interlocutor. "I should try," he replied gravely, "to interpose my own body."

As he lay dying at his home, Ham Spray, near Hungerford, Berkshire, a house guest, Dora Carrington Partridge, who had adored Strachey for years, crept down to the garage in despair and tried to kill herself by breathing exhaust fumes. Saved in the nick of time, she was watched closely thereafter. Strachey had been ill since early December 1931 with what was believed to be either colitis or enteric fever. Told that the doctor would soon be making another visit, the barely conscious patient responded that he would be delighted to see him, "but I'm afraid I shan't be able to do much socially." As he sank into oblivion for the last time he murmured, "If this is dying, then I don't think much of it." He died at about 1:30 P.M. on 21 January 1932 of what the autopsy showed to be a cancer that had perforated his colon. Strachey was cremated and a bronze plate commemorating him was placed in the Strachey Chapel at Chew Magna Church, Somerset.

The vigilance with which Dora was observed in later days and weeks inevitably diminished. On 11 March 1932, while alone in Ham Spray, she calmly ate breakfast and then, setting the butt of a borrowed rifle on the bedroom floor, fired into her side. The bullet missed her heart, and she died painfully a few hours later. Her farewell letter was not produced at the inquest, and her death was ruled an accident. *See* M. Holroyd (1968).

Swinburne, Algernon Charles (1837–1909).

When the English poet Swinburne was dying of alcoholic dysentery in 1879, an admirer of his poems, Theodore Watts (later Watts-Dunton), took him into his care and gave him thirty years more of stable, healthy life. They rented a house at The Pines,

Putney, and Watts' care was exercised so tactfully as to be almost imperceptible; for instance, he weaned Swinburne from strong liquor to pale ale. Their close friendship survived even Watts' marriage, at the age of seventy-three, to a twenty-one-year-old girl. Four years later, when his guardian was ill with influenza, Swinburne wandered off onto Wimbledon Common and, wet through, caught a fatal chill. When double pneumonia set in, the dying man refused to accept an oxygen mask until Watts sent word downstairs that oxygen was like a sea breeze and would do him a world of good. Whereupon, he inhaled it without another word.

Swinburne died quietly at 10:00 A.M., 10 April 1909, with a smile on his lips. He had had strong antireligious feelings, and had extracted a promise from Watts that a burial service would not be read over his grave. After a tussle with the family a compromise was reached. At Bonchurch, Isle of Wight, the vicar met the coffin as it left the hearse and read the services on the way to the burial site.

Tchaikovsky, Peter Ilyich
(1840–1893).

The Russian composer conducted his Sixth Symphony in St. Petersburg on 28 October 1893 (new style) and the following day added the descriptive title *Pathétique* to the title page at his brother Modeste's suggestion. On 2 November Tchaikovsky was unwell with a digestive upset but rose later in the morning and went out on business. At lunch he ate little but seemed recovered. Declining to have wine or coffee, he left the table to draw water from a faucet in the next room and, returning, drank it down rapidly. "Petia," cried Modeste, "that wasn't boiled. What crazy folly!" It was the annual cholera season in the city, but Peter simply shrugged his shoulders. A few minutes later, however, he rushed from the table and was violently sick in his room. By late that evening he had suffered chest constriction and stomach cramps. Evidently, he had picked up the cholera bacillus somewhere on the way from Moscow, and the cold drink had triggered the onset of the acute stage, but the patient was not immediately told the nature of the illness.

As men in white hospital uniforms arrived in the sickroom

with their carbolic soap and antiseptic powders, Tchaikovsky relived the frightening memory of his mother's death in precisely such circumstances. "Here she is then, the cholera," he cried, and a moment later screamed as the pain returned. The small iron bed had been moved into the living room to give the numerous nurses more room. On the 3rd, great thirst succeeded the pain, and Tchaikovsky felt somewhat better, though he told the doctors, "Leave me, I shan't recover." The next day he slept a great deal and murmured the name of Nadejda von Meck, the wealthy friend and patron who had always refused to meet him face to face and who, in ill health, had broken with him in 1890. He began to sweat profusely on Sunday 5 November 1893, and his pulse weakened. He probably never heard the priest praying over him. At 3:00 A.M. on 6 November the three physicians and Peter's brothers and nephews were alerted by a slight sound. Approaching the bed, they saw the composer's face clear and his eyes open. According to Modeste, "An indescribable look of clear recognition lighted up his face—a gleam which only died away with his last breath."

Contrary to the rules of cholera hygiene, Tchaikovsky's body lay in state in his brother's apartment and hundreds of mourners filed through the room kissing the dead man's face and hands. The body was taken in a closed coffin to Kazan Cathedral for funeral services. Peter had wished to be buried in the churchyard of the tiny village of Frolovskoe, but this was not done. Instead he lies in St. Petersburg in Alexander Nevsky Lavra Cemetery.

Tecumseh (1768?–1813).

When and where the American Indian leader died is known precisely, but the story of who killed him and what became of his body is wrapped in mystery. The cowardly British commander, Brig.-Gen. H.A. Procter, retreated from Detroit after Capt. O.H. Perry's decisive naval victory over the British on Lake Erie, 10 September 1813. Tecumseh, though serving under Procter, upbraided him and ordered him at gunpoint to make a stand at the Thames River against Maj. Gen. W.H. Harrison's pursuing force of 3,500 men. The site of the battle (present-day Thamesville, Ontario) was protected on the British left by the swift-flowing river, on the right by Tecumseh's men.

At 4:00 P.M. on 5 October Harrison sent in his Kentucky cavalrymen. The first line of British regulars broke and Procter fled in a waiting carriage. Demoralized and without reserve ammunition, the force of 600 was soon surrounded and captured. Their 1,000 Indian allies made a resolute stand. Tecumseh was wounded again and again but, with blood pouring from his mouth, he repeatedly reloaded his rifle and fired on the cavalry while rallying his men in their own language. With their ammunition exhausted, the survivors resorted to fighting with their tomahawks as they were driven into a great swamp. By then, Tecumseh's voice was no longer to be heard.

Many, including Harrison and Perry, later searched for his body. Glenn Tucker, in his 1956 biography, believes that a U.S. officer, Maj. Thomas Rowland, saw the great Indian warrior before darkness fell on the continuing battle. "There was something so majestic, so dignified, and yet so mild, in his countenance as he lay stretched on the ground, where a few minutes before he rallied his men to the fight, that while gazing on him with admiration and pity, I forgot he was a savage...." Rowland mentions a bandaged arm that would seem to clinch the identification (Tecumseh had received an arm wound at Chatham and wore such a bandage).

Tucker further writes: "As the years passed, the Indian story emerged. Naw Naw, Shabbona, Black Hawk, Noonday and others told how in the dead of night Tecumseh's faithful little band went over the battlefield examining the bodies until they found the chief's. A bullet had passed through his heart. His skull had been crushed by a gun butt. Otherwise his body was not mutilated. They lifted it carefully and carried it four or five miles away before they buried it in an unmarked grave." Tucker's best surmise is that Tecumseh was killed by sixty-four-year-old Colonel William Whitley at the same moment Whitley himself was shot dead by the Indian leader.

Tennyson, Alfred, Lord
(1809–1892).

The great English poet died slowly at his home, Aldworth, near Haslemere, Hampshire. Two days before his death, he was asked if he felt better; he replied, "The doctor says I do." His last requests were for his favorite Shakespeare to be brought to him.

He read a little from *King Lear* and *Cymbeline* before beginning to sink. "Have I not been walking with Gladstone in the garden, and showing him my trees?" he murmured. "No," answered his son. "Are you sure?" Always considerate to those who attended him, he told the specialist, Sir Andrew Clark, "This is the worst attack I have had;" but, knowing the doctor had left his Christchurch home at seven that morning, he added, "I hope you are not tired."

On his last evening Tennyson asked the doctor, "Death?" Doctor Dabbs bowed his head. "That's well," said the poet. His last words were a farewell blessing to his wife and son, Hallam Tennyson. The latter, whose wife was also present, writes, "He was quite restful, holding my wife's hand, and, as he was passing away, I spoke over him his own prayer, 'God accept him! Christ receive him!' because I knew that he would have wished it." Tennyson had asked for the blinds to be raised, and during the hours of his passing the room was flooded with light from the full moon. It shone through the oriel window onto what Dabbs described as "a figure of breathing marble...his hand clasping the Shakespeare 'drawing thicker breath' irresistibly bringing to our minds his own 'Passing of Arthur.'" He died at 1:35 A.M., 6 October 1892, and was buried—with his copy of *Cymbeline*—next to Browning in Westminster Abbey. *See* H. Tennyson (1897).

Thackeray, William Makepeace (1811–1863).

A few days before his death, the author of *Vanity Fair*, who had been ill with "shivering fits," was talking with Sir Theodore Martin in the great hall of the Athenaeum Club when Charles Dickens passed by with no sign of recognition. The two novelists had been on poor terms since Thackeray, in his clumsy way, had tried to defend Dickens from the charge of having an affair with Georgina Hogarth, his sister-in-law. "No such thing," Thackeray replied. "It's with an actress." Now, five years later, he hurried after Dickens and begged him to end the foolish estrangement. The two shook hands and exchanged some cordial words. "I love that man," Thackeray said afterward, "and could not resist the impulse."

On 23 December 1863 Thackeray felt unwell and remained in

bed at his home at Palace Green, Kensington, working on the proofs of *Denis Duval*, which was to remain unfinished. The following morning, as his daughter, Anne, recalled the events, there was "a strange crying sound in the house & I went out of my room to the landing. Charles the servant met me. He is dead Miss he said he is dead." Thackeray lay in bed with his body stretched out, face upward, and with his arms above his head. His hands grasped the bedrail in a final paroxysm of pain, but his features were calm. The doctor's certificate recorded, "Disordered digestion 10 days. Excessive vomiting 24 hours. Cerebral effusion."

Dickens heard the news on his way to Gad's Hill for Christmas. Young Marcus Stone commiserated with him: "I know you must feel it very deeply, because you and he were not on friendly terms." Dickens put his hand on Stone's arm. "Thank God, my boy, we were." Thackeray lies in Kensal Green Cemetery, London.

Thomas à Becket. SEE BECKET, THOMAS À.

Thomas, Dylan (1914–1953).

When John Malcolm Brinnin became director of the YM-YWHA Poetry Center in New York in 1950, he naively invited the Welsh poet over to give readings and then assumed the role of tour manager. It was an association that soon evoked concern and ended in anguish. Toward the end, Dylan's drinking became uncontrollable. Attractive, even lovable, when sober, he became sober only to become drunk once more; and when drunk his unrestrained advances to strange women, his offensive language and generally intolerable behavior made his self-appointed guardians retreat from their posts, baffled and fearful.

Although Brinnin was in New York during only part of Thomas' fourth and final visit, his *Dylan Thomas in America* includes a frank, detailed account of the last tragic weeks. Thomas flew in on 19 October 1953 for a matinee performance of his still-unfinished *Under Milk Wood*. Waiting for the plane in London he was shocked to find himself racing the clock, drinking one whiskey after another. By the time of the performance on the 25th he was recovering from another spree and deeply depressed, confessing "my health is entirely gone. I can't drink at all. I always could, before...." Dr. Milton D. Feltenstein injected corticotropin, which temporarily relieved "the feeling of dread, the terrible pressure...as if there were an iron band around my skull." The dramatic reading was a critical success, but those around Thomas sensed an ominous change in the pattern of his behavior. Brinnin's assistant, Liz Reitell, who was close to the poet in the final days, sensed the coming disaster but was unable to disengage herself. A poetry reading at City College on the 29th, two days after Thomas's thirty-ninth birthday, was his final public appearance. The drinking continued and delirium tremens developed. According to Paul Ferris in his 1977 biography, Dr. Feltenstein, summoned three times to the poet's hotel, the Chelsea on Twenty-third Street, finally injected a large amount (a half-grain) of morphine sulfate into his raving patient. This may have precipitated the breathing difficulties that caused Dylan, in a coma from which he never emerged, to be admitted to St. Vincent's Hospital at 1:58 A.M. on 5 November. His wife, Caitlin, flew over in time to see him alive; "possessed of ten thousand raving demons," as she later described her state on arrival at the hospital; she smashed a crucifix and a statue and attacked Brinnin. She was confined to a private clinic over the East River by the time Dylan died, while being bathed by a nurse, at about 1;00 P.M. on 9 November 1953. The autopsy report cites bronchopneumonia with "pial edema" (fluid on the brain) as the primary cause, with a fatty liver as the contributing factor. Thomas' embalmed body was returned home and buried on 24 November in the village churchyard at Laugharne on the South Wales coast.

Thoreau, Henry David
(1817–1862).

When, early in July 1861, the U.S. poet–philosopher returned to his home in Concord, Mass., following a three-month trip to Minnesota, his health was not improved and he knew his life

Henry Thoreau's small tombstone in the family plot, Sleepy Hollow Cemetery, Concord, Massachusetts. Photo by Roger B. Smith.

STATE UNIVERSITY OF NEW YORK, GENESEO

would not be greatly extended. He made his last journal entry on 3 November, by which time his tuberculosis was well advanced; he was coughing and expectorating frequently and he had a wasted appearance. After an attack of pleurisy in December, his voice began to fail. Nevertheless, he was busy with his reading and note taking, and possessed a good appetite. He faced his approaching death with much cheerfulness and resignation: "It is better some things should end," he remarked.

Surrounded by flowers, pictures and books, Thoreau had a cheering effect on his frequent visitors. One of them, Sam Staples, said he had "never spent an hour with such satisfaction. Never saw a man dying with so much pleasure and peace." Thoreau refused opiates; to relieve his sleepless nights, he had his mother or his sister Sophia place the lamp on the floor and arrange the furniture to throw fantastic shadows. Although he referred to the hereafter (when a friend told him of seeing a spring robin, he remarked, "Yes, this is a beautiful world; but I shall see a fairer"), he discouraged religiosity. His Aunt Louisa, wanting to know whether he had made his peace with God, received the reply, "I did not know we had ever quarrelled, Aunt." Near the end he was asked whether he could see "the further shore." "One world at a time," he murmured.

On his last morning Thoreau smelled a gift of hyacinths appreciatively and asked to be raised up on his cane bed. In his last sentence, incompletely recorded, the words "moose" and "Indian" were recognized, presumably references to the Maine Woods papers he had been working on. His breathing became fainter and fainter until he died at 9:00 A.M., 6 May 1862. Sophia remarked, "I feel as if something beautiful has happened—not death." Following a service in the First Parish Church in Concord on 9 May, Thoreau was buried in the New Burying Ground at the foot of Bedford Street. *See* W. Harding (1965).

Thurber, James (1894–1961).

The U.S. humorist wasn't so funny in his later years, and the criticism that had given his humor direction was harder to take. His appearance on stage in eighty-eight performances of *A Thurber Carnival* in 1960 was helpful to his shaky psychological balance; it was the last good thing to happen to him. The *New Yorker* was no longer printing most of his pieces; his poorest book, *Lanterns and Lances*, came out in 1961 and he was dictating an even poorer one. "He thought it was his greatest writing," recalls his secretary, "but I knew it was just terrible...."

Thurber's blindness, which had begun with the loss of an eye in 1901 (in a game of "William Tell" with his brother in Falls Church, Va.), was nearly total by 1952. He drank too much, and his personality was quite changed. He continually insulted his wife, Helen, and many of his friends ("his gentleness was gone," said one of them.) He left his home in Cornwall, Conn., for a week alone in New York; Helen in turn spent a while in the hospital, simply to obtain bedrest. Reunited, they attended Noel Coward's *Sail Away* on 3 October 1961. A marathon series of insults to Helen later that night went on at least until 4:00 A.M., when their single guest left their Algonquin Hotel suite in disgust. Two hours later Thurber collapsed and struck his head. A large subdural hematoma was removed at Doctors Hospital; evidence of cerebral arteriosclerosis and a series of minor strokes

Thurber did not wish to be buried in Greenlawn Cemetery, Colum-
bus, Ohio, "in which my once bickering, but now silent, family
occupies a good square mile of space." But his ashes are indeed
buried there. Photo by Betty Donaldson.

was discovered. Pneumonia and a pulmonary thrombosis followed.

Thurber died on 2 November 1961. In a letter to the Van
Dorens written two years earlier, he had expressed the hope that
he would not be buried in Green Lawn Cemetery, Columbus, "in
which my once bickering, but now silent, family occupies a good
square mile of space." But his wishes were disregarded and his
ashes, in a bronze urn, were interred on a snowy Wednesday
morning, 8 November 1961, a few feet from his parents'
headstone. *See* B. Bernstein (1975).

Tojo, Hideki (1884–1948).

Major Paul Kraus and members of the U.S. Occupation Force
drove to a modest house in the Setagaya suburb of bomb-scarred
Tokyo on 11 September 1945. A well-known face appeared at

the window: shaven head, hooded eyes behind thick glasses, sparse mustache. A moment later it vanished and a shot was heard. The arresting force smashed the lock on the front door and raced inside. Japan's wartime prime minister lay in an armchair wth a bullet wound above the heart. He recovered, to be found guilty of war crimes and sentenced to death. At Sagamo prison he handed the Buddhist priest a haiku he had written for his wife. After a service, at which joss sticks were burned and cries of "Banzai" were shouted, Tojo mounted the steps of the gallows and at 1:30 A.M. on 23 December 1948 died.

General MacArthur declined the widow's request for her husband's remains, but after Tojo and six other war criminals, who were hanged the same day, had been cremated, Japanese workers scooped up some of the ashes and hid them. At the end of the American occupation the salvaged remains were turned over to the families. On 17 August 1960 a granite tomb was unveiled atop Sanganesan Hill at Hazu with the inscription: THE TOMB OF SEVEN MARTYRS. *See* C. Browne (1967).

Tolstoy, Leo, Count (1828–1910).

The great Russian novelist ran away from home at the age of eighty-two and died ten days later. Life with the countess, Sonya, had long been intolerable. He was adamant in his religious belief, a form of Christian anarchism based on the New Testament, which rejected equally the church, the government and the concept of private property. But life on his estate at Yasnaya Polyana (about a hundred miles south of Moscow, near Tula) was clearly at variance with these tenets, however simply he tried to live. His family violently opposed him, and resented the visits of his fellow converts, notably the interfering V.G. Chertkov. By 1910, Sonya's spying on him and her hysterical reproaches had reduced him to a baffled obduracy.

Determined to seek seclusion, Tolstoy crept out of the house before dawn on 28 October after leaving a note: "I ask you to forgive me all the wrongs I have done to you...." Accompanied by a physician friend, he traveled first by train west to Optina monastery with the intention of settling nearby. But his daughter and ally, Alexandra, persuading him that her mother would soon send the police, advised further flight. The insane plan of traveling 600 miles to Rostov-on-Don was embarked on, but the exhausted Tolstoy, already ill, was forced to leave the train—after only one day's journey—at the little village of Astapovo in Ryazan province. The stationmaster gave up his cottage to the famous invalid and a death watch began. Doctors, journalists and photographers arrived from Moscow. Sonya came, but was denied admittance. The count had pneumonia of the lower left lung, and was being further exhausted by hiccups. By the time his wife was permitted to kneel beside him, Leo Tolstoy was unable to recognize her. He refused the rites of the church to the end, which came at 6:05 A.M., 7 November 1910. Tolstoy was buried, as he had requested, at the edge of the Zakaz forest on his estate at Yasnaya Polyana.

Toscanini, Arturo (1867–1957).

At his last broadcast concert—an all-Wagner program—with the NBC Symphony Orchestra in Carnegie Hall on 4 April 1954, Toscanini stopped conducting for half a minute and the broad-

Toscanini conducting one of his final concerts.

U.S. NATIONAL ARCHIVES

cast was faded out. Then, as though waking from a trance, the maestro took up the beat once more and the broadcast was resumed. Toscanini's retirement had been announced that evening and his biographer, George Marek, suggests that this poorly timed action may have distressed the conductor. Thereafter, he spent some time, in both New York and Milan, reviewing his recordings for possible release. In his last year he was almost blind. His son, Walter, had a peephole bored in the bathroom door of their mansion in the Riverdale section of New York City so that he could help the failing old man in an emergency.

After a New Year's party Toscanini suffered a hemorrhage, then several more over the next week or so. He came out of a coma on the night of 15 January 1957 to sing a snatch from Verdi's *Aida*, the opera that had made his name when, at a moment's notice, he conducted it from memory at the age of nineteen. In the morning he was dead.

Following funeral services at St. Patrick's Cathedral, New York, the body was flown to Milan where thirty thousand people paid him homage at La Scala Opera House. After a Solemn Requiem Mass at Duomo Cathedral, Toscanini was buried in the Monumentale Cemetery. A 400-voice choir sang "Va, pensiero" from *Nabucco* by Verdi.

Toulouse-Lautrec, Henri de
(1864–1901).

The French artist's physique was apparently defective from an early age. In May 1878, when he was thirteen, he was rising from a low chair with the aid of his cane when he slipped on the waxed floor of his home at Albi and broke his left thigh bone. The following year he was walking with his mother near Barèges, a Pyrenean spa, when he tumbled into a shallow ditch and fractured the other femur. Thereafter, the bones ceased to grow and, though Lautrec's head and torso were of normal size, his final height was barely five feet. Osteologists are still unable to establish the nature of the bone abnormality from which he suffered. In a 1970 study, Sir Terence Cawthorne suggested one of two known conditions: either osteopetrosis ("marble bones") or the very rare melorheostosis in which only one or two long bones are affected.

In the 1890s, Toulouse-Lautrec became a prolific portrayer of Montmartre night life, including its bordellos. He worked all day, drank all evening and debauched most of the night. By 1898 the quantity, though not yet the quality, of his work began to decline. Early in 1899 he suffered an attack of delirium tremens and was committed to a private mental home in Neuilly; by that date he had been syphilitic for a decade. After just a few weeks he was released into the guardianship of Paul Viaud, a middle-aged man in reduced circumstances who had digestive trouble that prevented his touching a drop. But Viaud's genteel restraints could hardly prevail over a dipsomaniac's obsession.

In the end, alcohol and syphilis combined to kill Toulouse-Lautrec three months before his thirty-seventh birthday. After a slight stroke in February 1901, he put his Paris studio in order. In August after a second stroke, suffered at Taussat, his mother brought him to her home at Malromé, Gironde. Even then he had to work. Supported on a ladder, he strived in vain to complete a portrait of Viaud. He lingered until 9 September 1901, when he died with a quip on his lips. To the priest he said, "M. le Curé, I'm happier to see you now than I shall be in a few days when you come with your little bell." He was buried in the little cemetery of Saint-André-du-Bois near the gates of the estate of Malromé. Later, his mother had the body removed to the village churchyard of Verdelais, two miles from Malromé, where it lies today.

Tracy, Spencer (1900–1967).

The U.S. motion picture actor completed his seventy-fourth film just two weeks before his death. Worsening of his emphysema sent him briefly to the hospital in February 1967, a few days before production began on *Guess Who's Coming to Dinner*. The disease had gravely affected his heart, and the customary insurance coverage could not be obtained; producer-director Stanley Kramer went ahead without it. Tracy's wife in the movie, and his companion (for twenty-six years) in real life, was Katharine Hepburn. In reference to their screen daughter's desire to marry a black man, he turned to Hepburn and, his voice cracking, said, "If what they feel for each other is even half what *we* felt, then that is everything."

On Saturday morning, 10 June 1967, Tracy was up early as usual in the cottage he rented on George Cukor's estate in Beverly Hills, Calif. Shortly after 6:00 A.M. he suffered a heart attack and was discovered, still alive, by his housekeeper, Ida Gheczy. But, by the time his brother Carroll arrived with a physician, he was dead. His wife, Louise, with whom he had remained on friendly terms, was summoned, along with other members of the family and Miss Hepburn, whose acting in Tracy's last movie won her her second Academy Award. Tracy, after a Catholic service at the Immaculate Heart of Mary Church, Hollywood, was buried in Forest Lawn Cemetery, Los Angeles.

Trollope, Anthony (1815–1882).

The English novelist, creator of Barsetshire and Plantagenet Palliser, was dining quietly in London with his brother-in-law, Sir John Tilley, on the evening of 4 November 1882. He was, perhaps, overexcited by an altercation with the leader of a German band that had disturbed him during the afternoon by playing under the window of his room at Garland's Hotel. F. Anstey's *Vice Versa*, the fantasy of a schoolboy magically changing places with his father, had just been published. The book was read aloud to the general merriment, with Trollope laughing loudest of all.

Suddenly his laughter died and he was seen to be sitting silent and crooked in his armchair. He had suffered a stroke. At a nursing home at 34 Welbeck Street, he recovered sufficiently to walk about a little, though not to speak. But his condition worsened again and he died, after a coma, at 6:00 P.M. on 6 December 1882. Trollope was buried in the cemetery at Kensal Green, London, where his literary hero, Thackeray, already lay.

Trotsky, Leon (1879–1940).

The Soviet revolutionary and rival of Joseph Stalin was expelled from the U.S.S.R. in 1929 and lived his last three years in Mexico. In May 1940 his fortified house on the Avenida Viena in the Coyoacán suburb of Mexico City was attacked by a force of

Trotsky's tomb in the garden of his house on Avenida Viena in the Coyoacán suburb of Mexico City. Photo by David King.

twenty uniformed men, assumed to be Stalinist agents. Trotsky, his wife, Natalia, and his grandson, Seva, escaped injury from the fusillade of machine gun bullets by hiding under their beds. Then, during the summer, a young man who called himself "Jacques Mornard" in Paris but who in Mexico possessed a Canadian passport with the oddly spelled name "Frank Jacson," ingratiated himself with the Trotsky menage, including the guards, by paying court to and later living with Sylvia Agelof, one of their secretaries. This man, who was later identified as Ramón Mercader, a twenty-six-year-old Spanish Stalinist, called at the Trotsky home a dozen times and sometimes dined there.

On 20 August, Trotsky began his day by feeding his rabbits; later he answered some letters and dictated part of an article into a recorder. At about 6:00 P.M. Mercader called, hugging an overcoat to his body and looking nervous and ill. He was offered food but declined. Trotsky walked into the study with him to discuss an article Mercader claimed to have written. Natalia shortly heard a "terrible heart-breaking cry." When Trotsky had sat down to read the article, the killer took an ice ax from under his coat. "Closing my eyes," he stated later, "I brought it down on his head with all my strength." Though the blade tore through the parietal bone into the brain, the victim was able to spring to his feet and throw himself on his murderer, biting his hand and preventing use of the pistol or dagger with which he was armed. He was subdued by the guards a moment later. Trotsky's last words to Natalia at the hospital that evening before he lost consciousness were, "I do not want them to undress me... I want you to undress me." This accomplished, they exchangd kisses. He died, within twenty-five hours of the attack, at 7:25 P.M., 21 August 1940. On 26 August 1940 the U.S. State Department refused to receive Trotsky's corpse; his body was cremated on the following day and the ashes were buried in the grounds of the house on Avenida Viena.

The assassin was sentenced to twenty years, the maximum term of imprisonment. He was supplied with money by a mysterious source and spent the time in reasonable comfort. After his release in May 1960 he disappeared behind the Iron Curtain. His brother, Luis, on 18 October 1978, reported his recent death from bone cancer in Cuba on an uncertain date at the age of sixty-four; his ashes were flown to Moscow.

Trujillo, Rafael (1891–1961).

The dictator of the Dominican Republic had been in power thirty-one years when he was assassinated. As he grew old, his sensuality deepened, with high officials selecting up to forty women for him as often as three times each week. He did not lack courage, but some mental imbalance became evident in the last months. He foresaw death and betrayal. The conspirators were in daily readiness to kill him and on 30 May 1961 a signal came from a palace informant that the evening was auspicious.

As Trujillo was driven along the coastal highway from his palace toward San Cristóbal, his Chevrolet was overtaken by the assassins de la Maza and García Guerrero at a point one mile beyond the El Pony restaurant. They wounded the dictator with machine gun fire. He ordered his chauffeur to pull over, while the attackers sped ahead and turned on the grass divide. Trujillo got out, blood spurting from his back, firing his .38-caliber revolver. Two other conspirators, who had been waiting farther ahead in a second car, now drove up to cover the assassins. De la Maza worked his way around behind the Chevrolet and fired from that point. Trujillo's high-pitched shout, "Ay, ay, ay, ay!" was heard as he half-turned and fell to the roadway, dead.

The police found the dictator's body a few hours later in the trunk of de la Maza's car, parked in the garage of General Tomas Diaz. After embalmment it lay in state before being taken to Paris and buried on 14 August in the Père-Lachaise Cemetery. The conspirators failed to follow up on their action. Most of them were tortured before being shot; their bodies were thrown to the sharks.

Tutankhamun (1356?–1338 B.C.).

Although a minor pharoah who reigned only nine years and died at about eighteen (his wisdom teeth were just emerging), "King Tut" achieved modern fame when his unrifled tomb, with its magnificent ornaments of gold and carved wood, was uncovered by Howard Carter in 1922. The treasures were exhibited

The unwrapped mummy of Tutankhamun remains in his tomb in the Valley of the Kings.

GRIFFITH INSTITUTE, ASHMOLEAN MUSEUM,
OXFORD, ENGLAND

throughout the U.S. in 1977–79. The mummy itself was replaced in its tomb in the Valley of Kings near Luxor. Apart from some carbonization of the skin, the head is intact, even to the half-open eyes, and, judging from photographs made in 1925, its resemblance to the heavy, gold death-mask is striking. No reason for the King's early death could be determined by D.E. Derry and S.B. Hamdi in 1925. Press reports that R.G. Harrison and A.B. Abdalla, when they x-rayed the mummy in 1968, discovered a hole in the skull leading to suspicions of foul play were not borne out by the printed report (in the quarterly *Antiquity* in 1972). The skull is intact and the cause of death is still unknown.

Twain, Mark *(Samuel L. Clemens)* (1835–1910).

Fate was not kind to Twain in his last years, and his mood was often bitter. The final blow came on Christmas Eve 1909, when his second daughter, Jean, drowned in the bathtub during an epileptic seizure. He spent the early part of 1910 in Bermuda, playing clock golf with Woodrow Wilson and writing an occasional article. But his angina pectoris became increasingly severe and he determined to come home. The two-day journey was torture; he could not breathe while lying down and barely slept. "It's a losing race," he gasped. "No ship can outsail death." Later, in a calmer moment, Twain observed, "When I seem to be dying, I don't want to be stimulated back to life. I want to be made comfortable to go." His married daughter, Clara, came to Stormfield, his new home in Redding, Conn., to be with him.

Twain had been born when Halley's comet was bright in the sky, and he always wanted to die on its next appearance. The comet reached its greatest brilliance on 19 April 1910; Mark Twain died on the 21st. "Suddenly he opened his eyes," wrote Clara, "took my hand, and looked steadily into my face. Faintly he murmured, 'Goodbye, dear, if we meet——'" He then lost consciousness and died at sunset. After thousands had filed past the casket, where he lay dressed in a white suit, in Brick Presbyterian Church, New York City, he was taken to his old home at Elmira, N.Y., for burial.

Mark Twain's last days were saddened by domestic tragedy.

LIBRARY OF CONGRESS

Valentino, Rudolph (1895–1926).

The Italian-born screen idol was taken ill in a friend's apartment on Park Avenue, New York, on 14 August 1926 and the following day was admitted to Polyclinic Hospital. On the 16th he was operated on for a ruptured appendix and perforated gastric ulcer. As telegrams and flowers flowed in from thousands of star-struck women, Valentino made a normal recovery for several days. On the 21st, however, his temperature began to rise again and signs of pleurisy were evident on the left side. He slipped into a coma at 8:00 A.M. on Sunday, 23 August, and died at ten minutes after noon. The death certificate, made out in his real name (Rudolfo Guglielmi) listed ruptured gastric ulcer and general peritonitis as major causes, with septic pneumonia and septic endocarditis as contributing factors.

One hundred thousand people filed past the open casket in the Gold Room at Campbell's funeral chapel in Manhattan.

After a funeral service in Beverly Hills, Valentino, who had died deeply in debt, was placed in the family crypt of his mentor, screen-writer June Mathis, in Hollywood Cemetery. Though this arrangement was intended to be temporary, the planned mausoleum has never been built and his remains lie there still.

Verdi, Giuseppi (1813–1901).

After the death of his wife in 1897 the Italian opera composer was lonely and depressed. He wrote to his friend and librettist, Arrigo Boito, in the fall of 1900 "...I am not really ill but my legs barely support me, and my strength diminishes from day to day." Later that year he went to the Grand Hotel in Milan for Christmas. On the morning of 21 January 1901 Verdi suffered a stroke. He remained motionless and unconscious, except for brief moments, during the next six days. The Milan city council had straw mats laid outside the hotel. Close friends gathered anxiously and doctors conferred in whispers as, day after day, the sound of the musician's breathing filled the room. The

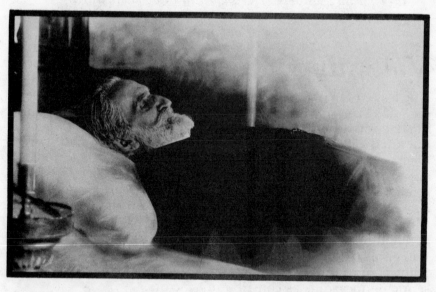

Giuseppi Verdi in death.

MUSEO TEATRALE ALLA SCALA, MILAN, ITALY

sound stopped at 3:00 A.M. on 27 January 1901; Verdi was dead.

In accordance with his wishes, he was buried quietly in a Milan cemetery. A month later the coffin was taken from the modest grave and reburied in the crypt of the "Casa Verdi," the name the Milanese gave to the home for retired musicians that Verdi had established shortly before his death. Toscanini conducted nine hundred voices in the "Va, pensiero" from *Nabucco,* a work that had made Verdi a national symbol almost sixty years before.

Victoria (1819–1901).

The year 1901 opened with the British queen in failing health. Cataracts were making her half-blind, but she still insisted on carrying out her duties, and "hideous mistakes" were made

Queen Victoria's funeral procession at Windsor. The new monarch Edward VII is walking behind the gun-carriage.

NEW YORK PUBLIC LIBRARY

when she misread state documents. She had been at a favorite residence, Osborne House, near Cowes on the Isle of Wight, since mid-December. She gave up keeping her diary (for the first time in sixty-nine years) on 14 January. On the 17th, mental confusion and speech difficulties were evident, and a heart specialist was summoned. That the queen was ill was first announced to the public on the 19th. The family gathered; her grandson Willy (the German Kaiser), with whom she had had difficulties, was now allowed to approach the bedside with the others to support his grandmother with his one good arm. Her last word was for her tearful elder son, who had caused her so much heartache: "Bertie," she whispered as she hugged him close. Her favorite hymn, Newman's *Lead Kindly Light*, was read to her.

As she drifted away to meet—she was certain—her long-dead Albert, Victoria's numerous children and grandchildren quietly identified themselves, then, after a while, fell silent. The end came a little after 6:30 P.M., 22 January 1901. As Prince Arthur lifted the body into her coffin he was amazed to find his mother "dwindled to a featherweight." Because she had agreed with Tennyson that a white funeral was best, she was dressed entirely in white with her wedding veil covering her face. Public buildings displayed white satin bows instead of the customary black hangings. After the public tribute, the family in a private ceremony on 4 February laid her to rest with her beloved husband at Frogmore, near Windsor. It took the nation a long time to adjust itself; few of her subjects could remember a time when Victoria had not been their sovereign.

Voltaire, François (1694–1778).

The great French writer, who fought against the clerical excesses of his time, died in Paris at 11:00 P.M. on 30 May 1778. During his final illness the clergy demanded that he renounce his antireligious writings, but despite his great pain he refused to do more than claim he wished to die a Catholic. "Then recognize the divinity of Christ," begged the parish priest. "Just let me die in peace," he replied. Accused of betraying his lifelong principles, he explained to his physician, "I do not want to be thrown into the carrion pit. These priests annoy me and bore me, but they

The funeral of Voltaire; a fanciful woodcut by G. Ansbeau.
NEW YORK PUBLIC LIBRARY

Leon Berard places Voltaire's heart in his statue at the National Library of France in 1924.

LIBRARY OF CONGRESS

Siegfried Wagner visits his father's statue at Cleveland, Illinois in 1924. Photo by Underwood and Underwood.

have me in their hands." Denied a Christian burial, his body was dressed in bathrobe and nightcap and driven away, sitting up, to Scellières, where a kinsman arranged interment at the abbey there before the bishop's prohibition was received. The abbé was later dismissed. A Mass was forbidden in Paris, but Voltaire's friend and pupil, Frederick the Great, had one sung in Berlin two years later. During the French revolution, Voltaire's body was brought to the Pantheon by a procession of 100,000 citizens, but royalists and priests rifled the tomb when Napoleon was exiled in Elba, stole the bones, and threw them into an unmarked grave. In 1924 his heart, preserved in liquid in a gilt container, was rediscovered in the National Library, Paris, but it was not examined.

Wagner, Richard (1813–1883).

The German composer of "music dramas" left the cold and damp of Bayreuth in September 1882 in search of the sun. A doomed, cantankerous figure on bad terms with many former friends, he spent his last months in the impressive Palazzo Vendramin-Calergi in Venice, where he had rented fifteen spacious rooms. His life's work was over, but he could barely tolerate to admit it, even to himself. On 11 February 1883 he began an essay on *The Feminine Element in Humanity* which, if he had finished it, would no doubt have proved to be a potpourri of the racial and sexual obsessions that had ruled him for so long. On the 13th, immersed in the task of relating his thesis to a Buddhist libretto he had toyed with over the years, he suffered a heart attack. A frantic summons on the bell brought his wife, Cosima, hurrying in. Resting in her arms, Wagner died at 3:30 P.M. When his body arrived back at Wahnfried, his Bayreuth home, his Newfoundland dog, Marke, greeted it with a great howl. Wagner's tomb in the garden at Wahnfried had been designed by the composer himself. *See* R. W. Gutman (1968).

Washington, George (1732–1799).

The first president of the United States (1789–1797) was a tall, vigorous man—he measured six feet three and a half inches at

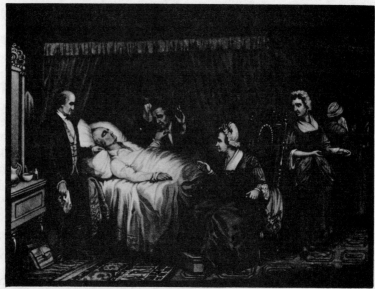

The death of George Washington, from a contemporary print.

LIBRARY OF CONGRESS

the time of his death—but he did not come from long-lived stock. He was frequently ill and lived much of the time in apprehension of dying. That he suffered malaria from his teens onward is not surprising, for the disease was prevalent in the southernmost American colonies at that time, but, in addition, he contracted smallpox in Barbados at twenty-one and hard on this he was stricken by a pleurisy that may have been tuberculous. However, during the Revolutionary War Washington's health was remarkably good and, though often exposed to British fire, he escaped injury.

Soon after his first presidential term began, his life was saved when Dr. Samuel Bard of New York incised a "malignant carbuncle" on Washington's left hip, but he was desperately ill for many weeks. In Boston a little later he caught a cold that seems to have turned to pneumonia. Tired and ill, he declined a third term and retired to Mount Vernon, Va., where malaria plagued him again. On his recovery, he enjoyed fairly good health. True, his hearing had been failing for some years; he employed spectacles for private reading and owned two famous pairs of false teeth made out of hippopotamus ivory.

On 12 December 1799, General Washington was in the saddle by ten o'clock to begin his ride around his plantation. The northeast wind brought snow, hail, rain and snow again before his tour ended five hours later. On his return, his faithful friend and secretary, Colonel Tobias Lear, remarked flecks of snow in the former president's hair and gleaming moisture on his neck, but Washington assured him that his greatcoat had kept him warm enough, and, because his dinner awaited him, he went in to eat without changing into dry clothes.

The following day, despite a sore throat, Washington marked some trees for felling and shrugged off the idea of taking medicine. "You know I never take anything for a cold," he told Lear. "Let it go as it came." During the night he woke his wife, Martha, complaining of ague but would not let her go through the cold house for help. In the morning, the general was given various gargles and vinegar mixtures which almost choked him. He was bled by the estate supervisor—a tolerably good man at veterinary work—and then three more times during the day by Drs. Craik, Brown and Dick. True, young Dr. Elisha Dick protested, but the senior physicians, supported by the patient, overruled him. Further dehydration of the sick man was perpetrated by means of calomel (a laxative) and tartar emetic. During the afternoon, Washington became weaker and, struggling for breath, changed his position in bed continually. Dr. Dick proposed a tracheotomy—opening of the windpipe—but the procedure was new and unproved, and his more conservative colleagues again turned him down. Instead, they applied blisters and wheat bran poultices to the legs of the harassed but obedient patient.

Washington's strangled breathing became easier at 10:00 P.M. and at about that time he turned to Lear, who was holding his hand, and said hoarsely, "I am just going. Have me decently buried and do not let my body be put in a vault in less than two days after I am dead. Do you understand me?...'Tis well." He lay quietly for a few minutes, then withdrew his hand from his secretary's to take his own pulse. His hand fell limp and without "a struggle or a sign" the father of his country stopped breathing. The time was about 11:00 P.M. on 14 January 1799. Washington's tomb is close to his home at Mount Vernon.

In a 1927 study, W.A. Wells assessed the diagnosis and treatment. Craik and Dick described Washington's illness as *cynanche trachealis* (quinsy of the windpipe), misleading in modern parlance but quite accurate at the time the diagnosis was made. Washington died of an acute inflammatory edema of the larynx, which causes painful swallowing and sometimes, as in his case, actual suffocation. In this most violent form it was, no doubt, caused by a streptococcal infection. The excessive bleeding weakened the patient, but was accepted practice and remained so for another fifty years. A tracheotomy might well have saved Washington's life, but it was considered a dangerous procedure until the 1820s.

Waugh, Evelyn (1903–1966).

The English author's mental instability was not confined to his last years, as his autobiographical *Ordeal of Gilbert Pinfold* (1957) demonstrates. Attending a nuptial Mass with his biographer, Christopher Sykes, late in 1965, he repeatedly murmured, "There's a man with a lot of lions behind me....It's dangerous," until Sykes told him to shut up. He confessed that the ability and desire to write had left him. "He spent his morning breathing on the library window and then playing naughts and crosses [tic-tac-toe] with himself [and] drinking gin in the intervals...." After Mass on Easter Day, 10 April 1966, Waugh and his family returned to their home at Combe Florey, near Taunton, Somerset. "It seems," writes Sykes, "that some time during the morning Evelyn went to the back parts of the house. While there he had occasion to raise his arms and this gesture brought on an instant and instantly fatal heart attack. Laura [his wife] found him dead." Waugh is buried at Combe Florey.

Weil, Simone (1909–1943).

The French philosopher and mystic spent the early months of 1943 in London. She was a tall, thin, bespectacled woman, more intolerant and difficult in her conversation than in her writings, many of which have been translated into English since her death. The Free French headquarters refused her request to be dropped into German-occupied France by parachute, and assigned her instead to a desk job. In her personal attitudes she had never deviated far from the pattern set when, at the age of five, she refused to eat sweetened food because her compatriots at the front had no sugar. Now she starved herself because, she said, the entire French nation went hungry. In April a friend found her lying weak and ill on the floor of her rented room in Portland Road, Holland Park. At the Middlesex Hospital she refused proper food and declined treatment for tuberculosis.

Born of Jewish parents, Weil had been attracted to Christianity but resisted baptism except on her own terms. "I can't admit that infants who die without baptism are shut out of Paradise," she declared, and there were other amendments to the faith upon which she insisted. "You are too proud," sighed a visiting priest. She was moved to Grosvenor Sanatorium at Ashford, Kent, on 17 August and the fight over proper nutrition was recommenced. She died on 24 August 1943. The certificate reads: "Cardiac failure due to myocardial degeneration of the heart muscles due to starvation and pulmonary tuberculosis. The deceased did kill and slay herself by refusing to eat whilst the balance of her mind was disturbed." At an inquest on the 27th the coroner recorded a verdict of suicide while the balance of the mind was disturbed. Her funeral would have pleased her; although buried at Ashford as a Catholic, the priest was absent, having missed his train from London. *See* J. Cabaud (1964).

Wellington, Arthur Wellesley, Duke of (1769–1852).

The British victor of Waterloo became a genial old man, a generous host and a great favorite of young children, whose boisterous games he loved to join. He was eighty-two years old when the Great Exhibition of 1851 opened in Hyde Park. No trees were to be cut down, and sparrows became a nuisance. "His country turned, as usual, to Wellington," writes Philip Guedella. "The duke was sent for, and the queen herself described the difficulty. 'Try sparrow-hawks, Ma'am,' he replied. It was Wellington's last victory."

On the morning of 14 September 1852 at his favorite home, Walmer Castle on the Kentish coast, he had not risen from his camp bed at the usual hour. His valet went in to him at 7:00 A.M. and was sent to Deal to fetch the apothecary. "I don't feel quite well, and I will lie still till he comes," said Wellington. His last words were, "Yes, if you please," when offered tea a little later. Thereafter a series of seizures began. Though unconscious, he was lifted into his wing chair at two o'clock because his valet believed he would be happier there. He died quietly at 3:25 that afternoon. In November the monstrous six-wheeled funeral car, devised by Prince Albert, became stuck in the mud in Pall Mall. Hundreds of thousands attended the interment of the embalmed body in St. Paul's. *See* E. Longford (1972).

Wells, H.G. *(Herbert George)* (1866–1946).

Long before his death, the English writer was out of spirits and out of favor. World War II was a great setback to his hopes for mankind, and his last book, *Mind at the End of Its Tether* (1945), is uncharacteristically somber. He refused to leave his London home, 13 Hanover Terrace (facing Regent's Park), during the Blitz, but Elizabeth Bowen found him visibly shaking with fright when she called on him late one night during an air raid alert. "It's not the bombs; it's the dark," he told her. "I've been afraid of darkness all my life." But he gave up the struggle reluctantly, describing himself toward the end as having "one foot in the grave and the other kicking out at everything."

Wells was a shrunken figure during his final months, consoling himself with Mozart on the phonograph. At about 4:00 P.M. on 13 August 1946, he rang for his nurse to remove his pajama jacket, but after a few moments of sitting on the edge of the bed changed his mind and climbed back in. "Go away," he said. "I'm all right." Ten minutes later she found him dead. Years before he had forecast that his death would be due to fatty degeneration of the heart, but it was cancer of the liver that killed him. After cremation at Golders Green, Wells' ashes were taken to the Isle of Wight by his two sons and cast into the sea.

West, Nathanael (1903–1940).

The U.S. writer, a notoriously bad driver, was returning home with his wife on 22 December 1940 after hunting duck and quail south of the Mexican border. The news that his friend, F. Scott Fitzgerald, had died the previous day may have distracted him. Traveling north on California Route 111, he failed to obey a stop sign before turning onto Route 80 and was struck by a westbound Pontiac. It was an hour before an ambulance arrived. The author of *The Day of the Locust* and other novels died at 4:10 P.M., shortly after admission to Imperial County Hospital. His wife, Eileen, was already dead; her watch had stopped at 2:55 P.M., the time of the collision. After a simple service at Riverside Chapel in New York City, West's casket, containing Eileen's ashes, was interred in Mount Zion Cemetery, Maspeth, Queens. *See* J. Martin (1970).

Whitman, Walt (1819–1892).

The U.S. poet was tall and heavy, but had a delicately textured skin which he bathed frequently in eau-de-cologne. He pre-

Walt Whitman in his Camden, New Jersey, home one year before his death.

THE BETTMANN ARCHIVE

ferred the company of men and never married, but it has not been shown that he was actively homosexual. Throughout his last thirty years Whitman was subject to minor strokes, and by 1891 looked much older than his seventy-two years. Even with the aid of a cane, he could barely walk about his Camden, N.J., home and suffered from indigestion, constipation and "bladder trouble." At the end of that year he took to his bed with a fever and lingered on until 26 March 1892, when he died without a sound. At autopsy advanced tuberculosis of the right lung and collapse of the left lung were discovered. He shared the disease with his mother and two of his brothers. After a nonreligious ceremony, Whitman was buried in Harleigh Cemetery, Camden.

Wilde, Oscar (1854–1900).

When the Irish writer and wit was released from Reading gaol in 1897, after serving two years for homosexual offenses, he went to live in France and Italy under the name "Sebastian Melmoth." At the time of his death he was living on credit in Paris in two small rooms overlooking the shady courtyard of the modest Hotel d'Alsace in the rue des Beaux Arts, whose proprietor had befriended him. A month after an ear operation in October 1900 he lay dying in his bedroom, the furnishings of which were not pleasing to the fastidious invalid. As he sank into a coma he was heard to murmur "This wallpaper is killing me; one of us has got to go." To a priest he was able by motions of the hand to signify assent to his admission into the Roman Catholic faith. After thirty-six hours of unconsciousness, Wilde died at 1:50 P.M., 30 November 1900.

In a 1966 study, Sir Terence Cawthorne dismisses the sometimes suggested diagnosis of neurosyphilis. Wilde had often complained of earache, notably after a fall in the prison chapel. Suppurative otitis media no doubt finally eroded the roof of the middle ear, spreading to the meninges and possibly to the adjacent temporal lobe. The death certificate correctly cites cerebral meningitis. Wilde was first buried in the Cemetery of Bagneux on the outskirts of Paris, but in July 1909 his devoted friend, Robert Ross, had the body moved to Père-Lachaise Cemetery, where the poet lies in a tomb designed by Jacob Epstein.

Oscar Wilde before the imprisonment which ultimately led to his death. Photo by N. Sarony.

LIBRARY OF CONGRESS

William the Conquerer (1027 or 1028–1087).

The corpulent William, duke of Normandy, was seriously injured at the French border city of Mantes during a foray in July 1087. After his army had set the buildings on fire, his horse stepped on an ember, throwing him hard against the iron pommel of the saddle. Back in Rouen he lay for weeks in the heat of summer suffering from what P.M. Dale believes was a slowly spreading peritonitis. He was moved to the relative cool of the hilltop priory of St. Gervaise where, in a little cell, he spent his remaining days recounting his life story to his sons.

At daybreak on 9 September 1087 William folded his hands in

prayer and quietly expired. His obsequies at Caen were thrown into confusion when the large body was being placed in its stone sarcophagus. The festering abscess burst, and the stench sent the mourners hastily to the church exit.

Wodehouse, P.G. (*Pelham Grenville*) (1881–1975).

The English humorist became a U.S. citizen in 1955 and lived his last twenty years in Remsenburg, on the far south shore of Long Island. On his ninetieth birthday he could still touch his toes and do his morning exercises. In the 1975 New Year's honors list, just two weeks before his death, he became Sir Pelham.

The creator of Jeeves, the perfect valet, was in Southhampton Hospital, a few miles from his home, for treatment of an irritating skin rash when his wife and sister-in-law visited him on the evening of 14 February 1975. "We saw him at 7:30 and he was fine...laughing." They had just returned home when the doctor called to say Wodehouse had died peacefully at 8:00 P.M., dozing in a chair in his room, apparently of a heart seizure. He was working on his ninety-eighth book, a Blandings Castle story. After a service in the local Presbyterian church, Wodehouse was cremated and the ashes were interred in Remsenburg Cemetery.

Wolfe, Thomas (1900–1938).

The U.S. novelist was already exhausted from an arduous motor tour when he sailed from Seattle, on an impulse, to celebrate the Fourth of July in Vancouver. He offered a drink to a fellow passenger who was shivering from the cold, then swigged from the whiskey bottle himself after a careless wipe with the palm of his hand. He was ill with chills and a fever next day, but arose in the afternoon to return to Seattle by train. He then entered the hospital there for what turned out to be an eight-week stay. Radiography showed a patch on the right lung, but the diagnosis was uncertain. Though Wolfe was intermittently wandering in his mind, his sister Mabel and a nurse friend were advised to take him across the continent to Dr. W. Dandy at Johns Hopkins

Hospital in Baltimore, armed with morphine to sedate him and a list of doctors in various cities through which the train would pass.

In Baltimore, Dandy relieved the intracranial pressure by trephination and on 12 September performed a craniotomy. Afterwards, Dandy told the waiting family: "The case is hopeless. He has miliary tuberculosis of the brain. His brain is simply covered with tubercles—there must be millions of them in there." An old sealed-off lesion of the lungs, disturbed by the pneumonia attack, had evidently released the microorganisms into the bloodstream, which carried them to the brain. Wolfe lingered semiconscious for three days more before dying peacefully on 15 September 1938. He lies in Riverside Cemetery, N.C. *See* E. Nowell (1960).

Wolsey, Thomas (1473?–1530).

By 1530 Cardinal Wolsey had lost the confidence of Henry VIII, and an indictment of praemunire (setting the Pope's authority over the Crown's) had been filed against him. He surrendered the Lord Chancellor's great seal in October 1530 and was ar-

Cardinal Wolsey's presumed grave in the ruins of the Abbey of St. Mary of the Meadows where he died in 1530.

LEICESTER CITY COUNCIL

rested for treason at his residence, Cawood Castle, near York, on 4 November. On his way south to face trial in London he was taken ill with abdominal pain and passage of black stools (melena). H.W. Syers in a 1901 study considers the most likely diagnosis to be a heavily bleeding duodenal ulcer.

As Wolsey lay dying at the Abbey of St. Mary of the Meadows, just north of Leicester, Henry sent to have him questioned about a certain L 1,500 that he was believed to possess, and that the king intended to take for himself. The cardinal died at 8:00 P.M., 29 November 1530. When his body was stripped for burial, a hair shirt was discovered below his fine linen garments. He was buried in the full robes and regalia of his office. Though Henry destroyed the abbey, there is a slab lying within the foundations which appears to mark Wolsey's grave; it bears the inscription: GIVE HIM A LITTLE EARTH FOR CHARITY.

Woolf, Virginia (1882–1941).

The English novelist's mental health was always at its most precarious after finishing a book. When *Between the Acts* was completed early in 1941, Leonard Woolf again saw in his wife the signs of depression and incipient madness, the worst since the suicidal episode of 1913. A family friend, a woman physician in Brighton, tried to reassure Virginia, who feared she would be unable to write again, but more forceful, distasteful steps were postponed. On 28 March 1941, Leonard was in their garden in Rodmell, a village between Lewes and Newhaven, Sussex; Virginia, he believed, was in the house. At lunchtime he found a note on the mantelpiece (a similar one was later discovered in her work room):

> Dearest,
>   I feel certain that I'm going mad again. I feel we can't go through another of those terrible times. And I shan't recover this time. I begin to hear voices and I can't concentrate. So I'm doing what seems the best thing to do....
>   I don't think two people could have been happier than we have been.
>
> V.

Leonard ran across the water meadows to the bank of the Ouse, where he found Virginia's cane. The police were called, but it was three weeks before children sighted the floating body. She had probably made a similar attempt a few days earlier. This time she improved her chances by thrusting a large rock into her coat pocket. Leonard describes in the final volume (1969) of his autobiography how he buried his wife's ashes at the foot of an elm in their garden. "There were two great elms there with boughs interlaced which we always called Leonard and Virginia. In the first week of January 1943, in a great gale one of the elms was blown down."

Woollcott, Alexander (1887–1943).

The American critic and wit was carrying nitroglycerin tablets for his failing heart when, on Saturday evening, 23 January 1943, he took part with four others in a CBS radio program—"The People's Platform"—in Manhattan. The question under discussion was, "Is Germany Incurable?" and he had just made a comment when he tried to push himself away from the microphone. "I AM SICK," he scribbled on a piece of paper. "I knew

"When Alexander Woollcott dies, he'll go to Hamilton," said Dorothy Parker. On 15 July 1943 a marble urn bearing the ashes of Woollcott, class of 1909, was interred in Hamilton College Cemetery at Clinton, New York.

HAMILTON COLLEGE LIBRARY

then that something was radically wrong," said Rex Stout, who was present. "A healthier Woollcott would have written 'I AM ILL.'" As Woollcott was helped from the studio he gasped "Get my glycerin tablets." But the heart attack was followed by a cerebral hemorrhage and he became paralyzed on the left side. He was rushed to Roosevelt Hospital, but it was too late.

The novelist, Marcia Davenport, used to say "not very nicely" that it was she who had killed Woollcott. He had insulted her regularly as a child when he visited her mother, Alma Gluck, and they continued to detest one another as adults. Called in as a replacement at the last moment, Mrs. Davenport exchanged bitter remarks with Woollcott until the microphones went live; a minute or two later he suffered his fatal attack.

Paul Robeson read the 23rd Psalm at the service at McMillin Academy Theater of Columbia University and Aleck's remains were then cremated. By mistake the ashes were sent to Colgate University in Hamilton, N.Y., and had to be forwarded to his alma mater, Hamilton College in Clinton. They arrived with sixty-seven cents postage due.

Wren, Christopher (1632–1723).

In later life, the great English architect was fond of traveling each year from his home at Hampton Court to visit his noblest creation, St. Paul's Cathedral. He would sit for some time under the great dome, perhaps in prayer, perhaps simply casting his mind back to the time of its building. On 25 February 1723, at the age of ninety, he was driven up to town through bitter weather to keep his vigil in the church. Home again, he dined, and afterwards fell asleep by the fire. There his manservant found him, dead in his chair, his face quite peaceful. His tomb in St. Paul's is marked by the inscription: *Si monumentum requiris, circumspice* ("If you seek a monument, look about you"). *See* R. Weir (1971).

Wright, Frank Lloyd (1869–1959).

On Saturday morning, 4 April 1959, the U.S. architect was busy at his drawing table at Taliesin West, Scottsdale, Ariz., when he was stricken with abdominal pain. He had been working on the

Donahoe project—three connected houses for a desert moraine—when he was forced to lay down his colored pencils for the last time. His physician drove him to St. Joseph's Hospital in Phoenix, where surgeons operated on the following Monday for an intestinal stoppage. On Thursday, 9 April at 4:45 A.M. he suddenly succumbed to a heart attack. His nurse heard him sigh—and he was gone. Wright's body was flown to Spring Green, Wis., where it lies in the tiny family burial ground next to Unity Chapel.

Wright, Wilbur (1867–1912) and Orville (1871–1948).

The Wright brothers were inventors of the airplane (1903). Nine years after the first successful flight of a powered heavier-than-air machine, the Wright brothers visited the site in Oakwood, a Dayton, Ohio, suburb, where their new home was planned. It was 2 May 1912. That evening Wilbur had to lie down, feeling decidedly queasy. Probably it was some contaminated fish he had

Orville Wright's funeral at Woodland Cemetery just outside Dayton, Ohio, thirty-six years after his brother, Wilbur, was interred in the same plot.

THE DAYTON JOURNAL HERALD

eaten a few days earlier in Boston, he thought. His illness, typhoid fever, grew steadily worse during the next three weeks, though a recovery was hoped for late in the month. With his old

The funeral of Wilbur Wright.

BAIN COLLECTION, LIBRARY OF CONGRESS

father (a retired bishop), his three brothers and his sister, Katherine, by his bedside, he died, at 3:15 A.M., 30 May 1912, upstairs in the little frame house where he had grown up in Hawthorn Street, Dayton.

Orville gave up his aircraft manufacturing interests after Will's death. Following a heart attack in 1947, Orville suffered a second, more severe one in the new year, and died in Dayton on 31 January 1948. Only in 1953 were the first of the Wright brothers' aeronautical papers published; not until then did it become clear that the vision, the theoretical knowledge and the organizing ability had been almost entirely Wilbur's, with Orville working under instructions as a junior assistant. Both Wilbur and Orville Wright are buried at Woodland Cemetery just outside the Dayton city limits. *See* J.E. Walsh (1975).

Young, Brigham (1801–1877).

The Mormon prophet who led his flock to Salt Lake City in 1848 after the murder of Joseph Smith (q.v.) had "married" twenty-two women before declaring plural marriage a tenet of the Church of Latter-Day Saints in 1852. His twenty-seventh and final wife was Ann Eliza Webb, a divorcee who fled from him in 1873 after four years' cohabitation and lectured across the nation against the evils and degradation of polygamous marriage.

Working at his desk in Salt Lake City on 23 August 1877, Young was beset by nausea. That evening, after leading evening prayers for his wives in the Lion House, he wearily took up his candle and retired. At 11:00 P.M. he became violently ill with "cholera morbus," defined by a daughter later as acute appendicitis. During the next four days the intestinal pain came and went as he grew steadily weaker. On 29 August 1877 he was moved to a bed near the open window. Shortly before he died he opened his eyes and called, "Joseph, Joseph," before losing consciousness. He died the same day at 4:01 P.M. His body lay in state in the Mormon Tabernacle while forty thousand people filed past. Among the four thousand who followed his coffin to the private burial place behind the Lion House on 2 September were sixteen of his surviving wives (only Ann Eliza was absent) and his forty-four surviving children. His legal wife, Mary Ann Angell, walked arm in arm with his favorite wife, Amelia Folsom.

Zola, Émile (1840–1902).

The French novelist and his wife returned from their summer vacation at Medan to their home at 21 *bis*, rue de Bruxelles, Paris, on 28 September 1902. A fire was lighted in their bedroom and they retired to rest early on the 29th, Zola, as was his habit, locked the door and tightly closed the windows. In the night, Alexandrine awoke to find her husband standing beside the bed. "I feel sick. My head is splitting," he muttered. She also felt ill. Begging him to lie down again, she saw him stagger across the room and collapse on the floor. She lost her senses a moment later. Deadly carbon monoxide from the smouldering coals was being diverted into the room by a blocked chimney.

The following morning, alarmed by the silence, the servants broke down the door to discover their master already dead, their mistress in serious condition. Mme. Zola recovered in the hospital. Though she had deeply resented Émile's young mistress during his lifetime, in 1906 she legally recognized the two children of the liaison, and gave them the surname Emile–Zola. Accusations that the chimney had been deliberately blocked by enemies of Zola—anti-Dreyfusards—were never proved. After a public funeral Zola's remains were laid to rest in the Panthéon, the vast mausoleum in Paris reserved for the great men of France.

Zweig, Stefan (1881–1942).

The Austrian novelist's depression deepened after his exile to Britain in 1934. In 1940 he settled in Brazil, latterly in a rented two-bedroom villa at 34 Rua Goncalves Dias, Petropolis, in the hills above Rio de Janeiro. He spent Saturday, 21 February 1942, writing goodbye letters, including one to his former wife, Friderike, and putting his affairs in order. His second wife, Lotte, went marketing as usual. On Sunday he wrote a final statement in German for the authorities. It was the servants' day off.

"That afternoon," writes D.A. Prater in his 1972 biography, "some time between midday and four o'clock, they took massive doses of veronal and lay down together for this last sleep, Stefan in his shirt, tie and trousers, Lotte in a flowered kimono she had

Emile Zola in his last days. Photo by Cautin and Berger.
NEW YORK PUBLIC LIBRARY

donned after a bath....Little Plucky, the terrier, lay down too, outside the room, to wait patiently for his master to wake and take him for the evening walk."

The bodies, locked in a final embrace, were discovered by the servants when the door was forced open late the following afternoon. During their years together, Zweig had twice suggested a suicide pact to Friderike. His particular need for a companion in this final act was fulfilled in Lotte's gentler, more passive nature. The Zweigs were buried in Petropolis cemetery at the expense of the Brazilian government.